GLOBAL TRANSFORMATIONS

GLOBAL TRANSFORMATIONS
Postmodernity and Beyond

ANANTA KUMAR GIRI

RAWAT PUBLICATIONS

JAIPUR AND NEW DELHI

ISBN 81-7033-427-6

Published by

Prem Rawat for *Rawat Publications*
3-Na-20, Jawahar Nagar, Jaipur 302 004 India
Phone: +91 141 651022 Fax: +91 141 651748

Delhi Office
G-19, Vijay Chowk, Laxmi Nagar, New Delhi 110 092 India

Typeset by Rawat Computers, Jaipur
Printed at Nice Printing Press, New Delhi

This anthology is dedicated to
Professors Andre Beteille, Chitta Ranjan Das,
Particia Fernandez-Kelly, Sidney W. Mintz, G.C. Pande,
Michel-Rolph Trouillot, J.P.S. Uberoi,
and to all my teachers in Sociology and Anthropology.

CONTENTS

PREFACE

The present collection brings together essays which were written over the period of last seven years. These essays were prepared for different occasions and some of them have been published. These essays touch upon diverse, sometimes seemingly unrelated, themes of contemporary life but what underlies them is a spirit to make sense of and contribute to the process of contemporary transformation. They take part in the contemporary debates on transformation, modern and postmodern, and at the same time strive to go beyond these by presenting the moral and spiritual frontiers of contemporary changes.

I have studied and worked in various places when these essays were written. I am grateful to my teachers, colleagues, friends and students in the following places where I wrote these essays: Department of Anthropology, The Johns Hopkins University, USA; National Institute of Science, Technology and Development Studies, New Delhi; Jamia Milia Islamia, New Delhi; G.B. Pant Social Science Institute, Allahabad; Ravi Matthai Center for Educational Innovations, Indian Institute of Management, Ahmedabad; and Madras Institute of Development Studies, Madras. Here I would like to especially mention the stimulating conversation I have had with Professors Sidney W. Mintz, Andre Beteille, Chitta Ranjan Das, Manorajan Mohanty, the late Bikram Nanda, S.P. Nagendra, G.C. Pande, Rajeswari Sunder Rajan, S. Neelakantan, Thomas Pantham, C.T. Kurien, M.S.S. Pandian, P. Radhakrishnan, S.S. Siva Kumar, Chitra Siva Kumar, Nancy W. Hanrahan, Betsy Taylor, Dr. Ranjit Nair, and Mr. Erick Mueggler, to all of whom I am grateful. I am grateful to Professor Roland Robertson, Professor of Sociology, University of Pittsburgh, for encouraging this endeavour by writing the 'Introduction' to this.

A grant from Ravi Matthai Center for Educational Innovations enabled me to prepare this manuscript for which I am grateful to its the then chairperson Professor Anil K. Gupta. I also thank Mr. I.V. Narayanan of Ahmedabad and Ms. Kalai Selvi of our Institute for typing the manuscript. Finally, I express my heartfelt thanks to Mr. Pranit Rawat, my enthusiastic and encouraging publisher, for his inetrest and encouragement.

I hope essays presented in this volume are of interest to the readers.

Ananta Kumar Giri

ACKNOWLEDGEMENTS

In preparing these essays I have incurred many debts. I am also grateful to the editors of the journals where they first appeared.

The first chapter, "Religious Movements in the Contemporary United States: A View From India", builds upon the work on religious revitalization in the contemporary United States that I had done at Johns Hopkins University, Baltimore, USA. The last section of the paper was presented as a lecture at Allahabad Museum, Allahabad and Indian Institute of Management, Ahmedabad. I thank Professors Gillian Feeley-Harnik, G.C. Pande and members of the audience at Allahabad and Ahmedabad for their comments and criticism. This has been published in *Sociological Bulletin* 43 (2), 1994 and I am grateful to Professor M.N. Panini, its managing editor, for comments, criticism and encouragement.

The second chapter, "The Portrait of a Discursive Formation: Science as Social Activism in Contemporary India", builds on the research that I had done with National Institute of Science, Technology and Development Studies (NISTADS), New Delhi. It is a revised version of my working paper on the subject published from NISTADS. I am grateful to Dr. Ashok Jain, its Director, and to Drs. V.V. Krishna and Ranjit Nair for many helpful comments and suggestions.

The third chapter, "Democratic Transition and the Challenge of Transformation", is the revised version of a paper presented at the national seminar on "Schools of Life and the Challenges of Tomorrow" at Thiruvanthapuram organized by Mitraniketan and Danish Folk High School Association. It has been published in *Economic and Political Weekly*, August 10, 1996 for which I am grateful to Mr. Krishna Raj, its editor.

The fourth chapter, "Social Policy and the Challenge of Post-Industrial Transformation", was presented at the national seminar on "Reconstructing Theories of Modernization and Development" held at Jawaharlal Nehru University, March 1991. I am grateful to Professors M.N. Panini and Nadu Ram, the organizers of the seminar, for their invitation. This has been published in *Indian Journal of Social Science* 6 (4): 371-393, 1992 for which I am grateful to Professor D.N. Dhanagare.

The fifth chapter, "The Dialectic Between Globalization and Localization: Economic Restructuring, Women and Strategies of Cultural Reproduction", was presented at the Annual Conference of Indian Association of Women's Studies on "The Dynamics of New Economic Policy: Implications for Women" at Mysore in June 1993. It has been subsequently published in *Man & Development* (Chandigarh) XV11 (2), June 1995 and *Dialectical Anthropology* 20 (2): 193-216, 1995.

The sixth chapter, "The Condition of Postmodernity and the Discourse of the Body", was first presented at the 1990 Annual Conference of American Ethnological Society's on "Body in Society and Culture". It has also been subsequently presented at The Center for Advanced Study in Sociology, University of Delhi and The Center for Advanced Study in Psychology, Allahabad University. I have been enriched by comments and criticisms that followed these presentations. I especially thank Professors J.P.S. Uberoi, Janak Pandey, R.K. Naidu, Drs. Yogendra Sinha, Rabindra

Ray, Mr. Suranjan Sinha and Monica for their comments and criticisms. It has been published in the *Journal of Indian Council of Philosophical Research* X111 (3), May-August 1996, and my thanks are due to Professors Daya Krishna and Prabal Dasgupta for their encouragement.

The seventh chapter, "Critique of the Comparative Method and the Challenges of a Transnational World", has been presented at the Department of Humanities and Social Sciences, IIT Kanpur; Center for Studies in Social Sciences, Calcutta; and G.B. Pant Social Science Institute, Allahabad. I am grateful to Professors S.P. Nagendra, B.N. Patnaik, Drs. Bijoy Baruah, A.K. Sharma, Anjan Ghosh, Amitav Ghosh and all the participants at these three presentations for their stimulating discussion and comments. It has been published in *Contributions to Indian Sociology* (n.s) 27 (2): 267-289, 1993 for which I am grateful to Dr. Patricia Uberoi, Professor Andre Beteille and the anonymous reviewer of the journal for their comments, criticism and encouragement.

The eighth chapter, "Some Contemporary Notes on Method," was appeared in *Man & Development* (Chandigarh) XV1 (2): 16-26, 1994 for which I am grateful to its consulting editor, Mr. Subrata Banerjee, for his interest and encouragement.

I have incurred many debts in the preparation of the ninth chapter, "Self, Other and the Challenge of Culture." An earlier version of this paper was prepared for presentation at the All India Sociological Conference, Jawaharlal Nehru University, New Delhi, December 19-21, 1994. I have benefited immensely from my discussion with Professors Marilyn Strathern and M.S. Nagaraj on its earlier version for which I am grateful to them. The present version has benefited from the comments, criticism, and encouragements of Professors C.T. Kurien, Michael Herzfeld, Rajeswari Sunder Rajan, Nancy W. Hanrahan, R. Hema, Janaki Nair, and M.S.S. Pandian and my thanks are due to them. It has also been presented at Center for Development Studies, Trivandrum and Department of Humanities and Social Sciences, Indian Institute of Technology, Madras and I am grateful to the organizers and the members of the audience for many enriching observations.

The tenth chapter, "Building a Global Covenant? The Overseas Work and the International Partners of Habitat for Humanity", builds upon my doctoral research, supported by grants from the Department of Anthropology, Johns Hopkins University, U.S.A., National Science Foundation, U.S.A., and from Mr. A.K. Kaul of Delhi. I gratefully acknowledge the help of these individuals and institutions. I am grateful to Professors Sidney W. Mintz, Michel-Rolph Trouillot and Dr. Niloofar Heiri of Johns Hopkins University for their help in the preparation of the dissertation on which the present paper is based. An earlier version of this paper was presented in the Department of Anthropology, Lund University, Sweden. I am grateful to Professor Jonathan Friedman, Dr. Anders Hyden, Dr. Rabi N. Dash, Ingrid Dash, and members of the audience for questions, insights and hospitality. I am also grateful to Professor Simon Harrison, Drs. S. Neelakantan, M.S.S. Pandian, Martin Bavink, Caroline and Fillipo Osella, and the two anonymous reviewers of *The Journal of Royal Anthropological Institute* for their comments and encouragement. I owe a special debt to Professor Roland Robertson for making available to me many of his published and unpublished papers.

The eleventh chapter, "The Quest for a Universal Morality: Jurgen Habermas and Sri Aurobindo", was prepared for presentation in the session on "Ethics and Morality" at the 1993 International Congress of Anthropological and Ethnological Sciences, held in Mexico City. I thank Professor Cynthia A. Sorti, the organizer of the session, for her encouragement. This has also been presented as a lecture at Indian Institute of Management, Ahmedabad and Allahabad Museum for which I am grateful to Professors Anil K. Gupta and G.C. Pande as well as to the members of the audience for their comments and criticism. Here I am particularly grateful to Professors Om Prakash, R.C. Tripathi, O.P. Malaviya, Yogananda Sinha, and Dr. Parichaya Das. I owe a special debt to Professor S.P. Nagendra who has read the manuscript and offered valuable suggestions. Professor Thomas Pantham has made very insightful and critical observations on this work, for which I am grateful to him. This has been published in *Indian Journal of Social Science* 1994.

The last two chapters have also been published earlier. While the twelfth chapter, "Units of Analysis and the Field of Study", has been published in *The Eastern Anthropologist* 45 (3): 205-214, 1992, the thirteenth chapter, "Connected Criticism and the Womb of Tradition", has been published in *Indian Journal of Social Science*. This was first prepared for presentation at the "The Congress of Traditional Science and Technology of India" organized by PPST, Madras at Indian Institute of Technology, Bombay, November 28-December 3, 1993.

INTRODUCTION:
GLOBALITY AND TRANSNATIONALITY

Roland Robertson

Although Ananta Giri is not directly concerned with the issue of globalization *per se*, his book—*Global Transformations: Postmodernity and Beyond*—is very relevant to it. I hope, then, that the reader will understand the appropriateness of my discussing some aspects of the current debate about globalization in this introduction.

We have witnessed a remarkable upsurge in writing about globalization in recent years. Much of this has involved use of the word "globalization" in ill-defined ways. It is in fact used in many quarters as a diffuse and vague indication of changes that have been sweeping the world as a whole. Thus, the time has arrived for us to begin to talk about *discourses of globalization*. In spite of a number of attempts on the part of social scientists and others to conceptualize globalization in a neutral, analytic and multidimensional fashion, there is so much variation in its employment that there is now an urgent necessity to delineate the variety of meanings attributed to the term.

So, in this introduction to Ananta Giri's book, I propose to sensitize the reader to the topic of discourses of globalization. It is, I think, particularly appropriate to do this because Giri's book does—as its sub-title clearly indicates—tackle certain aspects of the question of postmodernity. The central claim of advocates of postmodernity is, of course, that we now live—at the end of the twentieth century—in a circumstance in which there are no longer stable "grand narratives" concerning the general direction of change in the human condition. Rather, so the postmodernists claim, we live in a world of competing narratives of the history and future of human life.

I have myself attempted to show that the conspicuousness of discussions as to whether we now do indeed live in a postmodern condition can largely be accounted for in terms of the acceleration in processes of globalization (Robertson 1992: 128-45). Involving in its most basic sense the compression of the entire world, on the one hand, and a rapid increase in global consciousness on the other, contemporary globalization has produced a global circumstance in which civilizations, regions, nation-states, nations within or cutting across states, and indigenous peoples, are increasingly encouraged to "invent" their own histories and identities (the latter notion being distinctly western in origin). Indeed, I have been arguing in various publications that there are now various forces at work which are leading to the global institutionalization of the expectation of difference (e.g., Robertson 1995).

Nevertheless, around the world, we find the view often being expressed within new social movements that globalization is like a tidal wave sweeping over the world and obliterating local, including national, culture and national uniqueness, not to speak of the alleged undermining of national sovereignty. When globalization is seen in this way (often very ideologically) it is frequently represented in primarily economic terms, as a new type of economic and/or cultural imperialism, as westernization, or simply as Americanization. It should, however, be noted that social movements directed against economic and other dimensions of globalization are becoming increasingly conspicuous in the United States. Thus, non-western nations by no menas have a monopoly on anti-global movements. From the standpoint of globalization theory, anti-global movements should be seen as an interesting feature of the contemporary global arena, as one very significant *aspect of* the overall globalization process (Robertson 1992: 60- 84). That a movement is ostensibly anti-global shows in fact that there is an *increase* in global awareness (however ill-informed a particular movement's ideology may be) and that global consciousness is increasing. Having said this, one should recognize that the rise of anti-global movements certainly makes the theorization of globalization more challenging. The fact that some ostensibly anti-global movements are globally—or, at least, transnationally—organized illustrates the nature of this challenge.

Most of the theoretical work on globalization has been under-taken by sociologists in the United States or Western Europe. This has resulted in the tendency for non-western writers to talk of globalization as if it were another version of what has frequently been called westernization. This perspective has, intentionally or not, been encouraged by Giddens' declaration that globalization is a consequence of modernity and his presentation of modernity as a western product (Giddens 1990). In contrast, I have insisted that there have been a number of different sites and forms of modernity. In my own work generally there has been a continuing insistence during the past fifteen years or so that globalization should *not* be thought of as a form of westernization. I have been greatly con-cerned to address the issue of the ways in which particular non-western civilizations and societies have contributed increasingly to the overall globalization process. In a phrase, globalization is not simply a matter of structure. It is also, crucially, a matter of agency. The Giddensian view has in fact complemented a general perspective that one finds widely in the so-called Third World and other non-western regions of the contemporary world, as well as in "politically correct" circles in the West. This perspective centers on the proclamation that the West enjoys what is often called a hegemonic position in the world as a whole. In a certain sense, then, it is in the interests of those who maintain that they are representing subaltern groups to cast the West as very dominant and thus to conceive of globalization as a form of westernization, or, indeed, the new guise of imperialism. In this perspective non-western societies are *victims without agency*.

The position which I take is that the Giddensian standpoint when combined with the subaltern perspective is very misleading empirically. Together they serve to perpetuate an image of the global field (Robertson 1992: 8-31) that is centered upon the stratification of the world into dominant and relatively passive elements. This image, in turn, denies to the subordinate elements a positive and constructive role in the globalization process.

If, on the other hand, we start with the basic and simple proposition that globalization consists of the making of the entire world into "a single place"—a place which is the site upon which a new collective entity is created—then it behooves us to consider, in an analytically neutral way, the actual dynamics of the formative process. This means, in principle, that we must allow for the full range of actual and potential contributions to the formation of what has variously been called the world system, global system, world society, global society, global ecumene, global field, or whatever. It is not my purpose here to delve into the issue of the most appropriate master concept for the indication of the world as a whole. Rather, I am concerned with the ways in which the problematic of globalization is actually talked about; or, more accurately, how the rhetoric of globalization is discursively structured.

I suggest that there are at least three distinct, but empirically overlapping, aspects of globalization discourse. First, there are clusters of regional or civilizational discourses, such as those of East and South Asia, Eastern Europe, Western Europe, Latin America, and so on. Second, there are disciplinary discourses—such as those of economics, cultural studies, communication and media studies, political science, anthropology, sociology, and yet others. Third, there are ideological discourses of globalization. Here it is harder to give concrete examples. For present purposes I think we can talk simply about left and right discourses, emphasizing that there are both pro- and anti-globalization discourses on the ideological right, as well as the left.

As far as regional or civilizational discourses are concerned, I would stress that I include as discourses of globalization those which do not in fact strongly highlight the notion of globalization as such. For example, there has been much discussion of the theme of indigenous sociologies in sub-Saharan Africa in recent years. Much of this has been undertaken ostensibly in order to promote indigenous, alternative ways of doing sociology from particular African points of view and as a way of both injecting African worldviews into the global discourse of social science and creating "local' resistance to what are seen as hegemonic efforts to create and sustain a western form of universalistic discourse. I have myself argued that the discourse of indigenization is in fact a crucial *aspect* of globalization, but it is not my intention to pursue that argument here. It is worth adding that there is a discourse of indigenization that is not so much regional as it is global. In the early 1980s, the United Nations Organization began to formalize the issue of indigenous peoples. This has been largely responsible for the recent proliferation of global and "international" concern with the problems and deprivations of stateless, indigenous peoples. This has resulted in the formation of transnational organizations of indigenous peoples; although it should be emphasized that such organizations actually pre-date the formalization of indigeneity by the United Nations Organization (Wilmer 1993).

In disciplinary discourses of globalization one finds a tendency to reduce the globalization process to the referential domain of the relevant discipline. The most clear-cut example of this is to be found in the economic discourse of globalization. In this instance globalization as a process is seen in exclusively economic terms, with specific emphasis upon the growth and crystallization of the global economy. In the closely related discourse of business studies, one does find something of a departure from that standpoint, since there is much closer attention to the sociocultural distinctiveness of particular markets—indeed the creation of particular markets of categories of consumers. In any case, given the global ascendancy of economics and economists in politically influential national, international, and supranational contexts—a strong trend which cuts across all of the regions of the world—it is not surprising that the discourse of economic globalization is extremely pervasive; so much so that even practitioners in other disciplines not infrequently assume that the economistic stance is the definitive one. That is, even some sociologists have taken it as a given that when we speak of globalization we mean that it is *economic* globalization. Coming from a different angle, there are the sociologists of the world systems schools who have, during the past twenty years or so, declared the long making of the modern world system in terms of a special brand of economic history. So even from within sociology (although world system theory has not been promoted exclusively by sociologists) one finds a distinctly *economic* conception of globalization. Coming from a different angle, there are the sociologists of the world systems schools who have, during the past twenty years or so, declared the long making of the modern world system in terms of a special brand of economic history. So even within sociology (although world system theory has not been promoted exclusively by sociologists) one finds a distinctly economic conception of globalization. It should be pointed out, however, that world-system theorists and empirical researchers have not been enthusiastic about the concept of globalization as such.

I do not intend to provide characterizations of the whole range of disciplinary discourses of globalization, but the conception of globalization promoted particularly by those working within the field of communication and media studies should be briefly mentioned here. This is because the conception of the world as becoming a "global village" originated in the writings in the 1960s of

Marshall McLuhan, in reference to media trends. Even though it would be wrong to suggest that all of those working in the field of communication and media studies are McLuhan devotees the global village imagery has had a very great impact—indeed an impact that has extended far beyond this academic field. The conception of the world as a whole as being defined and shaped by global media—including, of course, the new electronic media of the Fax, Internet, and E-mail—remains very strong.

Interwoven with these regional and disciplinary discourses, there are, as I have indicated, ideological discourses. As I have also suggested, these discourses have appeared on both the left and the right in anti-globalization and pro-globalization forms. Thus, in world systems theory, one finds a predominant view that welcomes the making of the modern, capitalistic world system as the allegedly necessary prologue to the transition to world socialism. At the same time, one also finds on the left the frequent expression of the view that globalization disables emancipatory "local" movements and/or that globalization represents the triumph of the multinational (or transnational) corporation, as well as of world organizations such as the World Bank and the International Monetary Fund, which stifle "local" initiative and freedom. Here ecological concerns are often also to be found. If one looks at the right, one also finds such variation. Some on the right (particularly Christian Conservatives in the United States) are fond of demonizing "The New World Order", which they tend to see as the most effective way of symbolically representing what others may call globalization. Here again we find the view that "the local" (which notion may, as I have remarked, actually embrace the national) is being overridden by the global. But, on the other hand, we also find on the ideological right the argument that globalization constitutes the release of capitalism from its historic national containers and that it is also an enabling force for the economic success of particular capitalistic societies. In this case one finds a remarkable mixture of convergence with and divergence from the "internationalism" that has long been a major goal of many Marxists for many decades.

I have attempted here only the barest sketch of the array of discourses of globalization, which I am currently exploring in depth with Habib Khondker of the National University of Singapore. I must emphasize that I regard the discussion of discourses of globalization as an essential feature of the overall theorization globalization. In arguing that there is a variety of discourses of globalization I am not suggesting merely that there is a cacophony of voices and leaving it at that. To adopt the latter position would be to subscribe to an ultra-postmodern stance on the global circumstance. To say that we now simply have a lot of "global babble" (Abu-Lughod 1991) and regard the world as a Tower of Babel, without any attempt to analyze or interpret it, would indeed constitute a celebration of the clash of "small narratives" concerning the world as a whole. In contrast, I believe that we should and can include dissection of discourses of globalization within the project of achieving an empirically and historically sensitive theory of globalization, a theory which, moreover, is "critical" in the sense of showing how many of our presuppositions about the modern world and its history may be deconstructed and genealogized.

Ananta Giri's collection of essays does not take globalization as its pivotal theme, but there can be no doubt that he makes a contribution to the overall debate about globalization, largely from an Asian perspective. This is *not* to say that I classify, and thus relativize, Giri's work as simply a manifestation of an Asian discourse of globalization. Quite to the contrary, Giri's work clearly falls within the category of those who are seeking to transcend the particular discourses of which I have been speaking. What Giri does is to inject Asian, particularly Indian, considerations into the debate about modernity, postmodernity and globality. One cannot overestimate the importance of this kind of effort. It provides an Asian voice in the current deliberations on globalization, as well as an Indian Asian perspective on certain western trends. But, in Giri's case, that voice cannot be reduced to the status of being simply one discourse among others. Employing a transdisciplinary approach the chapters in this book amount, in varying degrees, to a serious contribution to what I would call the meta-discourse of globalization.

REFERENCES

Abu-Lughod, J., 1991, "Going Beyond Global Babble" in Anthony D. King (ed.), *Culture, Globalization and the World-System*, pp. 131- 8.

Giddens, A., 1990, *The Consequences of Modernity*, Stanford, CA: Stanford University Press.

Robertson, R., 1992, *Globalization: Social Theory and Global Culture*, London: Sage.

——, 1995, "Globalization: Time-Space and Homogeneity-Heterogeneity", pp. 25-44 in M. Featherstone, S. Lash and R. Robertson (eds.), *Global Modernities*, London: Sage.

Wilmer, F., 1993, *The Indigenous Voice in World Politics*, Newbury Park, CA: Sage.

Chapter One

RELIGIOUS MOVEMENTS IN THE CONTEMPORARY UNITED STATES: A VIEW FROM INDIA

INTRODUCTION

Our contemporary moment is characterized by a global resurgence of religion. This resurgence is taking place in all varieties of social systems—from the technologically most advanced to the traditional societies—and has manifested itself in many forms—from religious fundamentalism, even supporting terrorism, to a spiritual renewal of self and society. The public resurgence of religion has taken place in most advanced societies, contrary to the prediction of the prophets of modernity that with the march of time religion would lose its public significance and, if at all, would persist only as a residue in individual lives, as an aspect of personal faith. As one perceptive student of contemporary religious resurgence tells us: "Faith persists and in persisting allows us to build a world more human than one in which men, nations or economic systems have become gods. Twenty years ago it seemed as if religion had run its course in the modern world. Today, a more considered view would be that its story has hardly yet begun" (Sacks 1991: 93).

This story of the persistence of faith and the public resurgence of religion is as much true of the United States as it is true of a society such as India. Since the late 1960s a wave of religious movements have swept American society. These movements have been of various kinds—mystical, Christian fundamentalist, and evangelical left. These movements have brought religion back to the secular city and in the process have challenged various institutional and symbolic boundaries of modernity—the boundaries between religion and politics, private and public morality, religion and science, and state and society (Cox 1984; Wuthnow 1988).

The public resurgence of religion in the United States takes place at a time when life, culture, and society there is in the midst of a transition. Contemporary United States is in the midst of an all-pervasive restructuring which touches all the domains of lives and subsystems of society—from the script of life to the organization of economy and the discourse of politics. This restructuring is caused by the coming of a post-industrial society (Bell 1973; Block 1987). Economic restructuring has led to the "deindustrialization of America", political restructuring has led to the breakdown of the consensus regarding the welfare state and social democracy, and the rise of new forms of work arrangement has broken down the integration of the individual life course with a stable arrangement of occupation and employment (see Buchman 1989; Giri 1993a).

The resurgence of religion is taking place in this wider context of structural and discursive transformation in the United States. This resurgence, as we shall see in this paper, is a response to the challenges of contemporary changes, such as the colonization of the life world by the system world and the reduction of the meaning of life to measures of money and power. For instance, homelessness is a major problem in the contemporary United States which is directly related to its postindustrial transition and its valorization of capital through investment in the built-environment. Religious associations, church groups and religious movements have responded to this crisis by building shelters for the homeless and affordable houses for the low-income families. When the built-environment of life in the contemporary United States renders invisible inequality by "residential separation, and an often shocking indifference to human misery... religious associations are among the few institutions with large memberships that partly mitigate these tendencies towards segregated lives" (Bellah et al. 1991: 268). At the same time, religious initiatives are not simply responses to societal problems: they also provide a new identity to individuals as seekers of meaning, truth, and justice for both the self and the others. As Anthony Giddens writes: "New forms of religion and spirituality represent in a most basic sense a return of the repressed, since they directly address issues of the moral meaning of existence which modern institutions so thoroughly tend to dissolve" (Giddens 1991: 207).

RELIGIOUS FUNDAMENTALISM IN THE UNITED STATES: THE CASE OF THE NEW CHRISTIAN RIGHT

In his insightful essay "Religion in Postindustrial America" sociologist Talcott Parsons had written nearly two decades ago: "[when we look at contemporary United States] it is legitimate to speak of a fundamentally new phase in the development of western religious tradition. The most salient feature of this situation is the emergence of a movement that resembles early Christianity in its emphasis on the theme of love" (Parsons 1978: 313). When Parsons was writing he had in mind the religious movements of the 1960s which was part of the emergent counter-culture in the United States. He had not anticipated the rise of some other kinds of movements such as Christian fundamentalism, which has been one of the most important cultural forces in the contemporary United States in the recent times.

While looking at the cultural history of the United States, what strikes one most is the fight between the forces of liberal modernity and the forces of religious fundamentalism. This tension and fight is specifically visible when the United States was making the transition from its small town rural landscape to the culture and complexity of the big cities. During the early decades of this century fundamentalists, however, had an upper hand in setting the terms of the debate about the future of America, as exemplified in the leadership of W.J. Bryan, the famous political leader of his times (Cox 1984). But, from the 1920s onwards, the fundamentalists became side-tracked by the forces of modernity and had to live as a ridiculed minority. However, in the last decades, the Christian fundamentalist conservatives have made their presence felt in the broader political and cultural spectrum of the United States. The social and economic crises of the mid-1970s and late 1960s facilitated this revival of religion in American politics. With the election of Jimmy Carter, a compassionate born-again Christian, this evangelical entry into politics and other key institutions of the US society had a visible legitimacy. Towards the end of the 1970s, however, it is the Christian Right, more appropriately the New Christian Right, that took the center stage of evangelical activism and politics.

MORAL MAJORITY

The 'Moral Majority' is probably the most widely known among these fundamentalist Christian groups. It was founded in July 1979 by Rev. Jeny Falwell. Because of its chauvinist and anti-intellectual posture and fundamentalist stance Moral Majority has been usually defined as nothing but a "March of the Folly". But Moral Majority is more than this: it also embodies a struggle to redefine America. It does so by working as a cultural movement, bent on creating a new collective identity for the Americans. It fights against the philosophy of secular humanism and liberal Christianity—the main currents of thoughts in the American heartland. In its crusade against secular humanism, the Moral Majority characterizes it as godless, morally indecent and sexually permissive. Crucial to this anti-secular manifesto is Moral Majority's conviction that secular humanism has twisted the First Amendment to the Constitution of the United States to mean the separation of God from government and society.

The other major target of fundamentalism in secular humanism is modern science and its numerous authoritative and unquestioned social institutions. Specifically significant here is Moral Majority's opposition to the teaching of scientific evolution in the schools and its campaign for the inclusion of 'creationism' in the syllabus. But Moral Majority's critical posture to the logic of modern science is not necessarily a total rejection of it (Cox 1984). Its culture of anti-scientism is not the same as the closed minded anti-scientism of the early 20th century fundamentalists, which resulted in the infamous Scopes trial. For Harvey Cox, the Moral Majority advocates the teaching of creation on an equal basis with evolution not because the Bible teaches creation but because it believes that Biblical creationism can be established scientifically. Therefore, contemporary fundamentalists are not anti-scientists per se, but have an idea of science which is "the expression of a subculture that has refused to accept the modern division of labour by which theology was to deal with the inner life of faith and science with everything else" (Cox 1984: 55).

Egalitarianism and individual choice as aspects of the secular humanistic discourse are also Moral Majority's target. In place of the current egalitarian discourse of "positive discrimination" and "equality of opportunity", the Moral Majority emphasizes upon individual competition. Jerry Falwell defends capitalism even in the name of Christianity (Cox 1984: 63). However, it is to be noted that this pro-business and pro-establishment orientation of the present-day fundamentalists is at odds with the pro-poor and anti-corporation stand of the earlier fundamentalists of W.J. Bryan's generation.

AGAINST LIBERAL CHRISTIANITY

So much for Moral Majority's attack on secular humanism. Now some comment on this cultural movement's struggle against the liberal Protestant churches and liberal Christianity is in order. In recent decades, the National Council of Churches—the umbrella organization for mainstream Protestantism in this country—has become Moral Majority's main target. "The NCC has been attacked for representing a value system and worldview that appears to the New Christian Right to be much closer to secular humanism than to historic Christianity" (Heinz 1983: 135).

The first tenet of the fundamentalist anti-liberal theology is its literal reading of the scripture. The fundamentalists interpret the Bible literally and look to it for answer for almost everything. Fundamentalists also contend modern theology's understanding of faith by rejecting its interpretation that faith is a "personal encounter with God which carries with it no necessary cognitive content and needs no historical mediator" (Cox 1984: 57). "The fundamentalists insist that faith is not just a relationship; it also has a doctrinal content. God not only reveals himself. He also reveals certain truth about himself. Faith is substance as well as form" (ibid).

In its struggle to provide an alternative definition of America, different from that provided by secular humanism and liberal Christianity, the Moral Majority carries its fight to the symbol producing centers of the contemporary United States, mainly churches, schools, neighbourhoods and the family. Moral Majority fights for traditional family, law against abortion, autonomy and tax-exempt status of the fundamentalist educational and cultural institutions, and control over the secular ones. It legitimizes itself by bringing forth the theme of religious awakening in American history and presenting the current fundamentalist resurgence as harbinger of another great religious awakening (Lechner 1985). The second theme it employs in its search for legitimation is the notion of providential Americanism, which believes that the United States had always had a special "convenant" with God. The Moral Majority legitimizes its objective and agenda as a cultural movement by arguing that this covenant is now broken.

In their struggle to legitimize their definition of America Christian fundamentalists have made extensive use of television. In fact, televangelism is now an important cultural force in the contemporary United States, which embodies a "critical link between mass media and social movements" (Hadden and Shupe 1988: 40). While it is true that the communication revolution is now "reshaping American religion" (ibid) and "the move from the revivalist's tent to the vacuum tube has vastly amplified the voices of defenders of tradition" (Cox 1984:69) the mechanical reproduction of prayer and soul therapy in these electronic churches also detaches the people of faith from the bases of living tradition.

Contemporary fundamentalist resurgence has been misunderstood by its students—journalists, academic critics and social scientists—because they "fail to see that fundamentalism is an enclave, a little world that has been preserved by a range of schools, churches, colleges in which many of the assumptions of pre-modern world still obtain. In the subculture of fundamentalism people talk and think differently" (Cox 1984: 56). Nancy Ammerman's study *Bible Believers* provides us a thick description of this subculture of fundamentalism. In her study of Southside, a New England fundamentalist church, Ammerman found that for the fundamentalists, religion is grounded in an institution (the church) and in a document (the Holy Bible). Southside churchgoers are quite dogmatic about the literalness of the Bible. In fact, this uncompromising attitude to the literalness of the Biblical truth distinguishes them from their closest neighbors, the evangelicals (Ammerman 1987:4). For the Bible believers, all knowledge is contained in the Bible. For these fundamentalists any one who contradicts the "plain words of the scripture" is doing the work of Satan whether they know it or not (ibid).

"The assembling together of believers" in the church mainly on Sunday but also in other week evenings is a very important event in the life of the Southsiders. "Although they may not hear church bells calling them to morning prayers or evening vespers, their days and weeks and lives are no less regulated by the church's cycle of events" (ibid). As a Southside churchgoer says: "A good Sunday service gives me something for the whole week" (ibid). The various church fellowship meetings are also important where the participants tell each other stories about their success, ask for prayer about their needs. The way things are done at church provides the underlying structure for how believers expect the world to be. In this togetherness and fellowship, the shepherd is the pastor. The pastor has enormous authority and one of the situations where that authority is manifest is the preaching situation in the church. The pastor speaks to the believers and "they learn from what he says (ibid)." "None of them expects to have close personal friendship with the pastor; rather they expect to admire and imitate him" (ibid: 120).

The most important challenge for the Southside believers is to nurture their children in the line of the admonition of the Lord. In the early stages of childhood, the children of the Bible believers learn about religious initiative and guilt. From the religious culture at home, they get "substance over which to feel guilty: not going to church, forgetting to read the Bible, disobeying, or playing with an unsaved child" (ibid: 171). The children of the Bible believers go to their own Christian Church Academy. The parents of the Southside kids see public schools the greatest challenge to the transmission of the fundamentalist culture, because for them these schools are the repository of false ideas. However while being assured of a true Christian training in the church schools, the parents nevertheless worry about the prospect of such a predominantly Biblical education and the quality of training in the field of natural science and engineering.

The operation of the academy is a site for political activism and political contention for the Bible believers. As Ammerman tells us: "Much of the political activity at Southside, in fact, is aimed at defending fundamentalist's ability to establish and run Christian institutions as they see fit" (ibid: 201). Ammerman sees fundamentalism as basically a cultural movement. For her, "Fundamentalists are not defending declining prestige or economic position, but a culturally coherent way of life" (ibid: 193). She also places fundamentalism in the backdrop of social change in the contemporary United States when she writes: "When rapid technological change exceeds our ability to respond, feelings of lostness are to be expected. At such times, growth in fundamentalism can also be expected" (ibid: 192).

BEYOND FUNDAMENTALISM: A CRITICAL LOOK AT RELIGION AND SOCIETY IN THE CONTEMPORARY UNITED STATES

Fundamentalism is part of a broader movement in the United States, which has challenged some of the "secular assumptions" of American society and with it God has finally arrived in Washington (Ballah et al. 1991). But when God is brought to Washington does His followers lose some of His vision? According to Robert Bellah, yes they do. Bellah and his colleagues offer a profound critique of the tendency in Christian fundamentalism to bring God to Washington. In their words, "In mediating between State and the churches, so as to preach religious visions of a good society from pubic pulpits... specialized para-church institutions may have the effect of making the churches more like the state..." (ibid: 185). Moreover "in the process of learning the State's language of legal rights, cost-benefit utilities, and justice as due process, they have forgotten the language of covenant and communion" (ibid: 193). If Parsons had argued that new religious movements must achieve "a new level of integration with the secular society" (Parsons 1978: 322) Bellah and his colleagues show how some of the leaders of such movements argue that religions while positively relating to society must not be mere functional appendages to the integrated social system, it must offer a total critique of the contemporary condition, which stifles human spirit in many ways. Bellah et al. tell us how there is a sign of such a critical engagement in the contemporary religious resurgence in the United States.

The ideal of a "transformed Christ" is dear to many young church leaders who "grew in the 1960s" (ibid). Mary Hatch, one of the church leaders whose views Bellah and his colleagues discuss at great length tells us: "... the mainline churches have done a lousy job in naming the suffering of middle-class existence in our time. We haven't told the truth about it. That's the church's greatest sin-not saying that the competitive driven existence that divides what it is to be a man or a woman, a white or black, is a form of human suffering" (Bellah et al. 1991: 210). For Hatch, the church must educate its parishioners about the fact that "consumerism... denies the needs of the poor in the name of our anxious desire. But most of all, "consumerism kills the soul, as any good Augustinian can see, because it places things before the valuing of God and human community" (ibid: 211).

For Hatch, the mainline churches have stifled people's imagination and the preaching and teaching they provide "simply reify what people get from the newspaper and television" (ibid: 207). The reason for such stalemate lies "deeper than membership losses, and political controversy. A lot of it stems from assigning religion to the private realm..." (ibid). For Hatch, the churches should be "more like basic Christian communities on the liberation model" (ibid: 206). The church ought to form its worship and liturgy around waking people up and getting them moving in the spirit instead of putting them to sleep with a thirty-minute lecture" (ibid: 208). Hatch pleads for revitalizing the American social gospel tradition which she treats as a "uniquely American movement", which "uses American democratic norms and prophetic Christian ideals to criticize both society and the church, including the undemocratic aspects of American political economy and the privatization of bourgeoisie Christianity" (ibid: 210).

In the new religious movements there is now an effort to go back to the Bible. Hatch believes that people can use Bible as a "working document" because of the "incredible pluralism" that exists within it (ibid: 209). According to Robert Cooper, a Methodist Minister: "The buzzword today is 'spiritual formation'. You hear that all over the Methodist Church" (quoted in Bellah et al. 1991: 199). But mainline churches with their rationalist emphasis are unable to infuse the church goers with this living spirit. Hence, they are leaving the mainline churches to join the spirit-filled evangelical churches. In the words of Bellah and his colleagues:

> The crucial point in such trends is that the erosion of mainline religion's strength has been a matter more of ethos than of numbers. It remains numerically strong but with a growing consciousness of itself as a beleaguered cultural minority, caught between the widen-

ing free ways of secular city and the rising bastion's religious right, and divided from within by conflict between spirit-filled evangelicals and dispirited if still stubbornly principled liberals (ibid: 188).

THE SANCTUARY MOVEMENT

The above discussion points to the diversity within the resurgence of religion in the secular city. While the New Christian Right represents one spectrum of religious resurgence in the contemporary United States, the other spectrum is represented by many base-communities which are inspired by the Latin American movement of liberation theology and evangelical movements for social justice, human dignity and equality. One such initiative is the famous Sanctuary movement in the United States. Sanctuary movement is a broad-based Christian movement which strives to provide sanctuary to the refugees from Central America, who leave their homelands for threats of murder, political persecution and economic insecurity (Wiltfang and McAdam 1991). It was started by Jim Corbett of Tucson. Arizona Corbett and his friends decided to provide shelter to the refugees in the churches and they provided Biblical justification for their action by invoking the Book of Numbers where Moses was commanded by God to establish "cities of refuge for the people of Israel, and for the stranger and the sojourner among them..." (Tomsho 1987: 26). The pastor of the Tucson Presbyterian Church which was the first church to declare itself a Sanctuary wrote to the then US Attorney General: "We have declared (our) church as sanctuary for undocumented refugees from Central America... We believe that justice and mercy require that people of conscience actively assert out God-given right to aid anyone fleeing from persecution and murder" (ibid: 31). When we listen to the activists we get a sense of the conviction that animates the US citizens who defy US law in the name of biblical responsibility. In the words of one such activist who was arrested on the charge of smuggling illegal aliens and found guilty by the jury: "We have lost sight of the fact that when our sister and brother anywhere are hurt, we are hurt... I am a woman with a heart and a mind. My faith commitment connects me to people and injustice" (ibid: 149).

The Sanctuary refugees come from Central American countries of Guatemala and El Salvador where Christian base commu
nities are also active, providing assistance to people in their figh
against and flight from the military regimes. Base communitie
are characterized by lay control. These communities are places o
festivity which offers critical analysis of the secular situation i
the light of the Biblical message (Cox 1984). These base commu
nities are run on the vision of liberation theology, which als
provides a critical source of inspiration to the evangelical action
for social justice in the United States. Liberation theology stresse
on "orthopraxis", which favors the poor rather than "orthodoxy
(Cox 1984). In its theological imagination God is a suffering Go
who is suffering along with the humans in their confrontatio
with evil. Its "logos" (world) is a corporate world plagued b
corporate and class conflict (ibid; also see, Walzer 1985).

Base communities also exist in the United States (Praver
1981). Cox writes about one such Catholic parish in Cape Cor
Massachusetts: "Even a casual visitor to St. Frances Xavier cann
help notice that something is happening in the American cathol
church which could hardly have been foreseen two decades ag
(Cox 1984: 103). According to one of the Catholic Fathers, th
change lies in the fact that American Catholic Church is changi
from "one that in this century won national acceptance and ev
respectability to one that now, under very different and emergi
circumstances, dares to challenge the national and internatio
structures of injustice, selfishness and complacency of which c
nation is undeniably a part" (quoted in Cox 1984: 104).

HABITAT FOR HUMANITY

'Habitat for Humanity' is a broad-based ecumenical and no
denominational Christian initiative in collective action and cr
cal reflection, which builds houses for low-income families in
United States as well as in other countries around the world. As
January 31, 1993, the Habitat had house-building projects in 8
American communities and in forty overseas countries. Hab

for Humanity was founded as an international ministry of housing in 1976 by Millard Fuller, an ambitious young Alabama attorney "whose competence and drive made him a millionaire at a very early age" (Carter 1985). His wealth and reputation were rapidly expanding, when his wife got separated from him, who found no meaning in his pursuit of riches, Fuller reconciled with his wife by giving away his fortunes and starting their life anew in the service of Christ.

"No More Shacks" is "the daring vision of Habitat for Humanity" (Fuller 1986). In this striving Habitat is founded on the Biblical principles of "Economics of Jesus" and "Theology of Hammer" (Fuller 1991). Habitat's theology of hammer is put into practice in building houses. Theology of hammer not only celebrates intervention and embodiment but also prepares the context for transcending doctrinal differences and becoming genuinely ecumenical. For the German theologian Johannes Baptist Metz, Christianity can be ecumenical only when it strives to meet the practical needs of ordinary people and thus reclaims the "alien world" for the "Son of Man" (Metz 1970: 88). Metz's assessment enables us to appreciate the broader implication of what Millard Fuller says:

> One of the most exciting features of Habitat for Humanity is that people who do not normally work together at all are coming together everywhere to work in this cause: the affluent and the poor, ...Roman Catholics and Protestants, and every racial and ethnic group you can think of. We might disagree on how to preach or how to dress or how to baptize or how to take communion or even what communion is for. We may disagree on all sorts of other things— baptism, communion, what night to have prayer meetings, and how the preacher should dress... [However] We will agree on the use of the hammer as an instrument to manifest God's love (Fuller 1986: 127).

MORAL CRITICISM AND THE PARADIGM OF BUILDING

In their recent moral critique of institutional arrangement in the contemporary United States, Bellah and his colleagues tell us that contemporary American form of life minimizes seeking of any "larger moral meaning..." (Bellah et al. 1991: 43) and Americans have pushed the "logic of exploitation as far it can go" (ibid: 271). In this context, they plead for a new paradigm for the actors and the institutions of the United States—what they call the pattern of cultivation. This paradigm of cultivation refers to the habit of paying attention to the needs of one another and belonging to communities and traditions. Attention is described here normatively which refers to pursuing goals, and relationships which give us meaning, and is different from "distraction" and "obsession" (ibid). For the authors of *Good Society* and participants in its conversation while "channel flipping TV watching, compulsive promiscuity, and alcoholism is a form of distraction spending time with one's children, repairing the broken car of a neighbour and building houses for those who don't have a roof over their head is a form of attention" (ibid).

In Habitat we see such an idealism and attentiveness at work. If the actors in Bellah's conversation on good society express their idealism through the idiom of cultivation, the actors of Habitat express it through the idiom of "love in the mortar joints". The paradigm is a paradigm of building—building homes and building communities. Fuller talks about pursuit and building as appropriate models of the care of the self—as appropriate modes of being in the world and self-engagement. Like Bellah's actors Fuller also presents his idea of pursuit as a normative one and argues that "a spiritual dimension to our various pursuits is essential to make sense of what life is all about" (Fuller 1992b: 4-5). Fuller challenges the educated and affluent in North America: "Don't sell out for a big salary, a picket fence and 2.3 children. These things will take care of themselves if you aim high and go for the joy and reward of a life of accomplishment, excellence and building a better world" (Fuller 1992a).

Here it must be noted that many commentators of the emergent American consciousness point to a pervasive spiritual urge within a section of the population so that critical exhortations from interlocutors such as Millard Fuller do not fall only on the deaf ears. For instance, one observer tells us that a strong social ethic is emerging as a major component of the new spirituality. What she writes rings a bell in the discourse and practice of the actors of Habitat for Humanity. "This ethic might be called an activist form of mystical endeavor, for it supports transformative work in society as an outgrowth and manifestation of transformation of the self. Still further, movement people regard their immersion in transformational activity as a work of healing" (Albanese 1993: 138). Another observer of contemporary American religiosity argues that the religious scene is characterized by not only "pastiche styles of belief and practice, combining elements from such diverse sources as Eastern meditation, Native American spirituality [etc.].." but by a "profound searching" (Roof 1993b: 165). This profound searching is "not so much that of navel gazing, but a quest for balance—between self and others, between self-fulfillment and social responsibilities" (ibid)

THEORIES OF SOCIAL CHANGE AND THE DYNAMICS OF RELIGIOUS RESURGENCE

Two important theories of social change in the modern world, namely, secularization and Marxism, had predicted the demise of religion with the progressive modernization of society. Theory of secularization had spoken of the process of differentiation in social institutions by which religion would retreat from a privileged position in society to a private sphere of the individual. Differentiation and privatization were supposed to be accompanied by a third process, namely, the process of desacralization, which refers to the "tendency to explain the everyday world in terms of material reality rather than supernatural forces" (Wald 1992: 40). The theory of secularization also propounded that as a consequence of modernization people would "define their personal identity and political interests not in terms of religion but as a function of their standing in the market place..." (ibid: 5).

"The forecast of religious decline in the modern world has been reinforced by another influential theory of social change—

Marxism" (ibid: 6). Marx suggested that religion "appealed most strongly to the oppressed who desperately needed some explanation for their plight" (ibid). But with the end of oppression and the transformation of "intolerable social conditions" religion would simply evaporate along with these social transformations (ibid: 7).

Our preceding account of the dynamics of religious resurgence in the contemporary United States shows us, as pointed out in the introduction, not only the persistence of religion in technologically advanced contemporary societies but the crucial role religion plays in public life, including in efforts to make the "intolerable social conditions" more humane and just. At the same time, it also points to a very complex dialectic between religion and technology at work in the contemporary United States. Religion in the United States has not only gone through a process of rationalization of faith and practice but has used tools of advanced technology to present itself in the public. "...The very terms of religious discussion are increasingly being dictated by norms of technical rationality, as evidenced in such diverse developments as televised religion, creation science, the church growth movement, and religious nuclear disarmament campaigns" (Wuthnow 1988: 316). For Robert Wuthnow thus the survival and revival of religion has been made possible by the way religion accommodates itself "in perhaps irreversible ways to the dominant ethos of scientific technology" (ibid: 316). But our account also shows how the picture of adjustment between religion and technology constitutes only one part of the story. The other part of the story is a quest for spiritual renewal of self and society where religious resurgence indicates "perhaps not only regressions but also exploratory movements... beneath the threshold of the well-institutionalized orders of science and technology" (Habermas 1984: 25).

RELIGION, SECULARISM AND THE CHALLENGE OF SPIRITUAL RENEWAL: WIDENING THE UNIVERSE OF DISCOURSE

Indian intellectuals are currently engaged in a debate on the relevance of secularism for contemporary Indian society. For some of them, secularism is a western ideal and is not suited to the cultural ethos in India while for others the ideal of secularism is as much significant for modern India as it is for modern West, since secularism is not only at the core of our identity as citizens of a united India but also at the core of the organization of roles, occupations and institutions in contemporary India (Beteille 1993). But this debate is being carried out without paying attention to the process of retreat from secularism and the resurgence of religion and without realizing that the retreat from secularism that we are witnessing today in contemporary India is part of a similar global process of retreat and revival. But it is essential to pay close attention to the actual process of this simultaneous retreat from secularism and revival of religion and be sensitive to the hopes, fear and aspirations of actors which animate this reconstruction rather than take side hastily and see in the resurgence of religion the inevitable doom of humanity.

It is with this objective of bringing an anthropological view from afar that I have presented here the story of the religious movements in the contemporary United States, meant to provide us a different vantage point to rethink our taken-for-granted assumptions about the ascendancy of politics and the decline of religion in the modern world (Beteille 1980). The story that we have heard here is one of persistence of faith in the modern world; and is a response to the narrow view of human beings that utilitarianism, rationalism, and secularism have put forward before the modern man and his essential need for familiarity with the transcendent source of values. Thus, the retreat from secularism and revival of religion in the United States is taking place not simply because of the machinations of some apparent crooks such as Jerry Falwell but also because of the fact that more and more individuals are now realizing that science, technology, and rationality fail to give them meaning in both their personal and occupational lives. They are realizing that it is not just enough to play one's role efficiently in modern organizations but to ask the more fundamental questions of well-being, justice, and fairness. They are realizing the infinite fragmentation that modern and postmodern developments have caused in their lives and are striving to put these fragments back together again into a meaningful whole.

At the heart of many religious movements in the United States is an urge to participate in a spiritual transformation of self and society. Religions have always had two dimensions—social and spiritual (Pande 1989; 1991; 1992)—but sociologists have deliberately ignored the spiritual dimension of religion and its significance as a perennial source of criticism and transformation (Chardin 1956). Secularism is making a retreat because it has failed to resolve even some of the institutional problems of modern society, what to speak of providing a guide to our quest for ultimate concern—a concern which is not just abstract and isolated but an integral seeking, covering the whole space from food to freedom. Secularism has deliberately put us in the dark about the fact that there is a hierarchy of meaning in our lives and without a continuous touch with a transcendental sacred even the institutions which individuals are supposed to efficiently man become fossilized because individuals cease to be bearers of critical consciousness (Giri 1993b; Griffin 1988, 1989; Habermas 1984; Unger 1987).

But modern intellectuals have not cared to understand the spiritual dimension in the work of self, culture, and society. What is striking is that even Indian intellectuals have not looked at their secular assumptions critically. Thus it is no wonder that while talking about the career of secularism in modern Indian they can only talk of Nehru, not Gandhi (see Beteille 1993). It might be true that, as Beteille argues, "in trying to bring a secular India into being" Nehru did not turn his "back on religion" but it is also true that Nehru did not take religion seriously (ibid). But Gandhi took both religion and secularism seriously and sought to achieve both through spiritual *sadhana* and cultural movements. The story of the revival of religion in a technologically advanced society such as the contemporary United States shows us that there are multiple meanings of both religion and secularism and the Gandhian agenda of secularism through spiritual transformation is probably the only alternative we have as we are stirred by the call of faith in a complex and plural world. As T.N. Madan argues: "Perhaps men of religion such as Mahatma Gandhi would be our best teachers on the proper relation between religion and politics—values and interests—underlining not only the possibilities of interreligious understanding, which is not the same thing as an emaciated version of mutual tolerance or respect, but also opening out avenues of a spiritually justified limitation of the role of religious institutions in certain areas of contemporary life" (Madan 1992: 408).

For Madan, "In multireligious societies, such as those of South Asia, it should be realized that secularism may not be restricted to rationalism, that it is compatible with faith, and that rationalism (as understood in the West) is not the sole force of a modern state" (1992: 404). But Madan does not realize that this intermixture between secularism and faith is not simply a given one—as Madan seems to be suggesting—but has to be an object of a spiritual *sadhana*. Though it is true that "...in our participation in religious experience we can have immediate access to a distinctive kind of value realizable as spiritual freedom... exclusive dependence on religious participation [also] tends to encourage the error of intolerance, which fails to see an experience different from one's own as having claims to equal authenticity" (Pande 1991: 431).

But appreciating such an approach to religion and secularism requires us to adopt an appropriate stance to the worldview of modernity and an "interpretive stance towards religion' (Wuthnow 1991: 14). This does not mean that "we must abandon rigor, or view religious fanaticism with sympathy" but it means trying to "interpret the significance of contemporary movements in terms of hopes and aspiration of their participants, including their hopes for salvation and spiritual renewal..." (ibid). At the same time, taking an appreciative stance towards the significance of religion, especially its hidden spirituality, faces the daunting task of distinguishing between the wheat and the chaff—between religious bigotry and spiritual movements. Those who use the name of religion or God to break another believer's place of worship are making a misuse of both religion and politics; they represent what Heller and Feher (1989) call "bad conscience" of the modern world and destroy the spiritual essence of a religion. In our story of the religious movements in the US we have also seen them at work in the Christian fundamentalist movements (Harding 1987). But those Bible believers who make a chauvinistic equation between Christianity and the national destiny of the United States do not exhaust the scenario of religious revitalization there nor does American civil religion end up with their chauvinism since it has almost always incorporated vital international symbolism into its horizon (Wuthnow 1988). The challenge that Rienhold Niebuhr presents to religious bigots is as much true for the Indians as it is for the Americans:

> We cannot expect even the wisest of nations to escape every peril of moral and spiritual complacency; for nations have always been constitutionally self-righteous. But it will make a difference whether the culture in which policies of nations are formed is only as deep and as high as nation's ideals; or whether there is a dimension in the culture from the standpoint of which the element of vanity in all human ambitions and achievements is discerned. But this is the height which can be grasped only by faith... The faith which appropriates the meaning in the mystery inevitably involves an experience of repentance for the false meanings which the pride of nations and cultures introduces into the pattern. Such repentance is the true source of charity; and we are more desperately in need of genuine charity than of mere technocratic skills (Niebuhr quoted in Bellah et al. 1991: 231).

Destroying other people's faith and home in the name of religion is not fundamentalism and its critique is possible and in fact most effective when forwarded from within the horizon of faith. As Jonathan Sacks challenges us:

> Fundamentalism is the belief that timeless religious texts can be

translated into the time-bound human situation, as if nothing has changed. But something has changed: our capacity for destruction and the risk that conflict will harm the innocent... It is the virtue of those who believe unconditionally that rights attach to individuals as God's creation, regardless of the route he or she chooses to salvation. That is counter-fundamentalism, the belief that God has given us many universes of faith but only one world to live together (Sacks 1991: 81).

REFERENCES

Albanese, Catherine, 1993, "Fisher Kings and Public Places: The Old New Age in the 1990s", *Annals of the American Academy of Political and Social Science* 527:131-143, May 1993.

Ammerman, Nancy, 1987, *Bible Believers: Fundamentalists in the Modern World*.

Bell, Daniel, 1973, *The Coming of a Postindustrial Society*, NY: Basic Books.

Bellah, Robert et al., 1985, *Habits of the Heart: Individualism and Commitment in American Life*, NY: Harper and Row.

——, 1991, *The Good Society*, NY: Alfred A Knof.

Beteille, Andre, 1980, *Ideologies and Intellectuals*, Delhi: Oxford University Press.

——, 1993, "The Retreat from Secularism: The Defeat of the Intellectuals", *Times of India*.

Beyer, Petter F., 1990, "Privatization and the Public Influence of Religion in Global Society", in M. Featherstone (ed.), *Global Culture*, London: Sage Publications.

Block, Fred, 1987, *Revising State Theory: Essays in Politics and Postindustrialism*, Philadelphia: Temple University Press.

Buchman, Marlis, 1989, *The Script of Life in Modern Society: Entry into Adulthood in a Changing World*, Chicago.

Carter, Jimmy, 1985, "Hands for a Home", *Habitat Commentary*, Americus.

Chardin, Tielhard de, 1956, *Man's Place in Nature: The Human Zoological Group*, London.

Coleman, Simon, 1991, "Faith Which Conquered the World: Swedish Fundamentalism and the Globalization of Culture", *Ethnos* (1-2): 6-18.

Cousins, E.H., 1985, *Global Spirituality*, Madras: University of Madras Press.

Cox, Harvey, 1984, *Religion in the Secular City: Towards a Postmodern Theology*, NY: Simon and Schuster.

——, 1988, *Many Mansions: A Christian's Encounter with Other Faiths*, Boston: Beacon Press.

Deutch, Eliot (ed.), 1991, *Culture and Modernity*, Honolulu and London: University of Hawaii Press.

Featherstone, Mike (ed.), 1990, *Global Culture: Nationalism, Globalization and Modernity*, London: Sage.

Fuller, Millard, 1986, *No More Shacks*, Americus.

——, 1991, "Making Room at the Inn. The Church Confronts Homelessness", paper presented at the Bowen Conference, Handersonville, North Carolina.

——, 1992a, "Building a Better World", Commencement Address at Technical University of Novascetia, May 9, 1992.

——, 1992b, "Housing Things which Makes for Peace", *Baccalaurate Sermon*, North Park College, Chicago, Illinois, May 22, 1993.

Fuller, Millard and Linda, 1990, *The Excitement is Building: How Habitat for Humanity is Building Roofs Over Heads and Hopes in Hearts.* Americus.

Giddens, Anthony, 1991, *Modernity and Self-Identity: Self and Society in the Late Modern Age.* Cambridge: Polity Press.

Giri, Ananta, 1993a, "Social Policy and the Challenge of the Postindustrial Transformation", *Indian Journal of Social Science* 6 (4): 371-393.

——, 1993b, "Connected Criticism and the Womb of Tradition", Indian Institute of Management, Ahmedabad: Working Paper.

Griffin, David, 1988, *Spirituality and Society: Postmodern Visions,* Albany: State University of New York Press.

——, 1989, *God and Religion in the Postmodern World,* Albany: State University of New York Press.

Habermas, Jurgen (ed.), 1984, Observations on "The Spiritual Situation of the Age: Contemporary German Perspectives", Cambridge, MA: The

MIT Press.

Hadden, Jeffrey and A. Shupe, 1988, *Televangelism: Power and Politics on God's Frontier*, NY: Henry Holt and Co.

Harding, Susan, 1987, "Convicted by the Holy Spirit: The Rhetoric of Fundamentalist Baptist Conversion", *American Ethnologist* 14 (1): 167-181.

Heinz, Donald, 1983, "The Struggle to Define America", in R. Liebman and R. Wuthnow (eds.), *The New Christian Right: Mobilization and Legitimization*, New York: Aldine Publishing Co.

Heller, Agnes and F. Feher, 1989, *The Postmodern Political Condition*, NY: Columbia University Press.

King, Karen, 1982, *The Rhetoric of The New Religious Movements*, University of Iowa: PhD Thesis.

Lechner, Frank, 1985, "Fundamentalism and Socio-Cultural Revitalization in America: A Sociological Interpretation", *Sociological Analysis*, 46(3): 243-260.

Liebman, R. and R. Wuthnow (eds.), 1983, *The New Christian Right: Mobilization and Legitimization*, NY: Aldine Publishing Co.

Madan, T.N., 1992, "Secularism in Its Place", in T.N. Madan (ed.), *Religion in India*, Delhi: Oxford University Press.

Metz, Johannes B., 1970, "Does Our Church Need a New Reformation? A Catholic Reply", *Concilium* 4 (6): 81-91.

Newman, Katherine, 1988, *Falling From Grace: The Experience of Downward Mobility in the American Middle Class*, NY: Free Press.

Pande, Govind Chandra, 1989, *The Meaning and Process of Culture as Philosophy of History*, Allahabad.

——, 1991, "Two Dimensions of Religion: Reflections Based on Indian Spiritual Experience and Philosophical Traditions," in Eliot Deutch, Culture and Modernity, Honolulu and London: University of Hawaii Press.

——, 1992, "Culture and Cultures", unpublished manuscript.

Parsons, Talcott, 1978, "Religion in Postindustrial America: The Problem of Secularization", in Talcott Parsons, *Action Theory and the Human Condition*, NY: Free Press.

Pravera, Kate, 1981, "The United States: Realities and Responses", *Christianity and Crisis*, September 21, 1981.

Roof, Wade Clark, 1993a, "Preface to the Special Issue on Religion in the Nineties", *The Annals of the American Academy of Political and Social*

Science 527: 8-10, May 1983.

——, 1993b, "Toward the year 2000: Reconstructions of Religious Space", *The Annals of American Association of Political and Social Science* 527: 155-170, May 1993.

Sacks, Jonathan, 1991, *The Persistence of Faith: Religion, Morality, and Society in a Secular Age*, London: Weidenfield and Nicholson.

Tomsho, Robert, 1987, *The American Sanctuary Movement*, Austin, Texas: Texas Monthly Press.

Unger, Roberto M., 1987, *False Necessity: Anti-Necessitarian Social Theory in the Service of Radical Democracy*, Cambridge.

Wald, Kenneth D., 1992, *Religion and Politics in the United States*, 2nd Edition, Bombay: Popular Prakashan.

Walzer, Michael, 1985, 1985, *Exodus and Revolution*, NY: Basic Books.

Wiltfang, Gregory and Doug McAdam., 1991, "The Gifts and Risk of Social Activism: A Study of Sanctuary Movement Activism", *Social Forces* 69 (June): 987-1010.

Wuthnow, Robert, 1988, *The Restructuring of American Religion: Society and Faith Since World War II,* Princeton.

——, 1991, "Understanding Religion and Politics", *Daedalus* 120 (3): 1-20.

Chapter Two

THE PORTRAIT OF A DISCURSIVE FORMATION: SCIENCE AS SOCIAL ACTIVISM IN CONTEMPORARY INDIA

If there exists a philosophy in the face of which the question "Does philosophy still have a purpose?" need no longer be raised, then today, according to our reflections, it would have to be a philosophy of science that is not scientistic... It would incur a politically effective task in as much it went against the two-fold irrationality of a positivistically restricted self-understanding of the sciences and a technocratic administration isolated from publicly discursive formation of will.

—Jurgen Habermas (1981)

THE PROBLEM

The question of science and technology has been one of the most important interlocutors for critical movements of various kinds for, at least, the last quarter century in contemporary India. The questions related to modern science and technology—its genealogy, deep structure, global operation and its specific Indian manifestation—have created a broad discursive field in which critical scholars and social activists have participated in various ways: some with outright rejection, some with uncritical adoration and many with rather a pragmatic critical consciousness characteristic of the signs of our times. Here we can identify two broad streams of critical consciousness: The alternative science movement and the people's science movement. The alternative science movements in contemporary India spearhead a philosophical, civilizational and sociological critique of modern science and technology and plead for an alternative science which would be rooted in an authentic Indian tradition and be free from the evils of modernity. The people's science movement wants to use science as a tool for social emancipation and as an agent of social transformation. In this study of the question of science and society in contemporary India, I am engaged in an anthropological mapping of the discursive field of science and the modes of social criticism that several individuals and institutions are engaged in. In this study, I apply the idea of a "discursive formation" (cf. Foucault 1972; also, Giri 1994b) to the task of understanding science and society. My objective here has not been to create a monograph on science as a social movement but to create the narrative of science activism as a discursive movement. Science activism in contemporary India is not simply an organizational movement, each group having a well-defined membership and secured funding. Rather it is a discursive movement where activism starts with a discourse and does not manifest itself in a well-defined mobilizational space with which traditional social movement scholarship is so familiar and preoccupied with. Hence, besides taking note of the sociological questions of group and number, what has been attempted in this study is a conversation with various actors and through this (though not exclusively) to create the portrait of science activism as a discursive formation. This narrative sensitizes us to the rich complexity of the field where the alternative science movement and people's science movement simply do not constitute ideological polarities or even distinct social groups to which we can, with certainty, classify the actors participating in and entering inside this discursive domain. There are groups, individuals and institutions in contemporary India who are working at the interface of science and society but cannot be easily placed in an either/or framework. At one level, each is perhaps a node of this discursive formation embodying the rich complexity of the field and refusing to play a politics of easy fixations and familiar conclusions. For instance, Eklavya, a people's science group in Madhya Pradesh, while using science communication as an instrument for social change also promotes a deep-seated critique of the paradigm of development that has come to dictate the terms of our debate and destiny through the hegemonic voice of science and technology. Vinod Raina of Eklavya does not look at people's science as simply performing the task of communicating an unproblematic science to an ignorant and awestricken society.[1]

In this context, it is of no use simply putting the alternative science movements and the people's science movements in two separate boxes and drawing up "tables of differences" between them (cf. Foucault 1972: 37). What I have attempted here is not a presentation of the conflicting positions of the alternative science movement and the people's science movement but the description of "systems of dispersion" (cf. Foucault 1972: 37) that characterize science activism as a discursive formation in contemporary India. After constructing a portrait of this discursive formation, I have also made an attempt to locate the genealogy of science activism in the dissonance of the biography and history of the movement actors and in the wider cross-currents of the social movements of the sixties and the seventies, especially the Naxalite movement and the JP movement. I have also looked into the significance of science as a source of cultural criticism and social activism in contemporary India in terms of the opportunity for transformation it provides not only to individuals but also to institutions in contemporary India.

ALTERNATIVE SCIENCE MOVEMENTS: MAPPING AN INCOHERENT DOMAIN

Patriotic and People-Oriented Science and Technology (PPST)

The alternative science movement in India includes individuals and institutions who are engaged in a critical dialogue with modern science and technology and are exploring alternatives to its discourse and institutional structure. One of the earliest efforts in this domain of the emerging critique of science is a group called the Patriotic and People-Oriented Science and Technology, known as PPST, which is based in Madras. Sunil Sahasrabudhey, one of the founders of PPST, tells us about the birth of this critique of modern science: "Sometimes in 1979-80, a group of young scientists and engineers in Madras started reacting to modern science and technology and its consequences in a way which was quite different from other prevalent or previous responses to this overwhelming and overpowering phenomenon of the modern world. After extensive and hard discussions amongst themselves over months (most of them were bachelors and living together then), they arrived at a very board and tentative conclusion about the crisis in modern science and technology (S&T) perceived largely through its consequences in the Third World, particularly India" (Sahasrabudhey 1984: 1). These young men thought that it was the foreign domination in ideas and organization in modern India which was at the root of this crisis. They initiated a discussion on the question of modern science and technology through the distribution of draft statements of their positions among interested students and practitioners of science and technology in different parts of the country. "This effort culminated in a convention of such people at Madras between 28 and 30 June 1980. The name PPST was adopted at this convention and it was thought that the first phase of this struggle could be ideologically and organizationally developed around a bulletin called the PPST bulletin" (Sahasrabudhey 1984: 2).

PPST has a four-fold critique of modern science and technology. The first critique involves the larger question of the breakdown of traditional Indian society. Here British intervention is identified as the sole cause of India's degeneration. The second critique involves the argument that Indian science and technology had a flourishing and functioning tradition before the British intervention. Thirdly, PPST challenges the objective and universal claim of modern science and technology. According to Sahasrabudhey (1984: 37), "attempt is made to show that modern S&T, like many other S&T, is culture rooted and is part and parcel of a package deal, that is the colonial deal." Fourthly, as Sahashrabudhey again notes: "PPST refutes all the achievement claims of modern S&T. Claims of increase in efficiency, productivity, knowledge, wealth, etc., are rejected...Further, modern S&T is accused of depriving the people of their livelihood and rendering them helpless."

PPST has engaged itself in a reconstruction of the Indian past taking inspiration from the works of Dharampal. Scholars of PPST have undertaken to initiate a wider discussion on Dharampal's two books *Indian Science and Technology in the Eighteenth Century: Some Contemporary European Accounts* and *The Beautiful Tree: Indigenous Indian Education in the Eighteenth Century* (Dharampal 1971a, 1983a). PPST has also circulated among concerned scholar-citizens of India two of Dharampal's papers, "Some Aspects of Earlier Indian Society and Polity and their Relevance to the Present" and "Self-Awakening of India: The Context of the Past, the Present and the Future". In these papers Dharampal argues that just two centuries ago, India had a fairly functioning society in most parts. But British intervention destroyed this.[2]

The *PPST Bulletin* was the forum of reflection and intervention for the scholars of PPST. The pages of the *PPST Bulletin* during the 10 years of its existence have carried out many critical reflections on issues related to modern science and technology and the functionality of Indian society. These articles discuss many issues—from traditional health care to the strategy for technological self-reliance in contemporary India. On the question of health, PPST wants a reinvigorating operationalization of the tradition of the healing at work among people what it calls *Loka Swasthya Parampara* (Balasubramaniam 1989). A. V. Balasubramaniam's work shows how the elements of this *Loka Swasthya Parampara* are the only alternatives that the majority of the Indians have. According to Balasubramaniam, 60 percent of the child deliveries in India are still done by midwives. Another issue that has been passionately argued in the pages of the *PPST Bulletin* over the years is the question of the "Indian Tradition in Science and Technology" and the "Non-Western Perspective on Scientific Knowledge" (Bajaj 1989). Bajaj discusses at great length traditional Indian sciences such as linguistics, astronomy, mathematics, medicine, sciences of the matter (*padartha sastra*), metallurgy, architecture (*vastu sastra*), music (*sangita sastra*) and shows how a pragmatic attitude of "conceptual sophistication and operational simplicity" informs all the domains of Indian science. For Bajaj, the Indian approach to science and technology is "pragmatic-systematic," as opposed to the "theoretic-absolutist attitude of western science" (Bajaj 1985: 104). Bajaj articulates a broader civilizational critique of modern western science when he writes: "...the idea of modern science being the unique body of knowledge isomorphic to the structure of reality is...an integral part of the western view of the world. That is why continuous attempts at providing a justification for this belief have all throughout been made in the West. The non-western societies who have no reason to be enamoured with this western project must reject, at least, the idea of the West being the repository of absolute truth about nature and man" (Bajaj 1985: 105).

PPST's critique of modern science and technology is not simply a sociological or even a moral critique. Rather it is a civilizational critique trying to develop a "culture-rooted total critique of modern science and technology in the Indian context"

(Sahasrabudhey 1984: 38). In this civilizational trial, PPST does not make the distinction between science and technology (Sahashrabudhey 1984: 32). Both these frames of reference, i.e., a broader civilizational critique of science and the iconoclastic collapse of the rhetorical boundary between science and technology, inform varieties of efforts in the discourse of an alternative science the implication of which we would discuss, at great length, when we come to discuss the work Ashis Nandy.

The Voices Within PPST

M.D. Srinivas is one of the founders of PPST. Born in 1950, Srinivas had his studies in Bangalore and Rochester. Currently, he teaches at the University of Madras. Srinivas says about PPST:

> PPST is not a wholesale critique of modern science and technology, rather it is a critique of the way science has been done in modern India. We are not rejecting modern science. We are nobody to dismantle modern science and technology. We just want to set our house in order.

Srinivas is worried about the fact that most of the institutions in modern India are dysfunctional. He asks: "Why don't modern scientific institutions deliver? Perhaps these institutions are not expected to deliver much." For Srinivas, the problem is one of idiom—modern science and technology have not expressed themselves in the idioms of Indian society. Let us let Srinivas speak on the issues dear to him and PPST:

> A society which is continuous has no problem of self-discovery. In India, we had a major discontinuity in which our social fabric has been torn asunder. In India, we have gone to alien knowledge systems. But sadly, our understanding of the scientific tradition is not very different from what was between 1900-30, what we had learnt during the nationalist movement...The realm in which we got defeated is not simply in the realm of science and technology but in the realm of politics. Of course, India is not the only society to have a major disruption but our problem is the problem of a different

idiom that has come to rule. The modern idiom has impoverished our society both materially and spiritually. This problem of an illegitimate idiom has also led to the problem of dysfunctionality and disorientation of institutions in India.

From M.D. Srinivas, let us move to J.K. Bajaj. Bajaj has done his Ph.D. in theoretical physics from Panjab University, Chandigarh in 1978. Bajaj was in IIT, Kanpur, in 1974-75 where he had met Krishnan and Sahasrabudhey, two other founders of PPST. In fact many of the members of PPST were in residence in IIT, Kanpur, which had a radical student politics in the mid-1970s. Asked about the origin of his interest in the science question, Bajaj said:

> Personally, I was not interested in making science relevant to society. What was worrying me most was the dysfunctionality of most of our institutions including science. What we were reflecting upon is what made these institutions dysfunctional. I got this realization at a very early stage. For instance, in our university, we 45 students entered the B.Sc. (Hons.) in Physics. Now, only one or two have a career in Physics. This made me realize the problem of dysfunctionality of science which is a reflection of the dysfunctionality of modern institutions to begin with.

Engaging in anthropological conversation is not just a matter of passive listening. Regarding science question and Indian society, I offered a frame of interpretation to Bajaj towards the end of our conversation. I wanted to treat science as a cultural object and engage him in the anthropological perspective on the diffusion of cultural objects and the distinction between the origin of cultural objects and their diffusion. A cultural object might originate in a particular area, but when it diffuses to another area, it does acquire a life of its own and is not simply a passive reflection of the cultural property of the area of origin (Mintz 1985, 1987 and 1991). Similarly, modern science as a cultural object might originate somewhere but when it diffuses to India, it does not simply remain a western science; it acquires a life of its own. Bajaj concurred with this frame of interpretation and commented: "India could use western science as an artifact just as the West is using Ayurveda as an artefact."

Navjyoti Singh is another member of PPST. He currently works at the National Institute of Science, Technology, and Development Studies (NISTADS), New Delhi. For Navjyoti Singh, the key question in understanding PPST is how it took a Gandhian turn while most of its activists were influenced by Marxism during their student days. The role of the Marxist leaders and parties during the Emergency accounts for the disenchantment with Marxism of the young students of science and technology who later came to found PPST. This disenchantment also led these young students and scholars to realize that Marx was Eurocentric. Thus, this provided an occasion to turn to Gandhi and to articulate the agenda of a "patriotic and people-oriented" science and technology. During the initial phase, PPST was caught in a dilemma: whether it should organize itself into a science movement in the KSSP (Kerala Sastra Sahitya Parishat) model or it should discover a separate path for itself. As Navjyoti Singh says: "But we concluded that most of the protest movements are theoretically starved, they do not have theoretical maturity. We thought that we must not jump into some resistance activity before theoretical sophistication. In order to achieve this, we decided to concentrate our activity on publishing a bulletin."

Beyond Hegemony and Violence: Ashis Nandy and the Agenda of an Alternative Science

One of the most influential and important commentators on the science question and the Indian condition is Ashis Nandy who works at the Center for the Study of Developing Societies, New Delhi. Nandy's public polemic on science began in 1981 when he joined the debate on scientific temper. In opposition to the statement on scientific temper issued by some important scientists, technologists, and policy makers of India such as P.M. Bhargava, P.N. Haskar and B.M. Udgaonkar, Nandy issued a counter-statement on humanistic temper. Both the statements and counter-statements were published in *Mainstream* (Nandy 1982).

Nandy argues that his critique of modern science is part of his critique of modernity and it parallels his "rejection of the modern ideas of progress and history" (Nandy 1982: 17). Nandy's first major work on science, *Alternative Sciences*, was published in 1980 where Nandy still operated, as he told me in the interview I had with him in December 1990, with the distinction between the text and the context of science. But soon he shifted his position to argue that the obliteration of the distinction between science and technology, the text and the context of science is essential for a genuine and total critique of modern science. Nandy writes thus in a seminal paper published in 1983:

> Such dichotomy between the text and the context of science has worked well until quite recently. But it is now showing signs of breaking down. First of all, the coming-of-age of the social sciences has encouraged them to discount the nineteenth-century public image of the natural sciences. Imitative, self-hating and reductionist, the new sciences have nevertheless picked up from where medieval theology gave up. They have challenged the idea of science as a system of perfectly rational knowledge, separate from the imperfections of culture, politics and ethics. For the first time in human history a part of science itself, in the form of the social sciences, has begun to argue that science is not a fully autonomous, rational, affectless pursuit; it too has its myths, magics and rituals not merely in its culture as a context, but also in its core as part of a text (Nandy 1983: 324).

This collapse of the boundary between the text and the context of science is accompanied by Nandy's refusal to accept the distinction between science and technology. For Nandy (1988a: 4), "...it is only by distinguishing between science and technology that all social criticism of science can continue to be deflected away from science towards technology" (Nandy 1988: 4). "For technology comes to represent an escape from the dirtiness of politics" (ibid: 8). Nandy argues: "I do not see why I should blame only the society, the politician or big business when the fruits of modern science go sour, why for instance I shall have to say that

science did not build the nuclear bomb, only the military industrial complex did" (Nandy 1982). In this context, the crucial issue
for Nandy and his fellow contributors to the book *Science, Hegemony and Violence* is the fact that modern science has been
accorded unquestioned authority by the middle-class and the bureaucracy in contemporary India. Nandy articulates the agenda of
an alternative science movement in the Indian context: "...the
intellectual challenge is to build the basis of resistance to milita-
rization and organized violence, firstly by producing a better
understanding of how modern science and technology is gradually becoming a substitute for politics..., and secondly by defying
the middle-class consensus against bringing the estate of science
within the scope of public life or politics" (Nandy 1988a: 11).

Nandy makes clear that in his critique of modern science he is
concerned "with the frame of criticism, not with criticism only"
(Nandy 1988b: 64). Nandy is engaged in a criticism of modern
science from the vantage point of tradition: "Instead of using an
edited version of modern science for Indian purposes, India can
use an edited version of the traditional science for contemporary
purposes" (Nandy 1988b: 11).

In his writings as well as in conversations, Nandy makes clear
that his is not a position of anti-science: "...criticism of modern
science is not criticism of all science...Human beings have lived
with a plurality of sciences for nine-tenths of the life-span of
civilization, and many of them are still living with non-modern
sciences, and many of us survive the demise of modern science
and culture..." (Nandy 1982: 17). Nandy told me that he is interested in widening human choices through striving for the cause of
a non-modern and post-modern science.

Nandy's critique of science has become part of a wider debate
and discussion in India. Many concerned people in India are
familiar with it and have some opinion about it. In my fieldwork,
I had tried to find out how the discussants in this discursive field
look at Nandy's work on alternative science. A senior personnel
in the Department of Science and Technology told me: "Ashis

Nandy is another English-educated mystic. But he is not alone. There are a bunch of other jokers who talk about a Greek science and an Indian science." A professor at the Indian Institute of Science, Bangalore, says: "I agree with Ashis. But where does this criticism lead to? Ashis only moves from one book to another. But with us here, we have to devise concrete technological alternatives to the needs of the rural people." Says Dr. Anil Sadgopal, another important actor in the people's science movement: "I am not clear about the question Ashis is raising about the nature of modern science. If it were a critique of technology, then I would not have any problem. Because of my training as a scientist, I am not able to see how modern science is inherently hegemonic and violent. I think it is the manner in which you organize science is important. The issue is not science proper, but that of class and social structure. I can appreciate the gender problem in science, but not when it is argued that science is inherently violent." But Sadgopal told me: "I might not agree with Ashis but the fact that he is raising these issues are very fundamental even to the people's science movement."

In the review of Nandy's book, *Science, Hegemony, and Violence*, the reviewer (Jairath 1990) writes that the arguments of the book ought to be traced back to sociologist J.P.S. Uberoi's seminal work on the deep structure of modern science, *Science and Culture* (Uberoi 1978). In the discourse of an alternative science in India, Uberoi has asked many new questions. Uberoi shows the violence that is integral to the dualistic structure of modern science and pleads for a non-dualist science that would be genuinely Swarajist. Uberoi argues that modern science is not a monolithic structure and we must explore alternative traditions in the West and in western science itself. For Uberoi, India as a cultural area would be nowhere if she does not question the hegemony of modern science as the absolute repository of truth. This brings him to a dialogue with Goethe and through this Uberoi creates the portrait of "The Other Mind of Europe" for us (Uberoi 1984). For Uberoi, Goethe's method and world view is semiological as opposed to the positivist method of Newton. This semiological method is non-dualist and explores the homology among Man, Nature and God rather than reiterating the dualism among them.

Combining the Discursive Critique of Science with Practical Solution to the Challenge of Technology: The Case of MCRC and Professor C.V. Seshadri

Professor C.V. Seshadri, the founder-director of Shri AMM Murugappa Chettiar Research Center, is another important person in the alternative science movement. Unlike others Professor Seshadri combines philosophical and cultural critique of modern science and technology with creative innovation in technology and its diffusion in rural areas in and around Madras. His interests and activities are wide-ranging: from bio-chemistry to epistemology, from engineering to education. It is perhaps for this reason that a recent article has introduced him as "Scientist as Innovator-Epistemologist" (Seshadri 1990). Born in 1930, Professor Seshadri had his studies in the Universities of Madras, Bombay, and Carnegie Mellon. He obtained his Ph.D. in chemical engineering from Carnegie Mellon in 1958. After decades of teaching at the Indian Institute of Technology, Kanpur he left it in 1974 to set up India's largest yeast factory in Mysore. He founded the Murugappa Chettiar Research Center (MCRC) in 1977 to work on the problems of rural technology: its innovation and diffusion.

MCRC has pioneered the development of a number of innovative technologies to help the poor in various fields—from good roofing technology to the development of mass culture of microalgae nutrition. Indeed, MCRC is a center of technological innovation and its communicative diffusion to the rural people not only around Madras but also in quite far-off places like Tiruchi. Mrs. Wali, a senior technologist of MCRC, narrated to me the manifold activities of the Center during my visit in December 1990. MCRC has developed an algae called *spirulina* which has high nutrition value and can be grown in an organic medium by the villagers themselves in their backyards. In Tiruchi, MCRC has its pilot plant for the culture of spirulina algae. I visited a fishermen's village near Madras where MCRC has constructed small algae acculturation tanks in the backyards. Women and children work on these plants—they know how to process the algae and make use of it.

Another important innovation is the development of high-density polyethylene boats for fishermen. Compared to wooden boats, polyethylene boats are stronger and last longer. MCRC has also developed some high-quality fish-catching nets. Mrs. Wali says: "We are applying for a project which would help us in the mass production of this technology." MCRC has also done a lot of work in the field of low-cost housing. MCRC uses the mud block compressor developed by the Indian Institute of Science, Bangalore, to make stabilized mud blocks. MCRC has developed roofing types which can be used in place of reinforced concrete slabs. These are specially designed for rain harvesting. "Since no wood is involved, the system is fire proof; and since no technical personnel is necessary, this is of a self-help type" (Krishnamurti 1987: 15).

MCRC has many programmes for income generation for village women. One activity is the making of shampoos from ash. Another innovative exercise has been in screen printing. Women are taught to print messages and pictures on sarees. Besides helping women in income generation, screen printing has also been used as a tool for education and effective social communication. Mrs. Wali feels that messages printed on sarees (for instance, on environment or family planning) would have more effectiveness because they would flow through women. Besides screen printing, MCRC has developed many cloth books. These cloth books can be helpful in adult education. Mrs. Wali tells us about the larger implication of MCRC's production of cloth books: "Our main idea is that paper books are going to have a very disastrous effect on our forest resources." Professor Seshadri also told me during our conversations about his interest behind this project on cloth books: "We are concerned with environmental degradation and the depletion of our forest resources. But the struggle for conservation cannot be confined to the boundaries of the forests alone. If we consume paper at the rate we are doing today, then this would certainly have its disastrous consequence on the forests. This is why we are interested in cloth books. What it means is that the challenge for innovation is multidimensional and it has to link different disconnected domains."

Seshadri lays emphasis on technological innovation as an important agent of creative and genuine social transformation. According to him (1990: 91):

> There are two trends of thought: one emphasizes that the technological change is important, and that it must precede the process of social change; the other emphasizes the primacy of social change. Though I do not think I belong to either one of the trends, as a practicing engineer, I tend to lean towards the technology side... Besides radical social changes which have become necessary, we must also have radical changes in technology...We emphasize the connectedness of various technological issues, while our devices may offer local solutions. This has been the strength of our work with devices in technology intervention.

Seshadri and the Criticism of Modern Science

Seshadri's work has not been confined to the engineering task of developing technology. He is equally well known for his seminal work in exposing the cultural biases and vested interests that have gone into the making of laws and theories in modern science. His work in the realm of entropy and thermodynamics is indeed exemplary. According to him, the law of entropy is not only culturally biased but also biased in favour of the rich and the industrialist. Regarding the cultural bias in the idea of entropy, he (1990: 93) notes:

> Entropy has a profound history and is such a foundational concept of modern science that it would have been invented at any event. To me, it represents a compromise between the post-Galilean science and the church. The entropy concept has much to do with messianic Christianity which affirms that there is no cycle of birth and death-

these events take place once, and you go to heaven or hell thereafter; things happen once and for all... These beliefs give rise to a notion of unidirectional time, and entropy is the modern concept which 'fixes' that direction. I would point out the kind of hold that such a concept has on thinking at various levels: for example, political leaders in the Christian West often behave the way they do because in their vision, the destruction of the world is certain and they want to control the process. The entropy concepts and such beliefs, I believe, are mutually reinforcing" (Seshadri 1990: 93).

Furthermore:

The law of entropy, backed by authority, provides a criterion for utilization of energy available from various sources. This criterion, known as the concept of efficiency, is corollary to the law of entropy and came to existence along with the law. The efficiency criterion stipulates that the loss of available energy in a conversion becomes smaller as the temperature at which the conversion is effected is higher above the ambient. Therefore, high temperatures are of high value and so are resources such as petroleum, coal etc..." (Seshadri quoted in Álvares 1988: 89).

In this context, Seshadri's critique of the second law of thermodynamics calls for our special attention. In a critical appreciation, Sahasrabudhey (1988: 4) notes the following about Seshadri's critique of thermodynamics:

(i) that concepts of thermodynamics have a western bias being rooted in the culture and commerce of the place of origin, (ii) that the second law of thermodynamics is an energy-quality marker giving a concept of efficiency which is a guide to the utilization of resources to the grave detriment of the poor and generally all those who are outside the structure of opportunities in a country like India, (iii) that, this second law in fact is not only parochial, but patently false, and (iv) that there is need for the development of new energy-quality makers in the interest of the poor and the subjugated (Sahasharabudhey 1988: 4).

Concepts of energy, heat flows and unavailability or monotonic increase in entropy are central to thermodynamics. It is believed that heat flows involve a strict one-wayness in the sense of always increasing the entropy. Sasharabudhey (1988: 27) comments:

> Entropy changes are zero only when an isolated system goes through a cycle. This concept of an 'isolated system' or isobility is central to the formulation of the second law. [However] Sheshadri contends that a way of identifying the false content of thermodynamics is to recognize that strictly speaking isobility is not conceivable, meaning that isolate systems are not possible even in principle.

Regarding the implication of energy as value inherent in the second law of thermodynamics, Seshadri and Balaji (quoted in Sahashrabudhey 1988: 20) write:

> By its very definition, energy becomes available only through a conversion process and according to the most supreme law of entropy, a portion of energy is always lost in such a process. Further, under restricted conditions, the loss can be minimized and realization of such condition is, therefore, essential for operating a process efficiently. At this level, the concept, viz., energy cannot be viewed separate from its use and itself becomes a criterion for deciding the value of resources for utilization processes at hand. Energy becomes a quality marker in resource utilization in the same way that money becomes a marker in exchange.

But energy as value does not simply decide the nature of utilization of resources, it also determines the direction of flow of resources. As Sahashrabudhey (1988: 26) argues:

> ...energy as value...is a guide which in the name of science gives credence to sweeping transfer of resources from bahiskrit [excluded] to the paschimkrit [westernized] samaj. Modern energetics is only a tool to allocate resources so as to promote modern industry and modern lifestyles at enormous costs to those outside the modern structures (also see, Georgescu-Roegen 1971; Hornborg 1992).

It is in this context that Seshadri develops two important concepts: Shakti as a new energy-quality marker and the DNA model of development. Seshadri (1980: 22-23) develops his concept of Shakti with the postulate of mass energy:

> All forms of energy have mass equivalents (with suitable dimensionalizing factors). Thus, the internal energy or energy of combustion of a material can be considered to have equivalents in terms of mass. This enables us to redefine a new class of property functions, Shakti, that combines mass and energy in such a way that quality markers can be assigned to various materials for comparison on a common basis...Shakti is a property that combines the energy of combustion and, say, the food value of the material. It should be noted that combustion is a highly irreversible reaction that oxidizes the material rapidly and edibility is akin to combustion (especially of carbohydrates) but goes through a series of slower steps with conditions closer to reversibility, and leading to the same end products. Hence, in defining one kind of Shakti, we have really used the same oxidizing property of the material. It should also be noticed that Shakti is defined as a class of property functions that can combine various kinds of energy and their mass equivalents (Seshadri 1980: 22-23).

Seshadri's DNA model of development is a plea for social transformation which is generically multidimensional.[3] Seshadri develops his concepts of Shakti and the DNA model of development in the same paper. Is there a link between the two? He seems to be suggesting that a Shakti approach to energy is the basis for the multidimensional social development that would be DNA-like. Energy as value has led to a highly unequal pattern of development in Indian society. Moreover, energy conversion, according to the law of entropy, always leads to degradation and degeneration. Ultimately it leads to a degrading view of the cosmic situation and the human condition. In this context, the idea of Shakti proposes a transformative view of the human condition with a notion of time which is not only unidirectional and irreversible but also reversible and cyclical. This transformative model of Shakti can enable us to even transform the "waste" produced from energy generation to something useful. According to Seshadri (1990: 92),

> ...it is possible to conceive of interconnections or processes which would convert what is 'rejected' to environment, the 'waste' from energy use, into food. For example, the off-gas, the waste from combustion of fossil fuels (to generate useful energy) may be used in food production. Thus, we arrive at an important concept, namely, that in a country like ours, 'waste' is a free good, a resource. The whole science, or the knowledge system, will have to be modified to suit this view which enables use of waste as a resource.

Technologies for Rural Development: The Case of ASTRA

Another research center that encourages scientists and technologists to think with their hands for technological innovation and rural development is the Center for Application of Science and Technology to Rural Areas (ASTRA) of the Indian Institute of Science (IIS), Bangalore. ASTRA was created in 1974 to reorient the research and attention of the IIS to the technological needs of the rural people. ASTRA has been active in generating and diffusing technologies for the rural areas. ASTRA has extension centers in Bangalore and Tumkur districts where it interacts with villagers. ASTRA has projects in the areas of energy, building, agroprocessing, and transportation.

ASTRA's work in the field of building technology has been pioneering. The instrument designed by ASTRA to create compressed mud blocks is being used by other groups such as MCRC. ASTRA has also developed several alternative roofing designs. But what ASTRA seems to be doing is not simply the innovation of low-cost housing technology, but the innovation of a new grammar of architecture. The architectural scene in post-independent India shows the pervasive dominance of a western architectural idiom. Western architecture creates bounded spaces where individuals inhabit an enclosed tomb or a fortress. But vernacular architecture creates spaces which act as a meeting point between nature and culture, the external and the internal. The houses built by ASTRA reflect this sensibility (Basu and Jagdish 1988).

Professor A.K.N. Reddy was instrumental in setting up ASTRA. After working two decades in the field of electrochemistry in the IIS, Reddy felt that most of the work of an institution like the Indian Institute of Science is really irrelevant to the needs of the rural poor. Hence, he wanted to set up ASTRA where the resources and research can be reoriented towards the needs of the rural poor. He told me in the interview I had with him in January 1991:

> ASTRA is not a voluntary agency. It is a regular programme of the Institute. It is what we do as members of the Institute from 10 to 5. This is important. Most of the radical movements in our country used to think that in order to do something innovative, one has to act outside the system. But here in ASTRA, we want to show that what you can do between 10 to 5 as part of an Institute can really help people.

Reddy tells us about the lessons from ASTRA's experience in the field of technological diffusion and innovation. Technological innovators should not decide for the people what kind of technological package they should be given. Moreover, women have to be involved in the process of technology diffusion. Reddy gives us example about the work in the community biogas plant in a village where ASTRA has been working for long. ASTRA could feel that with the involvement of the women, collecting cow dung became much easier. ASTRA also learnt that the challenge is to create appropriate technologies because most of our traditional technologies do not meet the challenge of the present while most of our modern technologies are inaccessible to a large number of rural people.

PEOPLE'S SCIENCE MOVEMENT

The Discourse of People's Science

In the discursive field of science and society in contemporary

India, the people's science movement has emerged as another significant interlocutor. This movement in India consists of various groups and individuals working in several areas of popularization of science and technologies. The all India people's science movement has a network of groups which is called the All India People's Science Network (AIPSN). This has 30 groups as its members. Different PSM (people's science movement) groups had first come together under the auspices of the Kerala Sastra Sahitya Parishat in 1978. The PSM groups had again met in 1983 in Trivandrum under the same auspices to reflect upon their commonality of interests and decide a future course of action. This convention included even the groups such as PPST which has, in course of time, sought to distinguish itself as an alternative science movement, different from the people's science movement. In this convention, the operational agenda of the people's science movement was identified as fighting the feudal structure in social and economic spheres and the forces of obscurantism.

In 1987 different PSM groups organized a nationwide *jatha* (which means procession and mobilization) called the *Bharat Jan Vigyana Jatha* (Indian people's science mobilization) to mobilize nationwide interest on the burning issues of science and technology. This *jatha* covered a distance of 5,000 kilometers and mobilized thousands of persons and converged in Bhopal—the place of the Union Carbide gas disaster in 1984. This *jatha* was led by science activists who also performed theaters known as *Kalajathas* along the procession route to arouse people's interest in science, society, and technology in India. In 1990, the PSM groups participated in another nationwide mobilization called the *Bharat Gyana Vigyana Jatha* which mobilized an all India campaign for literacy. This *jatha* was carried out with the active support of the Ministry of Human Resource Development of the Government of India. In this nationwide mobilization, the people's science movement groups led the fight against illiteracy. Apart from these mobilizations or *jathas*, for the last three years, PSM groups have been participating in an annual convention called the People's Science Congress. In fact, the All India People's Science Congress is organized as an alternative to the Indian Science Congress which is thought of as a state sponsored *mela* and a *tamasha* by the activists of the people's science movement.

The people's science movement wants to create a scientific temper and sensibility among the masses. It looks at science as a universal phenomenon and ridicules the idea of a culture-rooted science as anachronistic. Professor B.M. Udgaonkar who plays an important role in the people's science movement, while speaking at the valedictory session of the All India People's Science Congress held at Bombay in 1990 said: "What is the meaning of the people's science movement? Does it mean people's science with a movemental dimension to it or does it refer to people's movement with science as an important ingredient?" Various PSM groups, perhaps, would answer this question differently. However, all of the PSM groups—be it the Kerala Sastra Sahitya Parishat or the Delhi Science Forum—would agree that the people's science movement combines the agenda of people's science and people's movement in varying degrees. Professor Udgaonkar pointed out in the same speech that people's science is not a different science, but science itself: "People's science is science but there is certain social purpose in the way you handle that science." Contra-PPST and Nandy, Udgaonkar argues that "there is nothing like Indian science or Japanese science." According to him, "all these distinctions must go away. I must emphasize this with all the emphasis that I can muster."

Is the people's science movement simply viewing itself as a communicator of scientific information and the harbinger of the scientific temper to the people? Many activists from within and observers from without the movement would argue that this, indeed, is the case. This interpretation seems quite convincing in the light of the fact that many of these groups are working also in the field of science education, especially among the children. Hence, the people's science movement is considered as a mere transmitter of *Balavigyana* (children's science) rather than *Janavigyana* (peoples' science) (Raina 1990a, 1990b). But within the people's science movement, the science question is not that uncritically handled as the rhetoricians in the field of alternative science movement would make us believe. Though it is true that PSM groups do not have a philosophical and epistemological critique of science as a form of knowledge from the vantage point of Indian tradition, it nevertheless has a class critique of modern science.

I had a discussion with Dhruv Raina, a PSM sympathizer, on this issue. Raina helps us understand the complex ways in which science enters the discourse of the PSM activists. He says that there are two generations of scientists and activists and they operate with two different mythologies of science within the people's science movement. The older generation of activists such as Parameshwaran of KSSP, Sethu Rao of the Karnatak Rajya Vigyana Parishad and Professor Radhanath Rath of the Orissa Vigyana Prachar Samiti operate with an old mythology of science whose chief proponent is J.D. Bernal. In this mythology, science, industrialization, and the big scale exist harmoniously and need each other. The younger activists operate with a different mythology of science where science is primarily a critical activity. For them it is the nature of this activity rather than some universalistic meaning of science that is the key issue in addressing the question of science and society in contemporary India. The second mythology, Raina is quick to point out, has nonetheless influenced the older generation. For instance, KSSP has recently taken keen interest in ecology and has effectively intervened to halt the environmentally disastrous Silent Valley project in Kerala. Earlier, KSSP could dismiss ecological questions as simply a middle-class obsession.

Let us now look at some groups who are important players in the all India people's science movement.

Kerala Sastra Sahitya Parishat

The Kerala Sastra Sahitya Parishat (KSSP) is the oldest active PSM group in India. It started as an organization of science writers in Kerala in 1962. KSSP has had undergone many turns in its reflection and social intervention. A KSSP writer in 1983 describes its history: "As an idea, it is 25 years old, as a body of persons it is 20 years old and as a movement it is 10 years old" (KSSP 1984: 3). In the initial phase, KSSP devoted itself solely to better and more effective science communication. In the first fifteen years, KSSP had solely confined itself to the production of popular science texts both for the students in the school as well as for the interested public at large. But, in the last fifteen years, KSSP has taken an activistic stance in the field of education, health, and environment. KSSP has used a novel form of communication—street theaters and *jathas*—to present its ideas before the masses.

Dr. M.P. Parameswaran is a key interlocutor of KSSP. Parameswaran has a Ph.D. in nuclear engineering from the Moscow Power Institute. Before leaving for the USSR, Parameswaran was working in an atomic energy establishment (which later came to be known as the Bhabha Atomic Research Center) in Bombay. Parameswaran has been interested in popular science and in popularizing science from a very early age. Early, in his career, while working at the atomic energy establishment, he had read a book called *Explaining the Atom* . After reading this book he thought he could write a similar book in Malayalam. In fact , he began writing on science related themes in Malayalam. As he told me during my interview with him: "When I went to Moscow, I took the Hindi dictionary of scientific words with me called the *Paribhasik Shabda Sangraha.* I tried to find the Malayalam equivalents for these technical words which were translated into Hindi." What led him ultimately to the field of science communication and popularization of science?

In 1968, the then Minister of Education of Government of India, Dr. Triguna Sen, had allotted some funds for the development of state languages. The Kerala State Government had formed the State Institute of Languages and I joined this to develop scientific literature in Malayalam. In 1969, I took leave from my work at the Bhabha Atomic Research Center and left for Kerala and stayed for four years. Gradually I became convinced that there is no meaning in doing nuclear physics. At that time, I came in close contact with the CPI (M) in Kerala. I resigned from my job at BARC and left for good for Kerala. I spent part of my time working for the party publication division and the rest doing voluntary work for KSSP. I did not have any salary. I used to publish party materials and make some money out of it.

Much is made of the close association between KSSP and the CPI (M) cadre in Kerala. Parameswaran does not hide his association with CPI (M):

KSSP did not have any problem whether it was Left government or not because KSSP people belong to all parties: Congress (I), CPI and even the RSS. KSSP does not take a political stand. Of course, KSSP takes stand by which it becomes political because the stand had political implications but it is not a political party. We get support from not only a large number of supporters of CPI (M) but also from the supporters of CPI and the Congress. Moreover, we have taken stand on issues such as the Silent Valley which has antagonized even the Left government in Kerala.

Parameswaran reiterates his interest in Marxist philosophy both as a student and as a political worker. Parameswaran says: "Marxist philosophy explains everything including atomic physics." He contrasts Marxist philosophy with Vedanta and says: "The Vedanta way is not only incompatible with social revolution but also incompatible with life itself." Regarding his interaction with Gandhi and Gandhism, Parameswaran says:

Gandhiji gave slogans which the individual can do. Gandhi gave us the challenge of khadi. We in the PSM are now speaking of literacy as a national challenge. Today spinning the yarn is not what is required. But today teaching somebody science and literacy becomes the 'charka' of Gandhiji. Another thing I thought significant in Gandhi, accentuated by my experience in KSSP, is that if the means of production are too large [if the scale of operation is too large], you cannot become a master of it and if you cannot be a master of something, then there cannot be true democracy. But I also think that "small is beautiful" would not work. In the present context, we need not only have the small which is beautiful but the small which is efficient and powerful to compete with the mega-multinational corporations. In my thought on the small scale, I am inspired by the Indian tradition because I think that smallness as a category is central to the Indian tradition.

Another aspect of Indian philosophy which ought to inform our scientific sensibility, according to Parameswaran, is the dictum of *Gita* which says: "You have only rights over work, not over its results." Parameswaran interprets this to mean:

You interact with nature but you cannot dictate the fruits of nature. The fruits are dictated by laws of nature, not by you. This is also beautifully explained by Marx and Engels in their statement: Freedom is the recognition of necessity. This aspect is easier to be taken [learnt] from Indian philosophy than from the western philosophy.

Regarding the argument that western science has the conquest of nature as its primary objective inspired by the Christian view that man is the master of nature, Parameswaran says:

The Christian character of conquering nature is the human character. Ultimately, what we are doing is transforming nature. The essence of science (eastern or western) is the same: you interact with nature, collate and generalize new ways of interacting with nature. This method is common to the Indian sciences like Ayurveda and Chemistry. There is absolutely no difference between Indian science and western science. Science means asking questions but the difference lies in who is asking questions, the Tatas or the tribals? Of course, the answer would be the same but the results would be used for different purposes.

KSSP had launched a campaign to make Kerala totally literate which became a reality in 1991. Regarding the overarching significance of literacy in the PSM mobilization, Parameswaran says: "Of course, there is a hidden curriculum behind literacy. We want to empower people with knowledge so that they can fight domination. You can also create a nationwide cross-class mobilization for literacy because everybody understands the significance of literacy while the defenders of establishment do not understand the meaning of this hidden curriculum." "Is this the reason why middle-class radicals abound in the people's science movement?" I asked Parameswaran. Parameswaran replied:

> In a way, that is correct. Literacy gives them a larger space than any other slogan. To read and to write is to work out a hidden curriculum. The knowledge you get gradually goes beyond literacy and continues to touch the question of social development. For instance, our literacy mission has created extraordinary level of confidence among the people of Kerala. Now our people are engaged in the resource mapping of each locality.

In the all India people's science movement, much is made about the uniqueness of Kerala and the uniqueness of KSSP as a science movement. Many argue that KSSP had the privilege to grow and mobilize in unique social circumstance and with the support of CPI (M) and the government. But when one talks to the activists of KSSP, one comes to realize the impediments they also faced. An idealized model of KSSP cannot help us understand how it operates synchronically with the challenges that any innovation faces in India and even in the paradise of Kerala. Parameswaran dispels the uniqueness myth of KSSP: "Of course, in Kerala, we have a strong tradition of social movements but how did these movements start in the first place? They are started by people. KSSP starts from a higher level, other groups can start from a lower level and come to this level. There is nothing unique. You are only in a running stream, you are at this level or at that level."

People's Science Movements and Pedagogy: The Case of Ekalvya

Eklavya is a PSM group in Madhya Pradesh. Eklavya was registered in 1982 to take up the pioneering task of science education initiated by two other voluntary groups in the state—Friends Rural Center and Kishore Bharati working in the district of Hoshangabad. Sudarshan Kapoor and Anil Sadgopal were then active with these two groups, which were established in the early 1970s. In 1972, Sadgopal and Kapoor along with their friends from the locality as well as from such premier institutions like the Tata Institute of Fundamental Research had launched an activity-based science teaching programme (HSTP) in 16 schools of Hoshangabad district. In 1978, the programme was extended to all the schools of the district. This expansion required more careful work on quickly expanding the science teaching programme to other schools and Eklavya was formed in 1982 to carry out this task. During the time of my fieldwork in January 1991, Eklavya had science teaching programmes in 16 districts of Madhya Pradesh.

Eklavya's creativity revolves around science teaching and its science teaching programme is the creative embodiment of the original HSTP programme. Key to HSTP is the idea of activity-based education. In this exercise of the mind and the heart, a learner is encouraged to participate in what Einstein had once called the "holy spirit of inquiry". Students are taken out to field visits and observe nature. For instance, one science teacher who teaches the HSTP curriculum in a middle school told me how specific subjects are taught only during the period when these phenomena occur in nature so that students have an opportunity to observe in nature what is taught in the class room. For instance, if the reproductive life of frog has to be taught in the class, then it is almost invariably taught in the rainy season so that students can observe it in nature. Even in the teaching of social sciences, activity-based education is encouraged. Social science teachers take the students out to the market and arrange meetings with village panchayat functionaries. Such activity-based teaching gives a new sense of discovery to both students and teachers. For Vinod Raina (1989: 7-8), a key architect of Eklavya, activity-based teaching breaks down the usual notion of child-teacher interaction:

Such breakdown includes the reorientation of class room architecture where rows of 'disciplined' and silent students sitting in neat rows are liberated into groups of excited and chattering bundles of energy and joy, engrossed in their activity at a level of 'indiscipline' or freedom, that is essential for the transaction of critical knowledge. Science at elementary school level also offers the opportunity to generate information through experiment and activity, making it less binding to supply it through comprehensive texts. Thus, it is possible to bring some of discovery into action, and this has been the major attempt at HSTP.

Eklavya is devoted to science education but it does not follow a canonical approach either to science or to science teaching. For instance, exactness seems to be occupying a sacred place in science especially when it is linked with the discourse of measurement. HSTP tries to free itself from a dogmatic attitude to measurement. HSTP tries to promote the idea that exactness is more contextual than absolute. Vinod Raina (1989: 9) tells us more about this:

> At training workshops, teachers are asked to measure the same length, say that of a class room, individually and record their observation on a piece of paper. All these observations are then written down together in a black board. The teachers are horrified to see the variation...So, by actual practice, students and teachers realize that no matter how careful you are, repeated measurements produce variations which are ultimately linked to the resolution of the measuring instrument

Along with activity-based education, Eklavya lays emphasis on the inculcation of a spirit of counter-hegemony among students which derives knowledge from popular folklore and common sense. In Eklavya's social science text book, one sees this in operation. For instance, while I was visiting a middle school in the district of Dewas, the social science teacher showed me Eklavya's social science text book for the eighth class. The chapter on the Mughal Empire entitled "The Amir of the Mughal Empire" begins with a very big picture of the Amir carried in a palanquin by eight people with one person carrying a pot so that the "Amir ' can throw his chewed betel nut into the pot. All of us present in the school had a hearty laugh while looking at this picture. The teacher observed: "Yes, students react in the same way. They laugh, laugh and laugh. Moreover, they quickly relate this to their immediate environment and are also able to jeer at the modern Amirs who consume and exploit like the emperors."

Ekalvya lays emphasis on teaching through a dialogue between students and teachers. However, this dialogue is not simply confined to the class room conversation: it is embodied in the very text itself. Many a time, dialogue in education seems to be boiling down to dialogically transmitting a text which is monological to begin with. But text books prepared by Eklavya are not monological. When one goes through its social science text books, one realizes this. A subject is discussed step by step following a question answer method. Several alternatives are suggested to discuss a particular issue. Then, after checking out that these alternatives do not contain the best explanation of the problem at hand, a final explanation is provided. Because the whole text is not written authoritatively, a student has the opportunity to create a space for dialogic imagination and critical intervention.

Eklavya has field centers in different parts of the state such as in Hard, Pipariya, Ujjain, Dewas, and Bhopal. Each of the field centers works on several issues such as science education and women's health and organizes games and different scholarly "corners" for school students. During my fieldwork, I had visited the Eklavya field center in the district town of Dewas just 30 km away from Indore. Eklavya runs a library at Dewas. It also hosts a monthly discussion forum called Eklavya Vichar Manch.

The Ekalvya field center at Dewas has two women resource persons, apart from other male workers, who work on the issues of women and children. But in their activities, these two women are not confined to the school setting; they work among the village women in diverse settings: from home to the field. But working on women's issues has not been easy for these two women Eklavya activists. One woman activist tells us about this:

Until recently, I was alone working on things which are so different [i.e., on the women's issues]. I do not organize a *jatha* or anything spectacular. Hence, I cannot show anything in terms of concrete results [i.e. I have been able to organize so many *jathas* this month]. Moreover, I have difficulty in organizing people, and even articulating very clearly what I want to do. But my male colleagues want me to work in a masculine way. Eklavya lacks an appreciation of women's issues. Having another female colleague recently has made a lot of difference. Now we want to form a women's group outside Eklavya.

But the gender bias, according to her, is not simply confined to organizational issues. It even permeates the text prepared by Eklavya. One of the insider observers of Eklavya has recently written:

Indeed, despite the ambient of S&T consciousness of the programme and the involvement of its participants in the activities of the People's Science Network, many uncomfortable beliefs have been seen to persist and surface quite unexpectedly even among the resource persons. For instance, ideas such as the biological determinism of the 'weaker' female sex, the indubitable superiority of the scientifically produced hybrid species...have often been confidently professed by responsible persons associated with the programme (Ramphal 1990: 1-2).

R.N. Shyag is the leader of the Eklavya field center at Dewas. Shyag comes from Punjab. He had first come to the HSTP training programme in 1978 on a UGC deputation and has been working with Eklavya as a key resource person since its resurrection and inception in 1982. Shyag emphasizes that what he is doing is not *seva* (service).

All of us get a good salary with which we can live in a city in a middle-class lifestyle. We have decided to have our field centers in the cities so that we can give good education to our children. In the field center, we do not believe in a campus life. Hence, we have our own places to stay. Having a campus is a kind of a limiting factor. If you stay on your own in a city, then you can freely interact with people.

We are basically a middle class group and our activities cater to the middle class. But working on education enables us to be engaged in some radical agenda. If you talk about minimum wage, you cannot mobilize many people. Moreover, you would face stiff opposition. There are so many problems, we cannot handle them all. Education is common and acceptable to all. There is no direct contradiction [confrontation?] involved and it is an entry point for working with people.

Hardy is another core activist of Eklavya. He has a Ph.D. in Physics from University of Delhi and was teaching in one of the colleges. Soon he realized that the answer to most of the questions that bothered him did not lie in physics. He had been associated with the Hoshangabad Science Teaching Programme even from his M.A. days. He resigned from his university job and joined Eklavya. Hardy tells us: "Being a part of a group brings clarity and confusion simultaneously. It brings confusion because your framework of understanding the world gradually starts widening. In Eklavya, one has learnt more than what one has learnt the rest of one's life. We have not only learnt physics, but sociology, economics, and politics. This is an experience which never could have been produced in a university kind of setting."

What has motivated Hardy in the first place to join Hoshangabad science teaching? Is there any factor in his life that can help us understand his trajectory as a social activist? Hardy says that his friends always pointed out that he suffers from a strange complex of always feeling that the world rests upon his shoulders. His mother is, perhaps, responsible for this chronic world-mindedness not taking a RSS-turn. "My mother was influenced by Gandhi, Subash, Ramakrishna and Ma Sarada. For me, options were clear: I could not join the RSS camp."

Hardy helps us to situate the politics of young students like himself as well as that of the initiatives like Hoshangabad Science Teaching Programme in its historical context:

> There is a connection with the Naxalbari movement. Coming to rural areas seemed what we could do at the most. There were a lot of ideas floating around in the wake of the Naxalbari movement. Many people in the academy felt that Naxalbari won't succeed unless people in the cow-belt are mobilized. The formation of groups like Kishore Bharati is, partly, influenced by these considerations. A lot of us did feel a sense of crisis of identity. A lot of people were reading existential philosophy. But I rejected part of existentialism because I thought individual salvation is not the answer. My decision to do my Ph.D. here and not to go abroad was part of an effort to define some identity for myself.

This brief biographical understanding of Eklavya can be enriched by the conversation I had with Dr. Anil Sadgopal, the pioneer of the Hoshangabad Science Teaching Programme, in December 1990. Sadgopal had developed an activistic attitude and concern quite early in his life. He developed a leaning towards Marxism during college days. After completing doctoral study in the United States, he came back to join Delhi University's Physics Department. He established Kishore Bharati in 1972. In the words of Sadgopal:

> In Kishore Bharati, we engaged young people to have critical awareness of their surroundings. We did social studies of drought and tuberculosis to show how these affect different social groups differently. In course of time, we got into organizing rural labour. But soon we came to realize that on issues such as this the feudal forces won't let you work. It is not that the government is directly putting pressure on you to stop. An institution has to decide whether it has

to organize rural labour or do educational work; in the case of the former, you have to have the backing of a large political party.

Regarding his association with the people's science movement and the PSM perspective, Sadgopal says: "Because of our interest in the question of development, we got in touch with KSSP in 1978. We went to Kerala and tried to understand what KSSP was doing." On the perspective that motivates PSM as a social movement, Sadgopal provides us his understanding of the problem:

> PSM calls for spreading the scientific temper. But this is something to which the government is also committed in principle. In fact, our Constitution was amended in 1976 to include scientific temper in our national agenda. But PSM groups have remained within the governmental framework and have not questioned the nature of science and technology. Government does not take seriously the issue of scientific temper. It is only interested in the popularization of science. This is because if people do not absorb scientific information then there is a limit to the spread of the state and the market.

In his 1981 Vikram Sarabhai Memorial Lecture, Sadgopal (1981: 15) argues: "...the primary role of science is enabling the people to comprehend the socio-political reality of their environment through the scientific method so that their struggle for justice and development can be planned on the basis of reliable data and logical thinking." For Sadgopal, scientific method and scientific temper are essential for the purpose of training cadres and creating people's organizations. According to Sadgopal (1981: 21): "If methods of science can thus be made part of people's thinking, there is hope that the domination of the educated elite and of vested interests can be challenged by the common people." Vinod Raina also wants to use science as an important instrument in people's struggle against the disastrous programmes of development. Thus, Eklavya's approach to science and Indian social reality is not simply that of making science fit for consumption as a packaged good of the establishment and state.

PSM and Policy Intervention: The Case of Delhi Science Forum

The Delhi Science Forum (DSF) is another active PSM group which came into existence in 1981. It involves many important scientists and technologists in Delhi and works with close collaboration with the Department of Science and Technology of government of India. DSF is a leading group in the All India People's Science Network. Its distinctive leadership lies in its pioneering work on several policy issues that involve the question of science and technology. Today, the operation of the state has become so complex that any critique of the state has to be informed by a deep knowledge of different policy formulations. Within the people's science movement DSF fulfills this responsibility and has published critical studies on health, drug industry, seed policy, the Pepsi deal, the nuclear holocaust, and the Bhopal disaster (Abrol 1990; Delhi Science Forum 1984, 1987, 1989, 1990; Rao 1988; and Sengupta 1986).

DSF has also worked in the field of technological innovation for the artisans, mainly for leather workers. For DSF, even though the country has witnessed, especially in recent years, a rapid growth of the leather industry, this growth has been mainly confined to the major urban industrial complexes. DSF wants to restructure the leather industry which would integrate the rural artisans with the overall structure. DSF had organized a workshop on "Technology for Artisans, Landless Laborers and the Other Poor" which was sponsored by the Department of Science and Technology. It then evolved a model which involved networking of flayers, tanners, and footwear makers setting up collective productive organizations of tanners for higher income and productivities. Tanning units and networks for supply of raw hides and utilization of vegetable-tanned leathers were set up in 1984 under the S&T sponsored research projects by it at Mandi (Himachal Pradesh), Dehradun (Uttar Pradesh) and Kavali (Andhra Pradesh). The units at Mandi and Dehradun reached break even in January 1986 and have been self-supportive since then.

DSF is striving for the widespread replication of its model for the leather industry. In fact, several S&T voluntary organizations have expressed interest in taking up the same sorts of projects and have approached DSF for technical collaboration as well as assistance in obtaining grants and projects from government agencies.

The Discourse of Science Activism in Contemporary India: Locating its Genealogy and Understanding its Significance

A discursive formation, like a social formation, has its origin in a particular intersection of space and time, the understanding of which requires what anthropologist Arjun Appadurai (1991) has called the "genealogy of the present". It means to start with key actors in the contemporary discursive terrain and move with them in their own constructed biography and reconstructed history to find out the origin and genealogical ground of the discursive formation. The narratives of actors such as Hardy help us in this task.

The Naxalbari movement forms the historical backdrop in which many activists in people's science movements formed their social commitment and have framed their social vision. In a recent insightful study of the Naxalite movement, sociologist Rabindra Ray (1988) has argued that the Naxalite movement precipitated the crisis of identity for people in institutions of higher learning. It raised basic questions regarding the relevance of university education including the expertise on science. At the peak of the Naxalbari wave, this growing sense of irrelevance led to a basic ontological doubt and political nihilism. The fire that arose in one's soul could be extinguished only with the liquidation of the class enemy. But once Naxalite terrorism itself was liquidated by state action, the souls in fire were perhaps forced to take recourse to some channels of creative social work and social transformation.

It is in this context that we have to understand how some turned to people's science and science activism. The emerging science and technology groups in the mid-1970s offered many young students of science and technology a social vision, a space for participation and intervention. Participation in social movements helps in the resolution of identity crisis of an actor which might have either biographical or historical origin or both (Giri 1989; Ginsburg 1989). The emerging science activism in the mid-1970s offered young students an ideal participatory platform.

It is in this historical context that we can understand how science activism touched a sympathetic chord in scientists and scholars belonging to both the people's science movement and the alternative science movement. For instance, Ashis Nandy tells us in the conversation that I had with him that his scholarship on science had emerged out of his existential dissatisfaction with the Emergency and was inspired by the JP movement. It is the Emergency and the JP movement which perhaps had converted young scientists and technologists with a Marxist leaning to Gandhism. Many of the activists of PPST, as Navjyoti Singh's narrative has already made it clear, started with Marxism but subsequently got disillusioned with it and became proselytizing Gandhians.

If Eklavya activist Hardy's comments help us to discover the genealogy of the discourse of science activism, Eklavya resource person Shyag's comments help us understand the ideological contours of people's science. Here we may remember Shyag's very insightful observation: "We are basically a middle class group and our activities are catered to the middle-class." The ideological space of radicalism and social intervention that the people's science movement in contemporary India creates is filled by the socially committed middle-class. The students of science and technology with a middle-class background and origin, perhaps, could not join a programme of total social revolution which might bring them into direct confrontation with the powers that be. Working with the PSM groups provides them a somewhat less threatening space where they can feel that they are contributing something important to the transformation of society without paying a heavy penalty for it.

It is the activists with a middle-class origin that proliferate the new social movements in advanced industrial societies (Kriesi 1989). The middle-class self world over is now in a historic need of openness and flexibility (Mankin 1978; Wood and Zurcher 1988). Besides helping in identity formation, participation in new social movements helps the middle-class actors attain a degree of flexibility of action and imagination which is not otherwise available. This idea of flexibility and openness might help us in our understanding of the middle-class activists in the people's science movement. They are educated and are experts in their fields of study and training. But they have deliberately chosen to work with PSM groups which provides them a sense of fulfillment and a horizon of possibility. Working with PSM groups, on the other hand, does not entail any material disadvantage. Many PSM groups pay well their full-time workers. Hence, if one is able to earn a comfortable livelihood without selling one's soul to the Devil of Lucifer, then why not go for it? At the same time, working with PSM groups means that one has the flexibility to make one's vision turn into social reality. Hence, participation in science movements is not simply a question of sacrifice. It is integrally linked to the opportunity for self-fulfillment that such participation provides not only in terms of resolution of one's identity crisis but also in terms of earning a livelihood where one's own deepest aspiration for self-realization becomes an instrument in actual or perceived social transformation.

In understanding the emergent ideology of any discursive formation, we cannot simply confine ourselves to the existential crisis of the actors, we must pay equal attention to the crisis of identity of the institutions themselves. Speaking of crisis of institutions, we must not simply be swayed away by the crisis as portrayed by critics of institutions but must be sympathetic to the existential pangs of the institutions themselves. Social movements not only help the individual actors in their resolution of the crisis of identity, it also helps concerned institutions in coming to terms with their dilemma of irrelevance. As the noted French sociologist Alain Touraine argues, social movements are not only agents of transformation of the actors they are also agents of transformation of institutions (Touraine 1981, 1988). The credibility of different PSM groups in terms of stewardship of social vision have enabled government departments to transform themselves, however limited it might be. In the eyes of the PSM activists, the Department of Science and Technology and the Ministry of Human Resource Development are less bureaucratic and less corrupt. Moreover, the personnel working in these two departments also feel that PSM groups are credible and funds provided to them would always have its desired effects.

Along with the issue of institutional transformation, what needs to be understood is that, in the last two decades, institutions of governance and state in India have attained a differentiated character which has created a novel space of mediation and interaction even for the critics of the system. In dealing with PSM groups, we must realize that these groups do not have an undifferentiated indictment of the whole structure. They get funds from government departments by not necessarily selling their souls. It is not fair to say, as some critics allege, that PSM groups funded by government are simply state-sponsored PSM groups. These groups occupy a negotiated space but the space of negotiation is also a critical space, it is different from a the space of total absorption. Moreover, the PSM groups have a different reason as to why they accept government fund. As one of the PSM leaders says: "It is people's money and we have a responsibility to use it for the real development of the people. Otherwise, who is going to be the beneficiary of this money? Contractors and corrupt bureaucrats!"

After a brief reflection on the genealogy and ideology of the discourse of science activism in India, some comments on its wider significance is in order. But before coming straight to a consideration of the significance of science activism, some general comments on their nature vis-a-vis voluntary organizations and organized politics would be helpful. For Dinesh Abrol, one of the key figures in the All India People's Science Movement, it is not true that a PSM group is simply another voluntary organization or an NGO showing abhorrence towards organized politics. Many of the PSM groups have linkages with political parties and when they organize a mobilization or stage a *dharana*, they receive help from the political cadres of some of the sympathetic political parties. Abrol also makes two other important observations regarding PSM groups. Majority of PSM groups start with a very humble beginning. In Abrol's own words, they start with a *jholla* (shoulder bag). But soon they mobilize resources, receive funds, and undergo a phase of institutionalization. They start with a charter but they continuously debate their own charters and modify them. According to him, nobody could dream of what KSSP today is compared to what it was in 1962.

But the most important significance of the people's science movement lies in preparing us in the domain of resource mobilization. Mobilizing resources continues to be high on the agenda of the people's science movement. But this mobilization does not refer to getting a grant or receiving government funds. It means mobilizing human resources of various kinds to meet the multi-dimensional challenges of science, technology, health, education and literacy. Different PSM groups strive to mobilize different kinds of human resources: some mobilizing teachers (Eklavya), some mobilizing active science volunteers (KSSP), and some scientists and technologists (Delhi Science Forum). Moreover, mobilization of resource is not very different from the quest for an identity. There is a great hiatus between those who look at social movements as agents of identity formation and those who look at them as agents of resource mobilization (Giri 1994a). But in many emergent collective actions, these boundaries are giving rise to a new politics of alignment and blurring of genres where the identity itself becomes a resource (Giri 1992; Rochon 1988). The specific groups that PSM groups educate and prepare not only give the actors a new sense of identity but also becomes a great asset and resource in the hands of PSM groups themselves. It must be stressed that understanding the wider significance of the people's science movement requires a much wider conceptualization of resources and resource mobilization.

The people's science movement in India is striving to create a wider conception of resources which is not simply bound by reality but is a constituent of possibility. It is this wider view which perhaps motivates the PSM activists to strive incessantly for total literacy. In another context, a noted sociologist of India has written: "It is essential to have a broad view of...resources and not define them narrowly in terms of the economic criteria of wealth and income" (Beteille 1991: 15). Hence, it is no wonder then that after total literacy, the Kerala Shastra Sahitya Parishat has undertaken the task of resource mapping for all the panchayats of Kerala. According to Parameswaran, "In Kerala, yet another programme to involve the village level people for a massive mapping of the entire state is being initiated. This should lead to the building up of natural resources data management systems, geographic information systems, and actual development planning at the panchayat level." This is hoped to be a great asset in the drive towards genuine and meaningful decentralization and local level planning. It is in this quest for possibility—a possible more humane India with an expanded meaning of both identity and resource—that the significance of science as a discursive formation lies.

NOTES

1. In the words of Raina (1989: 2):
   The role of a people's science movement..is...defined as not merely that of communicating and simplifying science (though that is essential) but also questioning each aspect of such [alienating] progress and development, in particular the S&T issues involved, and intervening wherever necessary with the active participation of the so called ordinary men and women.

2. According to Dharampal (1987: 38):

The society and the polity of India...was in a fairly flourishing state even as late as the 1750s, and in many areas still around 1800. The living standard of the people...seems to have been adequate and appreciably higher than that of similar classes in Britain around 1800. Productivity in agriculture was much higher than the British agriculture; agricultural tools, implements and practice were diverse and sophisticated; the crafts not only of the celebrated textiles, but also the production of iron and steel, of various chemicals and dyes, of gur and sugar, the construction of ships, the art of building or the craft of the digging of tanks as well as river and road transportation compared and, perhaps with advantage, to that which prevailed elsewhere in these spheres.

3. Seshadri discusses the significance of the two contrasting structural forms: the helix and the spiral. While the spiral as a form is two-dimensional, the "helix is a form that is purely three-dimensional and never-less" (Seshadri 1980: 31). According to him (1980: 34):

The most fundamental components of living systems are helical...the double helix of DNA, the triple helix of collagen and so on. In fact, the double helix of DNA is mechanically and structurally a strong form....It is this mechanical property of DNA that has been made use of in a wind motor at MCRC....When compared to a Darreus Triposkein wind device, the DNA device has a higher packing fraction and offers a greater surface to the wind. It can be conjectured that the most fundamental unit of self-organization, self-replication and repair must have evolved to be very sound mechanically, structurally and otherwise. Thus one asks the next question: if DNA is helical, larger living forms are helical or use the helix widely, can systems of organism be 'helical,' can society be DNA-like.

REFERENCES

Abrol, Dinesh, 1990, *GATT Astrophe: A Close Look: A Report on the Uruguay Round Negotiations*. Paper presented at the 4th All India People's Science Congress, Bombay.

Alvares, Claude, 1988, "Science, Colonialism and Violence: A Luddite View" in Ashis Nandy (ed.), *Science, Hegemony and Violence,* New Delhi: Oxford University Press.

Appadurai, Arjun, 1991, "The Global Ethnoscape: Notes & Queries for a Transnational Anthropology" in Richard G. Fox (ed.), *Recapturing Anthropology: Working in the Present.* Santa Fe, New Mexico: School of American Research Press.

Bajaj, J.K., 1982, "Green Revolution: A Historical Perspective", *PPST Bulletin,* Vol. 2, No. 2.

——, 1985, "Towards a Non-Western Perspective on Scientific Knowledge", *PPST Bulletin* No. 8: 97-105.

——, 1988, "Francis Bacon: The First Philosopher of Modern Science", in Ashsh Nandy (ed.), *Science, Hegemony and Violence: A Requiem for Modernity,* Delhi: Oxford University Press.

Bajaj, J.K. (ed.), 1993, *Ayodhya and the Future of India,* Madras: Center for Policy Research.

Balasubramaniam, A.V., 1989, "National Workshop on Traditional Medicine and Immunization", *PPST Bulletin* No. 18: 26-36.

Basu, Subash and K. Jagdish, 1988, "Vernacular Architecture in Karnataka", Indian Institute of Science, Bangalore: ASTRA.

Beteille, Andre, 1991, "Reproduction of Inequality: Occupation, Caste and the Family", *Contributions to Indian Sociology* (n.s.) 25 (1): 3-28.

Delhi Science Forum, 1984, *Bhopal Gas Tragedy*, Delhi.

——, 1987, *Impediments to Promotion and Spread of Scientific Temper*, Delhi.

——, 1989, *The Seeds of Dependence: A Close Look at the New Seed Import Policy*, Delhi.

——, 1990, *Action Under 301: Threat to India and the Multilateral Trading System*, Delhi.

Dharampal, 1971a, *Indian Science and Technology in the Eighteenth Century: Some Contemporary European Accounts.*

——, 1971b, *Civil Disobedience and the Indian Tradition.*

——, 1983a, *The Beautiful Tree: Indigenous Education in the Eighteenth Century.*

——, 1983b, "A Note on the Disruption and the Disorganization of Indian Society in the Last Two Centuries", *PPST Bulletin* 3 (2): 18-47.

——, 1987, *Some Aspects of Earlier Indian Society and Polity and Their*

Relevance to the Present, Poona: New Quest Publications.

Foucault, Michael, 1972, *The Archeaology of Knowledge and the Discourse on Language,* NY: Pantheon.

Georgescu-Roegen, N., 1971, *Entropy Laws and the Economic Process,* Cambridge, MA: Harvard University Press.

Giri, Ananta, 1989, "Narratives of Creative Transformation: Constituting Critical Movements in Contemporary American Culture". *Dialectical Anthropology* 14 (4).

——, 1992, "Mobilizing Resource: Towards a New Conceptualization", *Mainstream,* May 30.

——, 1994a, *In the Margins of Shacks: The Vision and Practice of Habitat for Humanity,* Johns Hopkins University, Baltimore: Ph.D. Thesis.

——, 1994b, "Some Contemporary Notes on Method", *Man & Development,* June 1994.

Ginsburg, Faye D., 1989, *Contested Lives: Abortion Debate in an American Community,* Berkeley: University of California Press.

Habermas, Jurgen, 1981, *Philosophical-Political Profile,* p. 17.

Hornborg, Alf, 1992, "Machine Fetishism, Value, and the Image of the Unlimited Good: Towards a Thermodynamics of Imperialism", *Man* (n.s.) 27 (1): 1-18.

Jairath, Vinod, 1990, Review of Ashis Nandy (ed.), *Science, Hegemony and Violence, Contributions to Indian Sociology.*

Jhunjhunwala, Ashok and B. Ramamurthy, 1990, "Technological Self-Reliance: Need for New Initiatives", *PPST Bulletin* No. 19 & 20: 45-57.

Kerala Sastra Sahitya Parishad, 1984, *Science as Social Activism: Reports and Papers on The People's Science Movements in India,* Trivandrum.

Kriesi, Hanspeter, 1989, "New Social Movements and the New Class in the Netherlands", *American Journal of Sociology* 94 (5): 1078-1116.

Krishnamurthy, Jayalakshmi, 1987, *The Jayaja Tile: A New Type of Roofing,* Madras: Shri AMM Murugappa Chettiar Research Center.

Habermas, Jurgen, 1981, *Philosophical-Political Profiles,* London: Heinemann.

Khandekar, Sreekanth, 1984, "The Lesson of Change", *India Today,* July 15 1984: 120-22.

Mankin, David, 1978, *Towards a Post-Industrial Psychology.*

Mintz, Sidney W., 1985, *Sweetness and Power: The Place of Sugar in Modern History,* Penguin.

——, 1987, "Author's Rejoinder", Symposium Review of "Sweetness and Power", *Food and Foodways.*

——, 1991, "Comments on the articles by Tomich, McMichael and Roseberry", Special Issue on Slavery in the New World: *Theory and Society* 20 (3): 383-392.

Mukund, K., 1988, "The Hoshangabad Science Teaching Programme", *Economic and Political Weekly*, October 1988: 2147-2149.

Nandy, Ashis, 1980, *Alternative Sciences*, Delhi: Allied Publishers.

——, 1982, "Science for Unafraid." *Mainstream*, June 26, 1982: 17-19.

——, 1983, "Towards an Alternative Politics of Psychology", *International Social Science Journal*: 324-338.

——, 1987, *Tradition, Tyranny and Utopia: Essays in the Politics of Awareness.* New Delhi: Oxford University Press.

——, 1988a, "Science as a Reason of the State", in Ashis Nandy (ed.), *Science, Hegemony and Violence: A Requiem for Modernity,* New Delhi: Oxford University Press.

——, 1988b, "(Alternative Science Movement) A Reply to Ram Guha", *Lokayan Bulletin* 6 (6).

PPST Bulletin, 1990, "The Alternative Decade and After: Report on a get Together Sponsored by the PPST Foundation", Issue No. 21: 51-67.

Rao, K. Ashok, 1988, *Public Sector: Critique of the Present Perspective and Framework for an Alternative*, New Delhi: Delhi Science Forum.

Raina, Dhruv, 1988, "From Bala Vigyana to Jana Vigyana: Towards Popular Science Movements", Paper presented at the 10th Anniversary Celebrations of Bala Vigyana, National College, Bangalore.

——, 1990, "Commoditised Science or Science for Consumption", *Economic and Political Weekly,* October 13, 1990.

Raina, Vinod, 1989, "Education within the Framework of People's Science Movement", Theme paper presented at the 2nd People's Science Congress at Calcutta.

——, 1991, "Formal and Non-Formal Communication Channels for Disaster Preparedness", Lecture delivered at the 1991 Annual Meetings of the Indian Science Congress, Indore.

Ramphal, Anita, 1990, "Images of Science and Scientists: Perceptions of Hovishika Teaching", Paper presented at the Seminar on "Science and Child-Centered Education", organized by Eklavya at Bhopal.

Reddy, A.K.N., 1988, "Lessons from ASTRA's Experience with Technologies for Rural Development", Karnataka Rajya Vigyana Parishad: Workshop on Identification of Minimum S&T Core for Common Man.

Rochon, Thomas, 1988, *Mobilizing for Peace,* Princeton: University Press.

Sadgopal, Anil, 1981, "Between Question and Clarity: The Place of Science in a People's Movement", Indian Council of Social Science Research: Vikram Sarabhai Memorial Lecture.

Sahashrabudhey, Sunil, 1984, *An Emerging Critique of Science*, Varanasi: Gandhian Institute of Studies.

——, 1988, *Freedom From Degrading Laws of a Degrading Order,* Varanasi: Gandhian Institute of Studies.

Sengupta, Amit (ed.), 1986, *Drug Industry and the Indian People,* Delhi Science Forum.

Seshadri, C.V., 1980, "Energy in the Indian Context", Invited Lecture at Madurai Kamraj University, September 8-9, 1980.

——, 1982, "Development and Thermodynamics: A Search for New Quality Markers", *MSEPS,* Vol. 11, MCRC, February 1982.

——, 1990, Interview with C.V. Seshadri, *PPST Bulletin*, Madras.

Touraine, Alain, 1981, *The Voice and the Eye*, Cambridge: University Press.

——, 1988, *The Return of the Actor*, Minneapolis: University of Minnesota Press.

Uberoi, J.P.S., 1978, *Science & Culture*, Delhi: Oxford University Press.

——, 1984, *The Other Mind of Europe: Goethe as a Scientist*, Delhi: Oxford University Press.

Viswanathan, Shiv, 1988, "Technology Transfer: Notes on a New Panopticon", *Lokayan Bulletin.*

Wood, Michael and Zurcher, 1988, *The Development of a Postmodern Self,* New York.

Chapter Three

DEMOCRATIC TRANSITION AND THE CHALLENGE
OF TRANSFORMATION

But the democratic process does not exist, and cannot, exist as a disembodied entity detached from historical conditions and historically conditioned human beings. Its possibilities and its limits are highly dependent on existing and emergent social structures and consciousness. Yet because the democratic vision is so daring in its promise, it forever invites us to look beyond, and to break through the existing limits of structure and consciousness.

—Robert A. Dahl (1989: 312)

But the typological differentiation between man and overman no longer makes sense, if it ever did. For the overman constituted as independent, detached type refers simultaneously to a spiritual disposition and to the residence of free spirits in a social space relatively insulated from reactive politics...If there is anything in the type to be admired, the ideal must be dismantled as a distinct caste of solitary individuals and folded into the political fabric of late-modern society. The 'overman' now falls apart as a set of distinctive dispositions concentrated in a particular caste or type, and its spiritual qualities migrate to a set of dispositions that may compete for presence in any self. The type now becomes (as it already was to a significant degree) a voice in the self contending with other voices, including those of resentment.

—William Connolly (1991: 187)

THE PROBLEM

Ours is an age of democracy. Democracy as a form of government, characterized by elections and the installation of a "representative" government, has been becoming a global phenomenon. The fall of the socialist world and domestic and global changes in Latin America, Africa, and Middle East have brought democracy to places and shores where it was undreamt of a few years ago, giving people a taste of freedom. But the globalization of democracy as a form of more legitimate representative government has not been accompanied by genuine efforts to tackle the problems of democracy (such as the tension between equality and liberty, the dictatorship of the majority, the actual as well as manufactured disinterest on the part of the so-called citizens not to participate in the electoral process resulting in as much as 50 per cent of them not fulfilling their constitutional obligation to vote[1]—the problems highlighted by no other than the most thoughtful observer of democracy as a practice, Alexis de Tocqueville—) and to widen the universe of democracy in accordance with the historical changes taking place in social systems as well as in the light of a desired agenda of transformation. The present paper aims at presenting some of the crucial gaps in the theory and practice of democracy and suggests ways we can rethink democracy as a prelude to a genuine transformative engagement.

Problems in the Existing Theory and Practice of Democracy

The demise of the socialist systems has led to euphoria on the part of the advocates of market and western models of democracy. But a majority of our legislators and interpreters have not subjected the existing arrangement of democracy in advanced industrial countries to a critical scrutiny nor they have looked critically at the process of political and economic liberalization in the peripheries. In fact, a narrow definition of both economy and politics in the existing discourse of democracy has reduced it to just a formal kind of political arrangement, whose most important function lies in ensuring regular (supposedly) legitimate reproduction of the existing system. But factors which are considered extraneous to the theory and practice of democracy such as economic inequality between citizens (which play a determinant role in the very process of politics), the deprivation of the actors, the immorality of the professionals who constitute an unquestioned elite in the management of social systems etc., have not been given systematic consideration in the agenda of democratization. But issues such as economic equality, professional morality, and entitlement of citizens are important ones for democracy at the contemporary stage of what Robert Dahl (1989) calls "third democratic transformation". It is perhaps for this reason that Dahl writes: "In an advanced democratic country the economic order would be understood as instrumental not merely to the production and distribution of goods but to a much more larger range of values, including democratic values" (ibid: 325). Therefore, economic democracy is an important theme which is conspicuous by its absence in our contemporary obsession with entrepreneurial rights and freedom of choice and requires serious attention from those who are genuine about democracy.

The Agenda of Economic Reconstuction

At present market economy is being portrayed as a natural ally of democracy. But as markets are being promoted as holding the panancea to all human ills their advocates are forgetting the challenge of making markets "people friendly" in their zealous drive to make governments market friendly (Streeten 1993). Few realize that "our current version of market institutions jeopardize freedom on both a large and a small scale"; and even fewer are interested in articulating an "alternative institutional definition of market" (Unger 1987: 482, 480).[2] Even after the supposed death of Marxism it is true that "we find the legal tools of privilege hold over capital reciprocally linked, through a series of mediating institutions and preconceptions, to the forms of privileged access to state power" (ibid: 490). In advanced capitalist societies, the stability of the established institutional arrangements, including the arrangements that define markets depend upon a "long-standing social demobilization" (ibid: 491)—not very different from the viled Soviet case. For Roberto Unger, such social demobilization is being encouraged and even deliberately sought "by the constitutional organization of government" (ibid).

Unger provides us a blueprint of the desired economic reconstruction that should be an integral part of the democratization process. In order to reorganize the economy Unger stresses on "the rotating capital fund and its democratic control" as well as on decentralization and the recovery of the small-scale as a unit of creative economic production. Unger, like Streeten (1993), believes that the state has a moral responsibility to preserve the small-scale (which is subject to the threatening logic of international capital) and create conditions for its better functioning in the contemporary context. This retrieval of the small-scale, which is not meant simply for museum display, has to be accompanied by institutional encouragement towards decentralization, upholding the "broader commitments of empowered democracy" rather than merely handing over decisions to local elites (Unger 1987: 475). Its objective is no less than facilitating "the self-organization of society outside government" (ibid: 476). "Decentralization refers, at a minimum, both to the number of agents who are able to trade and produce on their initiative and for their own accounts and to the extent of their independence" (ibid: 503). An empowered democracy, taking decentralization seriously, encourages "both more economic deconcentration and more innovation in the organizational form of production and exchange..." (ibid: 383). It must encourage "variety in the ways of doing business, and organizing work" (ibid) and multiple strategies of production and reproduction—including those which are not guided by market and follow the idioms of its exchange—rather than subject them to the control of the market (Giri 1993c).

In this context Unger's idea of rotating capital fund also ought to draw the attention of those who look at democratization as promotion of market in the economic sphere as well as those who look at democracy as a process of seeking for total transformation. Unger argues that the key idea here is the "breakup of control over capital into several tiers of capital takers and capital givers" (Unger 1987: 491). For instance, "the collaboration among small-scale and medium-scale farmers on the basis of government supported arrangements for the pooling of financial, marketing, and technological resources modestly prefigures the multi-tiered system of rotating capital allocation the program of empowered democracy embraces" (ibid: 436).[3]

Such an agenda of economic reconstruction does posit a great deal of significance in government, which has almost been made a taboo in the current discourse of privatization. This agenda is integrally linked with efforts to revitalize governments and transform the state.[4]

The agenda of economic reconstruction cannot dispense with public institutions and takes seriously the task of enhancing the "functioning and capability" of individuals through welfare programs, which are meant not to reduce them into clients but transform them into agents of well-being and freedom (see Sen 1986, 1989, 1991). Therefore, the neo-liberal view that "in any government's war on poverty, it is poverty that always wins" (Streeten 1993: 1284) cannot be allowed as an excuse to disband the welfare functions of government since the ultimate justification of such welfare engagement lies "not on grounds of social justice or human needs, but on grounds of human capital formation, of reducing barriers to income-earning opportunities, and of promoting social stability" (ibid: 1284). In fact, a stress on functioning and capability of individuals, instead of on the discredited modes of justification such as the fulfilment of basic needs can help the government "struggle against the tendency of some of its constituents to adopt a clientelist attitude to state..." (Unger 1987: 435).

Collective Mobilization as Collective Creation: Transformative Movements and the Building up of New Institutions

Imagining Alternative Institutional Arrangements

The agenda of economic reconstruction briefly outlined above requires building up of new institutions. For realizing the program of empowered democracy it is not "enough to change the way in which we describe and explain the formative contexts of social life; it is also necessary to imagine institutional arrangements now available in the world" (Unger 1987: 365). But this requires a shift in the way we think about institutions, namely, institutions as legal entities. For this, among other things, we need to make a shift from the model of analytical law that provide the foundational vision to modern institutions. For instance, David Apter argues that now there is a need to make a move from "law as an analytical discourse" to law as an emancipatory and enabling one.[5] Institutions of a democratic society ought to be founded upon a broader conception of law and rights whose model of law "cannot be confined to the realm of criminal justice, as Herbert Spencer and the state minimalists would prefer" (Whitehead 1993a: 1257). In the agenda of an empowered democracy law "must be expanded and adapted to govern the very different issues raised by the welfare state and the mixed economy—to universalize full citizenship—and therefore Bobbio in *From Structure to Function* regards shrinkage of the scope of public law as an indicator of social decay" (ibid). Insofar as the realization of full citizenship is concerned, it is important to realize that "citizenship does not stay within the confines of the political" (O'Donnell 1993: 1357). The inherently public dimension of private relationships is "violated when, for example, a peasant is *de facto* denied access to the judiciary against the landowner. This 'private' right must be seen as no less constitutive of citizenship than the 'public right' of voting without coercion" (ibid). "Even a political definition of democracy... should not neglect posing the question of the extent to which citizenship is realized in a given country" (ibid: 1361).[6]

Speaking of law, citizenship, and institutionalization of democracy Unger argues that it is essential to grant citizens in an empowered democracy immunity rights and destabilization rights. Urger's discussion of rights is part of his argument that economic and social reconstruction must be integrally linked with efforts to create a new constitution. The same argument is also offered by Claus Offe and Ulrich Preuss who emphasize upon "new constitutional procedures which will help to improve the quality of citizens' involvement in the democratic process" (Offe and Preuss 1991: 170). While "immunity rights protect the individual against oppression by concentrations of public or private power, against exclusion from the important collective decisions that influence his life, and against the extremes of economic and cultural deprivation" "destabilization rights protect the citizen's interest in breaking open the large-scale organization or the extended areas of social practice..." (Unger 1987: 524, 530).[7]

Beyond Instutionalism: Incorporating the Creativity of Culture and Communities

Bhikhu Parekh has argued that "strictly speaking liberal democracy is not representative democracy but representative government" (Parekh 1992: 167). In fact, democratization has been a statist agenda and even the institutionalists in the discourse of liberal democracy have not gone beyond state and taken seriously the work of culture and communities (Apter 1991). In the words of Apter: "Democracy tends to separate the state from society at a decision-making level even as it becomes closer to it in terms of public support. In so far as this renders the content of politics relatively empty of meaning, it becomes precisely what critical theorists consider false consciousness" (Apter 1992: 166). In this context, the Latin American experiment of bringing back community to the discourse and practice of democracy deserves our attention. Liberation theology and the base community movements in Latin America have striven to revitalize communities as locales of action, dialogue, and critical intervention. The search for lost community in Latin America has been accentuated by the disintegration that has taken place in society as a result of its globalization and transnational integration (Lechner 1991).[8]

Of the Latin American experience, one observer tells us: "The majority of citizens in our countries prefer democracy to any other regime. In practical terms, this preference appears to be motivated by identification of democracy with the restoration of community" (Lechner 1991: 548). But the same observer thinks that since "community emphasizes a monistic view of society which represses both particular interests and a comparison of alternatives" and does not permit a creative view of conflict "it is problematical whether a political culture of this kind can build a sound democracy" (ibid: 546). This objection also reminds us of the Indian debate on this issue and the same skepticism of liberals such as Ambedkar and Nehru towards the Gandhian agenda of making village community an unit in the democratic process. It is true that the "emphasis laid on the expression of the collective curbs any centrifugal movement" in communities but this cannot be the reason for throwing the baby along with the bath water. The challenge here is to introduce the desired concerns such as "creative view of conflict", "recognition of pluralism" (Lechner 1991) and the issue of human rights within communities through the work of transformative movements.[9]

Building Communities as a Transformative Striving: The Revitalization of Public Space and the Recovery of Public Morality

It is here that Unger's plea for a transformed conception of community holds the key to the genuine dilemma that the above critic has highlighted. For Unger, "a transformative conception of community" constitutes a "unifying theme of the cultural-revolutionary program" (Unger 1987: 560). For Unger, the kernel of the revised ideal of community is "the notion of a zone of heightened mutual vulnerability, within which people gain a chance to resolve more fully the conflict between the enabling conditions of self-assertion..." (ibid: 562). Reconceptualizing communities as zones of mutual vulnerability also helps us to re-imagine and relive the familiar categories of modern democracy such as the "public sphere" (Habermas 1989) and "public spaces" (Melucci 1992) as communities of discourse rather than simply a locale for bringing the possessive individuals for half an hour, only to disperse to their respective shells later. For Melucci (1992), consolidating independent public spaces—whose main function is "rendering visible and collective the questions raised by the movements" (Melucci 1992: 72) and which (i.e., this act of consolidation) is a reflection of the "collective signifying processes in everyday life" (ibid: 71)—can go a long way in retrieving and creating community in complex societies where it does not exist as a natural datum.

The resurrection of community in the institutional reconstruction of democracy has also a potential to creatively respond to the short-circuiting of the flow of time that takes place in liberal democracy. "Democratic institutions generate time: for example, they space out future time in a schedule of successive elections" (Lechner 1991: 546). Thus, elections constitute the markers of time and after elections people in power usually forget the promises of a longer-time horizon that they had given during elections. While it is true that "democracy makes it possible to forecast the future on surer foundations than the *de facto* duration of dictatorship" it is also true that "liberal representation can cope with substantive complexity (interdependence) but not with temporal complexity (permanence of decision making)" (Kitschelt 1993: 25). But culture and communities usually have a longer-time horizon than state and market and, in fact, they only hold the key to the resolution of the problem of contemporary "space-time compression" (Harvey 1989). Thus, it is no wonder that Lechner writes: "The time factor shows clearly that, over and above institutional difficulties, a reform policy comes up against obstacles which may be described as of a cultural nature. Paradoxically... the major challenges to democracy in Latin America come from the cultural context" (Lechner 1991: 546).[10]

The revitalization of the public space as an object of transformative seeking must go hand in hand with a recovery of public morality. The process of "consolidating democratic institutions and stabilizing market relationships is not just a matter of extending the machinery whereby individuals are empowered to make autonomous decisions, it also involves the affirmation of a revised and elaborated code of conduct" (Whitehead 1993a: 1248). Here we can take note of the re-entry of public morality to the stage of modernity in general and democracy in particular (ibid; also see, Etzioni 1988; Giri 1993a; Habermas 1990). For Whitehead, "one manifestation of this is the prominence of the religious sentiments emerging in the course of many democratic transitions, and the influence (at least in Latin America) of Catholic social thought as a counter-weight to the doctrines of unfettered market liberalism" (ibid).[11]

Institutions as Educators of Desire

Institutions of democracy must aim at providing transformative challenges to individuals so that it is not only their egoistic preference which becomes the criterion of accountability but their enlightened preference. Democratic institutions must refine and educate the preference of the actors and must create conditions for a new trend of "enfranchising" where the conflict is not only between different social groups but between different kinds of desires—the "inner conflict between what the individuals themselves experience as their more desirable and their less desirable desires" (Offe and Preuss 1991: 166). The challenge is to build institutions which would create opportunity for refining one's preference since such preference learning is a democratic way of creating enlightenment within citizens—a moral resource, which is absolutely essential for institutions of transformed democracy. Institutions should "upgrade the quality of citizenship by putting a premium on refined and reflective preferences rather than 'spontaneous' and content-contingent ones.[12]... Such reflectiveness may be facilitated by arrangements that overcome the monological seclusion of the act of voting in the voting booth by complementing this necessary mode of participation with more dialogical forms of making one's voice heard" (ibid: 170). At the same time, the challenge for those concerned is to strive towards building institutions which are transparent and accountable to people.[13]

Institutional Reconstruction and Transformative Movements

In putting into practice an alternative institutional design transformative movements have played and continue to play a significant role. Transformative movements, first of all, affirm the "primacy of institutional reforms over the redistribution of wealth and income" (Unger 1987: 433). "By engaging people in conflicts and experiments required for the development of new institutions, the movements give them a focus of concern other than immediate redistribution. It thereby establishes a bond with ordinary working men and women stronger than the gratitude or love that people may be expected to show a paternalist welfare state" (ibid: 433). Exploratory movements contain germs of "de-differentiation" "beneath a politics reduced to administration, and on the periphery of a highly mobilized economic system" (Habermas 1984: 25) and offer a "more complete experience of self-assertion through attachment than we can find in the everyday world of work and exchange" (Unger 1987: 431). According to Kitschelt, "some residues of direct democratic practice persist in the self-transformation of contemporary social movements, even though in a muted and constrained way" (Kitschelt 1993: 23) when direct democracy refers to the process where "actors discover their common objective in a communicative process of political deliberation" (ibid: 20).

But proliferation of critical social movements in advanced democracies does not mean that movements can replace complex economic and political institutions. The emergent configuration in advanced democracies "indicates less a polarization of different modes of participation and democratic decision-making than the opportunity for a new complementarity" (ibid: 28). Kitschelt helps us make sense of the contemporary predicament and possibility vis-a-vis institutions and movements:

In advanced capitalist democracies, citizens' personal resources to engage in direct democratic practices have increased. At the same time, the scope and depth of policy issues that give rise to discrete point decisions vulnerable to challenge by social movements appear to have increased... Advanced democracies face the problem not of replacing complex political and economic institutions with social movements but of finding way to accommodate spontaneity, individuality, entrepreneurship, and responsiveness in a bureaucratic and commodified society (Kitschelt 1993: 28).[14]

Building Movements and Institutions: The Transnational Challenge

The challenge of building new institutions of democracy is no where more urgent than in the emergent transnational sphere. Democracy today is no longer confined either to the boundaries of the city state—as was the case in the first stage of democratic transformation—and to those of the nation-state as it was the case in the second stage of democratic transformation (Dahl 1989). Democracy now is part of a transnational process since all societies are now part of a transnational world, characterized by the globalization of their economies and polities. "The proliferation of transnational activities and decisions reduces the capacity of the citizens of a country to exercise control over matters vitally important to them by means of their national government. To that extent the government of countries are becoming local governments" (ibid: 319). The democratic idea must be "adapted to the new change in scale" (ibid: 320). For Dahl, "the most obvious is to duplicate the second transformation on a larger scale: from democracy in the national state to democracy in the transnational state" (ibid).

But the existing practice of democracy is still bound to the models of state-centric discourse. Ours is the "Age of Democracy" and now there is a global euphoria about the emergent democratic spaces in the East and in the South. But "nations are heralding democracy at the very moment at which changes in the international order are compromising the possibility of an independent democratic nation-state" (Held 1991: 138). Nation-states have usually been treated as self-contained units, but democratic theory and practice bound within the logic of the nation-state is incapable of preparing us to face the challenge of living in a transnational world. Democratic politics remaining fetishized, even fossilized, within the electoral politics of the nation-state, offers outmoded statist solutions to the global contingencies—be it global warming or global terrorism. While "the very process of governance seems to be escaping the categories of the nation-state" (Held 1991: 147), "the state deploys... diverse set of objects to organize discourse" (Connolly 1991: 210).

Connolly (1991) provides us a picture of the theatre of the nation-state playing out familiar responses to the contemporary global contingencies. The state receives a fund of resentment from those whose identity is threatened by the play of difference (such as represented by the terrorists and the welfare underclass) and then construct differences as the dangerous Other to protect identities they represent. Thus electoral politics in advanced capitalist societies becomes a "closed circuit for dogmatism of identity through translation of difference into threat and threat into energy for the dogmatization of identity" (ibid: 210). This process of scapegoating and the late capitalist state's culture of sacrifice is easily noticeable in its construction of terrorism and welfarism. The erasure of the external Other in the construction of terrorism coincides with the erasure of the internal other in the construction of welfarism. Terrorism is now a global phenomenon which "challenges or supersedes legitimacy, explodes conventionality" (Apter 1987: 42). But the construction of terrorism in the discourse of the state provides an easy excuse to both the state and citizens. The state protects its sovereignty and veils its inability to modify its action while the domestic constituencies are provided the security of an agent of evil to explain the experience of danger. Construction of welfarism in the late-modern state also creates a "culture of sacrifice" by constructing the welfare class as dependent and inefficient which "becomes a dispensable subject of political representation and an indispensable subject of political disposability" (Connolly 1991: 208). It is in this context that there is a need to build new institutions that enable actors and governments to resolve global contingencies which defy state boundaries democratically as well as address the so-called internal problems in a moral and universal manner.[15]

New Democratic Institutions and the Complexification of Social Systems

The interconnectedness among societies and the rise of transnational processes, including global contingencies, which heighten the urgency of a global democracy has gone hand in hand with the evolution of social systems in the advanced industrial societies. Social systems have become increasingly complex now, with science and technology becoming crucially important in determining their scale and organization. At the same time, the rise of the complex systems in all domains of our everyday life has made professionals with expert knowledge of these complex processes important in not only managing these systems but also in determining their destiny. But the increasing systemic significance of professionals has not been accompanied by any institutional effort to arouse moral consciousness within them not to use their expert knowledge and power for exploiting the ordinary people who don't have such power and knowledge. In fact, apart from legislation there has been not much effort to suł ject professionals into a public scrutiny as a result of which professionals have become the new demigods in the system world.

But the distortion that professionalism introduces in the work of a democratic polity is no less, and in fact more dangerous, than the factor of economic inequality. However, the existing practice of democracy has not taken adequate steps to come to terms with this threat to democracy. As Dahl cautions us: "...I am inclined to think that the long-run prospects for democracy are more seriously endangered by inequalities in resources, strategic positions, and bargaining strength that are derived not from wealth or economic position but from special knowledge" (Dahl: 333). Now important policy issues are so complex that not only the government seeks the help of the professionals to come to a satisfactory and convincing judgement but also the ordinary citizens themselves who "no longer understand what would best serve their interest (ibid: 337). In the context of the complexification of not only social systems but also the issues which affect the actors of these systems the uncritical advocates of democracy have to recognize the gap in the existing practice, since "complexity threatens to cut the policy elites from effective control by the demos" (ibid: 335).

Thus the challenge of institutional reconstruction at the contemporary phase of democratic transition is immense and our creative response would determine whether the contemporary democratic transition is going to be ephemeral or enduring.[16]

The Challenge of Self-Transformation

The commonsense that moral quality of citizens and their enlightened understanding is crucial to democracy becomes an imperative when we reflect upon the complexification of social systems. The complexification of social systems at the contemporary juncture is part of what Daniel Bell (1973) called two decades ago "the coming of a post-industrial society". Post-industrial societies are characterized by the proliferation of what Roger Benjamin (1981) calls "collective goods", which requires an ability within the citizens to overcome the temptation to be a "free rider" and to contribute meaningfully towards their creation, maintenance, and appropriate imagination. In fact, an "enlightened understanding"[17] on the part of the citizens is essential to the idea of the common good. The same challenge for enlightenment and self-transformation seizes us when we are confronted with the need to expand democracy, for example, to a transnational universe, as discussed before.[18]

Rethinking Citizenship

Thus, it is not enough just to reiterate the familiar themes of citizenship and civil society but to ask what is the model of man (woman) that underlies the aspired for citizenship in a democratic polity. If democracy, as Alain Touraine argues, "is not just a competitive market; it implies the ability of each individual to act as a citizen" (Touraine 1991: 261) then the question that is often ignored is what is the model of citizenship that underlies the discourse and practice of democracy? Here it is important to realize that models of citizenship differ from one model of democracy to another. While liberal democrats look at citizens as "self-regarding individuals who experience political involvement as a burden to be delegated to a specialized group of professionals" organizational democracy looks at them as "other-regarding and therefore contributing to mass-parties" (Kitschelt 1993: 20). But it is only in the framework of a direct democracy that a new model of citizenship is promoted where citizens are viewed as "other-regarding [but at the same time] involved in politics as an opportunity for self-realization and self-transformation, not as a burden on one's time and energy" (ibid).

In direct democracy "an alternative definition of the spirit of the constitution emphasizes an ideal of personality and psychological dynamic" (Unger 1987: 575). For Unger, "the citizen of the empowered democracy is the empowered individual. He is able to accept an expanded range of conflict and revision without feeling that it threatens intolerably his most vital material and spiritual interests" (ibid: 579). What makes him participate in struggles is not just the urge to improve "the material circumstances of his life but nature and structure of groups to which he belongs and even his pre-existing sense of personal identity" (ibid). At the same time, the citizen is prepared for renunciation and has "learned the secret of how to be in [conflicts] but without being entirely of them" (ibid: 579). But this perpetual readiness for renunciation is not perceived as a sacrifice by the citizen not only because of "the guarantee of immunity afforded by a system" but because of a spiritual commitment to transformation. In the words of Unger: "Its higher spiritual significance consists in the assertion of transcendence as a diurnal context smashing" (ibid).

But the citizen renounces not to make himself a hero but to give herself more meaningfully in this world, conceptualized as a perpetual celebration of the sacrifice of creation.[19] An urge to share rather than to dominate rescues him from the vicarious pleasure and danger of "the aesthetic of empowerment" (Unger 1987: 584). It also frees him from the "corrupting association with the cult of leaders and of violence" since his "driving force is the desire to do justice to the human heart, to free it from indignity and satisfy its hidden and insulted longing for greatness in a fashion it need not be fearful or ashamed of" (ibid: 585).[20]

The ideal citizen is able to resolve the dualism between individuals and collective rationality and embody in his transformative striving the moral resource of reciprocity. But this requires a change in the way we think of actors, institutions and discourse. The standard route here is one of dualism, reduction and fixation and if "reciprocity" is the ideal and also the saving language then we would have to go beyond a reductionist view of the relationship between individual and institutions, self and the other. The challenge is no less than to work out a transformative view of the self. In terms of political theory the task is to realize that a theory of discourse, when discourse by definition means only those utterances which have political significance, is not a theory of self-transformation[21] and the language of need is inadequate to describe the moral topography of the self. Democracy is not an instrumental mechanism to satisfy human needs, when these needs themselves have been let loose from the beginning to be limitless, but a process of cultivating a more meaningful and caring self, where the development of the individual becomes a precondition for the development of society.[22]

Widening the Universe of Democracy: Self, Other, and Beyond

In widening the universe of democracy the starting point is a reflection on self, which strives to put food and freedom and the local and the global in the same space of transformative strivings. The challenge here is to start with an alternative account of the self, not simply as a locus of desire, utility, and interest but as a seeker of transformation. But "providing an alternative account of the self, however, has so far proved more difficult than critique. Part of the reason is that expansive democratic theories also suffer from *underdeveloped assumptions about the self*" (Warren 1992: 11; emphasis added).[23] Thus, we have to have a transformative view of the self in order to widen the universe of democracy. This is possible only when we take the moral and spiritual dimension within the self (which is usually conceptualized as a mere functional role and a sociological individual) seriously and try to cultivate it through our individual strivings including our conduct in the public sphere. Thus, democratic theory and moral theory have to be relinked. As Warren argues:

> I assume that a description of the self in terms of interests can be redescribed in moral terms, in this way linking democratic and moral theory. This is because self-identity includes ideal representations of the self to self, anchoring a person's conception of their interests in a moral representation of who they would like to be (ibid: 17).

Democracy, Self and the Ideal Representation of the Scheme of Becoming

Thus the ideal representation of our scheme of becoming is important here. Important also here is a characteristic of the self, which seeks to and has the courage to be, and has the capacity to distinguish values from appetites and interest. Democratic theory is now in need of a transformative self, and this we find in the work of Mahatma Gandhi, Sri Aurobindo, G.C. Pande, and Charles Taylor among others. G.C. Pande argues that "it is only a self which is conscious of its ideal universality that can distinguish value from appetites, pleasures, and selfish interests and can become the moral subject. It is the notion of the ideal self which is the source of the moral law on which social unity and cohesion depend" (Pande 1982: 113). For Gandhi, the self is characterized not only by the political and economic dimension but also by the *dharmic and satyagrahic* dimension. It is this moral dimension within the self, with its desire for truth, that democracy must put it at the centre of the social system, as it must help develop this dimension. Gandhi's political practice of satyagraha, civil disobedience and attachment to non-violence provides help in expanding the universe of democracy and anchoring it in a truth-seeking moral self, which is courageous to fight evil in a non-violent manner. For Gandhi, "the highest moral law is that we should unremittingly work for the good of mankind..." (quoted in Pantham 1989). Such practice of the self is neither a reiteration of the existing opposition between self and other nor a submission of the self to the appetite and ego of the other. As Pantham interprets the Gandhian agenda of emancipation: "unlike the cultural relativists who assert and cling to the radical essential separateness or otherness of the to-be-colonized other from the ethnocentric-imperialist self, Gandhi bases his emancipatory struggle of satyagraha on a post-liberal/post-relativist conception of the human 'self', namely, a self that is hermeneutically implicated with other selves" (Pantham 1989: 15).[24]

In this search for a hermeneutic self Charles Taylor (1989) provides us probably one of the rare modern accounts of the work of the self as an agent of critique and construction. For Taylor, a moral and a spiritual intuition characterizes the work of self and when we reflect upon "the self in moral space" "the sense that human beings are capable of some kind of higher life forms part of the background for our belief..." (Taylor 1989: 25). Self provides us an identity and to work on self is to know what one is.[25] The moral space of the self is a space of orientation, having a "crucial set of qualitative distinctions", which tells us that "some action, or mode of life, or mode of feeling is incomparably higher than the others which are more readily available to us" (ibid: 19).

Life Politics and the Reflecitve Mobilization of the Self

Ronald Inglehart's (1990) description of the culture shift in advanced societies around the axis of the emergent postmaterial values and Anthony Giddens' (1991) work on self and society in the late modern age provides us some engaging descriptions to relate these ideas of self to the agenda of a desired democratic politics. Giddens stresses that "the self in high modernity is not a minimalist self..." (Giddens 1991: 181). For Giddens, "the reflexive project of the self generates programs of actualization and mastery," which is manifested, among other things, in the choice of a particular lifestyle and participation in new social movements (ibid: 9). The reflexive project of the self, "which consists in the sustaining of coherent, yet continually revived biographical narratives" is not an "extension of the control systems of modernity to the self" but a project of moral choice and transformative speaking which gets manifested in the actors' participation in transformative movements.[26]

In this context, Giddens speaks of "the emergence of life politics" (ibid: 209). Giddens argues that life politics is a politics of choice—"a politics of lifestyle", rather than "a politics of life chances" (ibid: 214). It is a politics of self-actualization where the power that defines the field is not hierarchical but generative.[27] Life-politics brings to the fore "problems and questions of moral and existential type" because it centers on "how we should live our lives in emancipated social circumstances" (ibid: 224). In this context, Giddens urges us to take note of the significance of "new forms of religion and spirituality," which "represent in a most basic sense the return of the repressed, since they directly address issues of the moral meaning of existence which modern institutions so thoroughly tend to dissolve" (ibid: 207).

The reflexive mobilization of the self that is at work in life politics is different from the opposition between the Self and the Other as manifested, for instance, in familiar models of emancipatory politics. While emancipatory politics is usually a politics of negation life politics "is aimed not at reducing the negativity of otherness, as embodied in the colonial, the subaltern, the prisoner, vis-a-vis the mainstream, but to 'liberate' the mainstream from itself" (Apter 1992: 162). The task here is to simultaneously criticize the self and the other, thus going "beyond emancipation" and realize the dialectic between the dimension of dichotomy and the dimension of ground in the agenda of transformation (Laclau 1992).[28]

Beyond Emancipation and the Challenge of Freedom

The agenda of democracy is an agenda of freedom (see Dahl 1989). At the same time, the discourse of liberal democracy, especially in its current manifestation of libertarianism, is based upon a narrow view of freedom, and haunted by the problem of dualism. It has not addressed the question of the meaning of freedom as an object of transformative seeking. The work of Isiah Berlin and Amartya Sen have made us aware of the distinction between negative freedom and positive freedom (Sen 1989).[29] but even in Amartya Sen's continued quest for freedom the spiritual dimension within freedom has not received enough attention. But the dualism between negative and positive freedom is still a problem even in Amartya Sen, and there is a need to transcend this dualism at some level in order to be able to meaningfully imagine the agenda of democratic transformation. Only by having a view of freedom as a spiritual process of transformation and the agent of freedom as a transformative self, which begins with self-control[30] of one's lower self and cultivation of one's higher self, can we go beyond good and evil, positive and the negative. For instance Sri Aurobindo (1950) argues that standards of conduct and the practice of freedom must be anchored in a spiritual plane where the goal of freedom is not only to have the freedom to choose but also to transform our needs and desires. A spiritual seeking also helps us discover the "secret Godhead within us", a discovery that helps us create a universal ground within us where the social distinction between individual and the collective, negative and positive freedom get a new frame of reference for criticism and transcendence even if it does not get outrightly dissolved.[31]

Democracy and the Spiritual Transformation of Self and Society

The spiritual challenge of freedom is one of transcending the opposition between self and other and creating communities of discourse and practice where both can live as seekers of freedom. In fact, this act of creation of communities is itself a spiritual act. The challenge here thus is as much for religion as for democracy. While in religion the challenge is to realize that the contemporary competitive existence "that divides what is to be a man and a woman, a white or a black, is a form of human suffering" (Bellah et al. 1991: 210) in terms of actual challenges for the theory and practice of democracy it means looking at it primarily as a mode of paying attention (ibid). Democracy means paying attention to the needs and care of the self, family, neighbourhood, communities, country, mankind, and the mother earth. "Attending means to concern ourselves with the larger meaning of things in the longer run, rather than with short-term pay offs" (ibid). For Bellah *et al.* channel-flipping TV watching, compulsive promiscuity, and alcoholism is a form of distraction while spending time with one's spouse and children, and repairing the broken car of a neighbour is a form of attention.[32] Bellah et al. make it clear that we must understand this plea for attention in the normative sense. In their words:

> as in the religious examples, we mean to use attention normatively, in the sense of 'mindfulness', as the Buddhists put it, *or openness to the leadings of God*, as the quakers say. On the face of it, it may seem hard to tell the difference between attention and obsession. But as we shall use the term here, attention implies an openness to experience, a willingness to widen the lens of appreciation that is appropriate, and this obsession is incapable of doing. Obsessive 'attention' in this normative sense is not attention at all but distraction, an unwillingness to be genuinely attentive to surrounding reality (ibid: 256; emphasis added).

But this attention to the self and surrounding reality is hard to see in a democratic society such as contemporary American society. In the words of Bellah et al: "Americans have pushed the logic of exploitation about as far as it can go" (ibid: 271). This is manifested in addiction to conspicuous consumption where goods take precedence over man and God as objects of attention, the rise of homelessness and in the decadence of the built environment of the cities.[33]

In this context of dislocation, distraction and despair Bellah et al plead for a *politics of generativity and a pattern of cultivation.* For them, "The major problems that come to light require the virtue of generativity to solve—indeed, a politics of generativity. The most obvious problem is the perilous neglect of our own children in America: levels of infant mortality, child poverty, and inadequate schooling just as at or near the bottom in these respects among industrial nations" (ibid: 274). A pattern of settlement and cultivation is interested in creating communities. As Bellah and his colleagues say: "A pattern of settlement and cultivation allows not only the nurturing of ethnic and racial cultures within communities of memory but an open interchange of learning between such communities, a kind of global localism" (ibid: 275).

This concern for attention is very different from a preoccupation with either money or power as the ultimate measure of life. It is also very different from a clinical preoccupation with whether one's own country would continue to remain number one in the new global environment. Here a genuine transnational spirit must be our guide for action, reflection, and intervention.[34] Johan Galtung (1980) had argued long ago that transnational politics is a politics of individual human beings. Widening the universe of democracy means making a move towards both sides: towards the supranational collectivities as well as towards one's reflexive self which is not bounded to the dogmas of social roles and statist citizenship, and which has the capacity to criticize familiar institutions and turn them into islands of problematic justice (see Giri 1993a; Habermas 1990a). Bellah's agenda of democracy as paying attention and a pattern of cultivation falls in line with the argument of this paper that self-transformation is the key issue while coming to terms with the challenge of democratic transition and the complexification of social systems. It is a moral and spiritual awareness that can make professionals treat other citizens as human beings and with dignity and respect. It is a spiritual awareness that provides us "freedom from fear" in the context of the all-pervasive "fear of freedom" and help us realize what Aung Sun Kyi says: "It is not enough merely to call for freedom, democracy and human rights. There has to be a united determination to persevere in the struggle, to make sacrifices in the name of enduring truths, to resist the corrupting influences of desire, ill will and fear" (Kyi 1991: 153). It is this awareness which is crucial to build solidarity and "de-differentiation" (Beck 1992; Habermas 1984) in the infinitely differentiated but tightly integrated regime of the system worlds. It is the discovery of the universal self within oneself and the inner Godhead that is essential to build a transnational democracy. Thus, self-transformation is the key challenge in the face of the current democratic transition and evolution of social systems. Bellah and his colleagues best articulate this challenge for us:

> We can indeed try genuinely to attend to the world around us and to the meanings we discover as we interact with that world, and hope to realize in our experience that we are part of a universal community, making sense of our lives as deeply connected to each other. As we enlarge our attention to include the natural universe and the ultimate ground it expresses and from which it comes, we are sometimes swept with a feeling of thankfulness, of grace, to be able to participate in a world that is both terrifying and exquisitely beautiful. At such moments we feel like celebrating the joy and mystery we participate in. The impulse towards larger meaning, thankfulness, and celebration has to have an institutional form, like all the other central organizing tendencies in our lives, so that we don't dissipate it in purely private sentiment (ibid).

NOTES

1. Political scientists Frances Fox Piven and Richard A. Cloward (1988) make this observation about the voting pattern in American presidential elections.

2. As Unger argues, on a large scale market institutions leave a "restricted number of people with a disproportionate influence over the flows of investment decisions" while on a small scale these undermine freedom by "generating and permitting inequalities of wealth that reduce some people to effective dependence upon others..." (Unger 1987: 483).

3. Unger develops his idea of rotating capital fund thus:

   The ultimate capital giver is a social capital fund controlled by the decisional centre of the empowered democracy: the party in office and the supporting representative assemblies. The ultimate capital takers are teams of workers, technicians, and entrepreneurs, who make temporary and conditional claims upon divisible portions of this social capital fund. The central capital fund does not lend money out directly to the primary capital users. Instead, it allocates resources to a variety of semi-independent investment funds. Each investment fund specializes in a sector of the economy and in a type of investment. The central democratic institutions exercise their ultimate control over the forms and rates of economic accumulation and income distribution by establishing these funds or by closing them out, by assigning them new infusions of capital or by taking capital away from them, by charging them interest (whose payment represents the major source of governmental finance), and, most importantly, by setting the outer limits of variation in the terms on which the competing investment funds may allocate capital to the ultimate capital takers. The investment funds may take resources away from one another, thus forming in effect a competitive capital market, whose operations are also overseen by the central representative bodies of democracy (Unger 1987: 436).

4. David Osborne (1988) has described several experiments in the United States to make government competitive and fulfil its social obligation more efficiently (also see Giri 1993c; and Osborne and Gaebler 1992). In this context, what O'Donnell writes deserves our attention:

   There is no question that in most newly democratized countries the state is too big, and that this leads to numerous negative consequences. But, in this context, the antonym of big is not small but lean; i.e., an effective and less weighty set of public organizations that is capable of creating solid roots for democracy, for progressively solving the main issues of social equity, and for generating conditions for rates of economic growth suitable for sustaining the advances in areas of both democracy and social equity (O'Donnell 1993: 1358).

5. In the words of Apter: "The old institutionalists used law as an analytical discourse, both as history and system. Democracy, the systemic alternative to arbitrary power, consisted of law, participation, and accountability, so fashioned to produce a moving equilibrium in the political sphere parallel to the moving equilibrium in the economic (Apter 1991: 467).

6. In his words: "The denial of liberal rights to (mostly but not exclusively) the poor or otherwise deprived sections is analytically distinct from, and bears no necessary relation to various degrees of social and economic democratization. But, empirically, various forms of discrimination of extensive poverty and their correlate, extreme disparity in the distribution of (not only economic) resources, go hand in hand with low-intensity citizenship. This is the essence of the social conditions necessary for the exercise of citizenship" (O'Donnell 1993: 1361).

7. For Unger, "the theory of immunity rights rests, in part, on the empirical hypothesis that freedom from violence, coercion, subjugation, and poverty... enters into people's ordinary conception of essential security. These goods are rivalled in importance only by the more intangible sense of being accepted by other people as a person, with a place in the world" (Unger 1987: 524).

8. In the words of Lechner: "Latin American society becomes a 'two-thirds' society, with the remaining third of the population unemployed and living on what is cast off by the rest" (Lechner 1991: 542).

9. I owe this point of introducing the concern of human rights into the functioning of communities to a discussion I had with Shri B.D. Sharma, a tireless champion of the cause of the tribals and the downtrodden of India and the author of *The Webs of Poverty*, in March 1992 in Delhi.

10. Here it is worth remembering the seminal work of Anthur E. Mergan, one the most engaging advocates of community in modern times. It is no wonder that Morgan who pleaded for creation of communities in complex industrial societies also pleaded for understanding the significance of a longer-time horizon.

11. But Whitehead himself makes clear that "public morality is by no means reducible to religion" (Whitehead 1993a: 1248).

12. Offe and Preuss tell us what they mean by reflective preferences: "By

reflective preferences we mean preferences that are the outcome of a conscious confrontation of one's own point of view with an opposing point of view, or of the multiplicity of view points that the citizen, upon reflection, is likely to discover within his or her own self" (Offe and Preuss 1991: 170).

13. For instance, Whitehead believes that if institutions are "soundly based, with high professionalism and good standing in the society, i.e., 'transparent' and 'accountable', then they may serve to absorb and even reconcile clashes between economic and political liberalization." In the words of Whitehead: "Two of the most vital areas for liberal institution-building are the legal system and the apparatus of economic management. Both of these are often severely affected both by economic disorder and by authoritarian abuse. If the process of economic and political liberalization is to become routinized these institutions will have to be reformed and reorganized to provide the necessary continuity and support" (Whitehead 1993b: 1386).

14. Unger also makes a similar argument when he writes "Empowered democracy attempts instead to change the relation between large-scale, inclusive institutions and non-institutionalized collective action, to make the former into a more congenial home for the latter. The closer the movement comes to its moment of power—and therefore also to its hour of institutional definitions—the less room there is discrepancy between means and ends" (Unger 1987: 173-174).

15. Here I draw upon the arguments of Habermas. While discussing the problem of poverty within a country and inequalities between the North and the South, Habermas argues that "a dynamics self-correction cannot be set in notion without introducing morals into the debate, without universalizing interests from a normative point of view" (Habermas 1990b: 20).

16. A contemporary critic helps us understand this and go beyond the euphoria and illusion in the wall streets: "In the contemporary world, the joyful celebration of the advent of democracy must be complemented with the sober recognition of the immense (and, indeed, historically unusual) difficulties its institutionalization and its rooting in society must face... In addition, there are no immanent historical forces which will guide the new democracies toward an institutionalized and representative form, and to the elimination of their brown areas and the manifold social ills that underlie them. In the long run, the new democracies may split between those that follow this felicitous course and those that regress to all-out authoritarianism. But delegative democra-

cies, weak horizontal accountability, schizophrenic states, brown areas and low-intensity citizenship are part of the foreseeable future of new democracies" (O'Donnell 1993: 1367).

17. Here what Mark Warren argues deserves our attention:

    Public material goods present unique opportunities for self-transformation when compared with other goods. Although they are inherently conflictual and do not depend on commonality for their value, they can only be gained through common action. Combined with expanded democracy, this characteristic presents individuals with opportunities to change the way they make trade-offs between individual and public material goods, as well as to discover other, non-conflictual goods associated with the common deliberation and action that pubic goods require (Warren 1992: 21; emphasis added).

18. However, such an agenda of moral criticism and self-transformation has been peripheral to the discourse of modern democracy since it was preoccupied with supplanting the medieval hero worship and collectivism with people's verdict and individualism without thinking deeper about the nature of the person who is supposed to be at the centre of the drama of democracy, not simply as a viewer but primarily as an actor (see Ado 1984). But Warren argues that "transformations of the self are important for expansive democrats because they view democracy as justified not so much because it allows maximization of political wants or preferences as because it maximizes opportunities for self-governance and self-development" (ibid: 11).

19. Here I have in mind Rabindra Nath Tagore's line, *Jagate Anandajagye Amar nimantrana*, meaning "I am invited to the world of the sacrifice of Ananda [pleasure]".

20. David Harvey (1989) cautions us against aestheticization of politics.

21. I owe this argument to Mark Warren (1993).

22. As Warren argues:

    Fortunately, the self-transformation thesis requires only a very weak theory of needs, one that focuses on the general functional requirements of the self [what Amartya Sen calls 'functioning' and 'capability'] in relation to classes of goods that would satisfy them. This is because democratic theory is not a theory of welfare (although there are essential welfare requirements) but a theory of choice, public decision making, and self governance... A stronger account of needs is unnecessary and undesirable, since the point of expansive theories of democracy is to recommend institutional arrangements under which individuals develop control over their own need articulation... (Warren 1992: 16; emphasis added).

23. The same problem of underdeveloped accounts of the self haunts even anthropology and cultural studies even when they self-consciously want to be self-critical and transform themselves into critiques of culture. For instance, in anthropology the champions of self have not been able to go beyond the liberal-bourgeoisie model of individualism.

24. In the words of Pantham:

The satyagrahis regard their initial truth-claims as well as those of their opponents or oppressors to be relativistic. They then go through a rigorous discipline of hermeneutically testing the truths of the rival claims. The discipline of satyagraha includes hermeneutical and dialogic interpretations of the competing truth-claims and a set of actions based on the refusal to do harm even to one's opponents. These actions include self-purification and self-suffering, the vow of ahimsa, showing love and charity or doing good to the opponents, etc. In this way, for the satyagrahi, truth-seeking is not a mere attempt to secure a mirror copy of some out-there object. The attempt is rather to transgress the relativity of their initial truths as well as that of their opponents and thereby to move on to a postrelativist plane of truth. In this transgressive move from relativism, there is no submersion of the individuality of the satyagrahi. It is also not a passive or quietest stance. It is rather a hermeneutical move (Pantham 1989: 14).

Rolph Templin, writing about democracy and non-violence nearly thirty years ago, also acknowledges the signal contribution Gandhi has made to modern man's search for truth and says:

In the West, to experiment with truth is now practically unheard or, at any rate, not regarded as scientific. It is this lack in Western science that has given the phenomenon of Gandhi's life, movement, experiments and death their special significance against the western background. Future historians may regard Gandhi as the most consistent pursuer of his age of the truth which makes men free, and the most valiant experimenter with truth in the greatest of all laboratories, the human community (Templin 1965: 192).

25. In the words of Taylor: "To know who you are is to be oriented in moral space, a space in which questions arise about what is good or bad, what is worth doing and what is not, what has meaning and importance for you and what is trivial and secondary" (Taylor 1989: 28).

26. In the words of Giddens: "It becomes more and more apparent that

lifestyle choices, within the settings of local-global interrelationships, raise moral issues which cannot simply be pushed into one side. Such issues call for forms of political engagement which the new social movements both presage and serve to help" (Giddens 1991: 9).

27. In the words of Giddens, "life politics is the politics of a reflexively mobilized order—the system of late modernity—which, on an individual and collective level, has altered the existential parameters of social activity. It is a politics of self-actualization in a reflexively ordered environment, where reflexivity links self and body to systems of global scope. In this arena of activity, power is generative rather than hierarchical" (Giddens 1991: 9).

28. As emancipatory politics has shown us the significance of the particular and negation, now life politics must enable us to have a ground where we are concerned with "the destiny of the universal" (Laclau 1992: 132). Laclau helps us make sense of the challenge of the ground against the backdrop of modernity:

If, on the one hand, modernity started by strictly typing representability to knowledge, the constitutive opaqueness resulting from the dialectic of emancipation involves not only that society is no longer transparent to knowledge, but also—since God is no longer there to substitute knowledge by revelation—that all representation will be necessarily partial and will take place against the background of an essential unrepresentability. On the other hand, this constitutive opaqueness withdraws the ground which made it possible to go beyond the dialectic of incarnation, given that there is no longer a transparent society in which the universal can show itself in a direct unmediated way. But again, as God is no longer there, ensuring through his word the knowledge of a universal destiny which escapes human reason, opaqueness cannot lead to a restoration of the dialectic of incarnation either. The death of the ground seems to lead to the death of the universal and to the dissolution of social struggles into mere particularism (ibid: 131-132).

It is probably for this reason that Laclau concludes his engaging account of beyond emancipation with the following plea:

We are today coming to terms with our own finitude and with the political possibility that it opens. This is the point from which the potentially liberatory discourses of our postmodern age have to start. We can perhaps say that *we are at the end of emancipation and at the beginning of freedom* (ibid: 137; emphasis added).

29. For Sen, enhancing the "functioning and capability" of individuals is an engagement in positive freedom, while preoccupation with one's indi-

vidual rights and security alone is an instance of negative freedom (Sen 1989).

30. It has to be noted that no less a person than Joseph Schumpeter speaks of the significance of democratic self-control. It is important to read Schumpeter when he writes: "It is easier for a class whose interests are best served by being left alone to practice democratic self-restraint than it is for classes that naturally try to live on the state" (quoted in Whitehead 1993a: 1253).

31. Again the following long extract from Sri Aurobindo may clarify what I have in mind when I speak of the spiritual dimension of freedom:

all conduct and action are part of the movement of a power, a force infinite and divine in its origin... This power is leading towards the Light, but still through the ignorance. It leads man first through his needs and desires; it guides him next through enlarged needs and desires modified and enlightened by a mental and moral ideal. It is preparing to lead him to a spiritual realization that overrides these things and yet fulfils and reconciles them in all that is divinely true in their spirit and purpose. *It transforms the needs and desires into a divine will and Ananda. If transforms the mental and moral aspiration into the powers of truth and Perfection that are beyond them.* It substitutes for the divided training of the individual nature, for the passion and strife of the separate ego, the calm, profound, harmonious and happy law of the universalized person within us, the central being, the spirit that is a portion of the supreme Spirit... This is the high realization in front of all our seeking and striving, and it gives the sure promise of a perfect reconciliation and transformation of all the elements of our Nature. A pure, total and flawless action is possible only when that is effected and we have reached the height of this secret Godhead within us (Sri Aurobindo 1950: 193-194).

32. As Bellah et al. argue:

For we have not experienced the potentialities of ourselves and our relationships, and so we have not reaffirmed ourselves in the larger contexts that give our lives meaning. If, after a stressful day, we can turn our attention to something that is mildly demanding but inherently meaningful-reading a book, repairing a car, talking to some one we love, or even cooking the family meal-we are more apt to find that we are 'released'" (Bellah et al. 1991: 255).

33. In the words of Bellah and his colleagues:

The record of city growth [in the United States] over the last half-century graphically demonstrates that without sustaining institutions that make interdependence morally significant, individual attention becomes fragmented in focus and limited in scope. Vast social inequality is rendered invisible by residential separation, and an often shocking indifference to human misery and environmental degradation goes generally unremarked (ibid: 268).

34. As Bellah et al. argue: "The whole argument about whether the United States is in decline or is as strong as ever is also besides the point and fundamentally distracting. Clearly we are headed toward a future in which a number of highly successful national or regional economies will coexist; rather than worrying about where the united States is in the hierarchy, we should be worrying about creating a humane economy that is adequate to our real purposes and a healthy international economy that operates for the good of all people" (ibid: 272).

REFERENCES

Ado, H. et al. (eds.), 1984, *Development as Social Transformation*, Tokyo: United Nations University.

Apter, David, 1987, *Rethinking Development*, Sage

——, 1991, "Institutionalism Reconsidered", *International Social Science Journal*, No. 129: 463-481

——, 1992, "Democracy and Emancipatory Movements: Notes for a Theory of Inversionary Discourse", in Jan N. Perterse (ed.), *Emancipations, Modern and Postmodern*, Sage.

Beck, Ulrich, 1992, *Risk Society: Towards a New Modernity*, London: Sage.

——, 1991, *The Good Society*, New York: Alfred A. Knof.

Benjamin Roger, 1981, *The Limits of Politics: Collective Goods and Social Change in Post-industrial Societies*, Chicago University Press.

Block, Fred, 1987, *Revising State Theory: Essays in Politics and Post-industrialism*, Philadelphia Temple University Press.

Connolly, William E., 1991, *Identity/Difference: Democratic Negotiations of Political Paradox*, Cornell.

Dahl, Robert, A., 1989, *Democracy and its Critics*, Yale.

Etzioni, Amitai, 1988, *The Moral Dimension: Towards a New Economics*, NY: Free Press.

Galtung, Johann, 1980, *True Worlds: A Transnational Perspective*, NY: Free Press.

Giddens, Anthony, 1991, *Modernity and Self-Identity: Self and Society in the Late Modern Age*, Cambridge: Polity Press.

Giri, Ananta, 1992, "Social Development as a Global Challenge", *Social Action* 42 (3): 286-304.

——, 1993a , "The Quest for a Universal Morality: Jurgen Habermas and Sri Aurobindo", Indian Institute of Management: Ahmedabad, Working Paper.

——, 1993b, "Social Policy and the Challenge of the Postindustrial Transformation", *Indian Journal of Social Science*.

——, 1993c, "The Dialectic Between Globalization and Localization: Economic Restructuring, Women, and Strategies of Cultural Reproduction", Indian Institute of Management, Ahmedabad: Working Paper.

Habermas, Jurgen, 1989, *The Structural Transformation of the Public Sphere*, Cambridge, MA: MIT Press.

——, 1990a, *Moral Consciousness and Communicative Action,* Cambridge: Polity Press.

——, 1990b , "What does Socialism Mean Today? The Rectifying Revolution and the Need for New Thinking on the Left", *New Left Review,* No. 183: 3-21.

Habermas, Jurgen (ed.), 1984, *Observations on the "Spiritual Situation of the Age": Contemporary German Perspectives*, Cambridge, MA: MIT Press.

Harvey, David, 1989, *The Condition of Postmodernity*, Cambridge, MA: Basil Blackwell.

Held, David, 1991, "Democracy, Nation, State and the Global System", *Economy and Society.*

Inglehart, Ronald, 1990, *Culture Shift in Advanced Societies*, Princeton.

Kitschelt, Herbert, 1993, "Social Movements, Political Parties, and Democratic Theory", *ANNALS, AAPSS*, 528: 13-29.

Kyi, Aung San, 1991, *Freedom from Fear and Other Writings*, Penguin.

Laclau, Ernesto, 1992, "Beyond Emancipation", in Jan N. Pierterse (ed.), *Emancipations, Modern and Postmodern*, Sage.

Lechner, Norberto, 1991, "The Search for Lost Community: Challenges to Democracy in Latin America", *International Social Science Journal,* No. 129: 541-553.

Melucci, Alberto, 1992, "Liberation or Meaning? Social Movements, Culture and Democracy", in Jan N. Pieterse, (ed.), *Emancipations, Modern and Postmodern,* Sage.

O'Donnell, Guillermo, 1993, "On the State, Democratization and Some Conceptual Problems: A Latin American View with Glances at Some Postcommunist Countries", *World Development* 21 (8): 1355-1369.

Osborne, David, 1988, *Laboratories of Democracy,* Boston: Harvard Business School.

Osborne, David and Ted Gaebler, 1992, *Reinventing Government: How Entrepreneurial Spirit is Transforming the Public Sector,* New Delhi: Prentice-Hall of India.

Pande, G.C., 1982, "On the Nature of Social Categories", in Ravinder Kumar (ed.), *Philosophical Categories and Social Reality,* Delhi.

Pantham, Thomas, 1989, "Postrelativism in Emancipatory Thought: Gandhi's Swaraj and Satyagraha", Unpublished Manuscript.

Parekh, Bhikhu, 1992, "The Cultural Particularity of Liberal Democracy", *Political Studies* XL: 160-175.

Piven, Prances and Richard A. Cloward, 1988, *Why Americans Don't Vote,* NY: Pantheon Books.

Sen, Amartya, 1986, "The Standard of Living", In S.M. McCurrin (ed.), *The Tanner Lectures on Human Values,* Universities of Cambridge and Utah Press.

——, 1989, "Food and Freedom", *World Development.*

——, 1991, *Inequality Re-examined,* Oxford: Basil Blackwell.

Sri Aurobindo, 1950, *The Synthesis of Yoga,* Pondicherry: Sri Aurobindo Ashram.

Streeten, Paul, 1993, "Markets and States: Against Minimalism", *World Development* 21 (8): 1281-1298.

Taylor, Charles, 1989, *Sources of the Self,* Cambridge, MA: Harvard University Press.

Templhin, Rolph, 1965, *Democracy and Non-Violence: The Role of Individual in World Crisis,* Boston: P. Sergent Publishers.

Touraine, Alain, 1991, "What Does Democracy Mean Today?" *International Social Science Journal* 128: 259-268.

Unger, Roberto M., 1987, *False Necessity: Anti-Necessitarian Social Theory in the Service of Radical Democracy*, Cambridge.

Warren, Mark, 1992, "Democracy and Self-Transformation", *American Political Science Review*.

Whitehead, Lawrence, 1993a, "Introduction: Some Insights from Western Social Theory", *World Development* 21 (8): 1245-1261.

——, 1993b, "On 'Reform of the State' and 'Regulation of the Market' ", *World Development* 21 (8): 1371-1393.

Chapter Four

SOCIAL POLICY AND THE CHALLENGE OF POST-INDUSTRIAL TRANSFORMATION

The emergence of post-industrialization calls for a new look at the US response to need. The answer lies in the emergence of a set of innovations: reforms of unemployment compensation, a commitment to job training, and an exploration of public employment. The potential recipients of the future are not a narrow stratum of young men and women who have turned to lives of criminality, teenage motherhood, or drugs, but a broad cross-section of the population, experiencing the problem of part-time work, extended periods of unemployment, and the challenge of dislocation.

—June Axinn and Mark Stern (1988: 171)

What we may be seeing in the laboratories of democracy is the emergence of a new political paradigm, tailored to the realities of the new economy... Within the new paradigm there is a left, a right, and a center, but they have little to do with the left, right, and center to which we are accustomed. They have less to do with questions of spending and taking, for instance, than with how aggressive government should be in reshaping the marketplace, and whose interests should be protected in the process.

— David Osborne (1988: 321, 330)

THE PROBLEM

For the last two decades, advanced industrial societies have been undergoing fundamental transformations in their social economic, political and cultural domains. The ongoing process of this transformation is leading to the emergence of a new type of society whose full contour is yet to emerge. The trends of this emergent formation are looked at as part of "The Coming of the Post-Industrial Society" (Bell 1973). Along with the change from a predominantly industrial, manufacturing economy to a high tech and service economy, this transformative process has entailed some curious and shocking changes in the politics, administrative policy and culture in advanced capitalist societies. The post-war faith in the principles of "Welfare State" has yielded to a New Right redefinition of the priorities of state and society. Social policy in advanced capitalist societies in North America and Europe have turned increasingly "conservative" in the last decades. This reorientation is being justified as crucially necessary to confront the restructuring forces of post-industrialism and to instill dynamism and innovation to an otherwise lethargic and bureaucratic system (Dehrendorf 1988; Offe 1988).

In this realm of ongoing post-industrial transformation, the process of which has many painful consequences such as "deindustrialization", "unemployment", "underemployment", low-paying service job, what is to be the guiding principle and philosophy of a social policy? What is the role of state and different institutions in confronting the challenge of late capitalism? How and in which direction do the existing social policies have to be transformed in order to cope with the challenge of post-industrial transformation? Answers to these historically significant questions of survival require a critical reflection on the challenge of the post-industrial transformation and the accompanying need for transforming the theory and practice of social policy.

Post-Industrial Transformation and Contemporary Restructuring

The *"Great U-Turn"* that the post-industrial transformation has led to is best reflected in the domain of contemporary economic restructuring. In advanced capitalist societies, the decline of the manufacturing sector and the ascendancy of the service economy is also witnessing fundamental restructuring of the location of industries, where high technology has enabled the flight of capital from the snowbelt to sunbelt and to the safe havens of the Third World villages.[1] At the global realm, high technology makes possible the emergence of multinational corporations, a global assembly line, a global restructuring of industrial activities and spatial forms creating a "global-technostructure of production, ...investment and trade" (Bright and Geyer 1987: 1). This globalization of production, distribution and exchange has also been accompanied by the economic crisis of the advanced industrial countries in the 1970s (Cuomo 1988; Goldthorpe 1984). Moreover this global and regional economic restructuring has led to the spatial restructuring of the cities. Urban restructuring has been accompanied by the processes of "gentrification", "abandonment and displacement", creating "new homelessness"[2] and "hardship in the heartland"[3]. This restructuring has also led to the rise of the post-industrial cities as competitive units in the global economy (Harvey 1985; Sassen 1988; Savitch 1988).

But contemporary economic restructuring is not simply confined to the manufacturing sector. Deindustrialization is now being seen in the service sector as well; it victims are not solely the blue-collar workers of Detroit and Pittsburg but also the company managers and professionals who are "falling from grace" in the wave of the post-industrial restructuring (Newman 1988).

Post-industrial transformation is also restructuring the internal organization of industries. Industries now require workers with advanced technical skills for which they have to go beyond the boundaries of "the internal labour market".[4] "The new emphasis on high-skilled work and well-trained labour is partly responsible for the recent decline in the role of the internal labour market" (Noyelle 1987:2). The rise of the informal economy is also restructuring the internal labour market of the firms (Portes et al. 1989). Part-time job has also devoluted the internal labour market. At the level of firm, high technology is also leading to a general regime of flexible accumulation, specialization and exchange (Harvey 1987; Piore and Sabel 1991). As one commentator tells us: "Under vertical disintegration, firms tend to specialize in types of classes of production rather than in production of large quantities of specific outputs as in mass production. The essence of the firm becomes flexible production" (Nayelle 1987: 101).

Contemporary economic restructuring also manifests itself in a cataclysmic rise in speculative economic activity and flight from responsible assessment of risks. The economic crisis that the post-industrial transformation has created is an integral part of the coming of the "casino society" and the rise of "paper entrepreneurialism" (Blustone and Harrison 1988: 63). Now, it has been cheaper to acquire another company and its entire capital stock than to invest in new plant and equipment. In this incessant merger and acquisitions, new technologies also make possible the growth of corporate mega-structures (Derber 1982; Touraine 1988). But as anthropologist Marvin Marris (1981) rightly points out, the spell and appeal of particular products are lost in such faceless mergers and acquisitions which for him is one of the crucial reasons for the losing around of American products in the global market.

The economic crisis of the post-industrial transition has also given rise to fundamental political restructuring in late capitalism. The most visible development here is the rise of the New Right and its attack on the welfare state on grounds of its inefficiency as well as the current fiscal crisis. The conservative counterrevolution has supposedly come up to throw government off the back of the people and unleash their creativity and initiative to make the most and the best of the post-industrial opportunity. This political restructuring seems all-pervasive. Even in the exceptional case of

Sweden, there have been new divisions and anti-solidaristic strategies (Offe 1988: 217). But this political restructuring has taken place in the context of the restructuring of class and the "destructuration of collectivities" (Offe 1988: 215; also see Lash and Urry 1987). Here, as Offe tells us: "the primary significance rests with new forms of structural and cultural plurality leading to the virtual evaporation of classes and other self-conscious collectivities of political will..." (Offe 1988: 218). What Stuart Hall writes about Thatcherism makes clear the total revolution that this political restructuring strives to bring:

> Politically, Thatcherism is related to the recomposition and 'fragmentation' of the historic relations of representation between classes and parties; the shifting boundaries between state and civil society, 'public' and 'private', the emergence of new arenas of contestation, new sites of social antagonism, new social movements, and new social subjects and political identities in contemporary society (Hall 1988: 2).

But this conservative revolution and political restructuring have not been made possible solely due to image manipulation and conspiracy[5] since, as Hall argues, "in and through images, fundamental political questions are being posed and argued through" (Hall 1980: 261). The challenge here is to understand the structural foundations behind the dissatisfaction with welfare state and liberal democracy beneath the images of Thatcher and Reagan. Post-war democratic forces operated with the assumption that the expansion of the welfare state is in the best interests of the common people. "Post-war social democrats always talked in terms of the enabling and facilitating state and never explicitly faced the empirical evidence that the interests of the state—its officials and politicians—were in opposition to those of ordinary citizens" (Ignatief 1989: 69). When liberal forces not only defended the welfare state but also struggled for its massive expansion, "the New Right presented itself as the only party committed to oppose the exponential growth of the state..." (Hall 1988: 227).

But we have to realize that the New Right did not invent the dissatisfaction with the state in the first place.

It is undoubtedly true that the economic crisis of the welfare state which has generated individualistic political attitudes and orientations has translated into a political crisis of the welfare state. But was this translation inevitable and unavoidable? Claus Offe argues that "in all such cases, the decisive change occurs not only on the level of objective events but on the level of interpretive framework..." (1988: 215). In the context of the post-industrial crisis, the New Right was successful in providing an ideological alternative to the destructuration and ambiguity of post-industrialism.

Questioning the arguments of the inevitability of the conservative retrenchment of the welfare state enables us to understand the complex process in which the anti-welfare retrenchment has actually operated. Here it is crucial to realize that the beneficiaries of the welfare state are "Not only the Poor" (Goodin and Grand 1987) but also the middle classes who have a crucial role in creating, expanding, reforming and dismantling the welfare state. "The middle classes had significant interests in its preservation, interests neither politicians nor civil servants could safely ignore" (Grand and Winter 1987: 143; also see Hanson 1987). In Sweden, even the bourgeoisie coalition has not detracted from the philosophy and practice of welfare state (Fry 1979: 7).

But political restructuring in post-industrial society is not simply confined to reactive and defensive mobilizations but also includes those movements who are mobilizing for aspiration (Rochon 1988). Here the crucial trend is the restructuring of the relationship between political party, civil society and citizens and the rise of grassroots "critical social movements" (Walker 1988) as the agents of people's "need interpretation" (Fraser 1987). These social movements are agents of "self-production" (Touraine 1977) and historicity in programmed societies where "society's" work upon itself is no longer carried only in the economic order but almost always in the domains of culture" (Touraine 1981: 73).

As Touraine tells us: "In post-industrial society, social movements form around what is called consumption in the name of personal or collective identity, yet at the heart of the great apparatus of production and management—not in relation to the system of ownership" (Touraine 1977: 323). These movements "contest the administrative logic of the social state as they struggle for the power to interpret their members' needs and to institute democratic, dialogic and empowering communicative relations" (Fraser 1987: 31).

The restructuring process of post-industrialism is not simply confined to economy and politics, it is also restructuring "the script of life in modern society[6] and the boundaries of culture. According to Buchman, "unemployment due to structural (technological) change or economic factors undermine the "life long" integration in the occupational system that characterized male occupational careers since World War II. Thus, the individual's movement through the occupational system is gradually losing its highly standardized form" (Buchman 1989: 48). Moreover, "The rapidly decreasing half-life of the usability of acquired expertise gives rise to short-term work perspectives and induces a relatively low degree of calculability and predictability" (ibid.: 50). Hence, post-industrial transformation not only creates a flexible specialization on the shop floor but also engenders a flexible specialization in one's life course. Fred Block makes this restructuring of the lifecourse clear: "The patterns of social life consolidated in the country after twenties and thirties continued to organize people's lives around measured labour time, the basis of the old productive forces... All aspects of this organization of social life have been undermined by the progressive emergence of new productive forces over the past fifty years" (Block 1987: 109). Because of part-time work, informal economy and the home work, the relationship between work-time non-work time and leisure is changing (Fernandez-Kelly and Garcia 1989; Lozano 1985; Mankin 1978; Gross 1966). "This interpenetration of time structure leads to the reorganization of time in the entire life course" (Buchman 1989: 57).

But as in the case of political restructuring, this restructuring of the life course is not simply a reaction formation to the sweeping forces of post industrialism. In the domain of the post-industrial life-world, there has also occurred the development of a post-modern self, which embodies a "post-individualist"[7] "charismatic reaction to the contradiction between formal and substantive rationality embodied in the modern self" (Wood and Zurcher 1988: 137). Studies show that contemporary professionals have a process orientation towards themselves in relation to organization rather than a product orientation (ibid). This post-modern self has emerged in the context of the rise of the post-modern culture. Post-modern culture is accompanied by the destructuration of the great summarizing discourse and the rise of local narratives and local knowledge (Lyotard 1984; Portoghesi 1983). "Post-modernism is reflected in the post-Marxist socialist politics of the 'new social movements' or 'socialist pluralism'. It expresses itself in Foucault's micro-macro politics and the new politics of localities" (Graham 1988: 61). The emerging cultural sensibility in the contemporary "condition of postmodernity" (Harvey 1989) is striving to transcend the institutional and discursive boundaries of modernity and to imagine, explore and create alternative spaces in the contemporary landscape of despair (Cox 1984; Griffin 1988; Soja 1989).

Post-Industrial Challenge and the Imperatives for Policy Transformation

The overwhelming and all-encompassing restructuring that post-industrial transformation has brought urgently calls for a transformation in our weltanschauung and in our social policy. The logic of postindustrialism makes it inevitable transformations in social policy and in social institutions in order that the entry into the post-industrial world does not degenerate solely into disruption and dislocation. Post-industrial transformation has engendered crisis in existing social organization and representation. But it also has the potential of a renewal and reorganization of individual and society, the realization of which requires a transformation in self, institution and social policy.

The Need for Institutional Transformation

In coping with the challenge of postindustrial transformation and directing its restructuring towards a more humane social order, we have to realize that economic crisis is part of a larger social crisis and can not be solved through simple economic alternations, such as change in the budget allocation. Rather it calls for the growth of new social institutions and the development of a radically new social policy. Fred Block articulates very clearly the imperatives for a transformed social policy in contemporary restructuring:

> Post-industrial developments place institutional problems at the center of the policy agenda. Traditional macro-economic policies were purely quantitative—increase aggregate demand, slow the growth of the money supply, reduce taxes-but these measures fail to address the new problems. The new problems are institutional; how can firms be organized to make maximal productive use of human skills and technological advances; how can services like health care and education—which constitute a growing share of total consumption expenditures—be organized most effectively; how can we devise to infrastructure development-transportation, energy, communications-in a situation where neither the market nor centralized planning has proven its effectiveness (Block 1987: 28-29).

Post-industrial transformation makes it imperative the establishment of a regime of flexible accumulation and specialization which, in turn, depends on "the creation of institutions that resolve the micro-and macro-economic problems along new technological trajectories" (Piore and Sabel 1984: 263). In post-industrial societies, flexible specialization is better able to accommodate the fluctuations in exchange rates and commodity processes than is a regime of mass production. But there is an inherent incompatibility between the existing hierarchical and Taylorist forms of work organization and the operation of new technologies in the regime of flexible specialization. Advanced technologies have not only led to fundamental spatial and economic restructuring in postindustrial societies, they also make urgent a restructuring of work organizations. The new technologies of computer and micro-electronics are rapidly transforming the nature of work. But new technologies in many different realms—from the work place to genetic counselling—have been used as an instrument in the control of workers and ordinary people.[8] However, new technologies also have a more non-hierarchical and democratizing potential: according to Zuboff (1988), they simultaneously "automate" and "informate". Harry Shaiken's (1984) study of the Numerical Control Machine shows how in some cases, technology is viewed as a tool for the enhancement of the power of the machinist who often does a considerable amount of programming, rather than as a vehicle to control the worker. In the operation of new technologies, as one thoughtful observer of the contemporary condition of work and power tells us, "the questions that we face today are finally about leadership... Will they be able to create the organizational conditions in which new visions, new concepts, and a new language of workplace relations can emerge?" (Zuboff 1988: 12).

The operation of high technology is facilitated by the democratization of decision-making process in the workplace. The Cuomo Commission Report makes this imperative clear for us: The old fashioned assembly lines emphasize a hierarchical, top style approach but new technologies require a democratic way (1988: 199). Shaiken further challenges us: "A more participatory technology requires a broad public awareness and democratic involvement in defining the goals for designing automation" (Shaiken 1984: 64). The imperative for democratic work culture is very well-articulated in the words of David Obsorne: "Automated technologies not only require an educated workforce... they also require a more democratic workplace" (1988: 277).

Post-industrial development also *necessities* the building up of a post-industrial built environment and social infrastructure which, in turn, makes it urgent a transformation in the existing relationship between state and society. The post-industrial social infrastructure can not be built in the current social policy of retrenchment and general austerity. "Similarly, generalized austerity with the resulting decline in the physical and mental health of the population would undermine the capacity of organizations to expand the learning components of jobs" (Block 1987: 125). Moreover, without the accompanying policy transformation and institutional development to appropriate new productive forces, old forms of exploitation are intensified. The contemporary trend of high tech and low pay is a case in point.

Irrelevance of Existing Policies: Reconceptualizing Dependency and Poverty

In the contemporary condition which Cuomo has so aptly called "The New Realism" (Cuomo 1988), existing welfare policies have become irrelevant. According to Osborne, American "social welfare system is built on assumption of stability, that most workers will spend their entire careers in the same type of job. In today's world, these assumptions are obsolete" (Osborne 1988: 8). Moreover, American welfare system was created for a "particular age mix of dependents" when the major problem was the "cyclical unemployment" in the economy. But in the new post-industrial economy, vulnerability is all-pervasive and unemployment is built into the dynamics of the economy. But the challenge of the new economy has not been met in the US though some state governments have responded to these problems by "transforming their social welfare system into social adjustment systems" (Osborne 1988: 9). Thus, Osborne argues: "US social welfare program will have to adjust to new turbulence in the labour market..." (ibid: 6).

Transforming social welfare systems into social adjustment system calls for a redefinition and reconceptualization of dependency, poverty and disadvantage. In post-industrial societies, the demographic situation points to the increasing dependence of the aged and children. Because of the employment of both the parents, some provisions for day care of children has become extremely crucial. Post-industrial transformation, demographically, has also been accompanied by the greying of America. Moreover, poverty in post-industrial society is not simply confined to the non-working and the under-class. "The New American Poverty" (Harrington 1984) is a product of the systemic changes in the economy where, in the struggle between capital and labour, the needs of labour are losing ground. Downward mobility is not confined to the blue-collar worker; it has also cracked the American dreams of the middle class (Newman 1988). "The deregulated labour market poses risk for both the old and new working class" (Axinn and Stern 1988: 21). The growth of the low-wage job as a systemic feature of the post-industrial economy suggests that the next war on poverty will need to address both the non-working and the working poor.

A critical look at the emergent crisis of homelessness demonstrates the changing nature and structural foundation of disadvantage in post-industrial societies. The new American homelessness is not simply a transient phenomenon, among drug-addicts, alcoholics and the mentally ill. Rather it is produced by certain structural forces of contemporary American society, such as unemployment, the reduction of government benefit programs, abandonment and lack of production of low-rent housing (Kozol 1988). This homelessness "is not the result of general poverty. Rather it is occurring in one of the most advanced industrial economies of the world, in the midst of unprecedented wealth" (Marcus 1988: 72).

Post-industrial change not only makes it imperative a reconceptualization of disadvantage in the social policy agenda, it also calls for a critical rethinking of the appropriateness of the foundational assumptions of existing social policies. American social policy is built on a bifurcation between social security and public assistance. This bifurcation has, in turn, created two different representations of the beneficiaries of social policy: the citizens and the clients. "Social security by the stably employed majority of citizens had become by the 1960s institutionally and symbolically separated from welfare for the barely deserving poor" (Weir et al. 1988: 26). Moreover, the New Deal Welfare

System in the United States was "based upon commercial Keynesianism, not on social needs of the American workers" (Skocpol 1988: 302). It gave rise to compensatory welfare which ultimately helped in regulating the poor, rather than empowering them. In this context, the Reagan "Mean Season"[9] represents an "understandable culmination of the original failure of the New Deal to institutionalize social Keynesian policies..." (Skocpol 1988: 302). Even the Great Society Program of President Johnson did not transcend this New Deal bifurcation—it did not succeed in developing collective legitimation for social welfare, hence social welfare provisions were vulnerable to retrenchment. But the pervasiveness of dependence and poverty in post-industrial societies requires social policy to transcend the outmoded distinction between welfare and security.

Transforming the State

The imperative for a transformed social policy that post-industrialism heightens is no where more urgent than in the transformation of the state. The task of building a transformed social infrastructure to cope with the post-industrial challenge can be accomplished neither by the free market nor by the centralized state. Post-industrial societies are characterized by collective goods as opposed to public goods which not only presage a sharp rise in political conflict but also call into question the structure of government institutions themselves (see Benjamin 1980). The rise of the collective goods brings the question of a generalized social welfare and raises the question whether these collective goods are best delivered by centralized and bureaucratic institutions.

But the necessity for the increasing role of the government is not to be confused with the perpetuation of the bureaucratic and the corporatist state. What post-industrialism needs is a renewal, revitalization and transformation of state. As Marc Levine et al., write: "...time has come to revitalize the notion of a progressive, democratic state in the United States" (1988: 2). But they make clear what they mean when they advocate for a revitalized government: "This is not a book about statism. We are not advocates of stifling, centralized, and essentially undemocratic bureaucracies" (ibid: 2). The policy change that the post-industrial transformation necessitates calls for the transformation of the "state as an instrument of change and liberation, identity and dignity" (Kothari 1988: 7).

Designing an Appropriate Social Policy for Post-Industrial Society

Creating a Post-Industrial Society

The imperative for policy change that the coming of the post-industrial society creates challenges us to design an appropriate social policy. Social policy has to facilitate the growth of post-Toylorist and post-Weberian forms of organization both in the workplace as well as in other domains of social administration. As Block argues: "One of the signposts of postindustrial change are the efforts by corporations to devise new forms of organization that diverge sharply from classical Weberian bureaucracies" (Block 1987: 29). Various companies are developing work groups instead of hierarchies (Mankin 1978: 40). "The new bureaucracy" in contemporary advanced capitalist societies is characterized by managerial self-renewal (Skertchy 1977: 289) and "fewer levels of supervision, diminished deference to hierarchical authority, greater reliance on teamwork, and expanded decision making responsibilities for lower-level employees" (Block 1987: 29). For Block, the emergent "post-bureaucratic organizations are more effective than traditional bureaucracies in situations where changing technologies and changing markets create high levels of uncertainty and unpredictability" (Block 1987: 29).

Zuboff (1988) and Shaiken (1984) show how different companies using high technology have started developing non-hierarchical forms of work organizations. The Cuomo Commission Report mentions about an insurance company—Shenadith Insurance Company—which has organized clerks into teams of five to seven members with each responsible for all aspects of claim processing after realizing that internal bureaucracy had thrown a "monkey ranch" in the company's high-tech plans (Cuomo 1988: 175).

Service delivery, in the welfare system as well as in other areas, also have to be post-bureaucratic. In many instances, social movements among the welfare recipients have instilled the energy and dynamism of the life-world into the system world of the welfare bureaucracy and have transformed the clients from their passivity to a politically constituted collectivity (Hertz 1982; West 1981). Citizen movements, citizens groups and voluntary organizations present themselves not only as alternative agents of people's need interpretation but also as alternative agents of service delivery. Here, rethinking in social service delivery in post-industrial societies provides a model for designing an appropriate social policy. Experiments in social service delivery in Arizona under Governor Burce Babbit embodies initiatives for creating a post-bureaucratic social order. The state of Arizona, to deliver services such as meals, contacts voluntary organizations. Osborne articulates the broader significance of such an arrangement:

> The idea is not only to get more bang for the buck, but to get more compassion and more commitment from those delivering those services. It is also to promote competition, to use small units capable of more flexibility and humanity than large bureaucracies, and to take advantage of the diversity of community organizations to serve populations that are often beyond the reach of a state bureaucracy (Osborne 1988: 123).

But as the narrator of this experiment for the future, David Osborne, makes clear, such efforts should not be seen as movement for privatization and reprivatization of the functions of the state. What these creative leaps into future embody is the creation of a third sector, non-bureaucratic institutions as agents of transformation and survival. In the words of Osborne: "Today's governors search for non-bureaucratic solutions to problems; if reshaping the market place will not suffice, they turn to third-sector organizations" (Osborne 1988: 327). Partnership with these third-sector organizations is a significant step in the *debureaucratization of the state*. The agenda for creating a post-bureaucratic society has to realize that "the democratization of civil society is as important as dismantling the bureaucracies of the state" (Hall 1988: 231).

Debureaucratizing the state represents an "alternative to the arbitrary exercise of government power on the one hand and regulatory paralysis on the other" (Block 1987: 30). This also represents a "shift from a procedural to a substantive concept of regulation that is implemented through link between state agents and organized groups in society" (ibid). Concerning the partnership between state and organized groups in society, Alan Cawson's dictum seems very provocative: "The password of this new age must be self government, not for nations or for individuals, but for individuals-in-groups" (Cawson 1982:112). In Scandinavian countries, in the areas of occupational health and safety, we see the emergence of such partnership. Here the principal agents in the regulatory process are the health and safety committees which monitor government action. This regulatory process could be applied in other areas of social administration where frontline government regulators would work with workplace or citizen committees. The creation of a post-bureaucratic state requires reliance on an increased level of activity and organizations among non-state actors. It "depends on a renewal of political participation in which the citizenry plays a more active role in the regulation of social life" (Block 1987: 32).

Social policy in creating a post-bureaucratic society can also derive inspiration from the recent initiatives in "taming the bureaucracy" by the government and the citizen movements (Gromley 1989) in the past decades. The recent efforts in taming the bureaucracy, as William Gromley Jr. tells us, has involved both strategies of coercive and catalytic controls, both muscles and prayers. Each strategy has its own advantage though the strategy of prayer helps in creating a creative democracy. When the bureaucrats know which interests they want to represent, but don't know which policies they ought to pursue, "prayers make a lot of sense... prayers may encourage self-actualization and discourage pork barrel politics. A final advantage is that prayers promote bureaucratic creativity, flexibility, innovation, and experimentation" (Gromley 1989: 231).

A Positive Government

The idea of a "positive government" (Cumo 1988) is central to the design of an appropriate social policy for the post-industrial society. In recent years, the conservative attack on government and government regulation has struck populist chords. But the institutional transformation that the post-industrial challenge heightens cannot be accomplished by the retreat from the creative role of government. Governor Bill Clinton of Arkansas reflects a mature understanding of the post-industrial policy goal when he argues: "We may want the government off our backs, but we need it by our sides" (Osborne 1988: 109). Martin Carnoy et al. also write: "The ideal is not to get government off people's back, rather, it is to put government in people's hands" (1983: 214). But this revitalization of the government has to occur within the context of the extended political participation and a renewed democratic culture. Corporatist policy can not work in the post-industrial societies (Kushma 1988: 36). The state has to build partnership with various groups in society—business and labour—and provide leadership in confronting the dislocation of the post-industrial transition. The need for a expanded and reformed welfare state has perhaps never been greater when the central political question is: "Who will bear the hardships associated with transition to a postindustrial economy?" (Block et al. 1987: xiii).

In the post-industrial economy, the government has to provide leadership in creating an ethos for production and productive investment in a "casino" climate of speculation and merger. "The fundamental issues of the 1990s will be economic" (Osborne 1988: 20). But the economic problem of contemporary advanced capitalist societies is not simply produced by the macro economic disequilibrium of forces (Cuomo 1988: 21). "In the last analysis what matters is production" (Cuomo 1988: 21), and positive goernment has to play a creative role in transforming the immediate dislocation of post-industrialism into an asset in "Creating the Future" (Dukakis and Kaneter 1988). But in this challenging domain, "more than the federal governments, states have recognized the demands of a global economic environment and have taken steps to meet them" (Cuomo 1988: 107). Many states in the US have already launched such partnership ventures which R. Kanter so aptly characterizes as "Investment Economics and the Politics of Partnership" (Kanter 1988). Here rather than targeting specific industries or products, most states are targeting processes: technological innovation and capital formation.

An exemplary model of this politics of partnership is Ben Franklin Partnership Program in Pennsylvania, initiated by former Governor Dick Thornburgh. This is a joint venture of the state and business groups which strives to create capital formation for investment in high-technology and applies it to firms and industries. The program operates closely with research universities. Lehigh university, in particular, plays a critical role and has developed itself into a remarkable example of the post-industrial university.

In post-industrial societies, capital formation for investment is problematic and here state initiatives are important. The existing financial institutions are not meeting the need for capital on the part of the small business and other social groups. Perhaps for this reason, Michael Dukakis as Governor of Massachusetts had created many quasi-public finance agencies. The Massachusetts Housing Partnership, a distinguished board of forty public and private groups, is a case in point. Governor Jim Blanchard of Michigan has also established a Michigan Venture Capital Fund to assist in the economic revitalization of the cities abandoned by deindustrialization. These state developmental initiatives are comprehensive but decentralized. These programs are local, "they have the capacity to make decisions quickly, the flexibility to respond to a wide variety of problems, and the credibility that can only be earned thorough the daily contact with the people" (Osborne

1988: 261). Such investment economics and the politics of partnership help in the recovery of communities and cities, hard hit by post-industrial restructuring. Because of Ben Franklin Partnership even Pittsburg, hard hit by the decline of the steel industry, is remarkably well positioned for the hightech economy of the future.

Welfare and Efficiency

Two crucial policy agendas in the post-industrial societies are: creating economic growth and bringing the poor into the growth process. Governments can stimulate production by promulgating an investment tax credit "tailored to encourage investment in new process of technology and equipment" (Cuomo 1988: 121). It has to build a solid educational infrastructure by creating postindustrial universities and making education a lifelong process on the part of workers in particular and people in general. In the regime of flexible specialization, the urgent "task is to develop community-based approaches to social and economic problems" (Osborne 1988: 13). Governments have to create partnership banks and companies which invest in private-public partnerships that would assume a longer-time horizon. There must be national standard for social spending and revenue sharing coupled with national economic policies that provide for full employment (Carnoy et al. 1983: 209). In late capitalism, the state has spent a disproportionate amount of its energy and enthusiasm in armament production. But an appropriate social policy designed for postindustrial societies requires "a well-planned expansion of the public sector in non-military areas" (Carnoy et al. 1983: 160).

But this transformed state should not be confused with the corporatist state. "Only the national government—with a grassroots movement behind it—has the power to make such reforms as requiring workers representatives on the boards of corporations" (Carnoy et al. 1983: 9). But, first of all, the government has to earn credibility on the wealth-creating front (Hall 1988). But redistribution and the task of bringing the poor into the growth process has also to be accorded equal primacy and urgency. The fundamental challenge for the post-industrial state is attaining a creative balance between efficiency and equity, economic prosperity and fair economic share. In transcending the false division between welfare and efficiency that conservatism has created, the states have to convince people that social welfare is not an hindrance to economic growth, but an important tool for a prosperous and productive economy. Traditionally, we have thought of social welfare policy as not vitally linked to the agenda of economic development of a country. "Yet social policy can not be hermetically sealed from economic policy and economic analysis. Indeed the post-war tendency to leave 'welfare' issues entirely to students of social policy has had a number of consequences" (Charles and Webb 1986: 238). Boris Frankel also writes: "...no significant improvement in 'social wage' programs (whether locally organized or centrally administered) can be conceptualized if 'the economy' is seen to be separate from social welfare" (1987: 99).

Here the challenge is to create a board-based political support for a transformed social welfare policy that enables people to cope with structural disadvantage and creates opportunities for education and mobility. Global competitiveness has become a major issue for many economies in advanced capitalist countries and a reformed social welfare system would enhance the competitive positions of the troubled economies such as contemporary American economy. As Block argues: "Greater employment and income security, more democracy at the workplace, greater option for adult education and training, more extensive family and community services, and more flexible working time are all aspects of a post-industrial transformation of work that would make the economy more efficient" (Block 1987: 154). In this regard, experiments in the state laboratories of democracy embody the emergence of a new social welfare paradigm. In the words of Osborne: "Where as liberals in the 1960s thought primarily in terms of incomes of the poor, governors such as Dukakis and Cuomo have sought to increase their economic activity through education, training, employment and investment" (Osborne 1988: 1988).

Flexibility is the key word in the post-industrial transition and social policy designed to cope with its challenge must strive towards the institutionalization of a flexible life-course. To cope with the deindustrialization of post-industrialism, it seems that early retirement to ensure full employment is a move in the right direction. "This has already become a major concern of social policy in Western Europe..." (Block 1987: 134). Moreover, there needs to be a flexibility in the structuration between work time, family time and non-work time. The flexible restructuring of time in division of labour is also a demand of the New Christian Right in general and the pro-life movement in particular. The pro-life movement wants companies to "hire people in ways that will allow mothers and fathers to take care of their children" (Ginsburg 1989: 185). However, the concern with the family is not simply a New Right concern. Even Mikhail Gorbachev pleaded for the significance for articulating the needs of the family with the imperatives of the public domain and industry (Gorbachev 1987).[10] In this regard, what Weir et al. write about the future of social policy in the United States deserves our careful attention:

> As part of a comprehensive national family policy, new ways must also be found to make domestic obligations more compatible with work. For employed women, paid maternity leaves with right to return to similar work must be mandated by national legislation, although the financing might well occur through contributing insurance systems as well as through general tax revenues. Beyond guaranteed maternity leave, flexible work schedules and optional extended parental leaves are policies that would allow employees and society as a whole to shoulder some of the burden of children... (Weir et al. 1988: 444).

The particulars of an appropriate social policy are certainly important but what is much more crucial is developing a broad framework for policy analysis. Here, the fundamental thrust of a post-industrial social policy has to be its comprehensiveness: targeting both the middle class and the lower class. This comprehensive social policy would enable individuals, groups and classes to cope with the growing polarization of the post-industrial transition. This social policy has to be empowering, rather than compensatory. This empowering social policy in the post-industrial society has to create space for a dialogic "Life World" (Habermas 1987) and has to make the ongoing "Return of the Actor" (Touraine 1988) possible. The social policy designed to cope with the challenge of post-industrial transformation has to implant a post-industrial theory of justice[11] by making a creative balance among production, income and distribution.

Social Policy and Social Politics: Beyond the Illusion of "End of Ideology" and the Emerging Political Paradigm

Though post-industrial societies are highly technological and though there are compelling imperatives in this high-tech social order for policy transformation, technological compulsions are not going to determine the nature of policy change in the advanced societies. It is the nature of configuration of political and ideological forces that is going to determine the feasibility and the practicability of the proposed policy transformation. As Osborne so perceptively argues: "The fundamental task we face in adjusting to the post-industrial economy is not in the realm of policy and program, but in the realm of perception and ideology. It is the task of redefining our core problems" (Osborne 1988: 288). But, simultaneously, there is no simplistic ideological solution to the contemporary challenge of technology and society. As Cawson argues: "The task of understanding how politics and economics are enmeshed in the working of the late capitalist economy demands a complex explanation which eschews simple remedies based on faith—either in free market or in the inevitable collapse of capitalism" (1982: 8).

The attempts at policy transformation in contemporary societies have to be part of a broad-based political movement. As Skocpol argues: "In the shifting political circumstances of the 1980s, advocates of a revitalized American system of social provision have yet to find political metaphors of collective compassion simultaneously appealing to black and whites, to traditional and structured families, and to the middle class and the poor" (Skocpol 1988: 311). Eventhough structural trends in contemporary advanced societies are pointing towards a growing polarization of the class structure (Wright 1978), there is nothing deterministic in this structural polarization that would lead to the success of a progressive movement. Hence the issue of consistent and conscious political and ideological struggle is preeminently important. Thus, Hall argues: "Appealing to the 'real experience' of poverty or unemployment ...won't do the trick. Even poverty and unemployment have to be ideologically defined" (Hall 1988: 262). We require a movement like the civil rights movement that is capable of conscientizing the American people towards creating an "economic democracy" (Carnoy 1980) and meeting the needs of post-industrial poverty.

Such a movement can derive inspiration from the practices of "creative democracy" (Burn 1989) in the grassroots social movements under late capitalism. But citizen movements (Schmidt 1989) in different backyards need to be part of a national political movement (Boyte 1986; Mollenkopf 1983). The predominantly "middle class radicalism"[12] of the "backyard revolutions"[13] must incorporate the genuine need of the working men and women. The new social movements are on the forefront on the issue of democratization of civil society. But, as one of Alain Touraine's informants in his ethnography of anti-nuclear protest puts it: "The ecology movement has been totally incapable of explaining to workers and discussing with them the importance of these themes for their day-to-day problem" (Touraine 1983: 71). Hence, grassroots social movements becoming part of national progressive coalition have to be more sensitive to the issues of socio-economic justice and the needs of the working men and women.

The dynamics of institutional change in contemporary developed societies point to "basic reorganization (or attempts at reforms) of local and regional government" (Dente and Kjellberg 1988: 1). State and local governments are conducting creative and progressive experiments to cope with the challenge of the post-industrial transformation. These experiments in the laboratories of democracy are part of an "Emerging Political Paradigm" (Osborne 1988: 319). This emerging political paradigm is manifested in the policy agenda and political struggles of many state governors, both Democrats and Republicans, whom David Osbrone calls "the new paradigm governors." Chunck Rob, a former governor of Virginia, best articulates the agenda of this new political paradigm: "Just as we did in the New Deal, the time has come to negotiate a new social contract, to insist on economic growth with economic equity" (quoted in Osborne 1982: 331). A broad-based national progressive coalition can take imprisation from this emerging political paradigm. In the words of Osborne, "Those who would bring the new paradigm to Washington... will have to tell the American people a new story about where we, as a society, are heading. That story must deal with the new realities of the global economy and the new roles necessary for government, business, labour and the American people. It must resonate with the experience of the average voter" (Osborne 1988: 338).

But there should be no ambiguity on the point that it would be difficult to bring about this broad-based, progressive national coalition. Destructuration of classes and collectivities by the restructuring forces of post-industrial transformation poses the main challenge here (Gans 1988, Offe; 1988). But "cultures of solidarity" (Fantasia 1988) emerging among contemporary American workers also provide hopeful glimpses for the future. Efforts in creating a broad-based political movement and designing an appropriate post-industrial social policy have to point to both the challenges and the challenges and possibilities in the emerging social condition. But responding to the challenges of destructuration and dislocation requires an intimate participation with the cultures of solidarity in the laboratories of democracy. As Jurgen Habermas tells us:

> Yet beneath the threshold of the well-institutionalized orders of science and technology, law and morality, art and literature, beneath a politics reduced to administration, and on the periphery of a highly

mobilized economic system, it is possible to detect processes of de-differentiation in praxis itself, new symbolic forms in everyday life where the cognitive-instrumental once again touches upon the moral-practical and the aesthetic-expressive indicating perhaps not only regressions but also exploratory movements (Habermas 194: 25).

NOTES

1. Unless otherwise mentioned, all italics and emphasis in this paper are mine.
2. See Hopper et al. for the link between the contemporary homelessness and deindustrialization.
3. I adapt this term from a critical commentary on American homelessness; see D. Salerno et al. 1984.
4. Michael Buroway (1979) argues that existence of the internal labour market is a significant feature of the industrial social order. Hence, the significance of its breakdown in postindustrial transition has to be noted.
5. Mark Miller (1988) argues that the fascination with Ronald Reagan is a product of television and its manipulative culture. But such a view does not take into account the structural foundations behind the fascination with the so-called sweet faces of "Ronnie" and "Maggie".
6. I am adapting this phrase from Buchman (1989).
7. Fred Block (1987: 109) makes this restructuring of the lifecourse clear: "The patterns of social life consolidated in their country after twenties and thirties continued to organize people's lives around measured labour time, the basis of the old productive forces... All aspects of this organization of social life have been undermined by the progressive emergence of new productive forces over the past fifty years."
8. I am adapting this term from Dellmayr (1981).
9. See Rapp (1988) for an ethnographic portrayal of the use of new technologies for controlling ordinary people.

10. I am adapting the phrase from Block et al. (1987).
11. Gorbachev writes: "We are proud of what the Soviet government has given women the same right to work as men; equal pay for equal work... But, we failed to pay attention to women's specific rights and needs arising from their role as mother and home-maker, and their indispensable educational function as regards children... This is a paradoxical result of our sincere and politically justified desire to make women equal with men in everything" (1987: 103).
12. I am adapting this phrase from Kann (1986).
13. I am adapting this phrase from Kann (1986).
14. I am adapting this phrase from Boyte (1980).

REFERENCES

Akinn, June and Mark Stern, 1988, *Dependency and Poverty: Old Problems in a New World*, Laxington, MA: Laxington Books.

Baye, Hansik, 1982, *A Theory of Distributive Justice in Post-Industrial Society*, Florida State University: Ph.D. Dissertation.

Bell, Daniel, 1962, *The End Ideology*, Cambridge, Mass.: Harvard University Press.

——, 1973, *The Coming of the Post-Industrial Society*, NY: Basic Books.

Benjamin, Roger, 1980, *Collective Goods and Political Change in Post-industrial Societies*. Chicago.

Block, Fred, 1987, *Revising State Theory: Essays in Politics and Post-Industrialism*, Temple.

Block, Fred et al., 1987, *The Mean Season: The Attack on the Welfare State*, NY: Pantheon.

Bluestone, B. and B. Harrison, 1988, *The Great U-Turn: Corporate Restructuring and the Polarizing of America*, NY: Basic Books.

Bright, Charles and M. Geyer, 1987, "For a Unified History in the Twentieth Century", Ms.

Brown, Michael (ed.), 1988, *Remaking the Welfare State: Retrenchment and*

Social Policy in America and Europe, Temple.

Buchman, Marlis, 1989, *The Script of Life in Modern Society: Entry into Adulthood in a Changing World*, Chicago.

Burn, Tom et al., 1989, *Creative Democracy: Systematic Conflict Resolution and Policy Making in a World of High Science and Technology*, NY: Praeger.

Buraway, Michael, 1979, *Manufacturing Consent*, Chicago.

Carnor, Martin and D. Shearer, 1980, *Economic Democracy: The Challenge of the 1980s*, NY: ME Sharpe.

Carnoy, Martin et al., 1983, *A New Social Contract: The Economy and Government After Reagan*, NY: Harper and Row.

Cawson, Alan, 1982, *Corporatism and Welfare: Social Policy and State Intervention in Britain*, London: Heinemann Books.

Chodak, Szymon, 1989, *The New State: Etatization of Western Societies*, Boulder et al.: Lynne Riener Publishers.

Cox Harvay, 1988, *Religion in the Secular City: Towards a Postmodern Theology*, NY: Simon and Schuster.

Cuomo, Mario, 1988, "Changing Values Under Mrs. Thatcher", in *Thacherism*, edited by R. Skidelsky, London: Charter and Windus.

Dellmayr, Fred, 1981, *The Twilight of Subjectivity: Contributions Towards a Post-Individualist Theory of Politics*, Amherst.

Dente, Bruno and F. Kellberg, 1988, *The Dynamics of Institutional Change: Local Government Reorganization in Western Democracies*, Sage.

Derber, Charles, 1982, *Professionals as Workers*, Boston: G.K. Hall.

Dukakis, Michael S. and R. Kanter, 1988, *Creating the Future: The Massachusetts Comeback and its Promise for America*, NY et al.: Summit Books.

Fantasia, Rick, 1988, *Cultures of Solidarity: Consciousness, Action, and Contemporary American Workers*, California.

Faux, Jeff, 1988, "New Institutions for the Post-Reagan Economy", in M. Levine et al., 1988.

Fernandez-Kelly, M.P. and A.M. Garcia, 1989, "Informalization at the Core: Hispanic Women, Home Work and the Advanced Capitalist State", in Portes et al., 1989.

Frankel, Boris, 1987, *The Post-Industrial Utopians*, Polity.

Fraser, Nancy, 1987, *Social Movements vs. Disciplinary Democracies: The Discourse of Social Needs*, Minnesota.

Fry, John (ed.), 1979, *Limits of the Welfare State: Critical Views on Post-War Sweden*, London: Saxon House.

Gans, Herbert, 1988, *Middle American Individualism: The Future of Liberal Democracy*, London: Macmillan.

Ginsburg, Faye, 1989, *The Contested Lives: The Abortion Debate in an American Community*, California.

Goldfarb, Jeffrey, 1989, *Beyond Glashnot: The Post-Totalitarian Mind*, Chicago.

Goldthorpe, J.H. (ed.), 1984, *Order and Conflict in Contemporary Capitalism*, Oxford.

Goodin, R. and J. Grand (eds.), 1987, *Not Only the Poor: The Middle Classes and the Welfare State*, London: Allen and Unwin.

Gorbachev, Mikhail, 1987, *Perstroika: New Thinking for our Country and the World*, NY: Harper and Row.

Graham, Jullie, 1988, "Postmodernism and Marxism", *Antipode* 20 (1): 60-66.

Griffin, D. 1988, *Spirituality and Society: Postmodern Vision*, Albany: SUNY Press.

Gromley, William, 1989, *Taming the Bureaucracy: Muscles, Prayers, and Other Strategies*, Princeton.

Gross, Betram, 1966, *Space-Time and Post-Industrial Society*, Syracuse: Maxwell School of Citizenship and Public Affairs.

Habermas, Jurgen (ed.), 1984, Observations on "The Spiritual Situation of the Age", *Contemporary German Perspectives*, MIT Press.

Habermas, Jurgen, 1987, *The Theory of Communicative Action*, Vol. 2: Life World and System, Cambridge: MIT Press.

Hall, Stuart, 1988, *The Hard Road to Renewal: Thatcherism and the Crisis of the Left*, London: Verso.

Hanson, R.L., 1987, "The Expansion and Contraction of the American Welfare State", in Goddin and Grand, 1987.

Harris, Marvin, 1981, *America Now: The Anthropology of a Changing Culture*, NY: Simon and Schuster.

Harvey, David, 1985, *Urbanization of Capital*, Johns Hopkins University Press.

——, 1987, "Flexible Accumulation Through Urbanization Reflection on Postmodernism in American City", *Antipode* 19 (3): 260-286.

——, 1989, *The Condition of Postmodernity*, Basil Blackwell.

Hertz, S., 1982, *The Welfare Mothers' Movement*, Washington, D.C., University Press of America.

Hopper, Kim et al., 1985, "Economies of Makeshift: Deindustrialization and Homelessness in New York City," *Urban Anthropology* 14 (1-3): 183-236.

Ignatieff, Michael, 1989, "Citizenship and Moral Marcissism", *The Political Science Quarterly* 60 (1): 63-74.

Kann, Michael, 1986, *The Middle Class Radicalism in Santa Monica*, Temple.

Kanter, R., 1988, "Introduction: Investment Economics and the Politics of Partnership," in Dukakis and Kanter, 1988.

Kerr, Clerk, 1980, *Industrialism and the Industrial Man*, Cambridge, Mass: Harvard University Press.

Kelley, Donald R., 1986, *The Politics of Developed Socialism: The Soviet Union as a Post-Industrial State*, NY: Greenwood Press.

Kothari, Rajni, 1988, *Transformation and Survival: In Search of the Humane World Order*, New Delhi: Ajanta.

Kozol, Jonathan, 1988, *Rachel and Her Children*, NY: Crown.

Kushma, John, 1988a, "Participation and Democratic Agenda: Theory and Practice", in Marc Levine, 1988.

——, 1988b, "Realizing the Promise of Democracy in America's Third Century", The Marc Levine, 1988.

Lash, Scott and J. Urry, 1987, *The End of Organized Capitalism*, Wisconsin.

Levine, Marc et al., 1988, *The State and Democracy: Revitalizing America's Government*, Routledge.

Lozano, Beverly, 1985, High Technology, Cottage Industry: A Study of Informal Work in San Francisco Bay Areas, UC Davis: Ph.D. Dissertation in Sociology.

Lyotard, J., 1984, *The Post-Modern Condition*, Manchester.

Mankin, David, 1978, *Toward a Post-Industrial Psychology*, NY: John Wiley and Sons.

Marcuse, Peter, 1988, "Neutralizing Homelessness", *Socialist Review* 1: 69-96.

Millar, Mark, 1988, *Boxed In: The Culture of T.V.,* Northwestern.

Mollenkopf, John, 1983, *The Contested City*, Princeton.

Newman, Katherine, 1988, *Falling From Frace: The Experience of Downward Mobility in American Middle Class*, NY: Free Press.

Noyelle, Thierry, 1987, *Beyond Industrial Dualism: Market and Job Seg-*

mentation in the New Economy, Boulder et al: Westview Press.

Piore, Michael and C. Sabel, 1984, *The Second Industrial Divide: Possibilities for Prosperity*, NY: Basic Books.

Portes, A. et al. (eds.), 1989, *The Informal Economy: Studies in Advanced and Less Developed Societies*, Baltimore: The Johns Hopkins University Press.

Portoghesi, P., 1983, *Postmodern: The Architecture of the Post-industrial Society*, NY: Rizzoli.

Offe, Claus, 1988, "Democracy Against the Welfare State? Structural Foundations of Neoconservative Political Opportunities", In J.D. Munn (ed.), *Responsibility, Rights and Welfare: The Theory of the Welfare State*, Boulder: Westview Press.

Osborne, David, 1988, *Laboratories of Democracy*, Boston: Harvard Business School.

Rochon, Thomas, 1988, *Mobilizing for Peace*, Princeton.

Ross, George, 1988, "The Mitterand Experiment and the French Welfare State: An Interesting Uninteresting Story", in M. Brown, 1988.

Salerno, D. et al., 1984, *Hardship in the Heartland: Homelessness in Eight U.S. Cities*, NY: Community Service Society.

Sassen, Saskia, 1988, *The Mobility of Capital and Labor*, Cambridge.

Savitch, David, 1989, *Post-Industrial Cities*, Princeton.

Schmidt, David, 1989, *Citizen Lawmakers: The Ballot Initiative Revolution*, Temple.

Shaiken, Harry, 1984, *Work Transformed*, NY: Reinhart Winston.

Skerchly, A.R., 1978, New Bureaucracy: Reconstruction of State Government Bureaucracies to Meet the Needs and Expectations of the Post-Industrial Society, Perth, West Australia: Management Development Center.

Skocpol, Theda, 1988, "Limits of the New Deal System and the Roots of Contemporary Welfare Dilemmas," in Weir et al., 1988.

Soja, Edward, 1989, *Post-Modern Geographies*, Verso.

Touraine, Alain, 1977, *The Self-Production of Society*, Chicago.

——, 1981, *The Voice and the Eye*, Cambridge.

——, 1983, *Anti-Nuclear Protest*, Cambridge.

——, 1988, *Return of the Actor: Social Theory in the Post-Industrial Society*, Minnesota.

Walker, Richard, 1988, *One World, Many Worlds: Struggles for a Just*

World Peace, London: Zed Books.

Weir, M., S. Orloff and T. Skocpol (eds.), 1988, *The Politics of Social Policy in the United States*, Princeton.

West, Guida, 1981, *The National Welfare Rights Movement*, NY: Praeger.

Wright, Erik Olin and J. Singlemann, 1978, Proletariazation in Advanced Capitalist Societies: An Empirical Investigation into the Debate Between Marxist and Post-Industrial Theorists over the Transformations of the Labor Process. University of Wisconsin-Madison: Institute for Research on Poverty.

Zuboff, Soshanna, 1988, *In the Age of Smart Machine: The Future of Work and Power*, NY: Basic Books.

Chapter Five

THE DIALECTIC BETWEEN GLOBALIZATION AND LOCALIZATION: ECONOMIC RESTRUCTURING, WOMEN AND STRATEGIES OF CULTURAL REPRODUCTION

Technological change is a factor in women's lives everywhere in the world. This holds true whether one is referring to rural women in Third World countries or women from cities of the most technologically advanced countries. In an African village, introducing a water pump may save women hours of heavy labour, but all too often it is found that new techniques and technologies such as tractors, supplied through international aid projects, benefit men as a sex and remove women from traditional sources of income-generating work.

— Cynthia Cockburn[1]

The expert/non-expert polarity [of technology] thus corresponds internationally to the core/periphery distinctions, with corollary polarization of male/female and white/nonwhite. The shape of international industrialism is therefore shaped by capitalism, patriarchy, and colonialism... A predominantly young, non-white and female workforce executes production which is conceptualized thousands of miles away.

— Beverly Burris[2]

The continuing emphasis on export-led agriculture mostly ignores the resource requirements of millions of subsistence farmers whose needs are not satisfied through the mechanism of the market. Since scarce land, water, credit and technology are being promoted to the export sector, poor farmers lacking financial means and technical support, overexploit the natural resource base, including marginal areas to eke out a living. The result has been that the capacity of the continent to feed itself has been seriously hampered.

— Fantu Cheru[3]

THE PROBLEM

The economic arrangement of all social systems is now in the midst of a fundamental restructuring, necessitated by the crisis of varieties of command economies and bureaucratic regulations of production, distribution and exchange. Economic restructuring is meant to free the economy from the shackles of the state and create more opportunities for producers as well as consumers. Economic restructuring, which emerged in advanced industrial societies in the context of their economic and political crisis, is now in a phase of global diffusion. Contemporary economic restructuring, facilitated by the revolutionary manifestation of new technologies on the wake of a postindustrial transformation, is characterized by the breakdown of the standardized regime of mass production and the rise of "flexible specialization",[4] by a fundamental stress on increasing production and enhancing efficiency, and by globalization of production, distribution, and exchange. Contemporary economic restructuring valorizes a particular mode of production and social reproduction. It is needless to mention that this mode is the industrial and post-industrial mode, which based upon "valorization of capital",[5] promotes a culture of consumption. Architects of economic restructuring promote global integration of our societal economies but are blind to the problem of articulation, i.e., how "less familiar strategies of social reproduction" articulate with "world economic and political as well as cultural processes".[6] Economic restructuring very often leads to destruction of self-subsistent forms of livelihood. Integration with global market has meant the erasure of the less familiar strategies of what Alain Touraine calls "self-production of society".[7]

But the key question here is can the western style of life be universalized? Would our globe survive if the contemporary pattern of consumption prevalent in western Europe and North America is universalized? This provides the challenge to preserve multiple strategies of production and reproduction not only for the survival of little enclaves but also for the long-term interests of mankind and the Mother Earth. The present restructuring of economic life also calls for a critical reflection on the dialectic between localization and globalization, anthropology and economics.[8] The present paper describes the vulnerability of less "powerful" forms of live and sections of society in the regime of the global economy, with specific reference to the predicament of women. The paper first seeks to create a descriptive portrait of new economic restructuring and the global condition of which this is a part. It looks at the new economic mode as a global formation and describes the trajectory of its "dispersion" in multiple countries and communities—both advanced and the technologically backward and in multiple spaces and bodies. The paper specifically describes women's work and condition, their predicament and dreams, in the "emergent technocracy".[10] While looking into the vulnerability of women in the globalizing economy, the paper seeks to explore how we can preserve and universalize less familiar strategies of social reproduction by universalizing the feminine principle of *shakti* in the face of the power of the new economy and its global onslaught.

Contemporary Economic Restructuring

Contemporary advanced industrial societies are in the midst of an all-encompassing economic restructuring what two sensitive observers of the contemporary scene have characterized as the "Great U-Turn".[11] This economic restructuring, facilitated by the revolutionary manifestation of new technologies, has given rise to a new regime of flexible production, distribution and exchange. The economic recession of the advanced capitalist societies in the 1970s created a structural context for the deregulation of the Fordist mode of standardized production and the rise of flexible specialization, where firms tend to specialize in types of classes of production rather than a production of large quantities of specific output as in mass production. Under this condition, the essence of the firm becomes flexible specialization.[12] For Michael Piore and Charles Sabel, new technologies make "flexible specialization" a crucial sector of manufacturing in the advanced industrial countries.[13] Flexible specialization requires flexibility in organization of production—both its conceptualization and execution—and quick learning of new skills to cope with the challenge of new technologies. In the regime of flexible specialization production workers must be so broadly skilled that they may quickly shift jobs. Moreover, "...within a system of flexible specialization, firms depend on one another for the sharing of skills, technical knowledge, information on opportunities, and definitions of standards. Structure here shades into infrastructure, competition into co-operation, and economy into society".[14] Piore and Sabel further tell us: "In mass production it is the firm that organizes research, recruits labour, and guarantees the flow of supplies and credit. In flexible specialization it is community institutions—the community itself that are responsible for these tasks."[15]

While Piore and Sabel are optimistic about the possibility for prosperity in this emergent regime of flexible specialization other scholars have sensitized us to the destruction of communities and the deindustrialization of societies that has taken place as its consequence. To begin with the level of the firm, flexible specialization and its stress on high-tech mediated work is leading to the disintegration of the "internal labour market" of industries.[16] As

Noyelle tells us: "The new emphasis on high-skilled work and well-trained labour is partly responsible for the recent decline in the role of the internal labour market and the increasing reliance of firms on the external labour market."[17] This decline of the significance of the "internal labour market" of firms is being accompanied by the rise of part-time work and informal economy.[18] According to one commentator, "unemployment due to structural (technological) change of economic factors undermine the 'life long' integration of the occupational careers since world war II. Thus, the individual's movement through the occupational system is gradually losing its highly standardized form. The rapidly decreasing half-life of the usability of acquired expertise gives rise to short-term work perspectives and induces a relatively low degree of calculability and predictability."[19]

The disorganization of the previously standardized form in the life of both the actors and institutions that economic restructuring has brought about is also being accompanied by the decline of the manufacturing sector (for instance, in the US domestic employment attributable to manufacturing fell from 27 per cent in 1970 to 19 per cent in 1986), the ascendancy of the service economy, and a restructuring of the location of industries, where high technology has enabled the flight of capital from the snowbelt to sunbelt and to the safe havens of the Third world villages. At home in advanced industrialized countries deindustrialization of the previously industrial centers such as Pittsburg and Detroit has become a stark reality. Deindustrialization is now being seen in the service sector as well: its victims are not solely the blue-collar workers but also the company managers and professionals who are "falling from grace" in the wave of postindustrial restructuring.[20] At the same time, high technology makes possible the emergence of a global assembly line and multinationalization of capital, which operates through many forms of linkage: "co-production, licensing, out-sourcing, invisible partnerships to avoid arousing local anti-US sentiments."[21] For instance, American Airlines has a sweatshop in Barbados for entering computerized date, which is connected to Oklahoma by computers and satellite communications. "It is staffed by women who are paid wages that fall near the bottom of even Barbados's meagre pay scale."[22] Aihwa Ong best summarizes the contemporary scenario thus: "Since the 1972 world recession, new patterns of "flexible accumulation" have come into play as corporations struggle in an increasingly competitive global arena. Flexible labour regimes, based primarily on female and minority workers, are now common in the Third World, as well as in poor regions of metropolitan countries."[23]

Gender and Economic Restructuring: New Technologies and Women in Advanced Capitalist Societies

New technologies which continue to play a decisive role in current economic, industrial, and organizational restructuring work as double-edged swords. According to Soshana Zuboff, they simultaneously "informate" and "automate".[24] New technologies require a more participatory and non-hierarchical form of work-arrangement but without parallel institutional transformation via-a-vis the invidious distinctions of class, race, and gender new technologies are being used to oppress ordinary workers and women.[25] Indeed new technologies work as a new 'panopticon' where the distinction between the expert and the non-expert sectors in organizations seems natural-legitimized by the technocracy itself—and there managers rely on technology "to make behaviour transparent in the belief that people are more likely to do what they are told when they know their actions will be translated instantly and displayed as electronic text".[26] While the "information panopticon create the fantasy of a world that is not only transparent but also shorn of the conflict associated with subjective opinion" the electronic text "confronts the clerk with a stark sense of otherness".[27] At the same time, the electronic text for her is "impersonal; letters and numbers seem to appear without having been derived from an embodied process of authorship".[29] As Beverly Burris argues:

In offices, for instance, machines such as the typewriter presuppose some degree of worker pacing, whereas word processing technology has the capacity to be systematized. Such systems can be used by management to undermine worker autonomy; tasks can be fragmented and assigned to different workers, and work can be technologically paced and monitored for productivity and errors... Among the non-expert sector, whether clerical or production staff, computerized technology has typically been used to isolate and control workers. Predominantly male managers and technical experts control the labour of workers who are disproportionately female and non-white using technology to embody and promote social differentiation and managerial control, both domestically and internationally.[30]

In advanced industrial societies under the regime of an ascendant technocracy there is a bifurcation between the experts and non-experts but women in both the sectors have born more brunt. "Women are to be found in great numbers *operating* machinery... but women continue to be rarities in those occupations that involve knowing what goes on inside the machine".[31] In 1980, 95 per cent of the keypunch operators in the US were female but cnly 22 per cent of them were systems analysts.[32] In the export-processing zones of multinational corporations while young women comprise 80-90 per cent of operators, "men predominate within the smaller administrative and technical expert sector..."[33] Even within the expert sector the work of women managers is subject to patriarchal stereotyping. As Cockburn tells us: "...when the dust settles after the technological revolution, the same old male/female pattern can be seen to have re-established itself. The general law seems to be: women may press the buttons, but they may not meddle with the works... Always the person who knows best, who has the last say about the technology, is a man..."[34]

Here, it must be noted that although opportunities for women in advanced capitalist societies appear to have increased during the past two decades, their overall economic situation has deteriorated. "Currently in the US, two-thirds of all adults living in poverty are women, and more than half of all poor families are female-headed."[35] The reason for this in-built contradiction of poverty in the midst of unprecedented plenty is complex. Economic restructuring and the attendant process of deindustrialization has gone hand in hand with political restructuring, marked by the rise of "new conservatism" and the accompanying retrenchment of the welfare state. The "demise of the internal labour-intensive jobs disproportionately performed by women, have adversely affected both the present and future working lives of women workers in the nonexpert sector."[36] Burris argues that at the same time that technologies were exploring opportunities, "technocratic restructuring was undermining political victories."[37]

Economic Restructuring, Globalization and Gender

The restructuring of industries and work organization has not taken place in isolation. In fact this model of economic reform and structural adjustment is being globalized. In the 1960s developing economies, in their desperate bid to attract foreign investments, tried to improve conditions for the work of the transnational capital in their countries. With the failure of the earlier attempts at import substitutions international monitors of development including the United Nations put pressure on the developing economies to revert back to their earlier export functions. As Ong describes: "In addition to raw materials and crops, developing economies could export goods manufactured in 'Free-Trade Zones' (FTZs). To attract foreign capital, tax-free privileges in trade were combined with new incentives such as provision of building and utilities by the local government, and the ease of profit repatriation. Export-industrialization seemed to complement the 'green revolution' sponsored by the World Bank and International Monetary Fund."[38]

By the 1970s we saw global assembly lines at work in southeast Asia and the US-Mexican border. To achieve global dominance, Japanese and western companies bypassed high production costs, labour militancy, and environmental concerns at home by moving to other countries in south-east Asia, Caribbean and Latin America. In the locales of offshore production companies combine varieties of production-arrangements—mass assembly and subcontracting systems, firm work and home work. "In southeast Asia and Mexico, export manufacturing is not confined to FTZs but is increasingly dispersed in subcontracting arrangements that may include part-time work by peasants."[39]

While in Malaysia export-led industries operate mainly in FTZ, areas with 80 per cent of the female operators on the shop floor, in Hong Kong most of such production is undertaken by subcontracting family firms. Subcontractors also predominate such scenes in Taiwan and Philippines. "In the Philippines, where wages are among the lowest in Asia, subcontracting reduces the visibility of transnational firms, enabling them to bypass further political and economic costs. For instance, only a quarter of Filipino garment workers are based in FTZs; the bulk of garment manufacturing depends on a four-tiered subcontracting system that relies mainly on village home-sewers. Similarly, outside the Mexican *Mequiladora* zone, home work by housewives is part of the low-level of the segmented labour market; though, hidden behind illegalities and mixed forms of production, it is indirectly controlled by industrial capital."[40]

Daughters in Factories

Young women constitute the majority of the workforce in locales of off-shore production. Companies, as ethnographies of both Patricia Fernandez-Kelly and Oihwa Ong—anthropologists who have carried extensive fieldwork in the Malaysian coast and Mexican boarder—show, prefer single women.[41] In the Asian context these women come from the rural areas and they work under the moral and managerial custody of the male supervisors. These working daughters send money back to their families. But the income they earn from their hard work is meagre. Burris helps us understand this contradiction of high-tech and low-pay; "Gender and racial stereotypes combine to legitimate fast-paced and poorly paid work for Third World women. Young women are assumed to be working for supplementary income, where as increasingly, they are primary or sole breadwinners".[42]

The working daughters in south-east Asian global assembly lines who are breadwinners of their families and who also support their brothers' education are treated as "wards" in factories. As Ong tells us: "Japanese corporate policies in Malaysia defined Malay workers as "wards" under the moral custody of factory managers. By focusing on the young women's virginal status, the management capitalized on Malay fears about their daughter's vulnerability. Other techniques of control closely monitored workers' bodies. In mass assembly factories from South Korea to Mexico, operators were subjected to humiliating innuendos about menstruation, and were required to request permission to use the toilet."[43]

Not only these working daughters are subjected to "tight work discipline" that bodily constrained them they were used as replaceable instruments of labour. To maximize profit and production "quickly exhausted operators were replaced [by the company] by the next crop of school leavers".[44] Freshly recruited workers were routinely assigned work which required use of microscopes. This led to their early exhaustion and the deterioration of their eyesight. Ong tells us that industrial firms in Malaysia attempt to 'limit their employment to the early stage of their adult life, a strategy that ensured fresh labour capable of sustained intensive work at low-wages".[45] Sometimes new workers are employed on six months contracts so that they could be released or rehired at the same low wage rates. Ong's sympathetic description helps us envision the situation:

> The rapid exhaustion of the operators also resulted in most of them leaving of their own accord after three to four years of factory employment, although an increasing number remained working, even after marriage. Operators leaving the factories have not acquired any skills which would equip them for any but the same dead end jobs. The lack of legislative protection for women in the labour market and their low wages discouraged them from staying on longer in industrial employment. This weak structural integration of the women in the industrial sector, a situation fostered by corporate

employment strategy, has been used by male supremacists and capitalists to justify the low wages of operators in multinational corporations.[46]

The Body of Power, Spirit of Resistance

If such is the text of power written on the bodies of working women in global assembly lines then this writing is not without a difference. Workers make both overt and covert protests, which include attempts to damage the components they themselves assemble. As Ong tells us in her ethnography of such off-shore production in a Malaya village: "In one transistor factory, where about five million components were assembled each month, sometimes tens of thousands of transistors had to be rejected because of defects found. Occasionally, workers deliberately stalled the machine so that production was slowed down. A Malay technician reported that he was aware of these subversive acts but said that it was impossible to trace the workers responsible for them."[47]

Reactions of women workers also include overt forms of resistance such as displaying hysterial tendencies in the workplace. In Malaya villages women are considered especially vulnerable to spirit possession. Malaya women take recourse to such cultural beliefs to subvert the well-knit order that males have constructed for them. They get possessed with spirits in the work place, suddenly crying and screaming obscenities against restraining supervisors. In some cases the possessed exclaims: "I am not to be blamed" "Go away" "I will kill you, let me go", etc. Besides taking recourse to such spirit possession operators often attempt to seek relief from their dreadful work by asking permission to go to the locker room and to the prayer room, where as Muslims they could perform the obligatory worship five times a day. But managers also do not lay behind in such struggles. They dismiss women who are frequently subject to spirit possessions "for security reasons."[48] As Ong tells us of her case: "When the village elders protested, pointing out that the spirits in the factory were responsible for their daughters' seizures, the manager agreed but explained that the hysterical workers might hurt themselves in the machines, risking electrocution."[49]

In her comparative account of such regimes of control and forms of resistance Ong finds that South Korean women are among the most militant in Asia, "confronting a state more repressive of labour than other industrializing countries".[50] In the late 1970s when Korean economy was beyond the "take off" stage one of the major textile companies, the Dong-II Textile company, was engaged in a major labour dispute but the women didn't give in. Realizing that they have to organize themselves women rejected representatives of a puppet union led by men. In the words of Ong:

> Female workers, organized into different groups, have developed a whole repertoire of tactics and images expressing their struggles. In the Dong-II textile company strike, women protested 'miserable work conditions', poor food, imposed silence among coworkers, and prohibitions from going to the toilets. At the climax of their struggle against the company union, women on a hunger strike faced off against police by stripping and singing union songs.[51]

The above description shows that women do contest the categories and practices that treat them as mere extension of machines. But here we must not be quick to read these acts of resistance as markers of class consciousness or of a global anti-systemic ideology. "Working women rarely construct their identities or organize themselves in terms of collective or global interests."[52] However, "what we do find are attempts to escape from or live with industrial systems without losing one's sense of human dignity... In negating hegemonic definitions daily, factory women came to explore new concepts of self, female status and human worth."[53]

The complexity of the position of women in contemporary societies is evident by their above strategies of reproduction and resistance. It is true that women find dehumanizing their conditions of work in factories run by transnational corporations but their position at home is no less precarious. In her insightful essay, "Capitalism, Imperialism and Patriarchy: The Dilemma of Third-World Women Workers in Multi-National Factories" Linda Lim helps us to appreciate this complexity:

> Although women workers in these multinational factories are exploited relative to their output to male workers in the same country, and to female workers in developed countries, their position is often better than in indigenous factories and in traditional forms of employment for women. The limited economic and social liberation that women workers derive from their employment in multinational factories is predicated on their subjection to capitalist, imperialist, and patriarchal exploitation in the labour market and the labour process. This presents dilemma for feminist policy towards such employment: because exploitation and liberation go hand in hand, it cannot be readily condemned or extolled.[54]

Women's Vulnerability as a Mirror: The Sustainability of Privilege and the Challenge of Self-Subsistence

Structural adjustment of the economies of poor countries is another important aspect of the contemporary global economic restructuring. The International Monetary Fund now wants poor countries to improve their balance-of-payments position by liberalizing their economies, devaluing currencies, and increasing imports in proportion to exports. It is suggested that "by devaluation of local currency and frozen wages, the country's own exports would become cheaper in the international market".[55] But in reality, such structural adjustment programs bring havoc for the poor and vulnerable sections of society. Bolles' excellent study of the IMF program of structural adjustment in Jamaica shows how it devastated its manufacturing sector.[56] Bolles argues: "The IMF program has particular implications for Jamaica's manufacturing. The depression cut deeply into domestic sales because of higher prices. Devaluation costs (in local currency) of imported components—the essence of the screw driver type operation. Paying for and buying imported materials became more and more difficult and high interest rates raised bank loans beyond the reach of most manufacturers."[57]

The IMF packages of structural reform "depressed the standard of living of the majority of the nation".[58] It specifically made Jamaica's female production workers "vulnerable to events of international trade and finance."[59] Above all, structural adjustment program hard hit their kitchen. As Bolles says: "Food showed the most dramatic increment in price. For example,... the price of margarine rose from J\$ .50 per tub to J\$ 1.29: corned beef rose from J\$ .79 per tin to J\$ 2.00 and a large loaf of bread increased from 80 cents to more than dollar."[60] But the way women workers coped with such dislocations shows the resilience of their strategy of cultural reproduction. Economic crisis led to more reciprocal exchange of goods and services among the poor. Women revitalized their domestic network and widened its radius. "For example, one women in a visiting-union household supplied her neighbours and friends with cheese that she had bought at the commissary (of the multinational which employed her). In return her neighbour often provided child care on short notice, and her boy friend's sister performed small personal errands during the day while the woman was at work."[61] In this context what Bolles has written below helps us to understand the dialectic between globalization and localization and the creative power of existent forms of social reproduction to withstand the assault on people's standard of living:

> Thus, the reciprocal exchanges that take place in the domestic network of these urban working-class households provide mechanisms to compensate for the shortcomings of the wider economic system. The women industrial workers in these households take advantage of benefits available at their places of work to make their contribution to the exchange network. These household members not employed in the formal economic sector focus even more energy on exchange network activities to obtain for their households goods and services that would not be otherwise available to them, due to the lack of cash [caused by lack of employment] to obtain

them. These informal patterns of distribution and consumption have evolved in greater complexity as a response to provide increased access to the society's limited resources.[62]

What Bolles discusses in the context of the Caribbean region with reference to the manufacturing sector finds a striking parallel in Cheru's description of the devastation of African agriculture as a consequence of the IMF program of export-oriented capitalist agriculture.[63] For Cheru structural adjustment programs have led governments to "prefer large-scale mechanized farming to the detriment of the politically powerless small farmers."[64] Such mechanized agricultural mega-projects push monocropping instead of intercropping which devastates the fragile ecosystem. It also prefers cash crops to food crops. For instance, cotton or coffee production is accorded more governmental support than sorghum or cassava. The reason behind such discrimination is not hard to find. Cotton brings foreign exchange to finance the building of sky-scrappers of carnival for the pleasure of the local elite and their metropolitan mentors. Thus, it is no wonder that while agricultural production stagnated in Africa during 1990, having grown by 2.8 per cent on 1989, the food import increased.[65] "Africa spent $ 8 billion on food imports in 1986, a figure far greater than the total amount spent on oil import during the same year."[66] What is more food import "threatens to create a new and dangerous structural dependence on cereals such as wheat and rice that cannot be easily grown in many parts of Africa."[67] As a result, scarce land is being used to grow such crops which the poor usually cannot afford.

Cheru argues that "by putting valuable agricultural resources at the service of export markets in countries that are not self-sufficient in food, enormous pressures are created for local people to overexploit marginal lands".[68] At the same time, liberalization policy and international trade conventions such as GATT makes the pursuit of ecologically sustainable food security more difficult. Because of GATT poor countries "will be required to withdraw all trade restrictions—including quotas and tariffs designed to protect local food markets from cheap imports".[69] "The proposal would also deny the right of countries to restrict or inhibit export of agricultural food products to relieve food shortages, as now permitted under Article XI of the GATT treaty... On the other hand, the provision will do little to outlaw US and EEC food dumping."[70]

The implication of export-led capitalist agriculture for women cannot be ignored. According to Cheru, "women are responsible for 60-90 per cent of food productions, processing, and marketing in African countries, yet women have the least access to improved technology, credit, extension service and land".[71] Indeed such projects of development displace women "from productive activity" by appropriating or destroying "the natural resource base for the production of sustenance and survival".[72] The logic of market is now being applied to the use and the maintenance of even the commons, which in fact robs them. Indeed, wastelands development is an "euphemism for the privatization of commons".[73] The privatization of the commons along with the shift to capitalist agriculture brings havoc to ecology, which is evidenced by the increasing scarcity of water in all countries. According to Vandana Shiva, "ground water is drying up because it has been over-exploited to feed cash crops. Village after village is being robbed of its life line. Since women are the new water providers, disappearing water sources have meant new burdens and new drudgery for them".[74] Similarly, fodder collection takes longer with the destruction of the village commons. As a woman in the hills of Uttar Pradesh puts it:

> Since we were young, we used to go the forest early in the morning without eating anything. There we would eat plenty of berries and wild fruits, drink the cold sweet water of the *Banj* [oak] roots. In a short while we would gather all the fodder and firewood we needed, rest under the shade of some huge tree and then go home. Now, with the going of the trees, everything else has gone too.[75]

At the same time, the substantial increase in firewood collection time due to deforestation leaves women with little time for cultivation. Bina Agarwal draws our attention to the situation in Nepal where "substantial increase in firewood collection time due to deforestation has significantly reduced women's crop cultivation time, leading to an associated fall in the production of maize, wheat, and mustard which are primarily dependent on female labour in the region".[76]

The above examples show how contemporary economic restructuring with its logic of globalization systematically erodes locales of self-subsistence and modes of livelihood based upon principles of autonomy and "self-production" in the name of integration with a global market. Subsistence economies everywhere—whose primary example is peasant cultivation—serves basic needs through self-provisioning, and are very little dependent on the organization of market. Such modes of livelihood might look poor from an external point of view but for the participants in such a form of life it might not be so perceived. Vandana Shiva helps us to understand this:

> Culturally perceived poverty need not be real material poverty: subsistence economies which serve basic needs through self-provisioning are not poor in the sense of being deprived. Yet the ideology of development declares them so because they don't participate overwhelmingly in the market economy, and do not consume commodities provided for and distributed through the market...[77]

Market-oriented models of development perceive subsistent forms of livelihood as a danger and systematically try to destroy them. Indeed, the story of modernity is a story of the erosion of autonomous models of livelihood by the forces of industrialization and the accompanying mechanical worldview. It is a tragic story of the replacement of a "subsistence economy in which resources, goods, money, or labour were exchanged for commodities by the open-ended accumulation of profit in an international market."[78] As Carolyn Merchant tells us:

> Living animate nature died, while dead inanimate money was en-

dowed with life. Increasingly capital and market would assume the organic attributes of growth, strength, activity, pregnancy, weakness, decay, and collapse obscuring and mystiryeng the new underlying social relations of production and reproduction that make economic growth and progress possible. Nature, women, blacks, and wage labourers were set on a path toward a new status as 'natural' and human resources for the modern world system.[79]

The reduction of human beings to raw materials for production is an integral part of the logic of industrialism. The current heightened effort to subdue agriculture to the logic of industrialism has to be understood by the fact that the industrial mode is incapable of autonomous reproduction and cannot survive unless "low entropy is pumped from the environment into the economic process".[80] Industries have a thermodynamic need for extraction of resources from mining and agriculture—a point made clear by Georgescou Roegen's seminal study, *The Entropy Law and the Economic Process*,[81] in which he argues that industry is "completely tributary to agriculture and mining".[82] We are familiar with the second law of thermodynamics in which the law of entropy operates to create an eventual loss of energy. This creates a perennial thermodynamic constraint which compels the industrial mode to subject other self-subsistent modes of livelihood—which do not suffer from the same thermodynamic constraint—to its own logic of production and reproduction. While for the subsistent modes of livelihood useful things are encapsulations of the "strength of the earth" and "earth—and only the earth—provides the 'strength' or 'force' for life"[83], for the industrial mode use value is the product of the machine. But in reality the only "usefulness" which is at the heart of such a mode of production and reproduction is the sustenance of the technomass of industries. As Hornborg argues, "viewed as in some respects to living biomass, the super human "technomass" of industrial society must be fed specific kind of substances in order to grow. In industrial system, the structure in relation to which significant 'use values' can be ascertained is that of industrial, not human reproductions."[84]

Hornborg further helps us to understand this invisible logic: "Whereas hunter-gatherers, even in areas such as Kalahari desert, may retrieve 9.6 times the energy they spend on hunting and gathering. Industrial agriculture often yields only a fraction of the total, human-orchestrated energy input. Such a wasteful form of production can only continue so long as it is 'subsidized' by an asymmetric world trade in energy."[85]

Indian philosopher and scientist C.V. Sheshadri helps us to see this link as well. For Sheshadri, the second law of thermodynamics works as an energy-quality marker and provides a guide to the utilization of resources to the grave detriment of the poor and generally all those who are outside the structure of opportunities in a country like India. Sheshadri and Balaji argue: "By its very definition, energy becomes available only through a conversion process and according to the most supreme law of entropy, a proportion of energy is always lost in such a process. Further, under restricted conditions, the loss can be minimized and realization of such condition is, therefore, essential for operating a process efficiently. At this level, the concept, viz., energy cannot be viewed separate from its use and itself becomes a criterion for deciding the value of resources for utilization processes at hand. Energy becomes a quality marker in resource utilization in the same way that money become a marker in exchange".[86] But energy as value does not simply decide the nature of utilization of resources, it also determines the direction of flow of resources. As Sahashrabudhey interprets: "Modern energetic is only a tool to allocate resources so as to promote modern industry and modern life style at enormous costs to those outside the modern structures."[87]

The Dialectic Between Globalization and Localization: Towards a Recovery of the Principle of *Shakti*

Industrialism has an in-built need for "thermodynamics of imperialism" and its globalization has eroded autonomous modes of livelihood both within the West and East. The result has been devastating and we have seen this with specific reference to

women. The predicament of women in contemporary global restructuring is not confined to them; it is a mirror of the all-
pervasive process of dislocation and disruption that both woman
and men are subject to. In meditating upon contemporary predicament the last the feminists should do is to put a *purdah* around the
so-called women's issues. It is the dialectic between identity and
difference which constitutes both our dislocation and dream today. The multiple-level transformation that is taking place in the
contemporary world can hardly be captured by any form of essentialism. It is perhaps for this reason that Beverly Burris writes:

> However, despite the polarization and the persistence of politica
> issues, the technocratic system is a unified system, and one whicl
> unites, even as it divides, experts and non-experts, men and women
> whites and non-whites core and periphery. Although expert secto
> and non-expert sector women may face different specific issues, the
> more fundamental political questions which they confront are simi
> lar, and concern the structuring of technocratic organizations and
> the worldwide technocratic system. These concerns center around
> confronting polarization, centralization, and gender bias of techno
> cratic organizations, none of which is inevitable.[88]

But in confronting this common task Burris nonetheless ar
gues that women can bring their ventage point to bear upon in thi
task of epochal reconstruction. Burris thinks that "marginalit
within technocracy can be an advantage for women, well situatin
them to challenge technocratic norms, substituting feminist val
ues and organizational forms."[89] For Burris, "women's enhance
sense of connectedness, socially and ecologically, provides th
basis for a moral vision which can serve as an important correc
tive to the limitations of scientific rationality."[90]

Burris' arguments and hopes are shared by many feminist
One of the most creative among them is Vandana Shiva. Shiv
argues that the mechanical worldview of modernity, which ha
spelt the "Death of Nature", has also involved a radical concep
tual shift away from the traditional Indian commological view c

(animate and inanimate) "nature as *prakriti*", as "activity and diversity" and as an "expression of *shakti*, the feminine and creative principle of commos," which "in conjunction with the masculine principle (*purusha*)... creates the world."[91] Shiva pleads for a recovery of the feminine principle of *shakti* in order to reintegrate the division caused by science and technology.

From another perspective C.V. Sheshadri also pleads for a revitalization of the principle of *shakti* to find a way out of the entropic model of development. Sheshadri finds problems with the second law of thermodynamics which is at the centre of modern industrial and technological development. Sheshadri seeks to develop a new energy-quality marker which he calls *shakti*. Sheshadri develops his concept of *shakti* with the postulate of mass-energy:

> All forms of energy has mass equivalents (with suitable dimensionalizing factors). Thus, the internal energy or energy combustion of a material can be considered to have equivalents in terms of mass. This enables us to redefine a new class of property functions, *shakti*, that combines mass and energy in such a way that the quality markers can be assigned to various materials for comparison on a common basis, *shakti* is a property that combines the energy of combustion and, say, the food value of the material. It should be noted that combustion is a highly irreversible reaction that oxidizes the material rapidly and edibility is akin to computation [especially of carbohydrates] but goes through a series of slower steps with conditions closer to reversibility, and leading to the same end products. Hence, in defining one kind of *shakti*, we have really used the same oxidizing property of the materials. It should also be noticed that *shakti* is defined as a class of property functions that can combine various kinds of energy and their mass equivalents.[92]

Sheshadri's model of *shakti* as a new energy-quality marker proposes a transformative view of the human condition with a motion of time which is not only unidirectional and reversible, but also reversible and cyclical. It might seem an anachronism to juxtapose Shiva's idea of *shakti* and Sheshadri's but there are connections between them which are not difficult to identify. As a technologist Sheshadri provides us an alternative to the dominant industrial paradigm. Sheshadri's transformational model of *shakti* can enable us to transform even the "waste" produced from energy generation to something useful. As Sheshadri argues:

> It is possible to conceive of interconnection or processes which would convert what is 'rejected' to environment, the 'waste' from energy use, into food. For example, the off gas, the waste from combustion of fossil fuels [to generate useful energy] may be used in food production. Thus, we arrive at an important concept, namely that in a country like ours, 'waste' is a free good, a resource. The whole science, or knowledge system, will have to be modified to suit this view which enables use of waste as resource.[93]

From a cosmological point of view *shakti* is primarily concerned with the "capacity to bring forth life".[94] After all the debates in feminism about essentialism and universalism it is this "capacity to bring forth life" that still works as the differentiating attribute of women. Even though it is true that we are all hermaphrodites in some degree the revitalization of this principle of *shakti* within all of us, including the males, requires an appreciation of this distinctive feminine principle of *shakti*. It is the culture of *shakti*—its creativity and urge for synthesis—that we badly need today in our current phase of globalization which is bent upon making money and power the hegemonic language of the human condition. It only can introduce the much needed reflexivity to the dialectic between globalization and localization and can enable us to preserve our own cultural frame of production and reproduction in the face of the global onslaught of the new economy.[95] Universalization of this principle of *shakti* would provide us a creative alternative to the "flawed universalism"[96] of technocracy. This is a daunting task and at present can be best looked on as an utopia, given the actual asymmetries of the contemporary world. But we need high ideals before us and as we revitalize our own principles of *shakti* to take a step towards this creative realization it would be helpful to realize that:

> General-purpose money was the universal solvent which gave west-
> ern industry access to energy resources of the Third World... As the
> ancient 'loop' by which living-time was exchanged for food came
> to be mediated by industry, life had to be redefined as 'labour'.
> Perhaps, in the long run, the only way to liberate human bodies and
> soul from the grip of this parasitic, synthetic (industrial) biomass is
> to refuse to define nature as 'raw materials' and 'life as labour'.
> Such a cosmological shift might make us stop rewarding 'produc-
> tion' (i.e., destruction) for its own sake.[97]

NOTES

1. Cynthia Cockburn, "Technological Change in a Changing Europe: Does It Mean the Same for Women as for Men?" *Women's Studies International Forum* 15(3), 339-350, 1992, p. 85.

2. Beverly Burris "Technocratic Organization and Gender." *Women's Studies International Forum* 12(4), 447-462, 1989, p. 449.

3. Fantu Cheru, "Structural Adjustment, Primary Resource Trade and Sustainable Development in Sub-Saharan Africa", *World Development* 20(4), 497-512, 1992, p. 498.

4. Please see, Michael Piore and Charles Sabel, *The Second Industrial Divide: Possibilities for Prosperity* (NY: Basic Books, 1984): and David Harvey, "Flexible Accumulation Through Urbanization: Reflection on Postmodernism in American City", *Antipoode* 19(3): 260-286.

5. Ernest Mandel, *Late Capitalism* (London: New Left Books, 1975).

6. Please see, Scott Lash and Jonathan Friedman, "Introduction: Subjectivity and Modernity's Others", in Scott Lash and Jonathan Friedman, (ed.), *Modernity and Identity* (Basil Blackwell, 1992), p. 29.

7. Alain Touraine, *The Self-Production of Society* (Chicago, 1977).

8. Please see, Stanley J. Tambiah, *Culture, Thought and Action: An Anthropological Perspective* (Harvard, 1985).

9. Please See, Amartya Sen, "The Standard of Living", in S.M. McCurrin (eds.), *Tanner Lecture on Human Values* (Cambridge and Utah Universities press, 1986): and Ananta Giri, "Quality of Life and the Method of Science: A Contemporary Critique", *Gandhi Marg*, 1993.

10. Burris, op.cit., 1989.

11. Bennett Harrison and Barry Bluestone, *The Great U-Turn: Capitalist Restructuring and the Polarisation of America* (NY: Basic Books, 1988).

12. Thierry Noyle, *Beyond Industrial Dualism: Market and Job Segmentation in the New Economy* (Boulder et al: Westview Press, 1987), p. 101.

13. Piore and Sabel, op.cit., 1984.

14. Ibid., p. 298.

15. Ibid., p. 293.

16. Noyelle, op.cit., 1987.

17. Ibid., p. 2.

18. Please see A. Fortes, et. al. (eds.), *The Informal Economy* (Baltimore: The Johns Hoprkins University Press, 1989).

19. Marlis Buchman, *The Script of Life in Modern Society: Entry into Adulthood in a Changing World* (Chicago, 1989), pp. 48-50.

20. Katherine Newman, *Falling From Grace: The Experience of Downward Mobility in American Middle Class* (NY: Free Press, 1988).

21. Harrison and Blustone, op.cit., 1986, p. 32.

22. Ibid., p. 31.

23. Aiwa Ong, "The Gender and Labour Politics of Postmodernity", *Annual Review of Anthropology* 20: 279-39, 1991, pp. 279-80.

24. Soshana Zuboff, *In the Age of Smart Machine: The Future of Work and Power* (NY: Basic Books, 1988).

25. Please see, Harry Shaiken, *Work Transformed* (NY: Holt Rienhart and Winston, 1984); and Faye Ginsburg and Rayna Rapp, "The Politics of Reproduction", *Annual Review of Anthropology* 20: 311-42, 1991.

26. Zuboff, op.cit., 1988, p. 337.

27. Ibid., p. 349, 131.

28. Ibid., p. 132.

29. Ibid., p. 131.

30. Burris, op.cit., 1989, p. 449.

31. Cynthia Cockburn quoted in Burris, op.cit., 1989, p. 450.

32. Ibid.

33. Ibid., p. 455.

34. Cynthia Cockburn quoted in Burris, op.cit., 1989, p. 457.

35. Ibid., p. 456.

36. Ibid.

37. Ibid.

38. Ong, op.cit., 1991, p. 281.

39. Ibid., p. 283.

40. Ibid., pp. 283-84.

41. Maria Patricia Fernandez-Kelly, *For We Are Sold. I and My People* (Albany: State University of New York Press, 1983); and Aihwa Ong, *Spirit of Resistance and Capitalist Discipline: Factory Women in Malaysia* (Albany: State University of New York Press, 1987).

42. Burris, op.cit., 1989, p. 456.

43. Ong, op. cit., 1991, p. 291.

44. Aihwa Ong, "Global Industries and Malay Peasants in Peninsular Malaysia," in June Nash and Maria Patricia Fernandez-Kelly (eds.), *Women, Men and the International Division of Labour* (Albany: State University of New York Press, 1983), p. 40.

45. Ibid., p. 431.

46. Ibid.

47. Ibid., p. 436.

48. Ibid.

49. Ibid., p. 435.

50. Ong, op. cit., 1991, p. 302.

51. Ibid., p. 303.

52. Ibid., p. 296.

53. Ibid., p. 296, 305.

54. Linda Lim, "Capitalism, Imperialism, and Patriarchy: The Dilemma of Third-World Women Workers in Multinational Factories", in June Nash and Maria P. Fernandez-Kelly, op.cit., 1983, pp. 70-91.

55. Lynn Bolles, "Kitchens Hit by Priorities: Employed Working Class Jamaican Women Confront the IMF," in June Nash and Maria Patricia Fernendez-Kelly, op.cit., 1983, pp. 138-150, 142-43.

56. Ibid.

57. Ibid., p. 143.
58. Ibid., p. 150.
59. Ibid., pp. 156-157.
60. Ibid., p. 153.
61. Ibid., p. 150.
62. Ibid., p. 151.
63. Cheru, op.cit., 1992.
64. Ibid., p. 504.
65. Ibid., p. 499.
66. Ibid.
67. Ibid.
68. Ibid., p. 503.
69. Ibid.
70. Ibid., p. 502.
71. Ibid., p. 508.
72. Vandana Shiva, *Staying Alive: Women, Ecology, and Survival,* New Delhi: Kali for Women, 1989, p. 3.
73. Ibid., p. 86.
74. Ibid., p. 179.
75. Cited in Bina Agarwal, "The Gender and Environment Debate: Lessons from India", *Feminist Studies* 18(1): 119-158, 1992, p. 138.
76. Ibid., p. 140.
77. Shiva, op. cit., 1989, p. 10.
78. Carolyn Merchant, *The Death of Nature: Women, Ecology, and the Scientific Revolution* (London: Wildwood House, 1980), p. 288.
79. Ibid.
80. Alf Hornborg, "Machine Fetishism, Value and the Image of the Unlimited Good: Towards a Thermodynamics of Imperialism", *Man* (n.s.) 27 (1), 1-18, 1992, p. 7.
81. Georgescou N. Roegen, *The Entropy Law and Economic Process* (Harvard, 1971).
82. Hornborg, op.cit., 1992, p. 7.
83. Stephen Gudeman and Albert Rivera, "Colombian Conversations: The Strength of the Earth", *Current Anthropology* 30 (3): 267-281, 1989, p. 267.

84. Hornborg, op.cit., 1992, p. 6.

85. Ibid., p. 10.

86. C.V. Sheshadri quoted in Sunil Sahashrabudhey, *Freedom From Degrading Laws of a Degrading Order* (Varanasi: Gandhian Institute of Studies, 1988), p. 20.

87. Ibid., p. 26.

88. Borris, op. cit., 1989, p. 458.

89. Ibid., p. 459.

90. Ibid.

91. Quoted in Agarwal, op.cit., 1992, p. 124.

92. C.V. Sheshadri, *Energy in the Indian Context and DNA-Model of Development* (Sri AMM Murugappa Chattiar Research Center, Madras: Monograph Series on Engineering and Photosynthetic Systems, Volume 7, 1980).

93. Interview with C.V. Sheshadri, "C.V. Sheshadri: Scientist as Innovator-Epistemologist" *PPST Bulletin* Nos 19 and 20: 87-87, June 1990, Madras, p. 92.

94. Frederick Marglin quoted in Harvey Cox, *Many Mansions* (Boston: Beacon Press, 1988), p. 57.

95. Please see, Ananta Giri, "Social Development as a Global Challenge", *Social Action*, July-September, 1992.

96. Please see, Alvin Gouldner, *The Dialectic of Ideology and Technology* (London: Macmillan, 1976).

97. Hornborg, op.cit., 1992, p. 11.

Chapter Six

THE CONDITION OF POSTMODERNITY AND THE DISCOURSE OF THE BODY

Only a society governed by the principles of justice, a society structured for the realization of democratic pluralism, can fulfill the diverse needs deeply implicate in the nature of our bodies... given the fact that the order of our bodies is an order structured by reversibility, it is clear that what the body needs for its fulfillment is a social order governed, at the very least, by forms of reciprocity and an ethics of communicative rationality... Working for social justice today calls for 'promoting new forms of subjectivity'.. And this means collaborating with the pre-social order of our bodies to achieve in society at large a level of moral development in which questions of social justice, and the communicative procedures that reflection on these questions require, are of paramount concern: a possibility we cannot recognize, without understanding that neither the monadic ego (in the discourse of Cartesian metaphysics) nor the disorganized body of drives (in the discourse of Freudian psycho-analysis) should continue to represent for us the distinctive social character of the human self.

— David M. Levin (1989: 125)

[For Merleau-Ponty] The mind's body is not the objective body, not the body thought of the mind, but the phenomenal body, the field that reverses everything in it as sensible, as content or dimensionality of being-in-the world. The mind's body is a scheme of difference, of the doubling of the world's insides and outsides... Although I would warn against any anachronistic attribution of postmodernity to Merleau-Ponty, I think it is fair to say that his meditations on structuralism go beyond that paradigm... Merleau-Ponty's poststructuralism, if you will, lies on the side of his concept of the flesh of the world: the lived body whose structures of practical relevance necessarily sediments into body's habits and cultural gestures.

— John O'Neil (1989: 21)

THE PROBLEM

The postmodern condition is characterized by a particular discourse of and attitude to space and time, a particular configuration of "space-time compression" (Harvey 1989). As two of its most recent commentators write: "For the very foundation of postmodernity consists of viewing the world as a plurality of heterogeneous spaces and temporalities" (Heller and Feher 1989: 1). In the condition of postmodernity, it is space that is becoming the center of material practice and people's consciousness. Various commentators contrast this centrality of space in the postmodern condition with the preoccupation with "time" and "history" in the structure of modernity (Harvey 1989; McLuhan et al. 1989; Soja 1989). Heller and Feher go as far as to characterize the postmodern condition as a "post-historie" condition.

It is interesting to note that when David Harvey and Edward Soja make a contrast between the modern centrality of time and the postmodern centrality of space, Harvey Cox makes a contrast between the modernist preoccupation with mind and the postmodern celebration of the "body" (Cox 1984). Both space and body constitute the "unalterable" materiality of human existence (Kuper 1985). The similarities in the perspectives of Harvey and

Soja on the one hand and Cox on the other challenge us to explore the connection between the centrality of space and the centrality of body in the postmodern condition. While the discourse of space and time have been given much thought in the commentaries on the postmodern condition, this paper explores the discourse of the body in the condition of postmodernity. Here my objective is to paint a sketch of the discourse of the body in our contemporary times and then to locate the genealogy and contours of this discourse in the ongoing structural and cultural transformation of the advanced societies in particular and the world at large in general.

As we will see, the current understanding of the significance of the body as a creative agent has implication for the current debates about tradition, modernity and postmodernity. It has also its implication for rethinking political development and human development. A changed understanding of body as not simply the servant of the mind encourages us to create an embodied polity in so far as the challenge of political development is concerned. Human development also means a creative process of learning with a significant role of the knowledge of the body which is to some extent a-priori and "prehensive" (Neville 1974). But in this paper my objective is not to discuss and analyze all the significant correlations between rethinking body and rethinking politics, though I tangetially touch upon this issue. My objective here is to describe the "discursive field" (Foucault 1972) of body in the condition of postmodernity and then to locate this field in the wider context of social and cultural transformation.

Since the Second World War and especially for the last two decades, body has been thought of differently in various paths of human knowledge—from philosophy to anthropology. The works of philosophers like Wittgenstein, Ryle and Merleau-Ponty; anthropologists like Pierre Bourdieu, Emily Martin and Michael Jackson; and sociologists like Anthony Giddens and Bryan Turner show that body is not simply a constituted "thing" upon which the overwhelming power of culture and society write their script, but also and more fundamentally a constitutive and transformative agency of culture. In the social sciences, there is a growing challenge to the imperialism and determinism of the mind and an empowering effort to give back what is due to the body. In many fields of human knowledge, there is a concerted effort go beyond the body-mind dualism and to operate with a non-deterministic view of "embodiment" in the understanding of social and cultural reality (Shore 1991). In this context, it is worth exploring the significance of Derrida's philosophy of "differance" from the point of view of the discourse of the body. In the condition of postmodernity, body is perhaps the ultimate "differance".

From the point of view of sociology of knowledge, the key question here is what accounts for this particular shift in the discourse and representation of the body? In other words, why body is no more thought of as totally governed by mind and culture? This paper discusses the transformation in the structure of modernity that has made the transformed discourse of the body possible. In the modernist regime, the superiority of the mind was a legitimizing basis for the subordination of human categories and groups, (children, women, primitive people, the tribes and the colonies) thought of body-like. In this context, the changed relationship between center and periphery and structure and agency in the postmodern world might suggest a clue to the changed signification and discourse of the body. Moreover, the recent crisis of nation-state and the rise of creative grass-roots movements has created the sociological context in which the relationship between mind and body is being perceived in a new way by the ordinary citizens of the world.

RECENT TRANSFORMATIONS IN MIND-BODY DISCOURSE: THE PORTRAIT OF A COMMUNICATIVE BODY IN PHILOSOPHY AND SOCIAL THEORY

Mind-body dualism is a fundamental archetype of several deeply entrenched dualisms in western culture such as mind and matter, objective and subjective which constitute the fundamental elements of the deep structure of modernity. In western philosophy, this mind-body dualism can be traced more recently to Descartes and as far back as to Plato. For Descartes, there is not only a dualism between mind and body but also a supremacy of mind over the body. Descartes argued that mind's reports of its own affairs have a certain superiority to the best that is possessed by its reports in the physical world. But there have been "post-Cartesian meditations" (Marsh 1988) going on in western philosophy at least for the last five decades leading to important insights for reconceptualizing the human condition: the nature of language, thought, culture, body and praxis. Wittgenstein, Ryle and Merleau-Ponty have been significant pioneers in post-Cartesian meditations and have effected a marked transformation in mind-body discourse with their portrait of a "communicative body" (O'Neil 1989).

Gilbert Ryle (1969) finds many absurdities in Descartes' theory which he calls the "official doctrine". These absurdities are parts of a "category mistake": the mistake to represent the facts of mental life as if they belonged to one category. It also refers to the mistake of allocating concepts to logical types to which they do not belong. As Ryle writes: "My destructive purpose is to show that a family of radical category mistakes is the source of the double life theory" (Ryle 1969: 18). For Ryle, to be intelligent is not merely to satisfy criteria, but to apply them. In the words of Ryle: "Effective practice precedes the theory of it." Moreover for him, "intelligent practice is not a step child of theory. On the otherhand theorizing is one practice among others and is itself intelligently or stupidly conducted" (Ryle 1969: 26). Ryle argues that it would be quite possible for a boy to learn chess without ever hearing or reading the rules at all. This goes against the "official dogma" that an internal shadow performance is the real carrier of intelligence. But Ryle not only shows these category mistakes in Descartes but also traces their long pedigree. As Ryle tells us: "Descartes was reformulating already prevalent theological doctrines of the soul in the new syntax of Galileo. The theologian's privacy of conscience became the philosopher's privacy of consciousness, and what has been the bogy of pre-destination reappeared as the bogy of determinism" (Ryle 1969: 23).

Like Ryle's deconstruction of Cartesian "category mistakes",

Wittgenstein also shows the dangers in mistaking the unity of a supposed category such as language. For Wittgenstein, the word language is not the name of a single phenomenon, rather it is the name of the class of an indefinite number of language-games. Language is not the sovereign operation of mind, rather it is an aspect of human play, use and practice. Contrary to the mentalistic view of language, Wittgenstein argues that language does not simply depict the logical structure of facts. Of course, such a view of language as an aspect of human use rather than of mental dictation belongs to the later Wittgenstein rather than to the earlier Wittgenstein of the Tractus. For the later Wittgenstein of "The Blue and Brown Books" and "Philosophical Investigations", to discover the meaning of a statement is not to discover what it may describe or refer to, but to discover its use. As Wittgenstein puts it: "If we want to study the problems of truth and falsehood... we shall, at great advantage, look at primitive forms of language in which forms of thinking appear without the confusing grounds of highly complicated processes of thought" (Wittgenstein 1958: 17).

While Ryle and Wittgenstein have striven to transform the Cartesian mind-body dualism through meditations on body, mind, language, intelligence and thought process from the inside of western philosophy, Gregory Bateson brings his anthropological "views from afar" to bear on the body-mind problem (Rieber 1980).

If Ryle complains about "category mistake" in Cartesianism, Bateson is critical of the universalization of a particular cultural condition in the Cartesian agenda. Bateson shows that the personality of the Balinese character is illustrated at every joint of the body (Bateson and Mead 1942). In some Balinese characters, some one might have lost one's head, but one's body is animated. For Bateson, as for Ryle, the view that mind controls matter is a fake anyway. "It is one of those abstractions which is not represented by anything in the real world". As Bateson argues: "But when you separate mind from the structure in which it is immanent, such as human relationship, the human society, or the eco-system, you thereby embark, I believe, on fundamental error which in the end will surely hurt you" (Bateson 1973: 461).

Bateson argues that the step from mind to body is the step from state to difference. For Bateson, what perception depends upon is difference. This insightful phrasing of the problem by Bateson and the very occurrence of the term "difference" in his statement perhaps prepares the appropriate context for exploring the transformation in the mind-body discourse wrought by the deconstructionist philosophy of "diffe' rance". Deconstruction intervenes to displace the metaphysical subject and "his" hierar-chical system of modernist inequality where mind and its mirrors have the unquestioned sovereignty over body and its metaphors. As Pheby argues: "Deconstruction reveals what logocentrism con-ceals-domination-and the deconstructive posture reaches out to the exteriority of the absent, the other that the dominant culture relegates to the abyss of 'non-being' " (Pheby 1988: 9). The modernist project has been an evangelical and world-conquering project of incorporating all differences into a system of inequal-ity. This tradition also confuses "difference" with "opposition" (Pheby 1988: 102). On the other hand, deconstruction teaches one to attend to "gestures of exclusion" (Ryan 1982: 3). Derrida argues that "such philosophical oppositions as nature/culture, theory/practice, mental/manual, and life/death are differentially constituted" (quoted in Ryan 1982: 12). Differences resist incor-poration into a totalizing system of inequality through both spatial and temporal deferral (Barnett 1989). As Derrida writes: "We shall designate by the term differentiation the movement by which language, or any code, any system of reference in general, be-comes 'historically' constituted as a fabric of differences" (quoted in Ryan 1992:15). Moreover, the project of deconstruction does not privilege language, rather it shows how any such privileging (mentalistic and idealistic) is a "regional function produced by ...weave of differential relations..." (Ryan 1982: 24). Deconstruc-tion also denies that "there is any boundary essence between what

e call language and what we think of as non-language" (Statten
984: 21).

HE WORK OF THE "COMMUNICATIVE BODY": ETHINKING CULTURE AND SOCIAL THEORY

his discussion of postmodern social theory, John Murphy ar-
1es that for Derrida, space is a "diff'erance" (O'Neil 1989).
ollowing this, we can argue that for Derrida, body is also a
liffe'rance." Body provides a focal metaphor for a postmodern
ociological analysis. If mind and rationality were the fundamen-
l rhetorical constructs through which society, culture, state and
ructure used to be visualized in modernist sociology,
ostmodernism operates with a view of society and culture as
nbodiment. As Murphy explains: "As a result of ...Cartesian
fluence, ...sociologists have exhibited a propensity for concep-
alizing order as 'centered'... order is associated automatically
ith reason... society embodies reason, while persons are passion-
e... Reason, in fact, is given the power to suppress passion"
Murphy 1989: 57). But postmodernism displaces any such cen-
red rational construct. It displaces logocentric centers and part
this displacement "concerns a refusal to acquiesce to the power
the center, a refusal to adopt the belief that the dominant
ructures somehow have a privileged access to meaning and
uth" (Pheby 1988; 5).

The transformations in the discourse on body-mind dualism
s also its implication for rethinking the notion of culture. For
e postmodernists, "... culture is not the guardian of reason, but
mply imaginary. A specific culture represents a modality of
nagination... Postmodern society spawns a 'culture of imma-
nce'—a style of culture that embodies human inspiration"
Murphy 1989: 107). Here culture is not viewed solely as super-
ganic, but primarily as praxis,—as embodied praxis—as a field
r the Giddensian "structuration situation", where with the re-
urces of body and memory, structure and agency are engaged in
incessant transformative play (Bauman 1973; Giri 1989). To
derstand the emancipatory potential in such a reformulated and

transformed understanding of culture, it has to be noted that the mentalistic and the superorganic view of culture has tended to act in an exclusionary way. The view that culture is the sovereign domain of the mind and testimony to its "magical power" has "served as a token to demarcate, separate, exclude and deny; and although at different epochs the excluded 'natural' category shifts about among peasants, barbarians, workers, primitive people, women, children, animals and material artifacts, a persistent theme is the denial of the somatic, a turning of blind eyes on the physical aspects of Being where our sense of separateness and distinctiveness is most readily blurred" (Jackson 1983).

The very processes of human thought are also being re-thought and re-conceptualized in philosophy and social sciences. Now the emergent view is that thinking is not a disembodied activity. Rather we think through metaphors; our moral and linguistic universe is full of "metaphors we live by" (Lakoff and Johnson 1982). Metaphors, in most cases, are bodily and such embodied metaphors are not merely a figure of speech. All these bodily metaphors demonstrate the corporeal and sensible way of reading what the world means (Shore 1991). Anthropometric metaphors simply reflect the fact that, ontogenetically, the first language of life is gestural, postural and bodily. Moreover, metaphors show the unity of body and mind. For Jackson, the etymology of the most abstract words often refer to the body. However, Jackson makes clear that "this is not to say that all mental forms should be reduced to bodily practices; rather, that within the unitary field of body-mind habitus it is possible to intervene and effect change from any one of these points" (Jackson 1983). As Bourdieu so rightly points out: "The mind born of the world of objects does not rise as subjectivity confronting an objectivity. The mind is a metaphor of the world of objects which is itself but an endless circle of mutually reflecting metaphors" (Bourdieu 1977: 91). Lyotard also provides additional support to the argument that we think analogically and metaphorically, rather than logically (Lyotard 1988; also Shore 1991). Following Dreyfus, Lyotard characterizes human thought process as reflective rather than determinate. For Lyotard, analogical processes "constitute the experience of a body, of an "actual" or phenomenological body in its space-time continuum of sensibility and perception..." (Lyotard 1988: 81).

The postmodern reflection on body also finds its support in the contemporary striving of a postmodern theology and spirituality. Thus, it is no wonder that David Griffin writes in his *God and Religion in the Postmodern World*: "[The postmodern vision does not] suffer from the mind-body problem that undermined the first-stage of modernity, the problem of how experiencing mind could interact with non-experiencing matter. According to the postmodern view, the body itself is composed of experiencing individuals" (Griffin 1989: 24). In the postmodern view, all things are embodiments of creativity (Griffin 1989: 37; also Griffin and Smith 1989). David Griffin, perhaps reminding us of Gilbert Ryle, quite rightly points out that "the mind-body problem was paralleled by a God-world problem..." (Griffin 1989: 87). But for Griffin, "the postmodern God does not coerce, but persuades" (Griffin 1989: 25). Moreover, for him, twentieth century developments in science support a "new animism", a "postmodern animism", as Griffin calls it, where a "unit is first an experiencing subject expressing self-determination, then an experienced object expressing efficient causation" affirming a "non-dualistic interactionism" (Griffin 1989: 89).

But what is the nature of this body discussed so far? This body, following Merleau-Ponty, is a communicative body. As O'Neil tells us: "The communicative body is the hinge of our world; it establishes an identity-within-difference that overrides the subject-object dualism of transcendental phenomenology" (O'Neil 1989: 16). This communicative body is also a phenomenal body which is not only a vehicle of communication but also is a creative agent of communicative action.

Merleau-Ponty's idea of a "communicative body" avoids the dualism of objectivism and subjectivism through a focus on the lived body as a mode of being in the world. But this communicative body is not to be confused with the Foucauldian body despite

Foucault's illusive notion of bio-power. In Foucault, body i constituted by the discourse of bio-power, rather body itself con stituting this discourse. Here, "Discourse, thus, becomes the mono logue of power or, rather, the chorus of micropowers" (Ostrande 1987; also Hewitt 1983 and Lash 1984). Moreover, Foucault' idea of power is "disembodied" and reminds one of Talcott Par sons' view of power as the positive and enabling feature of a social structure (Kroker and Cook 1986). Foucault looks at powe as an aspect of discourse and addresses its play "within the dark underside of these very same [Parsonian] 'positive social organi zations' " (Kroker and Cook 1986: 216). Perhaps, for this reason Habermas argues that Foucault's discourse on power and body confines itself to the technology of power and lacks any medita tion on the technology of the self (Habermas 1987).[1] Foucault's subjects are formed by processes of subjection and his "concep tion of body makes it impossible for us to empower the body with any capacity to talk back to history..." (Levin 1989: 114).

THE DISCOURSE OF THE BODY IN THE CONDITION OF POSTMODERNITY: LOCATING ITS GENEALOGY AND CONTEXTUALIZING ITS SIGNIFICANCE

What is the sociological and historical genealogy of the recent transformation in the discourse of body-mind dualism? If, as Sohn-Rethel (1978) has shown us, the distinction between head and hand, intellectual and manual labor has something to do with the abstraction of commodity exchange under capitalism, then the challenge is to explore whether the contemporary transformation in body-mind discourse has something to do with the social and historical transformations of modernity. This requires meditation on the ongoing transformations in the structure of modernity leading to an embodiment of the condition of postmodernity. This requires a double tack on both modernity and postmodernity not so much as teleological historical phases, the latter inevitably supplanting the former, but as emergent cosmoses and perspective, contesting for generation and voice in a common historical womb. Before exploring the genealogy of the contemporary discourse of the communicative body, it is essential to remember that "postmodernity is an experience of 'the end of history' not the appearance of a different, or a newer, stage of history itself" (Vattimo 1988: xviii).[2]

The modern experiment in human history has been characterized by state formation at home and colonialism abroad. Both these processes have derived motivation from native western cultural resources and from native "folk psychologies". In his study of the cultural psychology of colonialism, Nandy (1983) has shown that the western folk cultural psychology of the superiority of the male over the female has provided impetus to conquer the supposedly feminine foreign virgin territories with the masculine forces of empire and industry. It is perhaps for this reason that Mahatma Gandhi in India did not fight back with the intimate enemy of colonialism on "his" own terms—on his masculine and rationalist terms. Rather he used the supposedly feminine indigenous resources such as non-violence and *satyagraha* and supposedly irrational devices such as myth to deconstruct the colonialist phallus and the mind (Bean 1989; Das 1985). The demise of the colonies, hence, precipitate challenges to the western folk psychologies of male domination. The revolutionary birth of postcolonial societies, hence, has played its role in challenging some of the deeply entrenched dualisms of modernity.

At home, in western societies, male-female dualism increasingly turned more oppositional with the march of modernity. New reproductive biology in 19th century had succeeded in establishing absolute dichotomy between the male and the female where once existed homology. Even the discourse of civic humanism in early 18th century Britain was an exercise in "the most authoritative fantasy of masculinity" which represented civic freedom not only as a freedom from servility but as an emancipation from the feminine desire (Barrel 1989: 103). Here it has to be noted that the male-female dualism in modernity is based upon the body-mind dualism. Hence, in the discourse of modernity, woman has been constituted as the body. In this context, it has to be noted that the feminist movement in the post-war era has not only challenged phallic authority but also what philosophers have said about mind-body distinction (Spelman 1982). Hence, it is not a coincidence that challenge to mind-body dualism has been precipitated in philosophy in the same post-war era which has also been characterized by post-colonial and feminist social struggles.

So much about the connection between the folk psychology of gender and colonialism, what about the connection among mind, modernity and state formation? One important place to look for this connection is to explore the link between the body and the French Revolution (Outram 1989). In her study of the French Revolution, Outram tells us: "... the Public body on which the middle-class founded its political legitimation during the Revolution was that of homo clausus, the male type validated by his separation of affect from instinct... Homo Clausus legitimated itself by his superiority to the somatic relationships enjoyed by other classes—aristocracy, peasants and workers—and by the other gender. In other words, what he possessed was a body which was also a non-body, which, rather than projecting itself, retained itself. In doing so, it became the location of abstract value systems, such as rationality and objectivity" (Outram 1989: 158). Hence, after the French Revolution, the state that came into being anchored itself upon the sovereignty of the mind rather than upon a communicative body. As Outram makes clear: "The history of [French] Revolutionary bodies is the history of a self-image of rationality, reflexivity, universality, autonomy..." (Outram 1989: 164). After French Revolution, both medicine and political culture tended to "desacralize the body..." (Outram 1989: 49). Hitler was perhaps able to make the best use of this modernist discourse of the "desacralized body". Hence, the desacralized bodies of millions of desacralized Jews could be easily dispensed with under the "rationalist" organization of the Holocaust. In the words of Zygmunt Bauman: "Modern civilization was not the Holocaust's sufficient condition; it was, however, most certainly its necessary condition... It was the rational world of modern civilization that made the Holocaust thinkable" (Bauman 1989: 13).

POSTMODERN STRIVINGS AND THE TURN TOWARDS THE BODY

If modernity characterized the triumph of the mind and the subjugation of the body, entry into postmodernity, in the wake of the post-war anti-colonialist struggles, civil rights movements, students movements and womens' movements precipitated challenges to the epitomes modernist rationality: nation-state and bureaucracy. The economic and political crisis of state and the bureaucratic manifestation of social democracy, welfare state and socialism, have led to the shrinking legitimacy of the state in the eyes of the common citizens of advanced societies. These continuing contestations have led to fundamental restructuring of the relationship between state and civil society—between the disembodied "system world" and the embodied "life world". In this restructuring and deconstruction of the state, "the new social movements" have played a transformative role. These movements have brought significant measure of participatory democracy to the "system world" of state and bureaucracy. Moreover, these movements embody a non-deterministic relationship between structure and agency making the "return of the actor" possible.

THE BODY OF POSTMODERNITY AND THE CRITICAL MOVEMENT OF THE BODIES

In contemporary collective actions vis-a-vis the operation of a monological State, body is an important tool of struggle. The communicative body of the actors work as both a medium and a message. In almost all the alternative movements what R.B.J. Walker (1987) calls "critical movements" in varieties of social order in the contemporary globe, body is being used as a very important tool and also perhaps as a mark of the ultimate "diff'erance". In the Chipko movement, a popular environmental movement among the hill women of Himalayas, the activists tie themselves to the trees preventing the contractors to touch the lived body of the tree. In the Baltic states in the former Soviet Union, the movements for independence made use of the strategy of the human chain: thousands of people holding hands over hundreds of miles to create a field of empowerment, embodiment and solidarity. These instances reiterate the centrality of the body in contemporary critical movements. The work of the communicative bodies in collective actions is now almost universal. In this connection, Dorinda Outram's observations are extremely insightful: "Even in western states it is increasingly true that the politics of even legal protest is becoming differentiated from establishment politics by its large-scale use of the human body; one thinks here of the tactics of CND and Greenpeace groups, of large-scale mass demonstrations, of human chains linking hands across Scotland, and of passive resistance. The construction and use of a dignified individual body which can be employed as a source of authority in conflicts in the public realm can thus be seen as a hallmark of late twentieth-century political change..." (Outram 1989: 23).

Besides the use of body in non-violent social and cultural movements, body is also being used decisively in the terrorist movements of our times where other people's bodies are mediums of contestation against the state. Though in its "construction of terrorism" (Connolly 1991), the late-capitalist state has created a sacrificial scapegoat to hide its inability to comprehend the roots of terrorism in the state-centric discourse and to cope with it as a global contingency, the significance of terrorism as a challenge to modernity and statism must be appreciated. Terrorist violence, as David Apter tells us, constitutes an "antitext, the object of which is to challenge or supersede legitimacy, explode conventionality, and 'deconstruct' that developmental 'structuration' that expresses that functional rationality of ordinary life" (Apter 1987: 40).

But while in terrorism it is the body of the other that is sacrificed, in some other sacrificial movements against the state, it is the body of the Self that works as both the medium and the message. Here, one instantaneously remembers the recent movement of self-immolation led by some sections of Indian students in September 1990 in their fight with the Indian State over its policy of caste-based reservation. The Union of India had promulgated a new policy of job reservation for the economically and socially backward classes which students from the middle-class origins felt as politically motivated. This led to a vigorous anti-government stir in which some students immolated themselves. In the anti-reservation stir, students deployed their bodies as a source of ultimate authority in their fight against a strong state which played the politics of number (Giri 1990). This movement of self-immolation can be looked at as a prime example of the contemporary significance of the body in the movement against the state.

The significance of body can also be appreciated in the movement of "glasnot" to create a "post-totalitarian mind" (Goldfarb 1989). Critical movements in the socialist societies challenged the very idea of the party invested with the mind and power to regulate ordinary citizens categorized as bodies. In socialist societies, the party used to be the head of the proletariat. According to Lefort: "[The party] merges with the body as a whole, while at the same time, it is its head" (Lefort 1986: 299). What is at stake here is the "integrity of the body" (Lefort 1989: 298) But the movement for democracy in these societies has led to the revitalization of the body (Lefort 1989: 305). Social movements in the former socialist societies questioned not only the mind of the political party, it also questioned the mind of the bureaucracy. The movement of perestroika challenged another epitome of modernist rationality, the bureaucracy, perhaps striving to create a "post-bureaucratic" social order (Giri 1992). The striving for creating a "post-bureaucratic" and "post-Taylorist" social order and work organization can also be found in the advanced capitalist societies. In advanced societies, there is an increasing realization that Taylorist forms of bureaucratic organization are incapable of coping with the reality of new technologies. In the words of Governor Mario Cuomo of New York: "The old fashioned assembly lines emphasize a hierarchical, top-down management style. The new technologies require a different style" (Cuomo 1988: 199). Taylorism had based itself upon the distinction between head and hand, conception and execution (Braverman 1974).

Hence, the emergence of post-Taylorist forms of work organizations and embodied groups of co-workers engaged in the innovative challenge and play of new technologies create the sociological context for rethinking body-mind dualism and experiencing one's labouring body as a "communicative body".

In contemporary movements for justice and peace, the communicative body is also becoming the model of law, polity and a just social order. Zillah Eisenstein (1988) shows that when this (communicative) body becomes a model of law, it leads to a reconstruction of the concept of equality. Eisenstein takes the pregnant body as the model of equality and community. She argues: "The pregnant body decenters the phallus without centering itself; instead, it allows a heterogeneous viewing of equality that recognizes the particularity of the human body and constructs a notion of diversity that is distinctively compatible with equality" (Eistenstein 1988: 4). The law that takes body as its model seems to be reconstructing the notion of equality "through a completely pluralized notion of difference(s), one that rejects a politics of inequality and demands a radical egalitarianism" (ibid: 5). This law also does not dispense with the contingent dimension of the case under review. Postmodernism reconceptualizes law as nothing more than "contingency formulae" (Murphy 1989: 93). The law whose metaphor is the body also engages itself in a process of self transformation transforming itself from the modernist legality to a postmodern interpretiveness (Bauman 1987).

The operation of this law and its moral reasoning is leading to a renewed significance of "casuistry" which refers to the mode of practical resolution of moral issues. Johnson and Toulmin argue that in the last few years "discussions of specific circumstances and cases have at last returned to favor" (Johnson and Toulmin 1988: 13). There is a revival of interest in case ethics. In this transforming situation, there is a renewal of interest in Aristotle. For Aristotle, ethics can not be a science rather it calls for "a recognition of significant particulars" (ibid: 19). What is striking about Johnson and Toulmin that, unlike many philosophers, they do not see it as simply an internal development within philosophy. They themselves write: "[The] moral ambiguities are only aggravated by the obsolescence of the nation-state..." (ibid: 311). They further note: "The historical reason for this change are complex and still are partly obscure, but they had less to do with developments within philosophy than with the challenges to authority and expertise that were evident in many other areas of life at this time" (ibid: 304).

In the social field of postmodernity, differences are proliferating. These differences are not simply surfacing to find their niche in a garland of surrealistic appearances, rather they are discovering their embodiments in a politics of contestations. Perhaps for this reason, Ihab Hassan writes: "Critical pluralism is deeply implicated in the cultural field of postmodernism" (Hassan 1987: 173). This critical pluralism constitutes the heart of the differential politics of our contemporary discursive as well as social movements. While in case of the discursive movements, this manifests itself in the "decontructivist critique of absolutist concepts" (Ryan 1982: 8), in case of social and cultural movements it involves the critique of the absolutist states. In both these critiques, we must note the significance of the body. Thus, John Murphy argues that the postmodern striving is a striving of radical democracy whose objective is to institute the body politics in the body of the people. In the words of Murphy: "Postmodernism is consistent with what might be called radical democracy. With the periphery suddenly everywhere, a decentralized polity is not an anomaly... With the omnipotence of authority placed in question, decisions can finally be made that embrace public sentiments... The body politic is thus instituted. This is the thrust of what Lyotard calls 'libidinal politics'—desire becomes real. And desire is not self-effacing... desire does not need to be infused with reason in order for society to survive; creativity is a sufficient political motive" (Murphy 1989: 147).

The dispersal of the centred authorities and the creativity of political practice that Murphy presents as characteristic of the body of postmodernity also constitutes the heart of the contemporary rethinking of development (Apter 1987; Kothari 1988). The contemporary discursive critique of modernist rationality finds a societal parallel in the critique of development as a sovereign operation of state and bureaucracy. Contemporary movements of development as an enchancement people's capabilities and as a pursuit of ever-widening webs of "positive freedoms" (Sen 1989; also Giri 1992) require an embodied politics which will have the courage and vision to combine "food and freedom" in a great saga of human liberation.

REALITY OF THE BODY IN THE POSTMODERN CONDITION

If such is the discourse of the body in the condition of postmodernity, then the question is whether such a discourse is only utopian? Of course, it is true that in the contemporary condition, "we need a utopian-emancipatory discourse on the body no less than we need the critical analytic discourse..." (Levin, 1989: 129). But still the question is whether the discourse of the body as a transformative agent is simply an utopian philosophical projection or has it some actual ethnographic referents in the contemporary world? This brings us face-to-face with the ethnography of the postmodern condition.

A FRAGMENT OF THE REALITY: EMBODIMENT, EMPOWERMENT AND ALTERNATIVES

In her study of the bio-politics of the menstrual women in contemporary American society, Emily Martin shows that the embodied experience such as menstruation provides some women (those who have not already been indoctrinated by the modern medicine) a vantage point to see the inequities of a gendered social world (Martin 1987). Moreover, their phenomenological experience of menstruation has the potential to give them a cyclical experience of time, as an alternative to the mainstream linear, industrial configuration of time. Cox also makes a similar point: "Because menstruation cycles link them [women] more closely to natural cycles than men, women hold a key to the past that men do not have... Kristeva believes this exclusively female vantage point enables women to touch the two forms of time consciousness that men, as non-menstruating creatures, can discern only with much greater difficulty" (Cox 1984: 258).

The processes of embodiment are also leading to the generation of a critical consciousness in other domains of contemporary advanced societies. Here, the abortion contest is a case in point. Ginsburg's (1989) study shows how the embodied experience of childbirth is central to the critical consciousness on the part of both pro-choice and pro-life activists. Childbirth gives rise to a sense of crises in these women's lives which is a product of the "dissonance" they feel between the conditions they face and the available resources to cope with it. As Ginsburg tells us: "In their (women activists') constructions, reproduction is a key turning point, not as a biological recurrence but as a class of life-cycle events that forced an encounter with the inequalities of a gendered social world. These encounters, as told in stories, lead the women to reconsider their relationship to and understanding of their assigned place in society. Subsequently, their activism took discursive shape as a concern not only with the place of procreation in women's lives, but with the reproduction of culture as a whole" (Ginsburg 1989: 143/144). The politics of embodiment in case of the pro-life movement is also leading to a profound cultural critique of the prevailing division of labor between home and work. It is to be reiterated here that this politics is not simply the conservative politics of the "Women of the New Right"—the conservative politics of the "reprivatizers".

The portrait of the body as a transformative agent is also becoming marked in varieties of postmodern theologies. Modern theology and modern Christian religious practice (especially as manifested in the mainstream Protestant denominations) is very rationalistic and cerebral. But the contemporary resurgence of feminine Christian piety seems to be transforming this. Commenting on the contribution that feminine spirituality is making to the generation of a postmodern theology, Harvey Cox writes: "Women speak frequently of the need to restore the human body with all its senses fully alive to a Christianity that has become arid and cerebral... Poor white church people do not theorize about it much; but what always strikes middle-class visitors about lower-class Protestantism, is its embodied energy" (Cox 1984: 210). This embodied feminine spirituality reminds us of the embodied spirituality of the medieval female Christian saints. Medieval women reflected in their visions a general sense of body as necessary for salvation. In the women saints' visions, "humanity included not merely senses and agonies but bones and flesh, even sticks and stones..." (Bynum 1986: 254). These saints also emphasized on the fact that "Christ's humanity is truly flesh and blood" which led to "an increasingly literal sense of what 'imitation' of Christ meant" (ibid: 255).

In another area of contemporary Christianity, imitation of Christ also refers to celebrating Christ's "flesh and blood"—celebrating the bleeding Christ as a symbol of the bleeding and suffering in the contemporary world caused by varieties of class and corporate conflicts. In liberation theology, it is the bleeding body of Christ that is being worshipped in an embodied way. The practitioners do not worship Christ individually, but as members of an embodied community, known as base communities. These base community movements with their embodied politics are transforming the fundamentals of modernist Christianity laying the ground for a second reformation (Metz 1981).

BODY AS A POSTMODERN SIMULACRUM

Contemporary ethnography of the postmodern condition also sensitizes us to the reality of the body as a postmodern simulacrum. For instance, the obsession of having a slim figure seems to be all pervasive among both males and females in contemporary American culture. In case of American women, this is sometimes leading to what Kim Chernin has called "the tyranny of slenderness" (Chernin 1981). As Brumberg tells us: "In the 1980s anorexia nervosa constitutes a modern credo of self-denial...it appears to be a secular addiction to a new kind of perfectionism, one that links personal salvation to the achievement of an external body configuration rather than an internal spiritual state" (Brumberg 1988: 7). She further writes: "A woman obsessed with the reduction of her flesh may be revealing the fact that... she has not been allowed to develop a reverential feeling for her body" (ibid: 2). This also reveals another fact about the late capitalistic cultural condition: the fact of the flight from concreteness and a new hegemony of the abstraction. Ewen shows the parallel between the flight from the body and the flight from cash exchange (as demonstrated in the craze for more and more abstract credit cards such as gold cards) as part of the same logic of flight from concreteness in contemporary culture (Ewen 1988).

Baudrillard has characterized contemporary condition as a simulacrum. For Arthur Kroker, body is also participating very passively in this postmodern simulacra. As the Krokers write: "Everywhere today the aestheticization of the body and its dissolution into a semiurgy of floating body parts reveal that we are being processed through a media scene consisting of our own (exteriorized) body organs in the forms of second-order simulacra" (Kroker and Kroker 1987: 21). The postmodern fashion style is contributing to the creation of this passive body. In postmodern fashion's "logic of planned obsolescence... the body is decoded and recorded [endlessly] in order to define and inhabit the newest territorialized spaces of capital expansion" (Faurschou 1987: 72). For Faurschou, "postmodernity then is no longer an age in which bodies produce commodities, but when commodities produce bodies: bodies for aerobics, bodies for sports car..." (ibid: 72). But even in the discourse of the body as a postmodern simulacrum, there is apparently a note of dissent. Charles Levin argues that body is not reducible to the structures and conventions of its "invaders" (Levin 1987: 107).

The Krokers show us how the postmodern simulated body is also invaded by all the languages of postmodern power—"from fashion scene and panic viruses to the proliferating signs of consumer culture" (Kroker and Kroker 1987). In this invasion, the nation-state in advanced societies is creating a post-modern panopticon which Arthur Kroker calls "Body McCarthyism" (Kroker et al. 1989).

BODY MCCARTHYISM OF ADVANCED NATION-STATES

Nation-states are now deploying new tools to incorporate bodies in a new mode of bio-power. As Terry argues: "[Now] the 'person' has become the site of illegal searches through the seizure of body fluids and other things that lie beyond the threshold of the skin" (Terry 1989: 17). The mandatory drug testing proposed by state is leading to the screening of even the urine. "Since quite a business has developed in the sale of drug-free urine, now there's talk of drug testing requiring urination under observation" (ibid: 232). In this "urinal politics", body is being constituted anew as "the target of the power of the panoptic" (ibid: 132). This also shows the evangelical zeal with which nation-state is pursuing the rhetoric of clean bodily fluids. In her ongoing work on immunology in contemporary American culture, Emily Martin records some of the similar operations of "Body McCarthyism". She shows how science portrays the body as a "nation-state at peril of being invaded by outsiders" (Martin 1990: A8). She relates this "imagery of the body to the fear of the nation-state's being invaded by outsiders in a world increasingly dominated by transnational capitalism" (ibid). Body McCarthyism also sustains itself "on generalized panic fear about the breakdown of the immunological systems of American society" (Kroker et al. 1989: 233).

Another arena of exercise of contemporary Body McCarthyism is the body of the pregnant woman. The pregnant woman is being screened to ensure that her body and blood is free from alcohol and drugs which might endanger the fetus. There are several instances of arrest of pregnant women on the charge of fetal abuse. A Michigan court has recently held that custody of a newborn could be seized by the state if there was evidence to show fetal abuse (Terry 1989). But these stances "heighten the imaginary division between fetus and the pregnant woman", a division which can only complicate the contemporary abortion debate (ibid: 22). This also gives an opportunity for the "adulterated" mixture of the rhetoric of the anti-abortionists and the neoeugenicists. This adulterated rhetoric endows "the fetus with a right to be born so long as it is to be guaranteed freedom from defect" (ibid: 37). In this strategy, the pregnant woman is constituted alone and the structures that have created her alcoholism and drug addiction are completely ignored.

In contemporary American society, there is also a growing effort to make one's body "fit". In contemporary United States, fitness has been a marketable commodity. A number of governmental agencies, councils, institutes and fitness clubs are engaged in the marketing of fitness. All of them are also engaged in appealing to what Bjorn Claesson calls "the notion of a deficient lifestyle" (Claesson 1989). Here individuals are alerted about their deficiencies and vulnerabilities. Consumption of knowledge of fitness does not necessarily increase the ability of the citizens to cope with their predicaments. Rather it produces a "deficiency of comprehension, increased anxiety and dependency of experts" (ibid). Now different companies and factories are also starting their own fitness programs and especially exhorting the workers to participate regularly in it. These companies strive to erase the boundary between the management and the workers and the operation of fitness centers. In one factory called Champion which Claesson has studied, "many workers choose not to use the fitness center because they strive to keep their distance from the company" (ibid). Commenting on the mandatory use of computers in the fitness centers, one of Claesson's informants says: "... there is nothing confidential there...if you know what the keys are, you could read my whole history...I do not have the trust in Champion" (ibid).

The fitness drive strives to create a feeling of vulnerability— a feeling of being "at risk" (Stone 1989). In this discourse of fitness and "being at risk" the nation-state and different corporations who deal with disease and disability have their own stake.

They reify "the risk factors, so that even when they are environmental (such as exposure to toxic substance) they are attached to the individual and counted as part of his or her portfolio of risks, as though each risk factor were located inside the boundaries of the person. The discourse refers to people as 'having risk factors', an expression that situates the factor in the person rather than in the socio-economic structure or in public policy" (Stone 1989: 626). While being at risk becomes a question of individual genesis, those who are at risk are constituted as a dangerous collectivity threatening not only themselves, but also others. Moreover, as Stone argues: "Health risk classification in insurance and labor markets cast off individuals who cannot make the grade and puts them outside the social-welfare pale" (ibid). People with good health risks are attended to by the insurance companies while those at risk take recourse to the welfare state. Such bifurcated paths followed by the citizens subsequent to their health risk classification further heightens the already shaky foundation of the American welfare state which, as Skocpol as clearly shown, is based upon a representational dichotomy between the citizens and the clients (Skocpol 1988). As Deborah Stone writes: "Using health-risk classification as an instrument of disease and cost control further fragments social welfare institutions..." (Stone 1989: 632-633).

DISCOVERING BODY AND TRANSFORMING THE SELF: MODERNITY, POSTMODERNITY AND BEYOND

Such is the complex picture of body in discourse and society in the condition of postmodernity. This shows us how modern man tired of the "hermeneutic circles" of the mind is coming back to body for concreteness and grounding. But, as fragments of the reality of the postmodern condition show us, the postmodern celebration of the body has also been narcissistic. Postmodernism embodies an urge to come to our senses but is not still very clear about an "anthropological revolution" (Heller 1967) that will address the vital question of whether we are going to be bound by our senses. The postmodern quest, it seems, despite the work of scholars such as Agnes Heller who writes in her *Beyond Justice* that "beyond has the connotation of 'higher', and not only of being different" (Heller 1987: 326) is still imprisoned in a narcissistic horizontality. Here a dialogue[3] with other cultures and traditions is important for a spiritual opening of our contemporary deconstructivist vision which will link sense and spirituality in ever-widening webs of creativity.

Much before the contemporary critique of modernity, Sri Aurobindo of India had sensitized us to the limitations of the mind. Sri Aurobindo's critique of mind and modernity also involved a celebration of the body where the body shall remember the secrets of our spiritual origins and spiritual transformation. But in Sri Aurobindo, the celebration of the body and the critique of the mind is part of a wider spiritual project of the transformation of self where the self will strive for the realization of a supramental consciousness and a "supramental time vision" (Aurobindo, 1950). Sri Aurobindo's critique of mind is part of a transformative striving of the self for the realization of the supermind. Sri Aurobindo's "supermind" is not an extension of the mind but a transmutation of the mind where both body and mind will discover their relationship of identity and difference in a spiritual quest of self and social transformation. The postmodern discourse of body can confront the challenge of "developing a more perfect and a divinely instrumental body" (Aurobindo, 1950:667).

NOTES

1. To be fair to Foucault, it must be noted that towards the later part of his life, Foucault was becoming increasingly aware of the problem of the self. Please see, Martin, L.H. et al. (1988) and Dews (1989).

2. Fred Dallmayr also makes a similar argument which disarms the simplistic critics of postmodernity who are bent upon making a caricature of it. For Dallmayr, postmodernism is "an event which has the earmarks of a quasi-spatial topology: rather than heralding a ₁ ₙ annex of structural addition, postmodernism refers to the discovery of a forgotten chamber..." (Dallmayr 1989: 96).

3. Asroft et al. (1989) show us the significance of this dialogue in their study of post-colonial literature. I have also discussed the significance of looking at post-modernity and post-coloniality as a global discursive formation in my review of Aschroft et al. (Giri 1992c).

REFERENCES

Aschroft, Bill et al., 1990, *The Empire Writes Back: Theory and Practice in Post-Colonial Literatures*, London: Routledge & Kegan Paul.

Apter, David, 1987, *Rethinking Development: Modernization, Dependency and Postmodern Politics*, Sage.

Aurobindo, Sri, 1950, *The Synthesis of Yoga*, Pondicherry: Sri Aurobindo Ashram.

Barnett, E.T., 1989, *Structuralism and the Logic of Dissent*, London: Macmillan.

Barrel, John, 1989, "The Dangerous Goddess: Masculinity, Prestige, and the Aesthetic in Early Eighteenth-Century Britain", *Cultural Critique* (Spring): 101-133.

Bateson, Gregory, 1973, *Steps to an Ecology of Mind*, NY: Paladin.

Bateson, Gregory and Margaret Mead, 1942, *The Balinese Character: A Photographic Analysis*, NY: New York Academy of Sciences.

Bauman, Zygmunt, 1973, *Culture as Praxis*, London: Routledge & Kegan Paul.

———, 1987, *Legislators and Interpreters: On Modernity, Postmodernity and Intellectuals*, Oxford: Basil Blackwell.

———, 1989, *Modernity and Holocaust*, Oxford: Basil Blackwell.

Berman, Marshall, 1989, *Coming to Our Senses: Body and Spirit in the*

Hidden History of the West, NY: Simon & Schuster.

Block, Fred, 1987, *Revising State Theory: Essays in Politics and Postindustrialism*, Philadelphia: Temple University Press.

Braverman, Harry, 1974, *Labor and Monopology Capital*, NY: Monthly Review Press.

Brumberg, Joan Jacobs, 1988, *Fasting Girls: The Emergence of Anorexia Nervosa as a Modern Disease*, Cambridge, MA: Harvard University Press.

Bourdieu, Pierre, 1977, *Outline of a Theory of Practice*, Cambridge: University Press.

Bynum, Carolyn W., 1986, *Holy Feast and Holy Fast: The Religious Significance of Food to Medieval Women*, Berekely: University of California Press.

Chernin, Kim, 1981, *The Obsession: Reflections on the Tyranny of Slenderness*, NY: Harper & Row.

Claesson, Bjorn, 1990, "The Cultural Politics of American Health", Paper presented at the Seminar in Atlantic History, Culture and Society, Department of Anthropology, The Johns Hopkins University.

Cuomo, Mario et al., 1988, *The Cuomo Commission Report on Competitiveness*, NY: Simon & Schuster

Das, Chittaranjan (ed.), 1985, *Gandhi and the Modern Times*, Cuttack: The Universe.

Das, Veena, 1986, "The Moral Foundations of the Abortion Debate", in D. Eck and D. Jain (eds.), *Speaking of Faith: Cross-Cultural Perspectives on Women, Religion and Social Change*, New Delhi: Kali for Women.

Dallmayr, Fred, 1989, *Margins of Political Discourse*, Albany: SUNY Press.

Dews, Peter, 1989, "The Return of the Subject in Late Foucault", *Radical Philosophy*, 37-41.

Eisenstein, Zillah, 1988, *The Female Body and the Law*, Berkeley: University of California Press.

Ewen, Stuart, 1988, *All Consuming Images: Politics of Style in Contemporary Culture*, NY: Basic Books.

Fraser, Nancy, 1987, *Social Movements vs. Disciplinary Bureaucracies: The Discourse of Social Needs*, Minneapolis: University of Minnesota Press.

Foucault, Michael, 1972, *The Archeaology of Knowledge and the Discourse on Language*, NY: Pantheon.

Faurschou, Gail, 1987, "Fashion and the Cultural Logic of Postmodernity", *Canadian Journal of Political and Social Theory*: 68-82.

Giri, Ananta, 1989, "Narratives of Creative Transformation: Constituting Critical Movements in Contemporary American Culture", *Dialectical Anthropology* 14.

——, 1990, "Understanding Self-Immolation", *Indian Express* (New Delhi): November 9.

——, 1992a, "Social Policy and the Challenge of a Postindustrial Transformation", G.B. Pant Social Science Institute: Occasional Paper.

——, 1992b, "Social Development as a Global Challenge", *Social Action.*

——, 1992c, *Review* of Bill Ashroft et al., *The Empire Writes Backs*, *Critical Sociology.*

Ginsburg, Faye D., 1989, *Contested Lives: Abortion Debate in an American Community*, Berkeley: University of California Press.

Goldfarb, Jeffrey, 1989, *Beyond Glashnot: The Post-Totalitarian Mind*, Chicago: University Press.

Griffin, David, 1989, *God and Religion in the Postmodern World*, Albany: SUNY Press.

Griffin, David et al. (eds.), 1989, *Varieties of Postmodern Theology*, Albany: SUNY Press.

Griffin, David and H. Smith, 1989, *Primordial Truth and Postmodern Theology*, Albany: SUNY Press.

Habermas, Jurgen, 1987, *Philosophical Discourse of Modernity*, Cambridge, MA: The MIT Press.

Harvey, David, 1989, *The Condition of Postmodernity*, Basil Blackwell.

Hassan, Ihab, 1987, *The Postmodern Turn: Essays in Postmodern Theory and Culture*, Ohio State University Press.

Heller, Agnes and F. Feher, 1989, *The Postmodern Political Condition*, NY: Columbia University Press.

Hewitt, Martin, 1983, "Bio-Politics and Social Policy: Foucault's Account of Welfare", *Theory, Culture and Society* 2 (1): 67-84.

Jackson, Michael, 1983, "Thinking Through the Body: An Essay in Understanding Metaphors", *Man.*

Johnson, Alfred and Stephen Toulmin, 1988, *The Abuse of Casuistry: A History of Moral Reasoning*, California.

Khare, R.S., 1984, *The Untouchable Unto Himself*, Cambridge: University Press.

Kothari, Rajni, 1988, *Rethinking Development*, New Delhi: Ajanta.

Kristeva, Julia, 1981, "Women's Time", *Signs* VII (1).

Kuper, Joseph, 1985, "Architecture: Building the Body Politic", *Social Theory and Practice* 11 (3): 265-283.

Kroker, Arthur and Marilouise, 1987, "Theses on the Disappearing Body in the Hyper-Modern Condition", in Arthur & Marilouise Kroker (eds.), *Body Invaders: Panic Sex in America*, NY: St. Martin's Press.

Kroker, Arthur et al., 1989, *Panic Encyclopaedia: The Definitive Guide to the Postmodern Scene*, NY: St. Martin's Press.

Lakoff, George and Mark Johnson, 1982, *Metaphors We Live By*, Chicago: University Press.

Lash, Scott, 1984, "Genealogy and the Body: Foucault / Deleuze / Nietzsche", *Theory, Culture and Society* 2 (2): 1-17.

Laqueur, Thomas, "Orgasm, Generation, and the Politics of Reproductive Biology", *Representations* 14: 1-41.

Lefort, Claude, 1986, *The Political Forms of Modern Society: Bureaucracy, Democracy and Totalitarianism*, Cambridge, MA: The MIT Press.

Levin, Charles Poli, 1987, "Carnal Knowledge of Aesthetic States: The Infantile Body, The Sign and the Postmodern Condition", *Canadian Journal of Political and Social Theory*: 90-110.

Levin, David M., 1989, "The Body Politic: The Embodiment of Praxis in Foucault and Habermas", *Praxis International* 9(1/2):112-132.

Lyotard, Jean-Francois D., 1988, "Can Thought Go On Without a Body", *Discourse* 11 (1): 78-88.

Marsh, James, 1988, *Post-Cartesian Meditations: An Essay in Dialectical Phenomenology*, NY: Fordham University Press.

Martin, Emily, 1987, *Woman in the Body: A Cultural Analysis of Reproduction*, Boston: Beacon Press.,

——, 1990, *Science and Popular Knowledge in the United States*: A Research Proposal.

Martin, L.H. et al. (eds.), 1988, *Technologies of the Self: A Seminar with Michael Foucault*, Amherst: University of Massachusetts Press.

McLuhan, Marshall et al., 1989, *The Global Village*, NY: Oxford University Press.

Metz, Johannes B., 1981, "Toward a Second Reformation: The Future of Christianity in a Post-Bourgeois World", *Cross Currents* XXX (1).

Murphy, John, 1989, *Postmodern Social Analysis and Criticism*, NY: Greenwood Press.

Nandy, Asis, 1983, *The Intimate Enemy: The Loss and Recovery of Self Under Colonialism*, Delhi: Oxford University Press.

O'Neil, John, 1989, *The Communicative Body: Studies in Communicative Philosophy, Politics, and Sociology*, Evanston: North Western University Press.

Osborne, David, 1988, *Laboratories of Democracy*, Boston: Harvard Business School.

Ostrander, Greg, 1987, "Foucault's Disappearing Body", *Canadian Journal of Political and Social Theory* XI (1-2).

Pheby, K.C., 1988, *Interventions: Displacing the Metaphysical Subject*, Washington, D.C.: Maissoneuve Press.

Rieber, R.W., 1980, *Body and Mind: Past, Present and Future*, NY: Academic Press.

Ryan, Michael, 1982, *Marxism and Deconstruction: A Critical Articulation*, Baltimore: The Johns Hopkins University Press.

Ryle, Gilbert, 1969 (1949), *On the Concept of the Mind*, London: Hutchinson & Co.

Skocpol, Theda, 1988, "Limits of the New Deal System and the Roots of Contemporary Welfare Dilemmas", in M. Weir and T. Skocpol (eds.), *The Politics of Social Policy in the United States.*

Sen, Amartya, 1989, "Food and Freedom", *World Development.*

Shore, Bradd, 1991, "Twice Born, Once Conceived: Meaning Construction and Cultural Cognition", *American Anthropologist* 93 (1): 9-27.

Sohn-Rethel, Alfred, 1978, *Intellectual and Manual Laobr: A Critique of Epistemology*, Atlantic Highlands, NJ: Humanities Press.

Soja, Edward, 1989, *Postmodern Geographies: The Reassertion of Space in Critical Social Theory*, London: Verso.

Spelman, E.V., 1982, "Woman as Body", *Feminist Studies* 8: 109-31.

Statten, H., 1984, *Wittgenstein and Derrida*, Nebraska.

Stone, Deborah A., 1989, "At Risk in the Welfare State", *Social Research* 56 (3): 591-633.

Terry, Jennifer, 1989, "The Body Invaded: Medical Surveillance of Women as Reproducers", *Socialist Review* (3): 13-43.

Touraine, Alain, 1988, *Return of the Actor: Social Theory in Postindustrial Society*, Minnesota.

Turner, Bryan , 1984, *Body and Society: Explorations in Social Theory,*

Oxford: Basil Blackwell.

Uberoi, J.P.S., 1978, *Science and Culture*, Delhi: Oxford University Press.

Vattimo, Gianni , 1988, *The End of Modernity: Nihilism and Hermeneutics in Postmodern Culture*, Baltimore: The Johns Hopkins University Press.

Voss, D. and J.C. Schitze, 1989, "Postmodernism in Context: Perspectives of a Structural Change in Society, Literature and Literary Criticism", *New German Critique* 47: 119-142.

Walker, R.B.J., 1988, *One World, Many Worlds: Struggles for a Just World Peace*, London: Zed Books.

Wittgenstein, Ludwig, 1958 *The Blue and Brown Books*, NY: Harper & Row.

Chapter Seven

CRITIQUE OF THE COMPARATIVE METHOD AND THE CHALLENGES OF A TRANSNATIONAL WORLD

We may compare Confucianism and Aristotelianism from a Confucian standpoint, or from an Aristotelian; or may compare both or either with some, third different, equally incompatible and incommensurable standpoint, such as that of Buddhism or of Kantianism, but we cannot find any legitimate standing ground outside the context of points of view. And when we have undertaken comparative study in a manner which recognizes this, we shall soon find that our task is not so much that of comparing Confucianism and Aristotelianism as that of comparing Confucian comparisons of Confucianism and Aristotelianism with Aristotelian comparisons of Confucianism and Aristotelianism. The key to comparative studies is the comparison of comparisons.

—Alasdair MacIntyre (1991: 121)

The problem of verification is not simply fraught with relativism, it is also one that could be resolved by resorting to an alternative form of comparative inquiry. In such an inquiry, national society is not the analytical point of departure, even though it may be a unit of observation of social processes that transcend national boundaries.

Given contemporary global realities, the ability to understand 'national society' as an ongoing historical entity, rather than a natural end (or arrival) in social evolution, is at a premium. An appropriate comparative method would therefore not assume its unit of analysis a priori, and would attempt to situate social processes (including state formation) within a broader historical moment or conjuncture.
—Phillip McMichael (1992: 358)

THE PROBLEM

The comparative method and the comparative project in the social sciences has received critical attention in the last several decades. It has been the subject of much of debate and discussion, critique and counter-critique. Scholars participating in this debate not only launch a frontal attack on the conventional comparative method but also strive to reformulate it in the light of our contemporary transformations in self, culture and society. While scholars from the advanced societies are more concerned with the question of reformulating and redesigning the comparative method which would enable us to make sense of our contemporary human condition, local and global, commentators from the developing societies spend much time in showing us the violence that the wholesale comparison of civilizations has done to the understanding of reality, western and non-western, modern and traditional (Appadurai 1989; Badie 1992; Beteille 1979; Kohn 1989; Oyen 1990 and Nader 1989). Critical social scientists from the developing countries have been at the forefront of launching a frontal critique of the comparative method. These critics have tried to demolish the myth surrounding comparative sociology. Critique of the comparative method has brought to the fore the ethnocentrism that has come in the garb of comparative sociology. Here we can take the recent debate on the use and the abuse of comparative method in Indian studies as an illustrative case. This debate has involved two thoughtful social theorists of our times, Andre Beteille and Louis Dumont. In several of his papers, the first on the subject presented in 1966 and published in 1969[1], Beteille has taken issue with what he calls a "distinctive feature" approach in the comparative sociology of India formulated by western scholars and prominent in the writings of Dumont. Beteille criticizes the comparative method of the kind provided by Dumont and pleads for being sensitive to both similarities and differences, structure and history in our pursuit of a genuine and benign comparative project. As Beteille (1987b: 675) writes:

> Dumont's comparative method is severely constrained by the symmetry of his own construction. By conscious choice that method assigns priority to contrast over comparison, to difference over similarity, and to discontinuity over continuity. It deals with the varieties of societies not as they actually exist but in so far as they exemplify certain constellations of value in their pure form. From the point of view of this method not all societies are of the same value: societies are valorized in the very acts of comparison and contrast.

In this paper, an attempt has been made to understand the contemporary predicament of comparative method through a critical study of the critique presented by Beteille and the debate between Dumont and Beteille that this critique has led to. At the same time, the paper also aims to go beyond the current critique and anti-critique to design a reformulated comparative method that would enable us to understand the interplay of identity and difference in our contemporary world. The paper presents a portrait of our present-day world as a transnational world, and looks at several contemporary attempts at reformulating the comparative method in line with the challenges of a transnational world.

CRITIQUE OF THE COMPARATIVE METHOD

The Case of Andre Beteille

The comparative method has provided an important and consistent orientation to Beteille's work in sociology and anthropology over the last three decades (Beteille 1991). Beteille has not only been engaged in a critique of the comparative method, but also has consistently used this method as a tool of "critical understanding" (Molund 1991). In this regard, it is not true that Beteille's criticism of the comparative method eschews it totally in favor of a "transcultural" one.[2]

Beteille's criticism of the comparative method can be traced as far back as 1966 to his paper entitled "Politics of Non-Antagonistic Strata" (Beteille 1969). This paper contains many important arguments which have been developed into more sophisticated forms in the later years, even though it is not explicitly a criticism of the comparative method. Here Beteille makes a general argument about the interrelationship between value and power, ideas and interest in the dynamics of and study of the social structure. As he wrote: "...the role of values themselves can never be fully assessed unless we study them in their continuous interaction with interests" (Beteille 1969: 30). For Beteille, one-sided accentuation of contrastive types in the conventional comparative sociology has been made possible by the one-sided accentuation of values in one's sociological framework, without relating these values to the dynamics of power in society. In this paper, Beteille also illumines the discussion on caste as essentially non-conflictual by invoking the Soviet discussion on "non-antagonistic" strata. This approach of illumining the comparison between two categories by invoking the character and process of a tertiary phenomenon is characteristic of Beteille's method which is most prominent in his recent comparison between caste and gender (Beteille 1990b).

Much of Beteille's critical reflection on comparative method has been born out of his debate with Dumont, though this is not confined to him. One of the earliest systematic efforts in this regard is Beteille's 1979 Kingsley Martin Memorial Lecture in Cambridge entitled "Homo Hierarchicus and Homo Equalis" (Beteille 1979). Here Beteille takes Dumont to task for the typological construction of India and the West as "Homo Hierarchicus" and "Homo Equalis" and the comparison between them as essences and unchanging structures. Criticizing Dumont's characterization of India as "Homo Hierarchicus", Beteille argues that hierarchy is more a theological than a sociological notion. Hierarchy as a value should not be given a sacrosanct place in the study of Indian society anymore than "The Great Chain of Being" can be a defining feature of the western society. Hierarchy is not an essential characteristic of traditional India; it existed in pre-capitalist Europe as well. Beteille presents the arguments of both Marx and Tocqueville to support his own arguments. Even though Tocqueville provides the intellectual heritage to Dumont's comparative sociology, Beteille argues that Dumont lacks Tocqueville's historical sensitivity when he reformulates his contrast between aristocracy and democracy as a contrast between hierarchy and equality. Thus:

> Dumont makes it quite plain that there was a historical break in Western society which led to the replacement of holism and hierarchy by individualism and equality....[But] having served its purpose in introducing the argument, traditional society in the West disappears from view in the rest of Dumont's discussion on Homo Hierarchicus...One is left wondering why the contrast with which the argument began, between the old and the new orders of western society—de Tocqueville's contrast—is never taken up at the end (Beteille 1979: 541, 542)

Why this is so? Beteille argues that this is because "the thesis about Homo Hierarchicus has...another implication as well. This is that homo hierarchicus is not only single-minded in his attachment to inequality but also deeply resistant to change" (Beteille 1979: 531). For Beteille, this is an act of "prejudice".[3] In this context, Beteille "would like to see a serious comparison made between the traditional West and traditional India" (Beteille 1979: 542). Despite his work on comparative history,[4] Beteille has not provided us this intended comparison between traditional India and the traditional West. The reason is not simply that Beteille is a sociologist, not a historian. There is a deeper reason behind this silence. Beteille's critique has been generated by the very structure of the argument against which he is launching a frontal attack. In "Homo Hierarchicus and Homo Equalis", Beteille provides us a critique of Dumont's construction of tradition, while in "Individualism and Equality", Beteille (1986) provides us a critique of Dumont's construction of modernity. But in pursuing Dumont to his edge, Beteille ignores the vital question of comparison between traditions—the traditional India and the traditional west. If Beteille's critique was not only generated by the structure of the argument set by Dumont, then Beteille himself would have taken up this as a worthwhile project of inquiry and could have used this as a frame of criticism.

In his critique of the comparative method, Beteille also provides us a critique of Dumont's construction of modernity. For Beteille, Dumont's construction of modernity ignores the tension between ideology and practice and also dissent and contestation within ideology. Beteille tells us that he finds Nehru's construction of modernity more insightful than the black and white contrast of Dumont. For Nehru, equality is characteristic of the spirit of modern times, but almost denied everywhere in practice. For him, this "provides a far more insightful approach to the structure of the modern world than a black and white contrast between homo hierarchicus and homo equalis" (Beteille 1979: 548). This black and white contrast, as applied to the modern side of the great divide, is the subject of critical analysis in his "Individualism and Equality" (Beteille 1986). Here he deconstructs the categories of individualism and equality which have been presented as essential attributes of the modern world, delinks the essential symbiotic relationship constructed between them and locates their genealogy in historical transformations, recent and contemporary. He also shows us how these modern ideas have diffused to other societies and how we must be sensitive to this diffusion in our method and analysis. As Beteille argues: "Individualism, equality and their relationship have so far been discussed almost entirely within the context of western culture. It is desirable to extend the discussion to cover not only the society in which these values were first clearly articulated but also others to which they have spread and in which they found some room for themselves" (Beteille 1986: 121). Thus, he hopes to bring to bear a "comparative perspective on the subject" (ibid).

In this paper, Beteille also questions the view (that he attributes to Dumont) that individualism entails equality. For Beteille, "...individualism is in the contemporary world linked more with the idea of progress than with the idea of equality" (Beteille 1986: 127). Moreover, for Beteille, Dumont has ignored the whole modern western experience of what following Simmel he calls "individualism of inequality" (ibid). For Simmel, "individualism might lead to either an appreciation of human equality or a preoccupation with the inequality of man" (ibid). Keeping this in view, Simmel distinguishes between "individualism of equality" and "individualism of inequality". What strikes Beteille is Simmel's argument that "the two kinds of individualism are historically related and products of the same social process" (ibid). For Beteille, those who are the votaries of individualism in contemporary western world are not champions of equality, but are ardent proponents of efficiency. Beteille discusses the ideas and positions of key contemporary interlocutors such as Hayek and Freeman who either dismiss completely the very project of equality or are "deeply mistrustful of distributive equality" (ibid: 127). Beteille here also sensitizes us to the crucial distinction between "equality as a right " and "equality as a policy". As he writes: "The concept of equality as understood today—and this is true both of United States and India—incorporates a component of distributive equality, even at some cost to formal equality of opportunity. The principle of redress, which has become a part of equality as policy, is opposed by strong individualists..." (ibid: 128).

If equality has its strong opponents even in those who are the dogged proponents of individualism in the West, then it has also its ardent supporters in India even in those who may be valuationally typed as "Homo Hierarchicus". Here Beteille refers not only to the architects of equality in twentieth century India such as Nehru and Ambedkar and the whole institution of the Constitution, but also to the 19th century protagonists such as Bankim Chandra.

The critique of the comparative method that Beteille puts forward in this essay begins with the same general problem of the dialectic between value and power. In his response to Dumont, Beteille tells us: "Dumont accuses me of denying value itself because I refuse to accept his own construction of the hierarchy of values. I view the matter differently. For me something is a value for people only if they are prepared to forego some other thing to secure it" (Beteille 1987b: 673). Here Beteille presents Wertheim's notion of "counterpoint" as an alternative to Dumont's idea of hierarchy, which enables one to work through "the co-existence of divergent values without seeking necessarily to place them in a hierarchical arrangement" (Beteille 1990a: 2261). While in the hierarchical construction of values, "values arrange themselves according to their internal logic; in the construction of values as fields of contending forces and counter-points different and even incompatible values may be characteristically associated with different groups, classes, and categories in the same society" (ibid).

Beteille's excurses into these broader questions of social theory[5] makes clear that in this engagement Beteille also has an agenda of his own. This becomes quite distinct in his two recent papers: "Some Observations on the Comparative Method" (Beteille 1990a) and "Race, Caste and Gender" (Beteille 1990b).

Beteille's essay "Race, Caste and Gender" contains both a critique as well as an agenda. It suggests some new and bold ways of comparing categories which might look dissimilar and illumining this comparison by understanding their relationship with a tertiary element. For Beteille, race and caste are comparable and this comparison can be illumined by looking at their attitude to and treatment of women. Beteille deplores the lack of systematic efforts in comparing caste and race not only in Indian studies but also in American studies. This is because of the same typifying approach at work: race typifying social stratification in United States while caste typifying social stratification in India. But for Beteille, "when we consider caste and race together, we are struck at once by the remarkable similarity in the contrasting attitudes towards women of lower and higher ranks characteristic of men in privileged positions in both systems. My argument is that in-equalities of caste are illumined in the same way as those of race by a consideration of gender" (Beteille 1990b: 491).

This leads Beteille to a discussion of the attitude to the purity of women and to blood in both the American and the Indian context. Here Beteille discusses the comparison between India and United States initiated by Mariott and his colleagues. Schneider's study of American kinship and his distinction be-tween "code" and "substance" has provided a framework for a particular construction of Indian kinship and society by American anthropologists and its comparison with the culture and kinship in the United States. But Beteille argues that this comparison often leads to typification. While he agrees with Mariott that Hindu thinking denies the "easy separability" of substance and code, this denial is not altogether absent even in contemporary American society. Here Beteille draws our attention to the American atti-tude (especially of the White Americans) to miscegenation. For Beteille, both in India as well as in United States, "the fact of miscegenation brings out deep-rooted fears about its effect on the purity of race or caste" (ibid: 499). Thus, if contra-Dumont, Beteille argues that hierarchy is not only a Hindu phenomenon, then Beteille's critique of the comparative method vis-a-vis Mariott and Schneider argues that "biological substantialism" is not the peculiarity of the Hindus alone (ibid).

This brings us finally to Beteille's agenda. Beteille concludes his self-reflexive introduction to his recent collection of essays: "Thus I end as I began, with the plea for a differentiated view of each and every society as a basis for comparisons and contrasts we make between them" (Beteille 1991: 17). He, further, chal-lenges us: "...in making comparisons we must try to deal even-handedly with similarity and difference, and avoid making it a dogma that either the one or the other is more fundamental of the two..." (Beteille 1990a: 2259).

Deconstructing the Critique and Understanding Dumont

Recent commentaries on the comparative method seem to reiterate the position that Beteille has put forward over the years. For instance, the editor of a recent impressive collection of essays on cross-national research tells us: "...lawful explanation of cross-national differences requires more explicit consideration of historical, cultural, and political-economic considerations than does the lawful explanation of cross-national similarities" (Kohn 1989: 80). Beteille's plea for being sensitive to the historical development of individual traditions, especially when they are made units of comparison, seems to be corroborated by the pioneering work of philosopher Alasdair MacIntyre on the comparison of traditions. For MacIntyre, traditions cannot be compared by simply translating their "incommensurable" standpoints "into the idioms of and presentation in terms of the forms of discourse of cosmopolitan modernity" (MacIntyre 1991: 187). For MacIntyre, if we want to compare "incommensurable" traditions—such as Confucianism and Aristotelianism—we must "realize that each has been confronted by successive sets of problems and difficulties, problems and difficulties identified by the standards internal to each of these developing modes of moral thought and practice" (ibid). This historical approach highlights the inner conflicts of tradition and renders our "own point of view as problematic as possible" (ibid: 121). Needless to say, such prolematization and the exposure to "counterpoints" that it makes possible is essential for a meaningful comparison of civilizations.

But while Beteille is correct in arguing that Dumont has ignored the historical development of Indian tradition and has not been sensitive to the "successive sets of problems and difficulties", to borrow the words of MacIntyre, in case of the western tradition, where history is given importance, Beteille's critique itself lacks a·critical sense of history. Hence, this critique has not really transformed itself into a reformulated and reinvigorated comparative method, capable of responding to the challenges of our contemporary world. In his critique, Beteille makes a distinction between "classification" and "typification" and argues that it is typification which sets the norms and objectives of conventional comparative method (Beteille 1990a). For Beteille, this kind of typifying comparative sociology is not only full of "intellectual errors" but also associated with "political mischief" (Beteille 1990b). But Beteille has not situated the specific manifestation of the distinction between "typification" and " 'assification" in the modernist project. Beteille does not ask the question why the universal aptness for classification is reified into typification as it is happening, as Beteille himself argues, in the case of modern comparative sociology. Is the specific unfolding of the distinction between "typification" and "classification" an integral part of the project of modernity?

For some commentators, the modernist project is characterized by an imperialistic and all consuming womb to incorporate all differences into a system of inequality (Giri 1990; Visvanathan 1988; Uberoi 1978). Beteille is not sensitive to the particular unfoldment of the craze for "typification" and erasure of difference, integral to the project of modernity. He pleads for intellectual detachment as central to the craft of sociology (Beteille 1991, 1992) but is not able to distance himself from his achieved modern identity. No wonder, Beteille writes, though in reaction to Dumont: "As to modernity, there is very little in that today—whether in India or in the West—to make the imagination soar. But I belong to the modern world, and I would be untrue to my vocation as a sociologist to disown the world to which I belong" (Beteille 1987b: 676). But a real deconstruction of the comparative project requires a critical sense of history and a sense of distanctiation in order to understand the genealogy of the comparative project in the deep structure of modernity.

In this deconstructive engagement, the key issue here is the issue of difference. Beteille takes issue with the formulation of the comparative method solely around difference. But here Beteille seems to be lacking an intimation with difference as a key symbol and a subversive language of our times, for instance, as proposed by the deconstructionist philosopher Jacques Derrida. For Derrida, the existence of the fact of difference and the act of differentiation is integrally linked with its movement and resistance against the system's efforts to erase and to incorporate it. In fact, for Derrida, differences are characterized by what he calls "spatial and temporal deferral" (see, Barnett 1989). For many commentators, our contemporary world is making a shift in both discourse and society from a system of inequality to an interplay of differences (Connolly 1991; Giri 1990). In this context, how to formulate a comparative method that would attend to the interplay of identity and difference in our contemporary world? Here Beteille's solution of a "limited comparative approach" (Beteille 1990a) seems to be an answer to the problems of the past, rather than an agenda for the future.

Here Dumont's response to Beteille's distinction between "individualism of equality" and "individualism of inequality" calls for a critical reflection. Dumont writes: "Identity and difference are more central to the opposition than equality and inequality" (Dumont 1987: 672)[6]. Regarding the criticism that he has ignored the process and ideology of "individualism of inequality" in his construction of modernity, Dumont argues that Simmel's original contrast can also be translated as "individualism of identity" and "individualism of non-identity" or difference (Dumont 1987: 671). Dumont also shows us the distinction between "individualism of inequality" and "individualism of difference." For Dumont: "...'individualism of difference' involves for the subject a duty to cultivate one's difference, and while to cultivate oneself as a unique individual may appeal to many, it is very much in its origin and development a German affair, as Simmel tells us" (Dumont 1987: 672). This leads Dumont to a consideration of the case of Germany in the modern world, especially her story of acculturation and modernization.

Dumont's treatment of the German case is important not only for the light it throws either on the specific German case or the general modern predicament, but also for its significance for the discourse on method. The comparative method that is at work in Dumont's anthropological treatment of modern ideology and in the study of modernization and acculturation of Germany shows a noticeable shift from his earlier approach. In his work on Germany, Dumont is interested in looking at it "as a national variant of the modern system of values and ideas" and writes: "this acculturation is similar in its form to that of countries such as Russia and India, and of the non-modern countries in general" (Dumont 1986a: 587). Dumont further tells us:

> The word 'acculturation' is normally used, of course, to describe the modern civilization and non-modern cultures. Yet it stands to reason that non-modern elements co-exist with the modern ones in the social as well as ideological make-up of European countries in various ways, and it is well known that change does not proceed at the same pace in all the countries and in all domains. On the micro-level as it were, or segmentally, we may look at the differences within modern civilization just as we do at differences between it and non-modern cultures (Dumont 1986a: 588).

Thus, Dumont himself tells us that essentializing the distinction between the modern and the non-modern is not tenable. For Dumont, "the conflicting values of holism and individualism combine in problematic ways in the present world as they did in German history" (Dumont 1986a: 601).

In his recent work, Dumont also challenges us to "maintain a double reference—a reference to the global society on the one hand, and on the other, a reciprocal reference of comparison between the observer and the observed" (Dumont 1986b: 5). If in "Homo Hierarchicus", Dumont was engaged in a radical comparison between the self and the other, in his recent work he is interested in a "reciprocal reference of comparison." Dumont writes: "Reversing the movement, one can see modern society against the background of non-modern societies" (ibid). The following argument requires a close reading from us not only to deconstruct Beteille's critique of Dumont and to understand him but also to understand our contemporary predicament:

> A more complex process...is found in the domains of cultures and results from their interaction. To the extent that the individualistic ideas and values of the dominant culture are spreading worldwide, they undergo modifications locally and engender new forms. Now-and this has escaped notice-the new, modified forms can pass back into the dominant culture and operate there as modern elements in their own right. In that way the acculturation of each particular culture to modernity can have a lasting precipitate in the heritage of global modernity. Further, the process is cumulative in as much this precipitate can in turn be transformed on the occasion of a subsequent acculturation (1986b: 18).

For Dumont, "the contemporary world is like a fabric woven by the continuing interaction of cultures" which calls for a "shift in perspective" and leads even to "certain uneasiness of vocabulary" (1986b: 19). Dumont tells us how he feels the need to modify his initial contrast in the light of a substantial body of facts which has to be "acknowledged". Reflecting upon his shift in perspective, Dumont further tells us: "At that stage I tended quite broadly to identify individuality with modernity.. But..in the contemporary world we find something other than what had been differentially been defined as modern. This is true even in that part of the world considered 'advanced', 'developed', or 'modern' par excellence, and even on the level of ideology itself" (ibid). It is easy to label this interpenetration of genres as postmodernity, but the real challenge, as Dumont articulates for us, is to "analyze these more or less hybrid representations" (ibid).

Thus, in his recent work, Dumont deploys a comparative method which is interested in hybridity, not solely in the black and white contrast. Dumont's recent work also shows a sensitivity to the dialectic between the local and the global in the constitution of modernity. Dumont does not propose to "reduce German thought to the conditions of its genesis" (ibid: 116). For him, "a feature is no less important for its being rooted in a particular tradition" (ibid). But Beteille does not take note of this shift in Dumont's position and, even when reminded, dismisses it on the ground of substantive veracity and interpretative accuracy. Beteille writes in his response to Dumont: "The argument about Germany's acculturation strikes me as unconvincing...I find the argument that the modernization of Germany has been marked by a 'synthesis' of holism and individualism rather lame" (Beteille 1987b: 675). Dumont's work on Germany raises both the question of history and the question of method. Beteille might disagree with the historical interpretation of Dumont, but is he justified in completely ignoring the question of method that Dumont's recent work poses?[7]

In this context, one wonders why there is no discussion of Dumont's recent work in Beteille's criticism. Dumont's work on German acculturation was first published in French in 1983 and Beteille's "Individualism and Equality" paper appeared in 1986. But one wonders why in this paper, there is no discussion of Dumont's discussion on the diffusion of modernity. This is particularly incomprehensible since this is also (i.e. studying the diffusion of a modern idea like equality) Beteille's objective. In his treatment of India, Beteille uses the concept of "spread" and in his treatment of Germany, Dumont uses the word "acculturation". Here one is struck by the similarity of method and objective between both of them. They are interested in their own ways in the same problem of diffusion and dispersion of modernity. But Beteille is not only silent on this similarity but also insensitive to Dumont's shift in position. In the critique of the comparative method, Dumont is rhetorically constructed in the act of valorization of criticism where there is an one-sided accentuation of Dumont, the author of "Homo Hierarchicus and Homo Equalis" and a total silence on Dumont, the author of "Essays on Individualism". Thus, Dumont replies back to Beteille's criticism with a charge of misrepresentation.[8]

But it is Beteille himself who has taken great care to show us the richness of Dumont's work vis-a-vis an ethnographic under standing of India. Beteille tells us about the rich ethnography of Dumont's "A South Indian Sub-Caste" and the discrepancy between this rich ethnography and the simplistic construction of India as "Homo Hierarchicus" (Beteille 1987c). But one wonders why the same sensitivity to Dumont's shift in perspectives is not shown in Beteille's critique of and observation on the comparative method. This raises the more general question of debate and dialogue in anthropology as a community of discourse. In many of our contemporary engagements of critique and anti-critique, there is a rhetorical construction of one's contestant's position as wholly different where ethnographies and substantial arguments demonstrate similarities between the two contestants, besides the much blown-out differences. In recent times, this problem faced us squarely in the debate between Mead and Freeman on the real nature of Samoa. As I have discussed elsewhere this debate as an instance of epistemological crisis in anthropology, the Mead-Freeman debate again points to us the problem of valorization in the act of criticism (Giri 1992c). The Beteille-Dumont exchange also raises the similar problem of the mode of participation in a debate and the challenge of striking a middle ground. This also shows the need for sensitivity to the richness and the nuanced differences within one's subject of criticism rather than to rhetorically construct the Other as an anti-hero.

Beyond the Critique and Anti-Critique: Comparative Method and the Challenges of a Transnational World

When one goes beyond the critique and the anti-critique, one is again struck by the remarkable similarity between Beteille and Dumont in their understanding of the nature and the process of our contemporary world. Both of them suggest important clues to understand our contemporary world as a transnational world of interpenetration of cultures and blurring of genres.[9] In his recent "Observation on the Comparative Method", Beteille draws our attention to the processes of interpenetration "that has become such a feature of the contemporary world" (Beteille 1990a: 2261).

These forces of interpenetration make societies field of conflicting forces rather than "discrete and bounded units" (Beteille 1990a: 2261). For Beteille, this is true not only of the nation-state, but also of societies in the broad sense. Beteille argues that in the contemporary context of interpenetration and mutual implication of societies on a global scale, there is the need for a reformulation of the method of classification and comparison. In the words of Beteille:

> It appears to me that if we treat societies as field of conflicting forces, rather than as discrete and bounded units, the classification of social types according to the rules of taxonomy may not be a very rewarding exercise. Those rules require that comparisons should proceed on a strictly graduated scale, first between the nearest neighbors, then between groups of neighbors and so on...Societies are implicated in each other to such a large extent in the contemporary world that one will find it hard to construct any simple scale of neighborliness with which to assess the interpenetration, in terms of ideas, beliefs, and values, of let us say, Britain and India, or the Netherlands and Indonesia (Beteille 1990a: 2262).

In this context, our reflection on the comparative method ought to enable us to make sense of the configuration of identity and difference unfolding in our contemporary world. This also requires us to understand our contemporary world as a transnational world. The contemporary world has a different configuration of "space-time compression" (Harvey 1989) and a different logic of the "mobility of capital and labor" (Sassen 1988). Contemporary world is a tightly intertwined system of production, distribution and exchange in which new forces such as multinational corporations, global assembly lines and different transnational agencies undermine the entrenched sovereignty of the nation-states. Contemporary transnational processes embody the twilight of subjectivity and sovereignty of the nation-states and the creation of a global space which is characterized not simply by the dominance of the nation-states in "The So-called World System" (Mintz 1977), but by people-to-people interaction without the mediation of the nation-states. As Connolly argues: "Globalization of contingency is the defining mark of late modernity" (Connolly 1991: 25) which shows the limits of the state-centred discourse and practice. It is in this space of predicament and possibility that many transnational movements such as the Ecology Movements, Human Rights Movements, Habitat for Humanity, The Sister City Movement have emerged to cope with our global challenge and contingencies (Giri 1992b). Transnational movements are multivalent symbols of our contemporary transnational existence. This transnational existence makes the formulation of a different kind of comparative method an imperative and a necessity. Therefore in his essay "The Imperfection of Comparisons", Oyen (1990) also speaks about the inadequacy of the nation-state as a unit of action and interpretation. At the same time, the comparative method should not be preoccupied only with similarity, but as Oyen (1990a:1) puts it, "comparative research may have to shift its emphasis from seeking uniformity among variety to studying the preservation of enelaves of uniqueness among growing homogeneity and uniformity."

If transnational movements are the archetypes of our contemporary world as a transnational world, then some of the important strivings towards transforming the comparative method have taken place in the case of the study of the transnational movements.[10] Transnational movements call for a "cross-national strategy" (Scheuch 1990: 29) in their study. Keeping in mind the predicament of these movements vis-a-vis the method of study, one recent commentator has written: "While nation-state, culture or society may be too large a unit for a causal attribution...or too small (as in the case of protest movements), it may also be too weak a context to account for differences observed within individual data" (Scheuch 1990: 29). But if the study of the transnational protest movements shows the necessity for a cross-national research strategy, they also embody a reformulation of this strategy. Daniel Betraux who has studied the transnational student movement of the 1960s argues that "the traditional quasi-experimental design [of comparative research] does not hold any more..." (Betraux 1990: 152). Oyen also argues that in comparative research "the dubious logic of quasi-experimentation is even less feasible in a world which has grown into an interdependent and intertwined world system" (Oyen 1990: 12). Betraux, further, tells us that the objective in his study of the 1960s student movements was not the comparison between student movements in different countries, but to follow the trajectory of this phenomenon as a global movement and through this to represent both the similarity and difference in the constitution of this global movement. In the words of Betraux: "The book was not meant to be an explicitly comparative study of these movements; our only aim was to retrace their history..." (Betraux 1990: 151). In this study he moves back and forth from one country to another which provided him a "wide-angle vision". But curiously enough this led him away "from a strictly cross-national, classically comparative perspective" (ibid: 152). In the pursuit of student movement as a global movement, what struck the author was not the difference in their national variations, but their "similarities". What Betraux writes about this transnational movement is important for understanding the dialectic between identity and difference in our contemporary transnational world: "...behind the obvious difference in style, content, claims and forms of discourse, the sensitivities of this generation of activists were variants of the same Weltanschauung—one and the same common subjectivity" (Betraux 1990: 153).

In my ongoing study of the global dynamics of a contemporary transnational movement, my method and objective has almost been similar. In my study of Habitat for Humanity, I have followed the trajectory of Habitat as a global movement. I have done fieldwork in four different places—two in India and two in United States. But in this study I have not begun with an explicit comparison between India and United States though like Betraux's study, my study has taught me important similarities and differences between contemporary India and United States as it is revealed through the pursuit of a global movement which works in both the countries and beyond. This is not the place for a detailed discussion of my work on Habitat for Humanity (Giri 1992b). But this study has shown the similarity between the Kerala construction of house and personhood as it is represented in the idea of "Taravada" and the American cultural construction of self-linked with homeownership.

Thus, the study of transnational movements suggests important clues towards rethinking the comparative method. What makes this possible? Here besides focusing only on their transnational mobilization, understanding their nature and emergent forms might help us to understand why the study of transnational movements has born the marks of a creative and transformed comparative method. Transnational movements as aspects of new social movements of our times embody the dialectic between "identity formation" and differentiation. New social movements, for many commentators, embody a new cultural identity, the identity of a constituted collectivity (Giri 1992a). But this identity itself is a mark of difference in Derrida's sense. The quest for a new identity in a social movement is also the creative practice of difference. Therefore it is no wonder that Derrida uses the very word movement in his definition of difference and differentiation.[11] Thus, Scot Lash shows us how the new class bears not only the mark of "invidious distinction" but also difference, which is manifested in the new class being the articulator of new social movements (Lash 1990; also Kriesi 1989). Of the new social classes and their quest for combining identity and difference in the practice of the new social movements, Lash writes: "...these same social groupings form in large part a constituency for the new social movements. Their habituses or identities can thus be constructed importantly along lines of gender, minority ethnicities, minority sexual practices and environmentalism...That is, along lines of difference rather than that of distinction" (Lash 1990: 23). Thus the new social movements embody the dialectic between "identity formation" and differentiation in their rhetorics and practice. As we have seen, one of the most important challenge before comparative method now is to combine identity and difference. Thus, the study of social forms such as the new social movements which combine identity and difference in practice provides us important clues to combine identity and difference in method. In this regard, what Giddens has recently written about sociology is primarily true of the comparative method. Giddens writes: "The challenges facing sociology at the end of the twentieth century reflect the issues the new social movements have brought to the fore" (Giddens 1991: 221). The interplay of identity and difference at a global level in the practice and ideology of the new social movements thus is a fertile ground for rethinking the comparative method and transforming it.

Another important example of a different kind of comparative research is the pioneering work of Johns Hopkins sociologist Melvin Kohn and his transnational colleagues in United States, Poland and Japan. In their study, "Position in the Class Structure and Psychological Functioning in the United States, Japan and Poland", Kohn et al. (1990) show a remarkable sensitivity to both uniqueness as well as to typical features in their construction of social class as a variable in cross-national research. What immediately strikes us is the distinction between the homogenizing cross-national research of scholars such as Kerr and the transnational spirit of Kohn and his colleagues. In this study, Kohn et al. seek to explore the relationship between social class and personality in a cross-national plane. The authors tell us:

> The analysis is cross-national, a major portion being to ascertain whether social class has similar or dissimilar psychological effects in western and non-western, capitalist and socialist industrialized countries. We don't claim that the United States is typical of western countries, Japan of non-western capitalist countries, or Poland of socialist countries. Nevertheless, if we find similarities in the psychological effect of social class in these countries, we can have considerable confidence that these findings have generality, not only beyond boundaries of any one of these three nations but also beyond any one type of society. If we find cross-national differences in the psychological effect of social class, our deliberate choice of such diverse type of societies will help us establish the

limits of generality of our findings and perhaps even to understand whatever differences we find (Kohn et al. 1990: 965).

What strikes a reader is that in this study there is a different kind of comparative method at work which is sensitive to the simultaneous unfolding of structure and history, similarity and difference not only in the comparison between societies but also in the very construction of the index of comparison such as social class. Occupational self-direction is a key variable in the relationship between social class and personality in this study. However, basing on this key variable, Kohn et al. construct a multidimensional model of class which is suited to the realities of the countries studied. For the authors: "Since social class is a multidimensional typology rather than a unidimensional rank ordering, this prediction does not imply a single rank ordering but rather a complex set of comparisons" (ibid: 966). This study is not aimed at showing either the homogeneity of class structure or their unique variance. However, the authors believe that it is necessary to "develop indices of social class that are attuned to the particular history, culture, and political and economic systems of each country..." (ibid: 968). The authors have conceptualized social class on the same theoretical basis, but have indexed social class in ways which have taken note of the differential character of these countries. Thus, they incorporate both similarity and difference in their cross-national research which helps them to "achieve meaningful rather than mechanical comparability" (ibid: 969).

Another recent study which is sensitive to our transnational predicament is a study on post-colonial literatures as a transnational genre. In this study, Aschroft et al. (1989) look at post-coloniality as a discursive theme and pursue its global trajectory. The authors proceed with a very broad characterization of the condition of post-coloniality which enables them to compare post-colonial literatures in such diverse countries as the United States, India and the Caribbean in the same space. The significance of this study is three-fold: (a) It shows that our transnational predicament is not simply the peculiarity of the present. We had a transnational web of identities long before, thus transnationalism as a theme can be taken up not only in the ethnography of the present but also in the archaeology of the past. (b) This study treats post-coloniality as a global discursive formation and shows how this formation is at work. Here, the authors suggest some very bold comparisons (not in a spirit of contrast) between post-coloniality and post-structuralism. They point to the similarity between the two and trace this method back to our initial moments of colonial encounter when the first phase of post-coloniality was integrally linked with the constitution of modernity. (c) this study shows us the specific embodiment of this global discursive formation in particular cultures and countries. This study again shows us how pursuing the trajectory of a sign in a global terrain, one can arrive at meaningful comparison and insightful understanding of the human condition.

Reimagining the Comparative Method: Building Upon Traditions and Creating New Genres

Important instances of a transformed comparative method discussed so far are either the studies of transnational movements or transnational themes such as Kohn et al.'s "social class and personality" and Aschroft et al.'s post-coloniality. In both these kinds of studies, the pursuit of a discursive theme in a global terrain is a very important strategy. As we are reimagining the comparative method, we can be enriched by Foucault's work on discursive field and "discursive formation". Foucault helps us to study the diffusion of a "discursive formation" without engaging in either/or comparison (Foucault 1972). Foucault also challenges us to identify the common thematic concern that permeates the ethos of two contrastive positions. Taking seriously Foucault's idea of discursive field and discursive formation would enable us to "describe systems of dispersion", rather than simply "reconstitute chains of inference" and "draw up table of differences" (Foucault 1972: 37).

In reimagining the comparative method, we have also to take

seriously the anthropological work on diffusion. Our contemporary period is marked not only by the global diffusion of the so-called imperial forms, but also by a global diffusion of themes, elements and processes which were once considered local and the vernacular. In this context, some creative retrieval of the anthropological tradition of diffusion is necessary. In his retrieval of what he calls the Boasian historiographical tradition, Sidney Mintz shows the significance of following the trajectory of the diffusion of cultural objects. For him, a cultural object might originate in a particular area, but when it diffuses to another area, it does acquire a life of its own and is not simply a passive reflection of the cultural properties of the area of origin (Mintz 1987). This perspective suggests new ways of comparing different cultural areas as they are linked through common cultural objects. Mintz's work on the global diffusion of commodities like sugar can provide us resource in reimagining the comparative method. Mintz follows the trajectory of sugar and through this is able to tell us the story of power in modern history (Mintz 1985). On a general methodological level, Mintz stresses on following the trajectory of particular substances in the modern world. For him, the integration of the Americas into a European economy was intimately associated with particular substances (Mintz 1991). For Mintz, we are accustomed to think in terms of big categories like political state and world market, hence "to start a commentary by attending to sub stances rather than to social formations may seem backward" (Mintz 1991: 383). But Mintz tells us the significance of following the trajectory of a commodity like coffee in the world market and insights in comparison that such a pursuit can yield: "Because the world coffee market was opening up while many new productive regimes were coming into picture, comparisons among them facilitate the simultaneous delineation of underlying likeness and local distinction. Such comparative treatment can go far towards stitching together analytically the sphere of world economy and local response, but does so without homogenizing the ideosyncratic features of each other" (ibid: 391).

Sidney Mintz's work is an example of a creative retrieval of tradition—building upon the tradition of Boas but also trans forming this in the face of the challenges of a transnational world. Here, it has to be noted that the current reflection on the comparative method has not lost sight of the Boasian tradition. But Beteille thinks that the Boasian comparative method is limited only to "neighbourly cultures" (Beteille 1990a: 2256). Moreover, Beteille thinks that this is a taxonomic approach which is incapable of taking note of the contemporary processes of interpenetration. Beteille remarks: "Neighbourliness is obviously not just a matter of geographical propinquity, although that was important to Boas. By making the conditions of comparability successfully more rigorous, we might find ourselves limited to the study of unique constellation of characteristics in a single society. It is in this sense that Boas's historical method might become opposed rather than complementary to the comparative method" (Beteille 1990a: 2256). While this might be true of Boas and the first generation of Boasians, this is not true of the second generation Boasians such as Sidney Mintz and Eric Wolf who through their creative retrieval of the Boasian tradition have combined the historical and the comparative method. In this context, a creative retrieval of certain traditions in American cultural anthropology which, as Arjun Appadurai has argued, "at least as far back as Boas and as recently in the voices of Sidney Mintz and Eric Wolf, has always seen cultural traits as shared and transmitted over large cultural areas..." (Appadurai 1988: 38) can help us reimagine the comparative method in the face the challenges of a transnational world.

Building upon these traditions of anthropology and discourse analysis, we can also take help from some current experiments in American cultural anthropology as we are reimagining the comparative method. The idea of a "multi-locale ethnography" is now being proposed by a wide range of thinkers in American cultural anthropology (Marcus 1986; also see Geertz 1988; Trouillot 1988) The research strategy of "multi-locale ethnography" helps us to study what Foucault would call "forms of division" or "systems of dispersion" of cultural forms which are in a "perpetually sensitive state of resistance and accommodation to broader processes of influences which are as much inside as outside the local context" (Marcus and Fischer 1986: 76). This "multi-locale ethnography" also involves a "strategic ethnography" where "the ethnographer constructs the text around a strategically selected locale, treating the system as background..." (Marcus 1986: 172). This kind of ethnographic engagement leads to the making of a "mixed-genre" text which evokes and describes the multiple genres of our contemporary condition in general and the "inner lives of the subject" and "the nature of world political economy" in particular (Marcus 1986). The strategies of "multi-locale ethnography" and "mixed-genre text" would help us weave together the multiple genres of self and society in our contemporary global condition neither in any mechanical integration nor in any contrastive presentation but in a creative delineation of the transnational discursive themes and a careful comparison of their local embodiments and manifestations.

As we are reimagining the comparative method, it has to be noted that both Beteille and Dumont, though located in a modernist framework, suggest important clues towards transforming the comparative method in the lights of contemporary transformations. But they can take more seriously the idea of "multi-locale ethnography" and meditate more systematically on the challenges of our emergent transnational forms. Dumont could follow the trajectory of "hierarchy-individualism" complex in a global terrain, doing fieldwork on the same discursive theme in the multiple locales of our contemporary transnational world, which as Dumont himself argues, has existed since the end of 18th century. The same could also be done by Beteille in terms of concrete anthropological engagement. Thus, the strategy of "multi-locale ethnography" would require both Beteille and Dumont to pursue the trajectory of the same discursive theme in a global terrain and to do fieldwork in a contemporary western society not simply in traditional and modern India. That would be an anthropological way out of the horizontal debate on the use and abuse of the comparative method and help us design a transformed comparative method.[12]

In our contemporary striving for an alternative, our fundamental challenge is to be enriched by the prevalent critiques of the comparative method and to design a transformed comparative method that is capable of coping with a transnational world where comparison involves not exclusive systems, but elements within a system, which is also often a global process, experienced as deterritorialized and spread in a global space. In the contemporary global ethnoscape, as Arjun Appadurai (1989) has written, "comparing entities which are interdependent in certain important regards poses challenges which are quite different from those which are relatively independent of each other..." (Appadurai 1989: 5). Our contemporary global change brings to the forefront the problem of "establishing the heuris tic boundaries of the units of analysis" (Arizpe 1991: 604). In fact, it also lays bare the lack of fit between "units of analysis and the field of study" (Giri 1992d). But the blurring of the boundaries between genres and units is not simply confined to the structural relationship between societies and nation-states in our contemporary transnational world, it is also at the heart of culture and subjectivity. As Clifford Geertz writes: "More concretely, moral issues stemming from cultural diversity...mainly between societies...now increasingly arise within them" (Geertz 1986: 115). In the contemporary world, marked not only by cultural diversity but also by "variant subjectivity" (Geertz 1986: 119, also Giri 1991a), "imagining difference ...remains a science of which we all have need" (Geertz 1986: 120). This calls for realizing the centrality of the "global cube" in our lives and to realize that "global change...is essentially a study of movement, of crossing historical thresholds into new domains" (Arizpe 1991: 603). Our critique of the comparative method and the making of a transformed comparative method ought to prepare us for the study of migrations and movements within our familiar systems and provide us "an imaginative entry into...an alien turn of mind" (Geertz 1986: 118). As we are reimagining the comparative method in face of the challenges of a transnational world, the following words of a philosopher provides us insight and challenge:

But to get a meeting going between people from two traditions more than presence is required. A lot of imagination is required also...the best vehicle for such imaginative flights will be texts which are neither comparisons and contrasts between previously-delimited domains within traditions, nor comparisons between traditions as a whole, but works of brilliant bricolage-books which insouciantly bring together bits and pieces of each tradition in ways which do not fit under any previously-formulated generic concept (Rorty in Balslev 1989: 53).

NOTES

1. In fact, this paper of Beteille was first presented in a seminar in Paris hosted by Dumont.

2. This is what is the reaction of Dumont towards Beteille's critique of the comparative method. See Dumont (1987).

3. Here we must note that Beteille begins his criticism of "Homo Hierarchicus" with the following lines: "The principal obstacle to its growth [i.e., the comparative method] is, in my opinion, neither lack of wits nor lack of words: it is prejudice" (Beteille 1979: 529).

4. I read Beteille's paper, "Harmonic and Disharmonic Systems" as an example of his work in comparative history. Please see this essay in Beteille (1983).

5. Beteille concludes his critique of the comparative method in "Individualism and Equality" with a general concern for theory. As Beteille writes: "If we are to take equality seriously, we must enlarge the concept of equality....It is the task of social theory to recognize the diversity of human ends and to understand and interpret the ways in which each society seeks, according to its own historical circumstances, to reach a balance between the different ends it values" (Beteille 1986: 128).

6. William Connolly's recent commentary on our times under the very

title "Identity/Difference" shows us how the pair of identity and difference is a defining mark of our contemporary condition.

7. In response to Dumont, Beteille, further, argues: "As far as I am concerned, the co-existence of contradictory values is a common feature of all societies, and there is nothing peculiar to Germany in this" (Beteille 1987: 675). But who is making the claim that the co-existence of contradictory values is peculiar to Germany? Is Dumont making such a claim? As we have seen in a detailed reading of Dumont's view on this subject, Dumont himself makes the same argument that the co-existence of contradictory values is characteristic of our contemporary world.

8. Dumont asks Beteille to show where he has made the assertion that individualism entails equality. In the words of Dumont: "What I have actually written is very different from the overimple, absolute statement that the critic attacks. To remedy his lack of evidence, I must be pardoned for quoting a whole page from the beginning of From Mandeville to Marx" (Dumont 1987: 669). In this page, Dumont writes:

> But first to clarify the relationship between the holism / individualism contrast. There is a logical relation, in the sense that holism entails hierarchy while individualism entails equality; but in fact it is by no means the case that all holistic societies stress hierarchy to the same degree, nor do all individualistic societies stress equality to the same degree. On the one hand, individualism entails not only equality but also liberty; equality and liberty are by no means always convergent, and the combination of them varies from one society to another (Dumont 1977: 4).

When one reads closely the above lines of Dumont, one can see that some of the propositions in Beteille's critique of Dumont are implied here. Of course, in the quoted passage, Dumont does not use Simmel's distinction between individualism of equality and individualism of inequality, but he is sensitive to the Tocquevillian distinction between liberty and equality. Here we must note that though Beteille refers to Simmel's distinction between "individualism of equality" and "individualism of inequality," he does not trace it back to Tocqueville's distinction between liberty and equality. I have discussed this in my "Tocqueville as an Ethnographer of American Democratic Practice" (Giri 1989a).

9. It is true that Beteille and Dumont do not compare nation-states, but cultures and civilizations. But the key issue is whether their model of culture is based upon a state-centric discourse. My position is that

Dumont's earlier comparative method was based upon such a model.

10. Our transnational world is a world in the making. Transnational movements are not only transnational in their structural and organizational forms but also strive to embody a transnational consciousness what the noted theologian Teilhard de Chardin once called "the planetization of consciousness." This striving for a transnational consciousness remains much to be desired in the more familiar transnational corporations and interstate organizations. That is why I take transnational people's movements as an archetype of our contemporary transnational condition. I have discussed these issues in my doctoral work on the transnational movement of Habitat for Humanity.

11. In the words of Derrida: "We shall designate by the term differentiation the movement by which language, or any code, any system of reference in general, becomes historically constituted as a fabric of differences" (Derrida quoted in Ryan 1982: 15).

12. Here we can take note of Berry's recent efforts in reformulating the comparative method which is similar to our agenda of reconstruction. Berry urges us to carry out comparative study neither solely through "emic" nor "etic" categories—insider's point of view and analytical concepts—, but through developing what he calls "derived etics" (Berry 1990). Berry urges us first to start with a question in our own culture (what he calls "emic A"), then to move "to an attempt to use the same concept in another culture" ("imposed etic"), then discover the native construction of the theme under investigation in another culture ("emic B") and then finally compare two cultures in accordance with their own points of view viz. comparing the emic of one culture with the emic of another. After such rigorous exercise, the commonality between two cultures gives rise to what Berry calls "derived etics," which is neither emics nor etics. Our conventional comparative enquiry proceeds in an either or fashion. The categories of comparison are either native categories or the universal categories of the analyst. But making "derived etics" the basis of comparison will save us from the either / or pitfall. But for this doing fieldwork in both the cultures with the research strategy of "multi-locale ethnography" is a must.

REFERENCES

Appadurai, Arjun, 1988, "Introduction: Place and Voice in Anthropological Theory", *Cultural Anthropology* 3 (1): 16-21.

——, 1989, "The Global Ethnoscape: Notes and Queries for a Transnational Anthropology", Paper presented at the annual seminar on anthropological theory, School of American Research, Santa Fe, New Mexico.

Arizpe, Loudes, 1991 "The Global Cube", *International Social Science Journal* 130: 599-608.

Aschroft, Bill et al., 1989, *The Empire Writes Back: Theory and Practice in Post-Colonial Literatures*, London: Routledge.

Badie, Bertrand, 1992, "Comparative Analysis and Historical Sociology", *International Social Science Journal* 133: 319-327.

Balslev, Anindita N., 1991, *Cultural Otherness: Correspondence with Richard Rorty*, Shimla: Indian Institute of Advanced Study.

Barnett, Eve T., 1989, *Structuralism and the Logic of Dissent*, London: Macmillan.

Berry, John W., 1990, "Imposed Etics, Emics and Derived Etics: Their Conceptual and Operational Status in Cross-Cultural Psychology", In Thomas N. Headland et al. (eds.), *Emics and Etics: The Outsider/Insider Debate*, Newbury Park, CA: Sage.

Bryant, C.G.A. & D. Jarry (eds.), 1991, *Giddens' Theory of Structuration: A Critical Appreciation*, London: Routledge.

Beteille, Andre, 1969, "The Politics of 'Non-Antagoinistic Strata", *Contributions to Indian Sociology* (NS): 17-31.

——, 1977, *Inequality Among Men*, Oxford: Basil Blackwell.

——, 1979, "Homo Hierarhicus, Homo Equalis", *Modern Asian Studies* 13 (4): 529-548.

——, 1980, *Ideology and Intellectuals*, New Delhi: Oxford University Press.

——, 1983, *The Idea of Natural Inequality and Other Essays*, New Delhi: Oxford University Press.

——, 1986, "Individualism and Equality", *Current Anthropology* 27 (2): 121-134.

——, 1987a, *Essays in Comparative Sociology*, New Delhi: Oxford University Press.

——, 1987b, "On Individualism and Equality", *Current Anthropology* 18 (5): 672-677.

——, 1987c, Review of Louis Dumont's "A South Indian Sub-Caste", *Indian Social and Economic History Review.*

——, 1990a, "Observation on the Comparative Method", *Economic and Political Weekly* XXV (40): 2255-2263.

——, 1990b, "Race, Caste and Gender", *Man* (NS) 25: 488-504.

——, 1991 *Society and Politics in India: Essays in a Comparative Perspective*, London School of Economics Monograph in Anthropology.

——, 1992, *Religion as a Subject for Sociology*, Department of Sociology, Delhi School of Economics: Working Paper.

Betraux, Daniel, 1990, "Oral History Approaches to an International Social Movement", in Oyen 1990: 151-171.

Calderon, Fernando and Alejandro Piscitelli, 1990, "Paradigm Crisis and Social Movements: A Latin American Perspective", in Oyen, 1990.

Connolly, William E., 1991, *Identity/Difference: Democratic Negotiation of Political Paradox*, Cornell.

Dumont, Louis, 1977, *From Mandeville to Marx: The Genesis and Triumph of Economic Ideology*, Chicago.

——, 1980 (1966), *Homo Hierachicus*, Chicago.

——, 1986a, "Are Cultures Living Beings? German Identity in Interaction", *Man* (NS) 21: 587-604.

——, 1986b (1983), *Essays on Individualism: Modern Ideology in Anthropological Perspectives*, Chicago.

——, 1987, "On Individualism and Equality", *Current Anthropology* 28 (5): 669-677.

Geertz, Clifford, 1986, "The Uses of Diversity", *Michigan Quarterly Review*, Winter: 105-123.

Giddens, Anthony, 1991, "Structuration Theory: Past, Present and Future", in Bryant & Jarry 1991.

Giri, Ananta, 1989a, *Tocqueville as an Ethnographer of American Democratic Practice*, Department of History, The Johns Hopkins University: Term Paper.

——, 1989b, "Narratives of Creative Transformation: Constituting Critical Movements in Contemporary American Culture," *Dialectical Anthropology* 14: 331-343.

——, 1990, "The Condition of Postmodernity and the Discourse of the Body", Paper presented at the American Ethnological Society's Annual Conference on "Body in Society and Culture".

———, 1991a, "Notes of a Traveller from an Andhra Village", *Mainstream* (New Delhi): February 9, 1991.

———, 1991b, The Portrait of a Discursive Formation: Science as Social Activism and Cultural Criticism in Contemporary India, Paper prepared for National Institute of Science, Technology and Development Studies, New Delhi.

———, 1992a, "Understanding Contemporary Movements", *Dialectical Anthropology* 17 (1).

———, 1992b, Transnational Movements and the Challenge of Shacks: Habitat's Excitement of Building and the Contemporary Global Ethnoscape, Manuscript.

———, 1992c, "Units of Analysis and the Field of Study: Anthropological Encounter with the Postindustrial Society", *The Eastern Anthropologist,* 15 (3): 205-14.

———, 1992d, *Epistemological Crisis in Anthropology: The Case of the Quest for the Real Samoa,* G.B. Pant Social Science Institute: Occasional Paper.

Harvey, David, 1989, *The Condition of Postmodernity,* Cambridge, MA: Basil Blackwell.

Hannerz, Ulf, 1990, "Culture Between Center and Periphery: Towards a Macroanthropology", *Ethnos* 3-4, 200-216.

Kriesi, Hans, 1989, "New Social Movements and the New Class in Netherlands", *American Journal of Sociology* 84 (5): 1078-1117.

Kohn, Melvin (ed.), 1989, *Cross-National Research in Sociology,* Sage.

Kohn, Melvin, 1989, "Cross-National Research as an Analytical Strategy", in Kohn 1989: 77-102.

Kohn, Melvin et al., 1990, "Position in the Class Structure and Psychological Functioning in the United States, Japan and Poland", *American Journal of Sociology* 95 (4): 964-1008.

Lash, Scott, 1990, *Sociology of Postmodernism,* London: Routledge.

Marcus, George, 1986, "Ethnography of the Modern World System", in James Clifford and George Marcus (eds.), *Writing Culture,* California.

MacIntyre, Alasdair, 1991, "Incommensurability, Truth, and the Conversation Between Confucians and Aristotelians About Virtues", in Eliot Deutch (ed.), *Culture and Modernity,* Honolulu: University of Hawaii Press.

Marcus, George and Michael Fischer, 1986, *Anthropology as Cultural Critique: An Experimental Moment in the Human Sciences,* Chicago:

University Press.

McMichael, Phillip, 1992, "Rethinking Comparative Analysis in a Post-Developmental Context", *International Social Science Journal* 133· 351-365.

Mintz, Sidney , 1977 "The So-Called World System: Local Initiative and Local Response", *Dialectical Anthropology* 2: 253-270.

——, 1985, *Sweetness and Power: The Place of Sugar in Modern History*, NY: Viking.

——, 1987, "Author's Rejoinder", Symposium Review of "Sweetness and Power", *Food and Foodways* 2: 171-197.

——, 1991, "Comments on Articles by Tomich, McMichael and Rosebarry", Special Issues on Slavery in the New World: *Theory and Society* 20 (3): 383-392.

Molund, Stefan, 1991, "Sociology as Critical Understanding: An Interview with Andre Beteille", Stockholm: Anthropological Studies (48).

Nader, Laura, 1989, "Comparative Method", Paper presented at the American Anthropological Association's Annual Meetings, Washington, D.C.

Oyen, Else (ed.), 1990, *Comparative Methodology: Theory and Practice in International Social Research*, Sage.

Oyen, Else, 1990, "The Imperfection of Comparisons", in Oyen, 1990.

Ryan, Michael, 1982, *Marxism and Deconstruction: A Critical Articulation*, Baltimore: The Johns Hopkins University Press.

Sassen, Saskia, 1988, *The Mobility of Capital and Labor*, Cambridge: University Press.

Scheuch, Erwin K., 1990, "The Development of Comparative Research: Towards Causal Explanations", in Oyen, 1990.

Tilly, Charles, 1992, "Prisoners of the State", *International Social Science Journal* 133: 329-342.

Teune, Henry, 1990, "Comparing Countries: Lessons Learned", in Oyen, 1990.

Trouillot, Michel-Rolph, 1988, *Peasants and Capital*, Baltimore: The Johns Hopkins University Press.

Uberoi, J.P.S., 1978, *Science and Culture*, Delhi: Oxford University Press.

Visvanathan, Shiv, 1988, "On the Annals of the Laboratory State", in Ashish Nandy (ed.) *Science, Hegemony and Viloence: A Requiem for Modernity*, Delhi: Oxford University Press.

Chapter Eight

SOME CONTEMPORARY NOTES ON METHOD

THE CHALLENGE OF CONTEMPORARY TRANSFORMATIONS

Self, culture and society in our times bear the marks of fundamental processes of structural and discursive transformations. Our existing modes of collective organization in traditional, modern and the postmodern societies have been subject to disintegration and our familiar modes of collective representation and rhetorical habits seem to be losing their authenticity. Both in the realm of culture and social structure, discourse and social formation, our lives are embodiments of fundamental changes at work. Everywhere in our contemporary world, the familiar boundaries of self, culture and society are breaking down in the face a global onslaught. Our individual lives, cultural practices and social zones are no more bounded locales but are fields of mediation between the concrete and the abstract, particular and the universal, the case and the cosmos and the pregnant moment and the eternal Beyond. At the root of our practice in the realm of culture, psyche and society at the contemporary moment lies a fundamental urge to go beyond—beyond the domains of rules and conventions—and to create new values by participating in what the noted theologian of our times Teilhard de Chardin had once called "the planetization of consciousness".[1] In almost all the societies in our contemporary world, fundamental changes are taking place in invariably all the domains of our lives, in all the sub-systems of our social order be it economy or politics. But while changes are taking place in both culture and social structure, transformation in cultural values seems to be lagging behind the changes in our economy and politics. This lack of match between the pace of change in the field of cultural and structural transformation seems to be accentuated by our insufficient attention to the challenge of developing appropriate "technologies of the self"[2]—the challenge of cultivating new modes of care of the self and articulating new modes of practice for the Being. However, it is the transformation of the Being, his or her willingness to participate in our contemporary global process of renewal and expansion of consciousness that holds the key to our future.

In the context of this predicament of the Being and the Becoming, what is the challenge for the study of self, culture and society? What methods we ought to devise and reformulate in order that we can understand the work of self, culture and society in all its mystery and splendour? As students of the human condition, it calls for transformation from us as human beings—transformation of both our habits of the mind and the habits of the heart. It calls for transformation from us as creative agents by participating in new social and cultural movements of our times and by making the *Return of the Actor*[3] and the return of the prodigal son possible in our lives. One important aspect of the contemporary challenge for creativity relates to our methodological imagination and methodological praxis. In the contemporary context, the challenge for the transformation of our beings calls for sharpening our "commonsense" as possible methodological resources, reformulating our traditional tools of method and creating new methods of looking at the self and the other and their everchanging and complex configuration in the dynamics of culture and society. As a prelude to participating in this epochal creativity, we have to realize that a discourse on method is not simply an exercise in techniques of empirical research and social investigation, it is part of a meditation on life and it is not simply a question of external strategy that we apply to the objects of our study while as subjects we cling to our outmoded habits and old rhetorics.

THE COLLAPSE OF GRAND THEORIES

With this as a background, let us look at the challenge for articulating new methodological imagination posed to us by the processes of transformation at work in our lives. Our last decade has witnessed many changes which were never anticipated by the prevalent theories of society. Until changes took place in the realm of social structure—be it the apparent or the real collapse of socialism, the restructuring of the nation-state and the rise of powerful ethnic movements all over the world, sociologists and anthropologists stuck to their own models and predicted that our present stage is inevitably going to lead to a pre-conceived teleological stage of history—either socialism or nationalism. Socialism and nationalism have been two powerful myths of our times and these two myths of the modern world have provided key metaphors to our theories of culture and society.[4] Socialism and nationalism (the discourse of the nation-state) have been the two great summarizing discourses or "metanarratives"[5] which have held powerful grips in our minds. But with the collapse of these two metanarratives of socialism and the ideology of the nation-state (as it is evidenced from the challenge nation-states are facing both from the sub-national forces as well as from the transnational processes), what has also taken place is a crisis of metanarrative as a totalizing genre of theoretical practice. The collapse of socialism and the disillusionment with "statism" is a testimony of the creativity of the "particular" in the face of the all consuming womb of modernity which had started a global mission to annihilate all differences of space and culture.

The challenge to the metanarratives of modernity has also posed fundamental questions to the idea of theory if it has not made it completely redundant. Now there have been serious challenges to the idea of theory as a historical redeemer and as a totalizing gaze which raise fundamental questions to the prevalent models of relationship between theory and practice. What the contemporary processes of transformation reiterate is the inadequacy of theories of all kinds, especially the theories of a universalist and globalizing variety, to understand the wonderful world of human creativity and imaginative praxis. Theories could be light posts in our journey in life, but when accorded absolute supremacy and unquestioned loyalty, they also make us blind to the processes at work in self, culture and society. An important characteristic of our times is a realization of the violence of abstraction and a sensitivity to the creative and enriched concreteness of our lives. This sensitivity is creating the genealogical ground for the rise of new kinds of theories, theories which are less infected with a missionary zeal of incorporating all facts into a pre-conceived mould and theories which are more ethnographic. Cultural anthropology with its tradition of sensitivity to the particularities of culture and their nuanced description, thus, seems to be playing a very important role in the contemporary restructuring of theory. In anthropology itself, there is now a distinct shift from structure to practice and process.[6] But the restructuring of theory as an all encompassing process of renewal of our times is not simply confined to the disciplinary prerogatives of the anthropologists. It is an epochal turning point, a turning point in our imagination, a point made very poignantly not by an anthropologist but by a philosopher. As philosopher Richard Rorty tells us: "Human solidarity is to be achieved not by inquiry but by imagination, the imaginative ability to describe our strangers, those who are different from ourselves and to redescribe ourselves.....This is a task not for theory but for genres such as ethnography. That recognition would be part of a general turn against theory and towards narrative."[7]

A TURN TOWARDS NARRATIVE

For Rorty, the most important question about method, at present, is not the usual quarrel as to whether social sciences are scientific or hermeneutical. For Rorty, to pose the problem of method in an either / or fashion—as a problem of choosing either between the Galilean natural science or the Aristotelian human science—is "misguided".[8] According to him, "the current movement to make the social sciences 'hermeneutical' rather than Galilean makes a reasonable, Deweyan point if it is taken as saying: narratives as well as laws, redescriptions as well as predictions, serve a useful purpose in helping us deal with problems of society...But this protest goes too far when it waxes philosophical and begins to draw a principled distinction between man and nature, announcing that the ontological difference dictates a methodological difference."[9] Thus, Rorty challenges us: "...if we get rid of traditional notions of 'objectivity' and 'scientific method' we shall be able to see the social sciences as continuous with literature—as interpreting other people to us, and thus enlarging and deepening our sense of community."[10]

DESCRIPTION AS CHOICE

Rorty brings description to the heart of the problem. Even though Habermas[11] jokingly remarks that with Rorty cultural anthropology would be the most successful contender for human imagination after the death of philosophy, the preoccupation with description seems to characterize the community of discourse of our times from economics to discourse analysis. A general turn against theory and a movement towards humane description and narrative is also visible in the hard and the dismal science of economics. Here the work of Amartya Sen who laments the victimage of descriptive economics under the imperialism of prescriptive and predictive economics can provide us an illuminating starting point. For Sen, description is a matter of choice, indeed a matter of committed choice. In his essay "Description as Choice", Sen comments: "Philosophical discussions in the social sciences have tended to concentrate on prescriptive and predictive exercises, and as a consequence, the methodological issues involved in description have remained largely unexplored."[12] For Sen, "...description can be characterized as choosing from the set of possibly true statements or a subset on grounds of their relevance."[13] Sen, further, tells us: "...description can be motivated by predictive interest or prescriptive interest, but it may also have other motivations, and to confine attention only to predictive interest impoverishes the traditions of descriptive economics."[14] Sen shows the need for a descriptive method on the part of the economists who are usually interested in statistical profiles and in an aggregate picture. But Sen argues that even in such areas as the study of poverty, description of human necessities is a must in order that we can have adequate understanding of the predicament of poverty from the vantage point of human experience. Sen writes: "...the measurement of poverty must be seen as an exercise of description assessing the predicament of people in terms of prevailing standards of necessities."[15] According to Sen, "description of 'necessities' may be far from ambiguous. But the presence of ambiguity in a description does not make it a prescriptive act only one of ambiguous description."[16]

Sen's plea for description is a part of his plea for having a disaggregated view of the human condition rather than simply remaining satisfied with the totalizing portrait of an aggregate picture. Sen makes us sensitive to the difference between statistical aggregation and descriptive disaggregation in his studies on famine and hunger. For Sen, the predicament of hunger could be looked at in terms of two approaches—the food availability approach and the entitlement approach. While the former is preoccupied with aggregate food amount available to a particular society or community, the later gives primary importance to the "entitlement" condition of particular individuals and families. The entitlement approach seeks to explore who have entitlements over food and who do not have and also aims at describing their actual predicament in a society whose total food availability might be enormous. Sen's following arguments on the challenge of description vis-a-vis the study of hunger and public action require a detailed quotation:

One of the central differences between the availability approach and the entitlement approach is the necessarily disaggregative nature of the later, in contrast with the inherently aggregative picture, presented by the former. While it is possible to calculate how much food a country can command, and while such aggregative calculations of 'total food entitlement' for the economy as a whole may have some analytical value as one of the constituent elements in understanding the food situation affecting a particular economy, the idea of entitlements applies ultimately to particular individuals and families. .....in analyzing famines and hunger, it is often important to make a more disaggregative view of the economy than one might get from standard class analysis. Since the particular reference of entitlements analysis is to families and persons, any aggregation in analyzing movements of analysis has to be based on identifying similarities of circumstances that make such aggregation viable and useful....The skill of entitlement analysis would lie in being able to make use of these advantages of aggregation in understanding in a tractable way the influences affecting the fortunes of persons and families, without losing sight of the fact that it is the families and their members to whom entitlement analysis must ultimately relate.[17]

COMMITMENT TO HUMAN FREEDOM

Yes, ultimately are the particular individuals and families whose predicament has to be described! But is description the end all and be all of analysis? What happens after the description of the human condition? Do the students of the human condition who believe in "description as choice" have any stake beyond description? In the kind of descriptive method proposed by Amartya Sen, description as a methodological strategy has to be part of a broader struggle for the enhancement of people's capacities and capabilities. If human beings do not have the basic capacities to survive with dignity and realize their divine potentialities, then the challenge for descriptive analysis is to accept human freedom and basic capability as a matter of value. That means it is a value to which the students of the human condition with a descriptive method must be committed. Reformulating the argument of Sen for our purpose here, we can say that description as a method must accept "entitlement of people and the 'capabilities' these entitlements generate" as a matter of value.[18] Here it is essential to note Sen's reflection on freedom, his articulation of the linkage between food and freedom and his distinction between negative and positive freedom. Sen looks at individual freedom as a matter of social committment[19] and writes: "The capability to function is the thing that comes closest to the notion of positive freedom, and if freedom is valued than capability itself can serve as an object of value and moral importance."[20] Thus, for Sen, description as a methodological choice ought to be linked with a concern for human capabilities and the pursuit of positive freedom as a matter of value.

But what is the basis of value in our method of study? Is commitment to a value possible or, in fact, should it ever be our ideal? The question of value in the social sciences has been a matter of debate for the last two hundred years and since then much water has flown down the river. In what way, can we cultivate a commitment to values and what kind of values they ought to be? Before we attempt a provisional answer to this very complex question, it must be stressed that the students of the human condition with a descriptive method have often shied away from the question of commitment to values. Here anthropologist Clifford Geertz's work is a case in point. Geertz had also challenged us for a "thick description"[21] of the human condition, but in majority of his works Geertz seems to be hybernating inside the beautiful world of rituals and symbols without sensitivity to victimage and human suffering. Geertz provides us a "thick description" of the Balinese cockfight, but where are the human beings who are sacrificed as cocks in the Balinese Negara, in the theatre state of Bali? But it must be noted that in his recent work Geertz, the master of "thick description", seems to be coming out of his phase of "symbolic involution"[22] and pleading for certain readjustment in our rhetorical habits. He also urges us to have an "imaginative entry...into an alien turn of mind" in order to cope with the challenge of diversity characteristic of our times.[23] Geertz is also pleading for resisting temptation to quick judgments and cultivating a habit for "capacious" seeing. Thus, in his recent work, Geertz proposes some broad frame of mind to be tied to thick description. Even though this might not be a vocal commitment to human capabilities, this is certainly a commitment to human imagination. As Clifford Geertz challenges us: "Imagining difference....remains a science of which we all have need."[24]

To come back to our question of value vis-a-vis description as a methodological strategy, the key question is what kind of value? What is and what ought to be our basis of evaluation? Here I propose a very simple framework. Those forces and processes which enhance and are capable of enhancing the forces of life on Earth are objects of positive valuation while those forces and processes which destroy the forces of life on earth have to be condemned. Celebration of life can be a source of ultimate values which can help us go beyond the limits of extreme cultural relativism. Cultural relativism has played a vital role in fighting bigotry and intolerance in the traditional and the modern world, but there is also the need for some commitment to human values as values beyond their specific cultural manifestation. Cultivation of a universal value in one's spirit and consciousness is possible. For Jurgen Habermas, with the work of what he calls "discourse ethics", it is possible to go beyond the coloration of a particular form of life and to look at the question of justice and ethics from a universal point of view. In the words of Habermas: "Under the unrelenting moralizing gaze of the participant in discourse,...familiar institutions can be transformed into many instances of problematic justice."[25]

Bringing Rorty, Sen and Habermas together for the purpose of our reflection here, we might say that description of the human condition and deep reflection on our local conventions based upon these descriptions and as embodied in the practice of our "discourse ethics" would enable us to look at human values beyond particular cultural constructions and accept human life as a sacred value in itself. Considered from this point of view, the question of commitment is not the sole prerogative of grand theories or metanarratives. Description has it own commitment built into our method and, in fact, is a source of critical consciousness in our contemporary times.

DESCRIBING SYSTEMS OF DISPERSION

Reflection on description as a methodological strategy aptly suited for the study of self, culture and society in our times can be enriched by the seminal work of Michel Foucault in the field of discourse analysis. For Foucault, the study of a discursive field or what he calls "discursive formation" must provide us a description of the system of dispersion at work. For Foucault, what defines a discursive field is not any single or homogeneous proposition rather than the persistence of a theme. This persistence is not simply a synchronic equilibrium of elements at a particular time, it is also a movemental persistence where a focal theme persists in its continuous flow and widening of horizons. Foucault challenges us to go beyond the either/or construction of the field. For him, an analysis of the discursive field "would not try to isolate small islands of coherence in order to describe their internal structure; it would not try to suspect and reveal latent conflicts; it would study forms of division."[26] In dealing with the thematic persistence of a discursive field, for Foucault, "one is confronted with concepts that differ in structure and in the rules governing their use, which ignore or exclude one another, and which cannot enter the union of a logical structure.. (in the discursive field) One cannot discern a regularity, an order in their successive appearances, correlations in their simultaneity, assignable positions in a common space, linked and hierarchized transformations."[27] In this context, the challenge in dealing with a discursive formation is not simply to "reconstitute chains of inference" and "draw up tables of differences," but to "describe systems of dispersion."[28]

Foucault's plea for describing systems of dispersion of the

pervasive themes of a discurive field can be better understood in
the light of Paulo Friere's stress on describing and analyzing what
he calls the "generative themes" of social and cultural life.[29]
Friere urges us to investigate people's "generative themes" which
ultimately would enhance the capacity for freedom on the part of
ordinary men and women. For Friere, in understanding the
"genreative themes" of a particular culture and society, one is not
engaged in a hypotheses-testing exercise. As Friere makes it
clear: "The concept of a generative theme is neither an arbitrary
invention nor a working hypotheses that has to be proved. If it
were a hypotheses to be proved, the initial investigation would
seek not to ascertain the nature of the theme, but rather the very
existence or non-existence of themes themselves. In that event,
before attempting to understand the theme in its richness, its
significance, its plurality, its transformations..., and its historical
composition, we would first have to verify whether or not it is an
objective fact; only then could we proceed to apprehend it."[30]
Such an exercise, rather, involves "description of the situation".[31]
In the words of Friere: "When an individual is presented with a
coded existential situation..., his tendency is to split that situation.
In the process of decoding, this separation corresponds to the
stage we call the 'description of the situation', and facilitates the
discovery of the interaction among the parts of the disjoined
whole."[32] Friere, further, tells us: "...the process of searching for
meaningful thematics should include a concern for the links between themes, a concern to pose these problems as problems, and
a concern for their historical-cultural context."[33]

But the investigation of people's thematic universe cannot
stop only at the description of the themes and the discovery of
their essential linkages; it must inaugurate "the dialogue of education as the practice of freedom."[34] "The methodology of that
investigation must likewise be dialogical, providing the opportunity both to discover generative themes and to stimulate people's
awareness in regard to these themes. Consistent with the liberating purpose of dialogical education, the object of investigation is
not men..., but rather the thought-language men use to refer to

reality, and their view of the world, which is the source of their generative themes."[35] The people whose thematic universe an analyst is trying to understand are not simply objects of investigation, but are "co-investigators".[36]

In a dialogical investigation of "generative themes," "the thematics which have come from the people return to them—not as contents to be deposited, but as problems to be solved."[37] Such an exercise ultimately leads to cultural action for freedom on the part of both the analyst and the people. As Friere makes clear:

> The investigation of people's generative themes or meaningful thematics...constitutes the starting point for the process of action as cultural synthesis. Indeed, it is not really possible to divide the process into two separate steps: first, thematic investigation, and then action as cultural synthesis...In dialogical theory, this division cannot occur...Investigation-the first moment of action as cultural synthesis-establishes a climate of creativity which will tend to develop in the subsequent stages of action.[38]

TRIGONOMETRY OF CREATIVITY: TOWARDS AN ECOLOGICAL EXPLANATION

Thus, what we are witnessing in the work of Richard Rorty, Amartya Sen and Michael Foucault is a generalized turn away from systems and theories and a movement towards description. While description has to be at the centre of our methodological praxis, we cannot lose sight of the two other important dimensions of our methodological life: observation and explanation. Observation, description and explanation constitute the trigonometry of creativity as it relates to our practice as students of the human condition. As regards observation, we have to sharpen our common sense of seeing and hearing and transform our observation into an ability to see things beneath the surface and to see things in their inherent interconnenctedness. Explanation is also a challenge and our focus on description cannot shy away from the responsibility of providing explanation of the phenomenon under study. But the key question here is what kind of explanation should we be engaged in? Should it be a causal explanation or an ecological explanation? Cause and effect are still at work even in our times and we cannot dismiss them. But should we explain them in terms of first principles? Should we explain the subject under study in terms of a deterministic causal framework? The question of succession and a particular construction of a unidirectional time is central to our causal explanation. But in our preoccupation with succession or with successive stages, we lose sight of the process of simultaneity constituting the reality at hand. Especially in our times, as human geographers such as David Harvey and Edward Soja have told us, time is being supplanted by space as the fundamental constituent element of our consciousness and society.[39] In this context, our explanatory framework must be sensitive to the total context in which transformation is taking place; it must also be sensitive to the process of simultaneity besides the process of succession.

The challenge for explanation in our times requires us not to be preoccupied with definite or conclusive explanations, but to explain process and reality in an ecological context and in a mode of probability. Probability calls for a flexibility of mind. In his provocative paper—"Eienstein, Renoir, and Greely: Some Thought About Evidence in Sociology"—, sociologist Stanley Lieberson tells us about the significance of the probabilistic mode of explanation and theoretical engagement.[40] For Lieberson, there is an "elective affinity" between a correct description of social life and a probabilistic mode of explanation. As Lieberson tells us: "The first step is to recognize that we are essentially dealing with a probabilistic world and that the deterministic perspective in which most sociological theories are couched and which underlies the notion of a critical test is more than unrealistic, it is inappropriate. If theories are posed in probabilistic terms, i.e., specifying that a given set of conditions will alter the likelihood of a given outcome, not only will the reality of social life be correctly described, but we will also be freed from assuming that negative evidence automatically means that a theory is wrong."[41] In studying any phenomenon and trying to specify its causes, Lieberson urges us to understand that "it is one matter to conclude that the data support a given theory; it is another matter to conclude that with these data we are confident enough about our explanation to rule out alternative interpretations."[42] For Lieberson, "explaining an event is very different from evaluating or testing a theory....It means describing the most likely processes that could have led to a given outcome."[43] In this way, "a probabilistic perspective is both liberating and more demanding. It is liberating because deviations are not automatically grounds for rejecting a theory...In this sense, it should make theorists data friendly....On the other hand, such a perspective is more demanding because tests per se are inconclusive for accepting or rejecting theory."[44] So, Lieberson tells us that "a more realistic view of our subject matter will result if we adopt a probabilistic view of both theory and evidence and if we use a probabilistic perspective to link them."[45]

The same argument is also made by Ramakrishna Mukherjee in his agenda of "inductive sociology". For Mukherjee, "even though a phenomenon may be regarded as an accomplished fact, several relevant but contradictory 'explanations' are now clearly available with the continual accumulation of knowledge on the contextual reality to answer 'how' and 'why' the phenomenon had emerged, disappeared or assumed a new form (and/or content) in the given place-time bound situation. The 'explanations' are thus turned into 'alternatives' and task becomes not a mere explanation but the search for and the diagnosis of the best possible explanation at the existing stage of knowledge."[46]

Thus, a phenomenon can also be explained in a probabilistic manner by means of description of the ecology where it occurs. As one recent insightful commentator tells us: "An ecological constuctionism thus fits with and is informed by....a contextual logic."[47] What I call ecological explanation is very similar to what Frederick Steir has recently called "ecological constructionism" and let us hear Steir in details:

> When the observer is placed within her or his inquiry, we have a beginning for a reflexive methodology for research. In attempting to

hear their voices in our stories, and to provide for the mutualness so necessary to contextualize our research...we take seriously the idea of ecology...I mean ecology here in Bateson's sense, of a 'context' constituted by a fitting together of ideas....I have proposed that we understand the various mirrorings involved in locating the researcher in such an ecosystem. It is this premise that allows the idea of a co-construction to be doubly relevant, in that both the relational processes of the researchers, as well as the reciprocator / researcher interaction are 'understandables' that allow for our claim to emerge.[48]

Description of the total ecological context unlocks another door of creativity not only for the analyst but also for the reader and the listener. A researcher provides us a probabilistic explanation of the genealogy and the dynamics of the reality at hand based upon the description of the ecology of the object of study. But since this kind of explanation is based upon description—description of the ecology and habitat of the phenomenon under study—the reader or the listener also is able to see how far the explanation holds ground especially viewed in the light of the description offered. The analyst offers an approximate explanation of a process and a reality out of a bundle of equally possible explanations and the reader or the listener is free to choose the one that is the most convincing. On the otherhand, a commitment to "discourse ethics" and critical rationality on the part of the reader or the listener helps to rescue this kind of flexibility of mind and method from degenerating into narcissistic arbitrariness and methodological solipsism. Thus description of the human condition and an ecological explanation based upon this has a potential to engage all of us in a trigonometry of creativity and widen the horizon of our familiar universe of discourse.

NOTES

1. Teilhard de Chardin, *Man's Place in Nature: The Human Zoological Group* (London: Collins, 1966).

2. In his discussion of Foucault, Jurgen Habermas makes a distinction between technology of power and technology of self. Please see, Jurgen Habermas, *Philosophical Discourses of Modernity* (Cambridge, Massachusetts: The MIT Press, 1987). Also see, L.H. Martin, H. Gutman & P.H. Hutton (eds.), *Technologies of the Self: A Seminar with Michel Foucault* (Amherst: University of Massachussetts Press, 1988).

3. Alain Touraine, *Return of the Actor: Social Theory in Postindustrial Society* (Minneapolis: University of Minnesota Press, 1988).

4. Ananta Giri, "Contemporary Crisis of the Idea of the System", *Man & Development* (Chandigarh, India), December 1991: 1-11.

5. J.F. Lyotard, *The Postmodern Condition* (Manchester, 1984).

6. Please see, Sherry Ortner, "Theory in Anthropology Since the Sixties", *Comparative Studies in Society and History*, 1984; and Joan Vincent, "System and Process, 1974-1985", *Annual Review of Anthropology* 15: 99-119, 1986.

7. Richard Rorty, *Irony, Contingency and Solidarity* (Cambridge University Press, 1989), xvi.

8. Richard Rorty, "Method, Social Science and Social Hope". in Mihael T. Gibbons (ed.), *Interpreting Politics* (Oxford: Basil Blackwell, 1987), pp. 241-259, 245.

9. Ibid., p.248.

10. Ibid., p. 252.

11. Jurgen Habermas, *Moral Consciousness and Communicative Action* (Cambridge: Polity Press, 1990).

12. Amartya Sen, *Choice, Welfare and Measurement* (Oxford: Basil Blackwell, 1982), p. 432.

13. Sen, op. cit., 1982, p. 433.

14. Ibid., p. 447.

15. Amartya Sen, *Poverty and Famines: An Essay on Entitlement and Deprivation* (Delhi: Oxford University Press, 1981), p.2.

16. Sen, op. cit., 1982, p. 19.

17. Jeane Dreze and Amartya Sen, *Hunger and Public Action* (Oxford: Clarendon Press, 1989), pp.30-31.

18. Amartya Sen, *Resources, Values and Development* (Oxford: Basil Blackwell, 1984), p. 497.

19. Amartya Sen, "Individual Freedom as Social Commitment", *India International Centre Quarterly,* Spring 1990: 101-115.

20. Sen, op. cit., 1984, p. 316.

21. Clifford Geertz, *Interpretation of Cultures* (NY: Basic Books, 1973).

22. In his recent interpretation of the urban space in Morocco, Geertz writes: "Meanings of any value in human life are inevitably sunk in materialities" (Clifford Geertz, "Toutes Directions: Reading the Signs in an Urban Spra," *International Journal of Middle East Studies* 21: 291-306, 1989, p. 301). I have also discussed Geertz's turn in positions and perspectives in my, "Theatrical Man: Some Critical Notes on the Symbolic Anthropology of Clifford Geertz", unpublished manuscript.

23. Clifford Geertz, "Uses of Diversity", *Michigan Quarterly Review* (Winter 1986), p. 118.

24. Geertz, op. cit., 1986, p. 120.

25. Jurgen Habermas, *Moral Consciousness and Communicative Action* (Cambridge: Polity Press, 1990), p. 108.

26. Michel Foucault, *The Archaeology of Knowledge and the Discourse on Language* (NY: Pantheon, 1972), p. 37.

27. Ibid.

28. Ibid.

29. Paulo Friere, *Pedagogy of the Oppressed* (Penguin, 1972).

30. Ibid., p. 69.

31. Ibid., p. 77.

32. Ibid.

33. Friere, op. cit., 1972, p. 80.

34. Ibid., p. 69.

35. Ibid.

36. Ibid., p. 78.

37. Ibid., p. 94.

38. Ibid., p. 148.

39. David Harvey, *The Condition of Postmodernity* (Basil Blackwell, 1989) and Edward Soja, *Postmodern Geographies: The Reassertion of Space in Critical Social Theory* (London: Verso, 1989).

40. Stanley Lieberson, "Eienstein, Renoir, and Greely: Some Thought About Evidence in Sociology", *American Sociological Review* 57: 1-15, 1992.

41. Ibid., p. 7.
42. Ibid., p. 1.
43. Ibid., p. 10.
44. Ibid., p. 9.
45. Ibid., p. 13.
46. Ramakrishna Mukherjee, *What Will It Be: Explorations in Inductive Sociology* (Allied, 1979), p.
47. Frederick Steir, "Flexibility and Methodology: An Ecological Constructionism", in Frederick Steir (ed.), *Research and Reflexivity* (Sage, 1991), pp. 163-185, 181.
48. Steir, op. cit., 1991, p. 180.

Chapter Nine

SELF, OTHER AND THE CHALLENGE OF CULTURE

In its essence, literature is concerned with the self ; and the particular concern of the literature of the last two centuries has been with the self in its standing quarrel with culture... This intense conviction of the existence of self apart from culture is, as culture knows, its noblest and most generous achievement. At the present moment it must be thought of as a liberating idea without which our developing idea of community is bound to defeat itself.

—Lionel Trilling (1955:118)

The essential view of culture was modelled on an essentialist view of *person*, both of which assume a monolithic identity defined in terms of *difference* vis-a-vis other cultures and other persons. The essentialist concept of 'culture' was, so to speak, an expanded version of the western person, i.e., an identity concerned in terms of invariance, boundaries, and exclusion. Paradoxically, a truly 'postmodern' personhood means a radicalized individualism, in that it implies greater openness, i.e., a greater capacity to 'bracket' one's own reference points and to relate to *specific* others in creative, nonstereotyped ways.

—Alf Hornborg (1994: 234-235)

...the theoretical recognition of the split-space of enunciation may open the way to conceptualizing an *inter*national culture, based not on the exoticism of multiculturalism or *diversity* of cultures, but on the inscription and articulation of culture's *hybridity*. To that end we should remember that it is the 'inter'—the cutting edge of translation and negotiation, the *in-between* space— that carries the burden of the meaning of culture...And by exploring this Third Space, we may elude the politics of polarity and emerge as the others of our selves .

—Homi K. Bhabha (1994: 39)

THE PROBLEM

We are now in a paradoxical situation in both theory and practice vis-a-vis the work of self, other and culture in our lives and our reflections on these. Self, other and culture are significant categories now; they are not merely categories of analysis but are emotionally loaded vehicles for us in as much as they deeply structure and affect our identities and differences and their multiple constructions today. The contemporary world of thought in many ways revolve around the questions of self and other, identity and difference. But contemporary reflection is not sufficiently reflective about the paradox and challenge in which we are vis-a-vis the questions of self and other and in this paper I aim at mapping this field of discourse with its inherent contradictions.

First, let us take up the question of self. Some commentators now draw our attention to the rise of a "reflective self" in what they call late modern times or in the condition of postmodernity (Dallmayr 1985; Giddens 1991; Inglehart 1990). For them, the "reflective self" is not the same thing as the "modern aggrandizing individual" (Giddens 1991:209); it is not a minimalist self but an actor which is critical of itself and appreciative of the other. But these commentators do not critically analyze the distinction between individual as a product of society and occupant of role identity and the reflective self as a historical process and an ontological question. Building upon their work, it is tempting to think about recent traditions in self, society and culture in such terms: if modernity was characterized by a preoccupation with "possessive individualism", then postmodernism is a movement for the discovery of the self.[1] But these commentators do not realize that the articulated shift from the "possessive individual" to "reflective self" is an evolutionary challenge and an ideal for us which requires multidimensional struggle in self and society, at least paralleling the struggle that involved the birth of the individual from the wombs of all-consuming and all-encompassing communities during the birth of modernity. In this chapter, I present a scheme of the transformative self that can potentially invite us to realize the distinction between us as sociological individuals and reflective selves. I present the ontology and cosmology of the "reflective self"—its webs of interlocution as well as its non-discursive constitution, its ideal universalism and interactive commitment drawing on the seminal works of two important interlocutors of our times, Govind Chandra Pande (1982, 1989) and Charles Taylor (1989).

I present the scheme of an ideal self at somewhat great length because I believe that insufficient attention to it and inadequate realization of it has colored the way we relate to the other. On the one hand, contemporary movements of thought which radicalizes differences give us an impression that now we are more sensitive to the other, rather than just being preoccupied with ourselves. But these moves which emphasize difference represent a reversal of move from self to the other without realizing that mere sensitivity or invitation to the other is not enough, the question is what is the nature of this invitation and what is the nature of the self.[2] Thus, without work on self and without the transformation of the individual from an egotistic monad to a reflective self is it possible to realize that the non-self is also part of the self? I address this question in my subsequent meditation on the challenge of the other in our contemporary times. I discuss contemporary efforts to systematically erase the other for the sake of self and the accompanying politics of resentment in the name of identity and difference. Building upon the seminal work of William Connolly (1991), I argue that it is a capacity for ethicality on the part individuals which can help us come out of the paradox of simultaneous rhetorical valorization of the other and its systematic social annihilation in our present times.

The paradox that we face vis-a-vis the questions of self and other is accentuated when we confront the predicament of culture. On the one hand, contemporary thought celebrates the present age as an age of appreciation of cultural diversity. But in reality, new boundaries and new rhetorics of exclusion are now being created in the name of culture (Stolcke 1995). In Europe, North America, and many parts of the world immigrants and aliens with a different culture are the targets of attack and exclusion. In the present chapter, I map this field of discourse but I argue that the contemporary "fundamentalism of culture", as Stolcke characterizes the new practice of exclusion, cannot be solved by electoral politics and state action alone; it also requires a reflexive mobilization of self as the actor of culture and its creative embodiment.

SOURCES OF SELF

What is the meaning of self in this presentation? It is that depth and reflective dimension within oneself which has the capacity to critically look at the given of social and cultural life and create a good society. It is that dimension within individual life which "generates programmes of actualization and mastery" (Giddens 1991: 9) and becomes an agent of criticism, creativity, and transformation. The nature and source of this reflective self has been recently described for us by Charles Taylor. Taylor's self is not simply a sociological individual, an occupant of social roles whom Ralf Dahrendorf had characterized as "Homo Sociologicus" long ago.[3] For Taylor, ".... we are selves insofar as we move in a certain space of questions, as we seek and find an orientation to the good. Our orientation in relation to the good requires not only some framework(s) which define the shape of the qualitatively higher but also a sense of where we stand in relation to this" (Taylor 1989: 35, 42). For Taylor, "the modern aspiration for meaning and substance in one's life has obvious affinities with longer-standing aspirations to higher being, to immortality" (Taylor 1989: 43). The work of self is characterized by a "radical reflexivity". Presenting the thoughts of St. Augustine, Taylor thus writes: "....radical reflexivity takes on a new status, because it is the 'space' in which we effect the turning from lower to higher" (Taylor 1989: 40). Self also has a depth dimension which is described by Taylor thus: "The inescapable feeling of depth comes from the realization that there is always more down there. Depth lies in there being always, inescapably, something beyond our articulating power" (Taylor 1989: 390). Thus an inquiry into self is "not only a phenomenological account but an exploration of the limits of the conceivable in human life, an account of its transcendental conditions" (Taylor 1989: 32).

In social thought the view that self is born of interaction has a long tradition and probably one of its most distinguished articulators in modern times has been George Herbert Mead who argues that the self is born of and realized in interactions with others. But though self is born of social interaction, Taylor argues that it nonetheless has a transcendental dimension. It is its transcendental dimension which enables the realization of what Mead himself states: "What is essential to communication is that the symbol should arouse in oneself what it arouses in the other individual" (quoted in Habermas 1987: 15). But a stress on the depth dimension or the non-reducible dimension of self cannot ignore its crucial dependence on interaction with the other either. In Taylor's view, the view of self as containing the universe but "bypassing any necessary relation to other humans" "do nothing to lift the transcendental conditions" (Taylor 1989: 39).

Taylor urges us to pay adequate attention both to the "webs of interlocution" or webs of interaction and the non-reducible transcendental dimensions in the sources of the self. Some protago-

nists of self such as the Romantics and the American transcen-
dentalists define themselves explicitly in relation to no web at all.
But Taylor argues that even though we may "sharply shift the
balance in our definition of identity, dethrone the given, historic
community as a pole of identity, and relate only to the community
defined by adherence to the good, this doesn't severe our dependence on webs of interlocution. It only changes the webs, and the
nature of our dependence" (Taylor 1989: 39). For Taylor, "...a
common picture of the self, as (at least potentially and ideally)
drawing its purposes, goals, and life plans out of itself, seeking
'relationships' only insofar as they are 'fulfilling', is largely based
on ignoring our embedding in webs of interlocution" (ibid). But at
the same time, to reduce self only to webs of interlocution is to
miss a great deal about the nature of the self. One important locus
of self lies in its detachment from webs of interlocution as well.
For Taylor, such a locus has been emphasized in the spiritual
traditions of western civilization, which "have encouraged, even
demanded, a detachment from the second dimension of identity as
this is normally lived, that is, from particular, historic communities, from the given webs of birth and history" (Taylor 1989: 36).
"In the writings of the prophets and the Psalms, we are addressed
by people who stood out against the almost obloquy of these
communities in order to deliver God's message. In a parallel
development, Plato describes a Socrates who was firmly rooted
enough in philosophical reason to be able to stand in imperious
independence of Athenian opinion" (Taylor 1989: 37).

This detached aspect of self has not received adequate attention in modern social thought. True, scholars such as Jurgen
Habermas (1990a) speak of the capacity of taking a hypothetical
attitude to culture on the part of an individual but they do not
explore the deeper sources of the self which makes this detachment possible (see, Giri 1995).[4] For Habermas, a critical insight
of cognitive distantiation is born of one's participation in rational
deliberation on the problems of life. Similar is also the approach
of a scholar such as Seyla Benhabib. In her project on self,

Benhabib (1992) states that the challenge is now to work out the agenda of an "interactive universalism", an importaᵣ. aspect of which is "the vision of an embodied and embedded human self whose identity is constituted narratively" (Benhabib 1992: 6).

But does the narrative of the self exhaust its sources? Probably not. Apart from interactive universalism, to talk of the self is also to talk of ideal universalism. This is a point emphasized by Indian philosopher Govind Chandra Pande: "It is only a self which is conscious of its ideal universality that can distinguish values from appetites, pleasures, and selfish interests and become the moral subject. It is the notion of the ideal self which is the source of the moral law on which social unity and coherence depend. The being or reality of person is in self-consciousness which contains within itself a tension between ideality and actuality. The ideal self is not an abstract model designed in the interest of social usefulness but the ultimately real transcendental subject in which immediacy and coherence or non-contradiction both coalesce" (Pande 1982: 113-114). The idea of ideal universalism is a "powerful ideal for us" even in modern times; though by no means it takes us out of the "original situation of identity-formation," it nevertheless "transforms our position within it" "however little we may live up to it in practice..." (Taylor 1989: 37).

Pande stresses on two aspects of "ideal universalism" as an attribute of the self, which deserves our careful consideration. First, though "an ideal is neither an actual thing nor a mere thought nor a logical form," yet its reality in society and history is "undeniable" (Pande 1982: 101). For Pande, "the socio-historical world would be inconceivable without the moving force of ideals" (ibid). Second, Pande urges us to realize the non-discursive dimension of self which is usually thought of as a product of discourse. Pande argues that the non-discursive dimension of self has been most poignantly articulated in the Indian philosophical tradition. Pande begins with an acknowledgment that the view that "knowledge and reality belong to several corresponding levels and that the way to the highest is prepared by philosophy as a dialectical examination of ideas is common to western idealism, as exemplified in Plato and Hegel, and the Indian traditions of Buddhism and Vedanta" (Pande 1982: 103). But while in Plato and Hegel self consciousness remains "continuous with human social experience" the Indian philosophical attitude, on the other hand, "interprets the absolute level of reality to correspond to non-discursive knowledge in which the sense of social difference is overcome by spiritual unity" (ibid). "Social reality thus corresponds to an intermediate level in the dialectic of consciousness, a level where the self is not seen as a mere object nor is the object seen as merely self" (ibid). Thus, for Pande, contra-Habermas, self is not constituted of language and discourse alone. Self is constituted of the dialectic between immanence and transcendence, silence and language, eternity and history, ideal universalism and interactive universalism.

How does such a self relate to the other? A self guided by ideal universalism considers it its duty to overcome the distinction between self-regarding activities and other-regarding activities.[5] In pursuing one's self-interest, a self conscious of its ideal universality and responsive to its interactive community, also helps or becomes a medium in the realization of the interests of the other.

THE CHALLENGE OF THE OTHER

Such a view of a reflective and transformative self is now crucial for dealing with the problem of the other. The "other" was once banished from the aggrandizing agenda of modern individualism. The colonialist self of the modern individual could only register the other in its map at the moment of conquest. But now because of decolonization and democratization as the colonialist self is slowly transforming itself into a sharing self, the other now refuses total incorporation into the self. To put this in the words of Derrida, differences now are transforming themselves into "differences" in as much they resist total incorporation into the system through a process of deferral (see, Barnett 1989).

Postmodernism is supposed to be a moment of celebration of the other, a moment of inviting the other into the self.[6] But despite the self-congratulation of postmodernism, the other at present is still being incorporated into a colonizing self and being erased from the face of the earth. The new racism in Europe, anti-immigration movements in North America, and ethnic fratricide in almost all parts of the world are vivid reminders of the unfinished task before us insofar as the question of inviting the other into self is concerned.

The other is still being systematically erased now and, what is more, democratic politics is contributing to this erasure. William Connolly provides us a graphic portrayal of the systematic erasure of the other in the political theater of late capitalism. Welfare recipients and terrorists are the most prominent others in the "culture of sacrifice" that politics in late-capitalist state creates (Connolly 1991: 210). In advanced industrial societies, the failure of welfarism "provides an outlet for generalized resentment" which electoral politics exploits. The welfare class becomes an other in the electoral politics of the state which becomes the object of erasure. In the words of Connolly: "The welfare class thus becomes a permanent demonstration project on the theatricality of power" (Connolly 1991: 208). "It becomes a dispensable subject of political representation and an indispensable subject of political disposability" (ibid). Similar is also the approach to the other "other" in late capitalist discourse, namely, the problem of terrorism. Terrorism as an other "provides domestic constituencies with agents of evil to explain the vague experience of danger, frustration, and ineffectiveness in taming global contingency" (Connolly 1991: 207). As Connolly argues, "terrorism, as the other constituted by the state system, allows the state and the interstate system to protect the logic of sovereignty in the international sphere while veiling their inability to modify systemic conditions that generate violence by non-state agents" (ibid). "The moral isolation of non-state violence from other modalities of violence produces multiple effects... it deflects attention from deficiency in state efficacy with respect to environment, inequality, and co-existence with third-world peoples" (ibid).[7]

Anti-welfarism, which aims at erasing the internal other from the space of attention and significance in advanced industrial societies, and anti-terrorism, which aims at erasing the external other, gives rise to a politics of resentment.[8] In such a situation, "electoral politics contains powerful pressures to become a closed circuit for dogmatism of identity through the translation of difference into threat and threat into energy for the dogmatization of identity" (ibid). One significant instance of this dogmatization of identity is the recent anti-immigration law in California which debars state benefits in health and education to the children of the illegal immigrants residing there.

If such is the incapacity of electoral politics to deal with the problem of the other what is required is a moral politics of the self which grants legitimacy to the needs and aspirations of the other. Jurgen Habermas's analysis of the problem of poverty and disadvantage in advanced industrial societies leads to such a suggestion. For Habermas, while in the classical phase of capitalism capital and labour could threaten each other for pursuing their interests, today "this is no longer the case" (Habermas 1990b: 19). Now, the underprivileged can make their predicament known primarily through a "protest vote" but "without the electoral support of a majority of citizens...problems of this nature do not even have enough driving force to be adopted as a topic of broad and effective public debate" (Habermas 1990b: 20). In this context, a moral politics of self is the answer as Habermas argues: "A dynamic self-correction cannot be set in motion without introducing morals into the debate, without universalizing interests from a normative point of view" (ibid). The same moral politics of self is required in dealing with the problem of terrorism as the other "other". Terrorist violence may represent some sub-national aspirations within a state-system which calls for sympathetic understanding of the systematic indignity that terrorists have gone through which is one of the factors for the rise of terrorism. It is a moral politics of self which is required in addressing other global contingencies such as environmental disaster, world poverty, and the inequality between the North and the South. In the words of Habermas: "The moral or ethical point of view makes us quicker to perceive the far-reaching, and simultaneously less insistent and more fragile ties, that bind the fate of an individual to that of every other making even the most alien person a member of one's community" (ibid).

We are indeed now in a paradoxical situation insofar as the problem of the other is concerned. The paradox is that "we cannot dispense with personal and collective identities, but the multiple drives to stamp truth upon those identities function to convert differences into otherness and otherness into scapegoats created and maintained to serve the appearance of true identity" (Connolly 1991: 67). For Connolly, ethicality—an ethicality whose main motive is an appreciation of difference—can disturb the self-closure of identity. By encouraging bonding through differentiation, ethicality can transform the demand for an "all embracing identity," leading to the loss of the power that a fixed moral code exercises over the self (Connolly 1991: 167). Connolly also believes that democratic politics can disturb the self closure of identity too. But given his own discussion of the degeneration of democratic politics into a politics of erasure of difference, what has to be stressed is the ethical problematization of the fixation of identities and the denial of differences. What is more, development of certain technologies of self can contribute towards a relativization of one's absolute identity. As Connolly argues: "Most people have experienced gaps between the identity ascribed to them and subversive orientations to life that press upon them...Attention to these gaps can encourage the cultivation of genealogical history, and genealogical histories can accentuate the experience of contingency in identity" (Connolly 1991: 183).

In this context, Connolly himself speaks of the need for the emergence of an "overman" in us. Connolly argues that in the contemporary condition, the "overman" is not a special caste or a social type but is a voice within the self fighting with other voices including the politics of resentment. Overman is a creative dimension in all of us which is critical of the motive to dominate, erase, and annihilate the other. Overman is not the Nietzchian Superman but the higher self in us and is not a vehicle of the "aesthetics of empowerment" (cf. Unger 1987; also Harvey 1989) but the vehicle of an "ethics of obligation" (Drucker 1993). At the same time, the overman is the universalized person in us which can help us develop a reflective stance towards our ego and an appreciative stance towards the predicament and possibility of the other. Moreover, the overman is that dimension in the self which provides us the capacity for self-sacrifice and renunciation—a capacity without which not only the primitive societies and their world of gift and exchange cannot function but also contemporary advanced societies. As Roberto Unger (1987) tells us, without the personalist program of sacrifice and renunciation which is a program of a creation of a "good society" (Bellah et al. 1991), the program of democracy is doomed to fail. But for Unger, a citizen renounces his need for security not only because of "the guarantee of immunity afforded by a system" but because of a spiritual commitment to transformation. "Its higher spiritual significance consists in the assertion of transcendence as a diurnal context smashing" (Unger 1987:579). It is no wonder then that in outlining his agenda of reconstruction and transformation Unger speaks of two kinds of sacred order—the social and the transcendental—and argues that once the social loses touch with the transcendental then we are bereft of our capacity for criticism and creativity. The social order then becomes a devil's world where God chooses to go into hibernation (Giri 1994; Hebermas 1981; Sri Aurobindo 1950).

Unger's outline of a reconstructive movement points to the spiritual foundation of our critical reflection and collective action in the context of the contemporary predicament of the self and the other. In my reading of Unger I would like to draw this lesson for the problem at hand that without spiritual work on the self it is difficult to accept the other as part of the self or to realize that the non-self is also self. Thus, we have to rethink our identity as the sociological individual and discover the transcendent and the universal dimension within ourselves.

THE PREDICAMENT OF CULTURE

If such is the predicament and possibility with regard to self and other, then what about the contemporary predicament of culture? On the one hand, contemporary changes urge us to recognize cultural difference which is articulated by Clifford Geertz thus: "Imagining difference remains a science of which we all have need" (Geertz 1986: 120). For Geertz, now that, "foreignness does not start at the water's edge but at the skin's", "there is need for a certain readjustment in both our rhetorical habits and sense of mission" (Geertz 1986: 119). But, on the other hand, now there seems to be a new process of creation of the other in the name of culture at work. Anthropologist Verena Stolcke tells us how new boundaries and new rhetorics of exclusion are now being created in Europe in the name of culture (Stolcke 1995). Stolcke characterizes it as a new racism which works through the logic of what she calls "cultural fundamentalism" and is different from the "old racism" which emphasized physical inferiority (Stolcke 1995: 4). In her view, "from what were once assertions of the differing endowment of human races there has risen since the seventies a rhetoric of inclusion and exclusion that emphasizes the distinctiveness of cultural identity, traditions, and heritage among groups and assumes the closure of culture by territory" (Stolcke 1991: 1). This creation of exclusion in the name of culture is most evident in the anti-immigration rhetoric and law in Europe. According to one commentator, "immigrants threaten to "swamp" us with their alien culture and if they are allowed in large numbers, they will destroy the 'homogeneity of the nation'. At the heart of this new racism is the notion of culture and tradition" (Barker quoted in Stolcke 1995: 3). While earlier racism inferiorized the other, the new racism, in the name of culture, can even assert the "absolute, irreducible *difference* of the "self" and the incommensurability of different cultural identities (Stolcke 1995: 4).

Stolcke argues that contemporary cultural fundamentalism's

rhetoric of exclusion and its reification of cultural difference draws, for its argumentative force, "on the contradictory 19th-century conception of the modern nation-state which assumed that the territorial state and its people are founded on a cultural heritage that is bounded, compact, and distinct..." (Stolcke 1995: 12). A way out of the erasure of the other in the name of culture requires going beyond such politicization of culture and the accompanying conflation between society and culture and state and culture. According to Stolcke, "genuine tolerance for cultural diversity can flourish without entailing disadvantages only when society and polity are democratic and egalitarian enough to enable people to resist discrimination (whether as immigrants, foreigners, women, blacks) and develop differences without jeopardizing themselves and solidarity among them" (Stolcke 1995: 13). But it is instructive that Stolcke herself writes in the very next line of her essay: "I wonder whether this is possible within the confines of the modern nation-state or, for that matter of any state"(ibid). Thus, Stolcke is sensitizing us to the limits of the state-centric approach in dealing with the problem of the other and the fundamentalism of culture though others characterize her diagnosis as utopian.[9]

It is precisely the utopian dimension in self and culture that needs to be retrieved, articulated, and lived by at the contemporary juncture. The tendency to erase an "other" because of difference of culture cannot be fought only at the level of state and now creative responses to it has to be explored in the domains of self and culture. Earlier in this essay while dealing with the problem of the erasure of the other, I have argued that the problem of the other[10] cannot be solved unless we also work on self—understand its depth dimension, and transform ourselves from mere "role identities" to "reflexive selves". Now I want to make a similar argument vis-a-vis culture. To creatively confront the predicament of culture, there is also a need to revitalize the reflective self as the creator of culture and as its creative embodiment. Every culture has a dimension of "beyond"[11] within it which resists its absolutization and political fixation and it is important to understand this ideal dimension of culture in order to be able to respond to the contemporary predicament of culture. Every culture has and ought to cultivate a "metaculture" which can radicalize both culture and self (Bidney 1967; Hannerz 1990; Robertson 1992; Nandy 1995).

Culture can play a transformative role in overcoming the distinction between self and other and in confronting the challenge of fundamentalism. But the significance of culture in the realization of freedom has not received much attention in the works of Connolly, Unger, and Taylor. For this, we would have to turn not to anthropologists who have abandoned their own ancestor Edward Sapir's distinction between "genuine culture" and "spurious culture" in the name of cultural relativism (see Bidney 1967; Giri 1992) but to the normative seekers of culture who look at it as a process of spiritual praxis or *sadhana*. Such an outline of culture is found in the seminal work of Govind Chandra Pande. According to Pande, "the awareness of culture begins with the discrimination of the ideal and the actual, of what is appropriate to the self or authentic and what is merely given or appears forced upon the self. It is the awareness of an ideal order which constitutes a worthy end or goal of man's authentic seeking. The ideal is not given or importunate like the actual, limiting human freedom since freedom lies in the voluntary choice of ends worthy of realization" (Pande 1993: 23).

As we proceed with the challenge of culture as a transformative seeking, it has to be noted that culture always has had two meanings— culture as a lived practice or a pattern implicated in a field of power and culture as a domain of seeking of values. As Edward Said argues, " 'culture' means two things in particular. First of all it means all those practices, like the arts of description, communication and representation, that have relative autonomy from the economic, social, and political realms. Second and almost imperceptibly, culture is a concept that includes a refining and elevating element, each society's reservoir of the best that has been known and thought as Matthew Arnold put it in the 1860s" (Said 1993: xiii). Explicating the second meaning of culture, Said tells us: "Culture palliates, if it does not altogether neutralize, the ravages of a modern, aggressive, mercantile, and brutalizing urban existence. You read Dante or Shakespeare in order to keep up with the best that was thought and known, and also to see yourself, your people, society, and tradition in their best lights" (ibid). But these two meanings are not mutually exclusive; in fact every lived culture contains within it a dimension of ideal seeking vis-a-vis self-realization, modes of inter-subjectivity, and the constitution of a good society. It is this dimension of meaning of culture which is in urgent need of recovery and reconstruction today to face with the challenge of the self and the other, a task in which we get enough resource and inspiration from Pande.

Continuing the reflective engagement with culture, Pande argues that "all cultural experience includes not merely a subjective but an intersubjective reference as well as a dimension of valuation" (Pande 1982: 22). "The sense of identification or alienation, appreciation or rejection, a sense of concern for what is significant for the self are pervasive ways of culture experience, which could be described as an experience of self-realization in some form" (ibid). Pande believes that "not only can one not tell the dancer from the dance, but the spectator must forget and rediscover himself in the spectacle" (ibid). For Pande, "the thinker incarnates himself in his thoughts, even the cook would be hurt if his cooking were not treated as representing him appropriately. Genuine participation in culture is a process in which the 'the subject is realized, the object idealized' " (ibid).

Reminding us of Taylor's "radical reflexivity", Pande argues: "It is only with reflective consciousness that the subjective-objective world of culture can be apprehended" (Pande 1982: 23). This reflective consciousness is characterized by a capacity to discriminate—"to discriminate right from wrong," "higher from lower emotions" (ibid). The "discriminative critical character of the consciousness" makes cultural seeking dialectical. Culture, for Pande, is a dialectical process of value seeking. In the words of Pande, ".. to seek a value is to seek progress in infinite direction, for it is in the nature of value to be a standard of perfection which judges all attainments to fall short of ideal. Thus, where as nature has no history, culture as value-seeking is inherently historical as it is bound up with a social and symbolic tradition within which its dialectical and 'developmental' process operates" (Pande 1982: 25).

For Pande, "value implies seeking, choosing, approving" (ibid). "Value seeking... tends to be a dialectical and progressive process where ideally one moves towards a perfect and infinite realization in which the immediacy of feeling and cognitive certitude would be found together. Such a state would be the unity of being and knowledge, in which the self or consciousness realizes itself fully... From the lower realization of the self in terms of finite accidents (*upadhis*) to their complete transcendence in pure self-experience, the human seeking follows a process of dialectical evolution" (ibid).

Pande urges us to realize that the "dialectic of value-seeking is the dialectic of self-transformation through the interaction of vision and praxis. It implies not merely progress within a plane of consciousness but a change in the plane of consciousness" (Pande 1982: 26-27). Indeed this change in the plane of consciousness is in fact the promise and challenge of culture. Let us hear Pande in greater details: "All praxis is designed to subordinate or sacrifice the lower to the higher so that the object to be used by the ego and ego itself are offered to and become the vehicle of a higher consciousness. Insofar as the lower is used to reveal the higher, it may be said to assume the character of a symbol. The primary origins of cultural traditions, thus, lie in the revelation or discovery of new meanings in phenomena given at various levels, a process which begins in individual psyche but enters social tradition creatively as a symbol" (Pande 1982: 28).

Pande argues that "culture as a pervasive moral order binds society and civilization and gives them a characteristic identity and direction" (Pande 1982: 28-29). "Whether it is the order or immediate affective relations as in a family or the cooperative and quid pro quo of the techno-economic order, or the legal-political order backed by force, the moral order is pervasive. Without an immediately felt but objectively recognized, coherent order of duties and obligations no society or civilization can even survive, let alone develop. This moral order presupposes the formulation of the vision of the good into a path of praxis leading up to it... It is as moral faith which mediates between vision and praxis that culture animates society and civilization" (Pande 1982: 29).

CONFRONTING THE CHALLENGE

Pande's outline of culture as a dialectical, transformative, and transfigurative seeking of values suggests a creative way out of the impasse revolving around the politics of identity and difference, and the predicament of the self and the other. But in order to appreciate the work of self and culture as transformative factors in our lives we need to be reflective about both nationalism and individualism which share the same "epistemology of entivity" and boundedness (Foster 1991). We have to give radically new meanings to familiar categories of self, other, and culture in both theory and practice. Revitalizing the reflective dimension in all these through the work of criticism and creativity is essential to take us out of the impasse in which we are today. This cannot be done by essentializing either the self or the other but discovering what Ashis Nandy (1995) calls "the other within" and Clifford Geertz (1986) calls our "variant subjectivity".

Culture is important from many different ends today. Culture plays an important role in the dynamics of the economy at present. As Scott Lash and John Urry (Lash and Urry 1987) argue, culture is not simply an object of production now, production itself is becoming increasingly cultural. Thus, it is no wonder then that the production of aesthetically beautiful and lofty apartments is a vital part of the speculative regime of late capitalism today. But Lash and Urry do not analyze the human cost of such an economy and the enormous problem of homelessness that the shift of capital from production to speculation in lofty real estate creates. Their account of the shifting trajectory of capitalism and its increasing cultural turn is devoid of a normative criticism. We here need a cultural criticism of contemporary capitalism as an institutional regime. As Alf Hornborg argues: "The counterdrive to total commoditization is the cognitive discrimination we know as culture" (Hornborg 1993: 317). Here again Pande's project of culture as a dialectic of "self-transfiguration" can be of immense help to all of us who believe that the task of social and cultural analysis is not merely to describe the systems which govern our lives but to provide them a transformative direction.

To speak of culture and the contemporary condition without speaking of the communications revolution underway in the present-day world would be an incomplete exercise. Now television is a household reality for many of us in all corners of the world. Television has helped to dissolve the distinction between the "high culture" and "low culture" and we must not fail to acknowledge the democratizing potential in this dissolution. But at the same time we have to realize that television has made us consumers of culture, making us believe that the vicarious consumption of culture is the same thing as its creation (see, Das 1984, 1993). But if many of us become consumers of culture when culture means soap operas, media-steered system images and advertisements for the system of money and power then what is the fate of culture as a source and process of transformation?

A contemporary meditation on self, other and culture cannot absolve itself of the obligation of what I would like to call criticism and creativity. The challenge for us is to continue to create culture in an age where culture itself has been made an object of consumption and commodification. When consumption of what on an average is understood as culture seems to be our new weltanschauung—our new *yugadharma*—the task for us is to recover the ground where cultural creativity as a *sadhana* of self and institutional transformation becomes a powerful ideal in our individual lives and in our public sphere. It is needless to mention that the realization of such a task requires multi-dimensional effort at both individual and collective levels.

Creation of culture is a work of *sadhana*. It is a work of

silence. But the culture of TV is the culture of the bombardment of words (Miller 1988). So the first step is to learn to be silent in our age of communications revolution. Silence would help us realize that if we watch television four hours a day or even two hours a day then even God cannot help us from being slipped into what Baudrillard calls the "silent majority" and Toyenbee called "the uncreative majority". But this desired silence may not come so spontaneously. The struggle for the meaning of culture in the next century may begin with the breaking of television sets which would complete the unfinished agenda of transformation inaugurated by the Luddite breaking of the machines of industrial production in the last century.

NOTES

1. Developments in social thought in the modern West in the past three hundred years demonstrate an oscillating preoccupation with the questions of self and other. The birth of modernity was characterized by the birth of the individual from the wombs of all-consuming and all-encompassing communities. Modern thought was intensely preoccupied with the problem of the individual—his genesis, her development, his autonomy, and her freedom. Modernity was a moment of the celebration of individualism. In this celebration there was very rarely a distinction made between individual and the self; it was assumed that individual as an occupant of social role identity exhausted the sources of the self and its design of becoming. In other words, modern thought confused the individual as a product of society with self which is something reflexive in nature. It is only with the case of some thinkers such as Marcel Mauss that we find a description of the work of the self in the project of modernity. Mauss tells us how modern western self has arisen in the context of many critical religious movements such as anabaptism. Mauss does not reduce self to the sociologically determined individual and gives it a critical dimension—a creative and

transformational dimension. But this stress of Mauss is not emphasized in the later commentaries on Mauss, especially by the contributors of *The Category of Person* and by Andre Beteille (1992) who also discusses Mauss's thought on the subject in his essay, "Individual, Person, and Self as Subjects of Sociology."

2. But in such moves of reversal, when the other is invited, who invites the other is still a "possessive individual" or a bourgeoisie individual whose main interest lies in the valorization of his own interest and power. Let us consider, for instance, certain developments in anthropological imagination which are called postmodern and reflexive. Postmodern developments within anthropology plead for listening to the voices of the Other and narrating that story without the control of the "ethnographic authority" of the anthropologists. But if the anthropologist himself does not have capacity for otherness, then the whole project of an anthropology inviting the other would fail. As Adam Kuper tells us in a recent critique: "The first wave of post-modernist ethnographies was largely about the ethnographer's own experience of cultural dislocation, inspiring the joke.. in which the native pleads with the ethnographers, "can't we talk about *me* for a change" (Kuper 1994: 542). Therefore an adequate attention to the reality and the needs of the other requires a transformation of ourselves—from the individual to the self.

3. The distinction between individual and self that I make in this paper is parallel to the following distinction between individual and person that Tim Ingold makes:

   ..to regard the human being simply as an individual culture-bearer is to reduce his social life to an aggregate of overt behavioural interactions, which serve to reproduce the elements of culture just as the phenotypic behaviour of organism results in the reproduction of elements of the genotype. But if he is regarded as a person, that is as a locus of consciousness, then social life appears as the temporal unfolding of consciousness through the instrumentality of cultural forms. Whereas the individual is a vehicle for culture, his mind a container for cultural content, the conscious life of the person is a movement that adopts culture as its vehicle. Thus, culture stands, in a sense, between the person and the individual; worked by one, it works the other (Ingold 1986: 293).

4. In this context, the following critique of the Habermasian approach to self is important for the purpose of our inquiry here:

   Unlike Freud, Habermas does not start with the demands of the self against society, but rather with *political* problem. His question is: What must we demand of the self *if* we wish our political life to be governed by talk rather than coercion... It is from this perspective that Habermas reaches into the self, but it is *only a reaching*, only an interest in those competencies that might best fit the demands of the self with the demands of political life which we have no a priori way of knowing to be the same. To the contrary, we must suspect that fit cannot be perfect; that because of their inherent demands for universality, public expressions can never exhaust the self. Public life stops where the inarticulate begins; a complete self, a healthy self, will always go beyond language (Warren 1995: 194-195).

5. Such a description of the work of the self is now available to us from the traditions of "deep ecology" as well. The following description of the work of "ecological self" by a sympathetic commentator calls for our attention here: "where interests are essentially connected and you desire someone else's flourishing for their sake, what is involved is not abandoning your own interest, because in pursuing the other's interest you also pursue, non-accidentally, your own" (Plumwood 1993: 153).

6. Zygmunt Bauman puts this supposed postmodern temper quite succinctly: "A postmodern ethics would be the one that readmits the other as a neighbour into the hard core of the moral self... an ethics that recasts the Other as the crucial character in process through which moral self comes into its own" (Bauman 1993: 84).

7. For Connolly, "the production of terrorism protects the identity of particular states and the state system as a whole more than it reflects an ethical imperative to apply general principles to distinctive instances on violence" (Connolly 1991: 207).

8. In the words of Connolly, "a circle of representation is formed here. The state receives a fund of generalized resentment from those whose identity is jeopardized by the play of difference, contingency and danger; it constructs objects of resentment to protect identities it represents; and then it receives a refined supply of electoral resentments aimed at the objects it has constituted" (Connolly 1991: 210).

9. For instance, Jonathan Benthall, in his comments on Stolcke's essay writes: "The last seven words of Stolcke's lecture suggest that she wants all state power to be weakened which sounds utopian" (Benthall 1995: 13)

10. It is in this spirit that we can critically interrogate Derrida's famous statement, "God is the wholly Other" (see Barnett 1989). But God is not wholly other, God is also part of the self.

11. In another way, E. Valentine Daniel, discussing the challenge that violence poses to the practice and project of culture, makes a similar point. Discussing the problem of violence and ethnic fratricide in his Wertheim memorial lecture, Daniel writes:

The counterpoint of which Wertheim wrote almost twenty years ago was a counterpoint of hope and human emancipation.... The counterpoint of which I have spoken today is one [i.e., violence] that r ·.ɔts all evolutionary streams, be they of action or of thought. It will and should remain outside of all (C/c)ulture, if for no other reasons than to remind us that (a) as scholars, intellectuals and interpreters we need to be humble in the face of its magnitude, and (b) as *human beings* we need to summon all the vigilance in our command so as to never stray towards it and swallowed by its vortex into its untouchable abyss. The first is a sobering point that concerns observation, the second is a cautionary one that concerns participation: the twin terms that, hyphenated, consisted the sine qua non of the anthropological method. It is time for cultural anthropology to lose both its Hegelian conceit and Malinowskian innocence (Daniel 1991: 16).

REFERENCES

Aschroft, Bill et al., 1989, *The Empire Writes Back: Theory and Practice in Post-Colonial Literatures*, London: Routledge.

Barnett, S., 1989, *Structuralism and the Logic of Dissent*, London: Macmillan.

Bauman, Zygmunt, 1993, *Postmodern Ethics*, Oxford: Basil Blackwell.

Bellah, Robert et al., 1991, *The Good Society*, NY: Alfred A. Knof.

Benhabib, Seyla, 1992, *Situating the Self: Gender, Community and Postmodernism in Contemporary Ethics*, Cambridge: Polity Press

Benthall, Jonathan, 1995, Comments on Verena Stolcke, in Stolcke, 1995

Beteille, Andre, 1992, "Individual, Person, and Self as Subjects of Sociology", in Andre Beteille, *Society and Politics in India: Essays in a Comparative Perspective*, Delhi: Oxford University Press.

Bhabha, Homi K., 1994, *The Location of Culture*, London: Routledge.

Bidney, David, 1967, *Theoretical Anthropology*, NY: Shocken

Carrithers, Michel et al (eds.), 1985, *The Category of the Person: Anthropology, Philosophy, History*, Cambridge: Cambridge University Press.

Connolly, William E., 1991, *Identity / Difference: Democratic Negotiations of Political Paradox*, Ithaca: Cornell University Press.

Dallmayr, Fred, 1985, *The Twilight of Subjectivity: Towards a Post-Individualist Theory of Politics*, Amherst: University of Massachusetts Press.

Daniel, E. Valentine,1991, *Is There a Counterpoint to Culture?* Amsterdam: Center for Asian Studies.

Das, Chittaranjan, 1984, *Sanskruti o Odisa* [Culture and Orissa], Bhubaneswar: Mayur Publications.

——, 1993, *Sukara O Socrates* [The Pig and the Socrates], Berhampur: Pustak Bhandar.

Drucker, Peter, 1993, *The Ecological Vision: Reflections on the American Condition*, New Brunswick, NJ: Transaction Books.

Foster, Robert, 1991, "Making National Cultures in the Global Ecumene", *Annual Review of Anthropology* 20: 235-60.

Geertz, Clifford, 1986, "The Uses of Diversity", *Michigan Quarterly Review* Winter: 105-123.

Giddens, Anthony, 1991, Modernity and Self-Identity: Self and Society in the Late Modern Age, Cambridge: Polity Press.

Giri, Ananta Kumar, 1992, "Genuine Culture, Middle class, and the American Project: Towards an Ethnographic Critique of Robert Bellah's *Habits of the Heart*", *Indian Anthropologist*, January-June.

——, 1994, "Connected Criticism and the Womb of Tradition", Indian Institute of Management, Ahmedabad: Working Paper

——, 1995, "Moral Consciousness and Communicative Action, From Discourse Ethics to Spiritual Transformation", Madras Institute of Development Studies: Working Paper.

Habermas, Jurgen, 1981, *Philosophical-Political Profiles*, London: Heinemann.

——, 1987, *A Theory of Communicative Action, Volume 2 : Life World and System: A Critique of Functionalist Reason*, Cambridge: Polity Press

——, 1990a, *Moral Consciousness and Communicative Action*, Cambridge: Polity Press

——, 1990b, "What does socialism mean today? The rectifying revolution and the need for a new thinking on the left today", *The New Left Review* No. 183:3-21.

Hannerz, Ulf, 1990 "Cosmopolitans and Locals in World Culture", in Mike Featherstone (ed.), *Global Culture: Nationalism, Globalization and Modernity*, London: Sage Publications.

Hornborg, Alf, 1993, "Money and Meaning: Towards a Multi-Centric Economy", in *Entropy and Bioeconomics*, Milano, Italy: European Association for Bioeconomic Studies.

——, 1994, "Encompassing Encompassment: Anthropology and the U-Turn of Modernity", *Ethnos* 59 (3-4): 234-247.

Harvey, David, 1989, *The Condition of Postmodernity*, Cambridge, MA Basil Blackwell.

Inglehart, Roland, 1990, *The Culture Shift in Advanced Societies*, Princeton: Princeton University Press.

Ingold, Tim, 1986, *Evolution and Social Life*, Cambridge: Cambridge University Press.

Kuper, Adam, 1994, "Culture, Identity and the Project of a Cosmopolitan Anthropology", Man (n.s.) 29 (3): 537-554.

Lash, Scott and John Urry, 1987, *The End of Organized Capitalism*, Madison: University of Wisconsin Press.

Mauss, Marcel, 1985, "A Category of the Human Mind: The Notion of Person; The Notion of Self", in Carrithers et al 1985: 1-25.

Miller, Mark C., 1988, *Boxed In: The Culture of TV*, Evanston, Illinois: Northwestern University Press.

Offe, Claus and Ulrich K. Preuss, 1991, "Democratic Institutions and Moral Resources", in David Held (ed.), *Political Theory Today*, Cambridge: Polity Press.

Nandy, Ashis, 1995, "The Other Within", in A. Nandy, *The Savage Freud*, Delhi: Oxford University Press.

Pande, Govind Chandra, 1982, "The Nature of Social Categories", in Ravinder Kumar, (ed.), *Philosophical Categories and Social Reality*.

——, 1989, *The Meaning and Process of Culture as Philosophy of History*, Allahabad: Raka Prakashan.

——, 1993, "Culture and Cultures", Unpublished manuscript (it is now published in *Journal of Indian Council of Philosophical Research* but my citation is from the unpublished text).

Plumwood, Val, 1993, *Feminism and the Mastery of Nature*, London: Routledge.

Robertson, Roland, 1992, *Globalization: Social Theory and the Global Culture*, London: Sage Publications.

Said, Edward, 1993, *Culture and Imperialism*, London: Chatto & Windus.

Sri Aurobindo, 1950, *The Synthesis of Yoga*, Pondicherry: Sri Aurobindo Ashram.

Stolcke, Verenna, 1995, "Talking Culture: New Boundaries, New Rhetorics of Exclusion in Europe", *Current Anthropology* 36 (1): 1-24.

Taylor, Charles, 1989, *Sources of the Self*, Cambridge, MA: Harvard University Press.

Trilling, Lionel, 1955, *Beyond Culture: Essays on Literature and Learning*, London: Seeker & Warburg.

Unger, Roberto M., 1987, *False Necessity: Anti-Necessitarian Social Theory in the Service of Radical Democracy*, Cambridge: Cambridge University Press.

Warren, Mark, 1995, "The Self in Discursive Democracy", in Stephen K. White, (ed.), *The Cambridge Companion to Habermas*, Cambridge: Cambridge University Press.

Chapter Ten

Building a Global Covenant?
The Overseas Work and the International
Partners of Habitat for Humanity

Alternative solutions are generally antistatist and usually have two, but not necessarily contradictory points of reference: the local community and the earth. The relevant actor on the local level would not be the state but issue-oriented social movements whose global operations transcend the nation-state as the dominant mode of political organization

—Bjorn Hettne (1990:34)

Yet the *Word of Life* is significant not so much for what it can achieve, but what it represents. Apart from illustrating one particular religious adaptation to the forces of globalization and secularization, it also indicates that globalization can imply not only the creation of a world order of meaning, but also a kaleidoscopic clashing of meanings and cultural orientations.

—Simon Coleman (1991:16)

THE PROBLEM

Globality, Transnationality, and the Task of Ethnography

Globalization has become the sign of our times but like most other contemporary signs it has become a contested one as its complex unfolding in the world and discourses about it have led to radically divergent debates, positions, and perceptions. Not long ago, the discourse of globalization was mainly confined to the domains of economy and politics. But of late there has been a broadening of focus to include the cultural and "subjective"[1] dimensions of globalization as global processes now touch upon the thresholds of self and culture, breaking down insularities, and creating new trajectories of flow and interpenetration, which deeply affect the everyday life of individuals (Appadurai 1990; Featherstone, Lash and Robertson 1995; Hannerz 1992; Robertson 1992). Scholars of globalization are now concerned with "socio-cultural processes and forms of life which are emerging as the global begins to replace the nation-state as the decisive framework for social life" (Featherstone and Lash 1995: 1-2). They provide us with a multidimensional view and a "perspectival"[2] construction of the contemporary global human condition. While for Robertson (1992), the constitutive variables in the global human condition today are self, national society, the world system of societies, and humankind, for Appadurai (1990) these are the global flows in mediascapes, ethnoscapes, technoscapes, and ideascapes. Hannerz (1992), meanwhile, perceives the cultural complexity today as a configuration of four non-reducible variables—state, market, movements, and forms of life.

However, the cultural broadening of the discourse of globalization in the work of the above scholars has been subjected to a trenchant criticism by Friedman, for whom cultural globalization is a product of the already existing global systems and models of it are as much of the "global researcher", "the cosmopolitan intellectual" as of the world (Friedman 1995: 87, 72; also, Friedman 1994).[3] For Friedman, globalization is not about diffusion and cultural flows but about global systemic relations in production and consumption (ibid: 75; also Friedman 1990). Friedman thinks it better to conceive of such "global processes in terms of positioned practices such as assimilation, encompassment and integration in the context of interaction" (Friedman 1995: 81) and argues that "it is the transnational structures and organizations themselves that are the locus of the transcultural" (Friedman 1995: 79).

In this chapter, I take issue with such a view of globalization coming from scholars such as Friedman by describing the cross-currents in the global human condition as it is being articulated by a transnational movement. Friedman's structural-deterministic approach has limits in helping us understand the work of the global processes because it cannot explain its own key category, what he calls "practice of identity" (Friedman 1995: 86). Friedman's approach to globalization does not interrogate the ontology of practice and its cosmology and it does not explore the process of identity formation (cf. Giri 1996; McAdam 1988; Neville 1974). Robertson's attention to self and humankind helps us to widen the universe of discourse here but Robertson's confusion between individual and self[4] or what Tim Ingold (1986) might call "individual" and "person"[5] does not enable him to explore the conditions of self-preparedness which establishes a positive link between globalization and planetary self-consciousness. It does not address the kind of self-preparedness or "technologies of self" (cf. Giri 1994b; Habermas 1987; Martin et al. 1988; Sri Aurobindo 1950) that is required of individuals which will facilitate a global orientation on their part and enable them to creatively participate in a global flow. Hannerz provides some help in this direction when he brings modes of self-engagement to the center of the discourse. As Hannerz argues, "a more genuine cosmopolitanism entails a certain metacultural position. There is, first of all, a willingness to engage with the other, an intellectual and aesthetic stance of openness towards divergent cultural experiences, a search for contrasts rather than uniformity" (Hannerz 1990a: 239).[6]

But what is still of anthropological relevance in Robertson's model of globalization is its rootedness in a "voluntaristic theory" and his stress that "it should not entirely conflate the empirical issues with interpretative-analytical ones" (Robertson 1995a: 4). The current discourse of globalization very rarely engages itself with ethnographic study of processes, movements and forms of life in the current globalized world. The present essay is an attempt to partly remedy this gap in our scholarship by describing the work of a transnational organization which presents itself as a transnational people's movement. Through this ethnography I hope to show how both "encompassment" and "relativization" are simultaneously taking place in the process of globalization. I also hope to show the dialectic between the local and the global as it unfolds in the life of a transnational initiative.[7]

This essay is concerned with these issues related to the process and discourse of globalization. However, I wish to enter inside this discursive field through the practice of critical ethnography and the question of transnationality. Transnational organizations and transnational movements are now important parts of the discourse and process of globalization; they point to the limitation of state-centric discourse and practice and the significance of global structures and consciousness. Ethnographies of transnational organizations, corporations, and movements can help us understand the multi-dimensional unfolding of globalization, especially from the perspectives of self and culture. Ethnography of transnational processes can help us not only to understand "how the rhetoric of globalization is discursively structured" (Robertson 1995b: 5) but also to discover the reality behind the rhetoric itself.

At present, many organizations, initiatives, and movements work with a proclaimed objective to reach out to the needy in the global terrain and much is claimed on behalf of these initiatives which are characterized as transnational. These transnational initiatives supposedly "transcend the nation-state in their global operations" (Hettne 1990: 34; also see, Chekki 1988; Frieberg and Hettne 1984, 1988; Hegedus 1990; Kothari 1987, 1988; Mansbach

1976; Zelinsky 1991) and facilitate people-to-people partnership across the globe, creating a global community of seeking souls.[8] In this essay, I wish to examine such claims through an ethnography of an international organization which presents itself as a transnational movement. Through an ethnography of an international organization I hope not only to examine the claims made on behalf of transnational initiatives—organizations and movements—thus contributing to an ethnographic grounding of the current discourse of globalization but also respond to the calls made within anthropology to transform itself into what is variously called "macroanthropology" (Hannerz 1990b), "transnational anthropology" (Appadurai 1991) and "cosmopolitan anthropology" (Kuper 1994). Paradoxically both the discourse of transnationalism and the plea for a transnational anthropology have not gone beyond rhetorical sketches and what is thus required now is to describe the work of culture and communicative action as a consequence of and in conjunction with transnational initiatives in the global terrain—an ethnography of global phenomena and transnational organizations in the multiple sites of their work (see, Marcus 1986). In terms of ethnographic engagement, it means following the trajectory of transnational forms and processes in the multiple sites of their embodiment—an engagement whose object of inquiry is the understanding of the "discursive formation" (cf. Foucault 1972; also Giri 1994b) across boundaries rather than just the comparison of the different locales which host its movement and the logic of its differential local embodiments.[9]

In this essay, I describe the overseas work of Habitat for Humanity International—an ecumenical initiative in the contemporary United States which builds houses in nearly 1,200 communities in the United States and in 47 other countries. Habitat builds houses for low-income families with the donated resource and the contributed labour of supporters and volunteers but it does not give these houses free of charge to the homeowners. It sells its houses "at no interest" and "no-profit" to the homeowners who are required to pay back the mortgage amount in installments in a period of twenty years. Habitat takes special pride in the fact that it builds for people in need of a house not only in the United States but also in many poor countries of the world in partnership with Christian social groups in these countries.

I describe the work of Habitat for Humanity International in two of its house-building projects in India, namely, Khammam in Andhra Pradesh and Koovappally in Kerala. I describe at great length the work of the Habitat Project in Khammam because it provides us with a counter example to the rhetoric of global partnership proliferating in both Habitat as well as in the discourse of transnationalism. I describe the work of Habitat at Koovappally to discover some differential features in both the structure of the sponsoring organization and the culture of the locality which make the embodiment of this transnational organization different in that project. My following description of the vision and activities of Habitat is based on my anthropological fieldwork in multiple sites of its operations: Americus (Georgia), Immokalee (Florida), Khammam (Andhra Pradesh) and Koovappally (Kerala), spread over a period of fifteen months. I have stayed in these places and carried out my research employing the methods of participant observation, life story, interview and questionnaire. My association with Habitat has been that of an academic researcher and it is in that capacity only (neither as a development worker nor as a staff of Habitat) I have participated in the house-building activities of Habitat.

The description of the differential trajectory of Habitat in Khammam and Koovappally is supplemented by bringing an actor's perspective to the center. In the overseas work of Habitat for Humanity International, international partners are a very important category of actors. The American volunteers of Habitat who work overseas are called international partners, popularly known as IPs. I describe the perception and work of some IPs in India and analyze these in the light of a critical framework of the "cosmopolitans" offered by Hannerz (1992). Description and critical analysis of such actors is meant to show the enormous signifi-

cance not only of structure and culture but also of self in determining the particular embodiment of a transnational organization.
As Robertson argues, "globalization is not simply a matter of
structure. It is also, crucially, a matter of agency" (Robertson
1995b: 4).

I realize fully that a concern with transnationalism requires of
one to examine the work of Habitat for Humanity not only in
overseas countries but also in the United States, i.e., the country
of its origin, legitimacy, and resource mobilization. But in this
essay, I am primarily concerned with the overseas work of Habitat
and its international partners because of my objective to examine
its discourse of global partnership. However, I describe below
briefly the evangelical discourse of Habitat and its work in the
United States in order to examine these issues in their characteristic transnational context.

THE TRANSNATIONAL AT HOME

Habitat for Humanity International in the United States

Habitat for Humanity was founded as an international ministry of
housing in 1976 by Millard Fuller and Linda Fuller who had
articulated its vision as "No More Shacks" (Fuller 1986a; also
Fuller 1977, 1980, 1994; Fuller and Fuller 1990). For Fuller and
the activists of Habitat, "obviously the nuclear question is a big
issue. Women's rights is a big issue. But one of the biggest issues
of our day is shelter" (Fuller 1986b: 42-45). They also articulate
the global dimension of the predicament of shelter and argue that
solving this problem is an important aspect of not only global
development but also the realization of "kingdom of God" on
earth. For them, though the global problem of lack of adequate
shelter is stupendous it is possible to make a difference "with the
partnership of God".[10]

Habitat articulates itself as a "God's movement" and locates
its foundation in two Biblical principles—"The Economics of
Jesus" and "Theology of the Hammer". While for Habitat follow-

ing "economics of Jesus" means not to charge interest in providing capital and building houses for the poor, the "theology of hammer" refers to the spiritual vocation to use the hammer "as an instrument to manifest God's love" irrespective of doctrinal differences. In its discourse, Habitat is also self-conscious in situating itself in a new frontier of Christian evangelism which emphasizes meeting human needs rather than conversion.[11]

Habitat for Humanity builds houses in different communities in the United States in partnership with the local affiliates and with the help of the volunteers. Volunteers of Habitat are characterized by their distance from government and zeal for fundraising. Their distance is manifested primarily in a non-compromising stance that Habitat should not accept government money because, for them, it hinders private and community participation—and all the economic, ethical, and social benefits of such participation. But their distance from government is matched only by their enthusiasm for fund raising. Fund-raising becomes a matter of deep joy for many Habitat activists and is an aspect of their identity and desire. They brag about the money they collect for Habitat and the uniqueness of each donation. Their distance from government and zeal for fund-raising is accompanied by their stress that nothing should be given to the beneficiaries for free: the homeowners must make regular repayment for the interest-free mortgage contract they have entered with Habitat.

The volunteers of Habitat are moved by the image of shacks. Upon their arrival at Americus, Georgia, the headquarters of Habitat's global operations, the new volunteers are first shown a video about how Habitat destroys shacks and builds decent homes. In fact, showing videos on the substandard housing situation in the developing world constitutes a regular feature of the community meetings at the headquarters of Habitat. In overseas projects, the picture of a prospective homeowner's old shack is first sent to Americus before the latter's destruction and the building of a new Habitat house. Thus shacks are the moving images[12] in the mobilization of Habitat. At the same time, in the drama of contestation that Habitat strives to create, these turn into what Kenneth Burke calls "scapegoats", operating not as evocative images but as scapegoats, arousing disdain to the very sight of the shack itself (Giri 1989; Simons and Media 1989; Stewart et al. 1984). During the process of initiation into Habitat and its rhetorical construction, every shack is constituted negatively as a scapegoat. Hence, it is not just a coincidence that the local Habitat project director in Immokalee, Florida, insists on the destruction of the shack before a prospective homeowner enters inside the newly constructed Habitat home. In this insistence on the destruction of the shack about which a poor homeowner has no choice[13] the image of the structure which has created shacks and trailer parks in a community in the first place is forgotten; only the scapegoat remains. Its destruction not only becomes a vital matter, but also a ritually empowering act for the leaders, who are otherwise powerless before the real estate establishment.

In Immokalee, Florida—the other site of my multi-locale ethnography of Habitat—the volunteers build and donate regularly so that the needy family can receive the "gift" of a home but this "gift" is mediated through the local Habitat project. The homeowners are happy and excited to receive the "gift" of a home but they also feel controlled by the local project in ways they do not articulate systematically (Giri 1994a). While a majority of the homeowners of Immokalee, Florida, are immigrants from Latin America and Central America, the volunteers are wealthy suburban homeowners who live in the affluent cities of Naples and Marco Islands and come to work in the poor community of Immokalee.

THE INTERNATIONAL WORK OF HABITAT

From Affiliates to the Sponsored Projects

Habitat projects in the United States are called affiliates. As affiliates, they are required to send 10 per cent of their contribution to Habitat's international headquarters in Americus, Georgia for international work. Habitat house-building projects in the overseas countries which receive funding for its work from the International are called sponsored projects.[14] These two kinds of projects have different status within Habitat International, affiliates mattering most in Habitat's scheme.

Insofar as the overseas work of Habitat is concerned, for launching a project, interested local Christian leaders must first submit a sponsored project proposal,[15] providing information regarding various aspects of the local population, as well the nature of the sponsoring local group and its understanding of and commitment to Habitat. The sponsoring group must be a Christian organization, be it a church or a Christian service society. The sponsored project proposal goes first to the Area Director of Habitat International and is then evaluated by the Board of Directors. In the meantime, the sponsored project's Habitat committee must sign a covenant with Habitat International, committing it to maintaining the integrity of the Habitat vision, and to honesty in its operation. For the actors of Habitat, this covenant is not a legal document, but a commitment of faith towards keeping up the spiritual and financial stewardship of Habitat. According to Millard Fuller, the covenant "sets out the basic principles or ideals of this ministry and to be officially recognized as a Habitat for Humanity affiliate, a covenant must be signed and the parties who make up the local affiliate must agree to abide by that covenant. Not abiding by the covenant can be grounds for disaffiliation" (personal communication).[16] If approved, the sponsored project has to wait till the arrival of the Habitat International Partners for the release of its funds.

The Overseas Work of Habitat: The Project in Khammam

Khammam Habitat for Humanity, located in the district town of Khammam in the state of Andhra Pradesh in India, is a sponsored project of Habitat for Humanity International. Habitat International reached Khammam under the auspices of an evangelical group called Christian Service Unit. Christian Service Unit (CSU) has been working in the Khammam area for the last 36 years, preaching Christianity among the high-caste Hindus and delivering varieties of services—helping children, widows, the elderly and the sick. Evangelist K. Azariah is the leader of the Christian service unit of Khammam who was instrumental in starting the Habitat project there.

The Salient Features of the Habitat Sponsored Project at Khammam

The Differential Incidence of Habitat in the Villages of Khammam

The local Habitat has built houses in eight villages of Khammam, besides the district town, but has arrived in each of these differently—in most cases through the evangelical followers of Azariah and only in a few cases independently on its own. In the case of the former, the work of Habitat is looked on as an extension of Azariah's evangelical work. For instance, a Habitat homeowner in one such village says that his village has been adopted by the American Missionary Society resulting in the flow of a lot of money to it, but neither Azariah Garu nor David Garu (the local evangelical leader) has told them anything about it. Another homeowner says that the Habitat missionaries are interested in converting them though they would not force them to convert. Some of the homeowners only know vaguely the purpose of Habitat. But in the villages where Habitat has arrived independently, it has a different significance: homeowners understand Habitat as a mission to build houses for the poor, and not simply as an extension of Azariah.

Palladugu is one such village where the Habitat homeowners are deeply involved in the work of Habitat. They are concerned about regular "mortgage payment" from the homeowners of the whole village. Seith Sahib, a Muslim homeowner and an enthusiastic supporter of Habitat, says that Habitat is a very good scheme and they must make regular payments. If somebody defaults in his house payment, he says, it is a slur on their entire village. He also thinks that if they make regular repayment, they can build at least one house every year in their village with repayment money alone. He told me how once all the Habitat homeowners of a village went to the house of a willful defaulter and told him straight that what he is doing was not good. Then he paid back his dues to Habitat.

Seith Sahib's narration shows that Habitat has a deep community penetration in this village which can be attributed to the fact that Habitat has not come to this village not through any of the strong evangelical followers of Azariah nor are Azariah's missionary programmes at work in this village. Probably because of this fact Habitat homeowners have been able to develop an autonomous identity of their own, not being over-shadowed by any of the influential actors of Azariah's evangelical network. In other villages, the presence of such local leaders has not facilitated the building of community solidarity around the cause of Habitat since local leaders almost invariably use their links with both Azariah and Habitat to consolidate their own positions and pursue their own interests in their villages.[17]

Defaulting in Mortgage Payment Collection

Regular mortgage payment is an all-pervasive concern of Habitat—from Immokalee to Koovappally and from leaders to the homeowners. But while on the part of the leaders regular mortgage payment by the homeowners is crucial to their "identity formation,"[18] for the majority of the homeowners their concern in mortgage payment lies in fear i.e. if they do not make regular repayment then they would not only be eventually forced to vacate their homes but also would become scapegoats in the eyes of the community.

Making regular house payments is a continuing problem for the Habitat homeowners of Khammam. In August 1990, as calculated by international partner Herod, 81 per cent of them were behind in their payments. While the representatives of Habitat International at Khammam look at the problem of default as a problem of lack of education on the part of the homeowners in the vision and philosophy of Habitat and as a case of willful withholding, the homeowners and the local leaders look at it differently. Azariah argues that it is not that the homeowners are unaware of the significance of Habitat, nor is it that they do not know that money comes from "America" and that they have to repay. They lag behind their mortgage payment because they are very poor. The homeowners express the same inc⁚ ¹city in addition to their preference for paying their mortgage only once a year—after the harvest season. Moreover, they do not like and find it difficult to pay every month. But for the international partners, if homeowners want to pay once a year, then they should pay in advance during the harvest season, not after six months of continuing default. For the homeowners this is making their already burdened lives more miserable, which even Azariah considers inconsiderate. Azariah Garu would like to extend the mortgage term to 22 years from the current term of 20 years.

Nevertheless, the representatives of Habitat International stick to the month as the unit of collection. Recently, there has also been a move at the Habitat headquarters to reduce the mortgage term to eight years, to protect Habitat's "Revolving Fund for Humanity" from the corrosive and disintegrative process of global inflation. In the context of Habitat International's continued stress on months as units of collection, the move for shortening the mortgage period considerably, and local Habitat's plea for a lengthier time, we are witnessing a cultural conflict, linked to the contemporary compression of time (cf. Harvey 1989). Compression of time is posing a constant challenge to the construction of solidarity and a longer time vision in advanced societies and a social movement originating in such a society is also pushing local Habitat to the edge to take swift legal action against the defaulters who are allegedly not properly socialized in this culture of compressed time.

As a response to constant pressure from the international headquarters, the local Habitat is taking various steps to make the repayment situation up to date: repossessing bullocks, taking out bags of rice from the beneficiaries' households and taking legal action against the defaulters. But the local Habitat has also been resisting the move to take legal action against the defaulters. It has recently constituted a legal cell. Azariah says that he wants to take legal action against only one person so that they are able to teach people that they are serious. He told me when I was visiting Khammam for the second time in July, 1991 that Khammam Habitat has 350 homeowners and he could not quarrel with all of them. Azariah also told me that he gives money to the defaulters from his own fund for evangelical work so that they can catch up with their mortgage payments and save the face of Khammam Habitat. Azariah has such arrangements with nearly forty homeowners. One such case is a poor widow who rents her house to a school. Classes are held there in the morning while she sleeps in the same place at night. Such arrangements not only help the homeowners but also help Azariah to show acceptable "statistics" to Habitat International.

The poor repayment record of the local Habitat has strained its relationship with Habitat International, resulting in the withdrawal of approval for its already-sanctioned fourth phase of house-building and forcing it to agree to build a low-cost model house (discussed in the next section). At the Fall 1990 board meetings, Habitat International approved the fourth phase of the Khammam project, allotting funds for building 200 more houses. Because of Khammam Habitat's chronic default in repayment, international partner Herod asked area director Sam Bandella to withdraw funding for its proposed "phase four" operation. This led to a considerable tension. Azariah was quick to withdraw the local Habitat's application for further construction, writing to the Area Director: "...we withdraw the phase four proposal, for the persons whoever they are that are responsible to authorize funding and stop funding showed no respect in dealing with the project."[19]

Under these circumstances, it is no wonder then that the local Habitat has recently attached special importance to collecting money regularly from the Habitat homeowners. The office organizes collection drives every now and then in which the office staff and some committee members go off in their jeep to a particular village, and spend the entire day there, moving from door to door. I was present at one such collection drive that was carried out in the village of Ashnogoru on 4 September, 1990, and led by Habitat vice-president Thomas. Before the drive set off to Ashnogoru, the whole Khammam Habitat team was summoned to a meeting with Habitat IP Herod. In this meeting, Herod instructed Habitat workers to strictly follow Habitat rules. He cautioned that the continuance of the project depended upon strict observance of the Habitat principles and policy. He urged the employees to collect Habitat money regularly so that house construction did not stop. Herod explained its far-reaching implication: "If the construction stops, then there would be no need of a work supervisor in the project, nor a driver, nor an office assistant." Thomas, vice-president of the local project, added an explanatory footnote: "Yes, just as he stopped the funding from America, one day you would not be surprised to find that he has also cut your salary or has thrown you out of your job". Herod further instructed the workers not to allow any deviation from the original Habitat design, by permitting any "extensions" in the Habitat houses. Herod also instructed the staff to keep a log book, both here at Golapudi and in the Khammam office, where Habitat employees had to regularly sign. He also wanted Habitat materials, such as cement and bricks, to be stored separately from those of the Christian Service Unit.

Paul: The Critic of Habitat

The local Habitat has issued legal notices to all the defaulters, but has taken legal action only against Paul. Paul has not repaid his Habitat dues for years, but his continued default is not the only reason why he has been the target of the local project. The primary reason behind taking legal action against him lies in the fact that he has a different understanding of the challenge of the Christian mission. If Millard Fuller bases his Habitat foundation on Exodus, Paul bases his critique of Habitat on Chapter Six of Luke which says: "and lend, hoping for nothing again..." Paul vehemently argues that it is not scripturally justified to ask for repayment money from the poor, for whom Habitat is meant to build. He resents the "fact" that Habitat not only collects "house payment" from the poor but also does not give them any priority in the sanction of Habitat houses. He also considers the dedication of houses by those who are not pastors as unscriptural.

Paul refused to repay Habitat in spite of its repeated requests and notices. In 1989, the confrontation between Paul and the local Habitat took a physically abusive turn, as Paul says, in the very presence of Azariah. When we look closely at Paul's conflict with Habitat, we can find that it is not only a conflict of interest but also a conflict of interpretation. The key issue here is a homeowner's challenge to the monolithic interpretation of Habitat not only by its local sponsors but also by their metropolitan mentors. Among the 356 Habitat homeowners of Khammam, Paul is the only homeowner who not only understands Habitat but also offers a profound critique of it based upon the same scripture upon which Millard Fuller had built the housing movement of Habitat. This is probably what enrages the leaders of Habitat International.

Problematic Relationship with the Homeowners

Paul's case draws our attention to the problematic relationship that exists between the local Habitat and the homeowners. After continuous pressure from the headquarters, the local Habitat has set up village subcommittees which include the homeowners. But members of village subcommittees are not to take part in the decision-making process, nor are they to attend the main decision-making committee meetings, held once a month at Khammam. They are only responsible for the regular collection of the Habitat money. Azariah thinks that such an arrangement is only to be expected since they are poor and illiterate. Making them members of the main decision-making committee means educating them, paying them bus fares to come to Khammam from their villages, and serving food to them during the meeting. "Then what about the idea of partnership?" I asked him. Azariah Garu told me that the homeowner is a partner to the extent that he is a beneficiary, making regular payments, thus helping Habitat grow. For him, Habitat partnership primarily refers to the partnership between those who are providing money in "America" and those who are building houses in Khammam.

No Attempt at Building Low-Cost Houses

At Khammam, those granted Habitat loans for house building do not stick to any set Habitat model or house design. Moreover, most of them borrow money from the moneylenders at high rates of interest to construct bigger houses. Since after house-construction their primary concern is to repay their interest bearing loan rather than the Habitat interest-free loan, they default in their Habitat mortgage payment. This is a point nobody understood better than the international partner Winston. Winston urged the local committee to build a low-cost model house. He faced stiff resistance from the influential members of the committee. When the International threatened that it would not release its due funds unless it built a low cost model house, the local project took up this task.

The model house built did not turn out to be a good one, however. The story of the model house in the village of Rebbavaram points to the complexity of the relationship between form and content in a social movement. For many, Habitat is primarily a "God's movement," housing being no more than its content. They join Habitat because it fulfills their spiritual needs. But when housing is considered simply a means towards one's self-actualization and spiritual fulfillment, the actors do not feel any need for cultivating an appropriate technical imagination. This is the case with the Habitat projects in India where leaders have not cared to pay attention to the question of building low-cost houses for the poor. There are now several science and technology groups in India developing varieties of low-cost housing technologies. There are many housing movements, such as the Baker Movement and the Nirmithi movement in Kerala, which combine sociological and technical imagination (Giri 1993a). But Khammam Habitat seems unaware of these developments.

Problematic Relationship with the International

The relationship between the local leaders and the representatives of the International in Khammam Habitat is a problematic one. The local leaders feel that the IPs are dictating terms to them and leading a luxurious life without doing anything while the IPs feel that the local leaders are using Habitat to solidify their position and extend the network of their benevolent patronage in the community. One Habitat IP talks about Azariah: "Oh, people here kiss Azariah's feet. They think of Azariah as a god. They think Azariah is giving them a house from his own pocket." On the other hand, Azariah says of the same IP: "He is 60 years old. He has been divorced five times which means that he lacks love and commitment."

There are visitors from the Habitat headquarters to Khammam every now and then and their subsequent reports are mostly critical of the state of things in the project. The local leaders find the language of these reports derogatory. When one looks at the file of Khammam Habitat, one notices many one-sided and domineering opinions in the correspondence between the Khammam local and Habitat International. In this context, one of the most respectful memoranda of Habitat International that I found in its files was the one submitted by Tom Schleiffer, then director of Habitat International's Programme in Appropriate Technology. In this report, Schleiffer asks who is to pay for the jeep and the pick-up truck that the local project has. In his view, "if the fund for humanity is to build houses for God's people in need on its own someday..we cannot burden it with huge vehicle expenses." Schleiffer urges the local project to realize that hiring a taxi is cheaper than owning a truck to move people.

DIFFERENTIAL MANIFESTATIONS OF THE OVERSEAS WORK OF HABITAT: FROM KHAMMAM TO KOOVAPPALLY AND BEYOND

The Habitat project in Khammam has had a ten year history but is still no more than a loan-giving unit and a mortgage collection agency. This is not the case regarding another Habitat project in

India which within a short span of two years was not only able to build 300 houses but also achieve a high degree of community participation. The Habitat project in Koovappally, a mountainous village in central Kerala, started in 1989. Habitat came to Koovappally under the auspices not of any evangelical group but of a development organization. The Society for Integral Development Action, known among the people in the locality as SIDA, had been carrying out developmental activities in various fields—sanitation, rural credit service and the rehabilitation of the displaced rubber tappers—since its inception in 1984. SIDA has self-help organizations (known as SHOs) in and around Koovappally. These SHOs are meant to generate self-help among the people, especially among women. They encourage village women to save in SIDA's Jan Vikash (people's development) scheme in return for which they are eligible to get interest-free loans from Habitat and receive preference in SIDA's other developmental programmes, such as the goat-loan scheme, self-help latrine scheme, and the housing scheme of Koovappally Habitat. The pre-existing SIDA networks serve to diffuse the idea and practice of Habitat. The workers of SIDA collect the monthly mortgage payment from the homeowners as well.

SIDA has its production-cum-office complex in Koovappally. SIDA's production unit prepares cement blocks which in turn are given to the homeowners. Unlike Khammam, there is no official mason in Koovappally and homeowners take responsibility for building their houses. But each homeowner is required to contribute a day's labor in the building of another homeowner's house. Those who apply for a Habitat house in Koovapally are required to attend the Habitat village meeting in Koovappally in which both the local leaders and the international partners explain the principle of Habitat and its non-compromising stress on regular mortgage payments. I attended one such meeting held at Koovappally in June 1991 in which 30 prospective homeowners were present. Both the international partners were present in this meeting and stressed the need for regular repayment on the part of the homeowners.

The Habitat project in Koovappally has been able to involve community leaders whose recommendation is valued highly in the selection of the homeowners. They become what the local project calls recommenders. The recommenders are those people who recommend the case of a needy family to the local project and also help it with additional money and materials. Some recommenders also become part of the board of directors of the local project, its apex decision-making body. But though Habitat builds for people of all religious faiths, the members of the board of directors of Koovappally Habitat for Humanity are Christians only. (In the case of Khammam Habitat too, all board members are Christians.) Khammam Habitat states that it has a Hindu on its board but, in fact, the member concerned is a converted Christian). The project director of Koovappally Habitat justifies his exclusion of people from other religious backgrounds in its board on the ground that what is important is not religious representativeness but the functional viability of the board and its efficiency in building houses. Interestingly, a similar reason was given to me by a leader of Habitat at its headquarters. To my question as to why the homeowners are not members of the decision-making board in any affiliate in the United States, he told me: "Why should a homeowner become member of the board? He needs a house and we must see that this need is most efficiently taken care of. It is immaterial whether he is a member of the board or not."

The high-degree of community participation of the Habitat project at Koovappally and its up-to-date repayment record presents a contrast with the one at Khammam. What is the reason behind this? The first is a structural reason having to do with the nature of the organization through which Habitat for Humanity International builds a "covenant" in the local area. In the case of Khammam, it is an evangelical group which undertakes the work of Habitat for Humanity International. The Christian Service Unit of Khammam, the organization which has sponsored Habitat's work in the locality, does not have either interest or expertise in developmental action. Its main interest has been in preaching about Christianity to those who have never heard about it, namely high caste Hindus. Its social programmes mentioned earlier are in the mode of missionary charity than developmental action. The situation is different in Koovappally where a development agency is the sponsor of Habitat for Humanity. This development agency is a Christian organization too but it has experience and interest in carrying out different development-oriented programs for the local people. Thus the nature of the sponsoring group plays a crucial role in determining the nature of the manifestation of the global covenant of Habitat for Humanity International. It is like the case of the medium of light which is as important as the light itself in determining the way light is reflected and refracted.

The second reason is a cultural one, having to do with the cultural significance of homeownership in the lives of the people of Kerala. In Kerala, it is felt important for couples to have homes of their own, after marriage, separate from one's ancestral home. When the younger brother marries, elder brothers and their wives do not feel at ease in staying in the same house where they were born and raised. They also know that people in the village do not think highly of elder brothers who do not try to form their own households, at least after the marriage of their younger brothers. Even under extremely trying material conditions, people try to build a roof over their heads which they can call their own. In Malayalee culture there is an intimate relation between self and house. It is perhaps for this reason that Melinda Moore writes: "More than any other unit of residence or locality in South Asia, the Kerala house stands in an intimate and literal association with its members" (Moore 1985: 533-534; also, see Moore 1989). Here, homeownership has a moral significance in the life-cycle of an individual, akin to the moral significance of homeownership in American culture.[20] It is this moral significance of individual homeownership in traditional *Malayalee* culture which makes it different from other parts of India including Andhra Pradesh where joint family and common household are still the preferred norm. It is this cultural significance of individual homeownership which suggests a clue to understanding why Koovappally Habitat for Humanity seems to have made a bigger impact in a brief span than what the project at Khammam has been able to make over a much longer period (see, Giri 1993b). The president of Koovappally Habitat for Humanity could never make the statement that the president of Khammam Habitat for Humanity in Andhra Pradesh had once made during our conversation: "Here in India, people can sleep on somebody else's veranda, but they need crucial support in food and medical care. In the US, Habitat is a movement to the extent that it involves and activates churches, institutions and individuals to the crucial task of meeting the needs of shelter. But in India, people do not think that shelter is an urgent need."

The differential manifestation of Habitat for Humanity in its overseas work in Khammam and Koovappally cannot make us blind to parallels in their links to the International. The lack of partnership between the local project and the international is also evidenced in the work of Koovapally Habitat. Thus the president of Koovappally Habitat also finds Habitat International self-assertive, with no serious desire to involve the local organization. For him, whereas an organization such as MISERIOR, a German Christian organization which has also been supporting the work of SIDA, wants to develop the local organization, Habitat wants to push it into the background. Both Khammam and Koovappally Habitat projects are also merely rhetorical in their "partnership" with the homeowners. Like Khammam Habitat, the homeowners, despite greater involvement, do not have much say in the decision-making process of Koovapally Habitat.

Bindoo Kutty is a homeowner of Koovappally Habitat. She has five sons and two daughters, and finds her two-room Habitat house quite inadequate. Though she urgently wants to expand her house, she is not getting permission from the local project to do so. Habitat policy is that one must pay back at least 50 of the loan before getting permission to make any extension. She does not take all of this kindly. She does not like the fact that she needs the permission of the office even to paint her house. After the house construction, Habitat wanted to put a sign board with the title: "This house has been built by SIDA Koovappally Habitat for

Humanity". But she did not allow this because she thought that it would tell everybody that her house had not been built by her.

Bindoo Kutty may not take kindly to Habitat's regulations about an extension, but homeowner Matthew's wife in Kanjirappally would not do anything without Habitat's permission. She says that she would never violate any rule. She is grateful to Habitat; she considers her house as a grace from God.

Paul Anthony is another homeowner of Habitat who is also a member of the board. Paul supports the policy of the local Habitat not to grant permission for building extensions to one's Habitat home unless 50 per cent of the loan is repaid. But unlike the local leaders, Paul does not think that Habitat International does away with the autonomy of the local project. In this regard he told me about recent advice from the international to stop construction because of financial problems, but the local Habitat proceeded with construction with its own repayment money, which finally made the international retract its steps.

THE INTERNATIONAL PARTNERS

The international partners (IPs) of Habitat are crucial to the overseas work of Habitat. In fact, without their presence the Habitat grant to a sponsored project cannot be released. International partners also symbolize Habitat's ideal of building a global covenant. They are symbolic of Habitat's seeking to build communities around the globe.

Shelly is an international partner of Habitat, working at Koovappally. She got her international partnership training provided at the Habitat headquarters in 1989 and began her overseas assignment in Koovappally in 1990 along with Mary, her classmate in the IP training. In spite of advanced notice, she was not prepared for the solitude or the material conditions. Construction had already started when she and Mary came, which is quite unusual for Habitat: local projects usually await the IPs. She and Mary had to redirect the work according to a more up-to-date Habitat manual than that was used on their own by the locals.

They soon experienced the concrete difficulties of applying Habitat principles to a foreign situation. Neither the leaders nor the homeowners were keen on physical labour or mutual help.

Shelly's testimony suggests lurking issues of control and misperceptions between the IPs and the local population. At any rate, she feels that local resident's perception of the white foreigners' benevolence contradicts Habitat's expectations of local self-reliance in the long-term. Meanwhile, social and cultural divides impose local readjustments. The returns from the Christmas 1990 fund-raising drive did not even cover the expenses for the campaign. Rich estate owners refuse to donate although they recommend their workers to the local project for the grant of a Habitat home.

The ground reality is indeed different from the writings of Millard Fuller, or even from the newsletters[21] of the international partners. In reality, IPs are rarely welcomed in local projects. Local leaders are pleased when the IPs play the role models to which they have been assigned but feel insecure when they start getting involved. The IPs also face the dilemma of allegiance: do they belong to the local project or to the international? Those who look at themselves as local supervisors for Habitat International have an easy answer but those who take the task of building a global partnership have serious difficulties in policing the local Habitat on behalf of the International. They identify themselves with the local project. IPs like Shelly are caught in the middle. She does not like the domineering edge with which Habitat International and its area director deal with local projects. However, she argues that Habitat has a logic when it asks for regular reports and accounts. For her, ultimately Habitat is accountable to thousands of donors in America and must ensure them that their money is being spent the right way. Her angst is sharpened by a built-in feature of the IP experience: their average stay of three years is too short for the human task required. She comments on the contradiction: "If I want to build this local project in the light of Habitat vision, I would have to work more with the local people".

Reality differs from expectations in more than one way. Shelly had thought that she would actually build houses when she landed at Koovapally with a hammer in her briefcase. But she has yet to find an opportunity to build. She has instead used her hammers only to break dry coconuts. She does not like this but the local committee is not sensitive to her feelings. In fact, all the Habitat volunteers who come to a Habitat project want to go right out with their hammers and build houses the very next day. Instead, most of them are given assignments in the office, which they do not like. This is as much true of the international headquarters as it is of a local project in India. In an Indian project, when an IP takes his or her commitment to "No More Shacks" literally—going every morning to build houses with the homeowners—s/he is even ridiculed. The president of a Habitat project in India speaks of one such IP: "He was going everyday to build houses in villages. But he did not mix with all the sections of the community. He favoured the lower class and maintained a distance from the rich and the upper class. Then what is the significance? I could have got more work from a labourer by paying him Rs. 20 a day".

The episode immediately points to the structural imbalance between the rich and the poor countries involved with Habitat. In the United States, labour is expensive, hence voluntary labour is so valued. But this is not so in a country like India where labor is relatively cheap. In any construction-work, whether building a house or constructing a road, people feel that the main problem is capital, not labour. Hence, some of the enterprising leaders of voluntary groups devote their energy towards securing the much needed capital from either the government or the international aid organizations rather than motivating people to volunteer their labour. This is probably for a variety of reasons. First of all, it is easier to hire labour if one has cash rather than to create a group of volunteers. To have volunteers means to share a space of mutuality and accountability for which most leaders of non-governmental organizations in India are not prepared. It is no wonder then that local leaders fail to appreciate the urge for physical labour that North American representatives have in the work site.

For the local leaders of Habitat, the primary significance of the international partners lies more in the fact that they bring much needed capital than in these Americans' urge to share their sweat with their less resourceful fellow beings.[22]

During our conversation, Shelly insisted that she viewed her stay in Koovappally not as a sacrifice but as a privilege and a blessing. Staying here has been a great asset in her continued spiritual quest, she said. God, not slogans, moved her to Koovappally. Habitat, for her, is just a medium: the real message for her has been God. This is also how Mary, Shelly's co-IP, feels. Mary appreciates the opportunity for spiritual growth that being an international partner provides. Mary's current journal in Trivandrum also reflects her contention, echoed in Shelly's previous comments and in a book that she read in her training class, *The American Cultural Pattern*, that Americans are unduly interested in 'doing' rather than in 'being'. As Mary puts it: "We do not allow the natural unfoldment of being".

Dolly is another IP of Habitat working in its newly started project in Trivandrum. Unlike most of the Habitat volunteers, Dolly does not have a strong Christian background, nor is she enthusiastic about Christianity. She was born to a Christian parent, but her step-father is a Jew who had a strong influence on her. She likes the Judaic tradition of strong family and close-knit community. She also likes the fact that unlike Christianity, there are no single answers in Judaism, which allows multiple interpretations—an orientation which makes her, as she says, interested in Hinduism.[23]

Dolly had joined Habitat hoping that it was a development organization, but now she finds it different. She is frustrated that she does not have much to do, even in the office, let alone in the field: the project has not started building. Like Shelly, Dolly uses her hammer only to break dry coconuts. Gone are her early hopes and expectations. She had expected to stay in a village where there would be no electricity and no running water, where she would know all the villagers well, where she would work 70 to 80 hours per week. Alas, she is not doing any of these things. She feels uncomfortable about her nice apartment and the indulgence of calling home every week and the expensive meals she takes in the continental restaurants of the city. She says: "If I were not learning Malayalam and doing something for Habitat, I could not justify my existence here".

Dolly is not alone in joining Habitat with the romantic hope of getting experience in real development work. One Habitat IP in India, Parry, formerly worked with the World Bank. This IP is Parry. Her work in the Bank in the context of its overture towards grassroots groups logically led her to Habitat. But her current quest with Habitat, she makes clear, is never of a fact-finding nature, or simply to learn some non-bureaucratic and people-oriented skills; it is to make large and resourceful global organizations like the World Bank more efficient. She feels that if Habitat can do so much on a global scale with so few resources, then governments and world-bodies with such massive resources can learn from its example.

After her training Parry was placed in a project in India, which she and her co-IP soon discovered as just a money-making organization, with little interest in either Habitat or housing development. For Parry, this is due to the Habitat principle that the sponsoring group must be a Christian organization, no matter whether it has either experience or interest in developmental work or not. She hopes that Habitat learns and insists on broadening its base if it is at all serious about its task.

Tom is another enthusiastic international partner of Habitat who works with his co-IP James in the Habitat project at Hubli. He writes about this movingly in his first newsletter, sent to family members and friends in April 1990:

> Of course there are times when I get a little depressed about the fact that I'll be away from y'all for two and one-half years. But I am usually out of that mood when God slaps me across the face and tells me to wake up and smell the sewage (not the coffee),...We in America struggle for comfort, for a better income, and for more

'toys'. These people struggle simply to survive today, so that they can see tomorrow....So think about this the next time you go to purchase a $30 pair of jeans.

Apart from the work for Habitat, Tom considers it unfortunate that despite his and his co-IP's enthusiasm he could not build a single house during his entire stay for one and one-half years in Hubli.[24] What still keeps Tom animated is his novel experiment of staying in a slum—an opportunity he thought he might not get in his entire life. Living in the slum he realized that even silence is a luxury that many are unable to afford.

Tom thinks that if the IPs really take the idea of financial stewardship seriously, then they ought to live more simply and frugally when in societies such as India. For him, if Habitat makes a rule that with Habitat money the national partners can only travel second class in the train, then the IPs should also travel second class. Tom says that he contributes regularly to Habitat from his IP stipend but feels that his co-IPs find him unconventional and resist his policy of austerity.[25]

Faith is another IP of Habitat in Koovappally. The bottom line for Faith, as for many of the partners, is that Habitat is primarily a spiritual quest. She does not like it when the overseas Habitat projects are bent upon getting more funds and build houses, but not concerned about making Habitat a spiritual realization in the life of the homeowners and the community at large. She warns that without proper community development, spiritual growth, and the "broad-basing" of the local committee, there is a real danger to the very foundation of Habitat. She says:

> The aim of Habitat is to help the poor. Those people who invite Habitat to come to a community and build for the poor are not any way better than the poor. Just imagine how this project would have been if the poor rubber tappers here had formed a co-operative and built partnership with Habitat.

Regarding the Habitat covenant Faith argues that it should more genuinely bind the relationship between the local and the

International Habitat but it may not extend to the homeowners since not all of them have the same conceptions of God. Still, the relationship between the local Habitat and the homeowners ought to be bound by a relationship of real partnership, which she finds lacking.

HABITAT'S INTERNATIONALISM: A CRITICAL ASSESSMENT

The international partners of Habitat are supposed to be messengers of Habitat as a God's movement to other—poor—parts of the world. The international partners are the actual interfaces between the local and the global. But their person to person contact is not necessarily accompanied by a greater degree of cross-cultural awareness and transnational sensitivity. Their attitude to local culture, people, and problems varies from sympathy to sugar-coated condemnation, the latter being the rule rather than exception. Their encounter with other people and culture is best described by what Hannerz calls the attitude of "home plus": "...many people travel for the purpose of "home plus". But the plus for the tourist often has little to do with curiosity about alien systems of meaning and a lot to do with facts of nature or quasi-nature, such as nice beaches" (Hannerz 1992: 247). Thus, the newsletters that the IPs send home are full of pictures of the local scene, of people, places, and houses but rarely describe and analyze their encounter with other cultures and traditions. Nor do they discuss the problems that they encounter in the local project. Surrounded by foreign culture they mostly try to keep it "at arm's length," to put in the words of Hannerz again.

But Hannerz (1992: 252) also tells us that a transnational cultural encounter could be a "personal journey of discovery" as well and it could involve "paradoxical interplay between mastery and surrender" (1992: 253). We also see this at work in Habitat for Humanity. Some Habitat IPs are animated by a genuine desire for new cultural experience. Some of them feel guilty at staying in home-like situations in the cities and want to live in the villages. It is perhaps for a sense of discovery that Tom and James decided to stay in a slum in Hubli, while "an interplay of mastery and surrender" characterizes the critical perspectives of some IPs. However, those who take their vocation seriously as a journey of discovery face the problem of dual allegiance. They also face hostility from the local project leaders (not necessarily from the homeowners and the local people) when they stress homeowner partnership and point out irregularities in the project functioning, which shows that the problems in the localization of Habitat do not solely lie with the donors.

Habitat's international work is an important part of the urge on the part of the American volunteers to come to terms with themselves not only in relation to American society but also in relation to the world at large. Habitat's mobilization involves the incorporation of vital "international symbolism"[26] such as "global village,"[27] "transnational walk"[28] and international partnership. But this incorporation has been more at the symbolic level, not accompanied by a genuine striving to put such symbolism into the practice of its own proclaimed goal of development and global partnership. Therefore, it is no wonder that the current chairman of the board of director of Habitat himself writes:

> We speak a lot about partnership, but our lines of authority and accountability aren't always clear... We like to talk about ourselves as an international organization, but we tend to act like a US organization with an international component.. If we want to be an international organization, we must be international people (Stosez 1993: 5).

In terms of Habitat building for the low-income families in poor countries, Habitat volunteers think that they belong to a "doing evangelism", rather than an evangelism interested in conversion. But though in Habitat's discourse there is a shift from old evangelism stressing conversion to new evangelism emphasizing concrete action for meeting human needs, in practice such a move is not divorced from pragmatic considerations: in a multireligious society like India to build only for Christians and to stress conversion overtly can be detrimental even to the interests of the mission itself. Habitat's emphasis upon coming to a local area only through Christian groups—churches or Christian organizations—no matter whether they have interest or expertise in house building and people's development, and the fact that these local Christian organizations do not have people from other religions in their board point us to the limits even in such "doing evangelism".

Such limitation is directly related to the way the volunteers of Habitat look at other religions. One volunteer in a Habitat project in the United States says: "As for other religions—I feel everyone is a child of God and is searching in his or her own way. However, as a Christian, salvation is in Jesus Christ, but those who don't have a chance to know him are not condemned." Sometimes this takes a nuanced form as another volunteer tells us: "I think each of the great religions contains some revelation of God. If a particular religion has meaning to people, we should respect that religion. However, as a Christian, I believe that God's most complete revelation of himself has been through Jesus Christ."

The weak internationalism of Habitat is also evidenced by the fact that in their attitude to other cultures and religions the actors of Habitat mostly operate with an idiom of "foreign policy" and diplomacy and not with one of genuine dialogue. Millard Fuller, the founder and the charismatic leader of Habitat, often says in his speeches that Jesus Christ was not an American citizen, and it is written in the Habitat International training manual: "For Christians, it means that we have to come to the point of realizing God's foreign policy—and enjoying cultural diversity". What is in fact pleaded for here is to accept the diverse cultures in which Christianity presents itself in the contemporary world rather than being prepared for accepting either religious or cultural diversity per se. Habitat's international partnership training programme is more interested in preparing IPs to be able to manage themselves in other cultures rather than genuinely taking part in these and being prepared to question one's own. It becomes an exercise in what Robertson (1995a: 31) calls the "instrumentally rational promotion of intercultural communication" (also, see Wallerstein 1991). Of course the international partners are advised in their training manual: "Compare your findings with your own culture and with the Bible. Become sensitive to the strengths and weaknesses of your's and their's. This helps overcome blind spots and ethnocentrism." But overcoming ethnocentrism is a remote concern in the vision and practice of Habitat for Humanity International. If "to step into real dialogue," as Harvey Cox (1988) argues, "is to step into a holy ground—[where] no one who enters—really enters—remains unaffected," then there is very little evidence of this taking place in the life of Habitat.

Of late there seems to be some introspection in Habitat about its international work. The board of directors of Habitat in its 1993 annual meeting has recommended that all Habitat projects be called affiliates, thus urging an abolition of the distinction between the sponsored projects and the affiliates (Fuller 1994). All Habitat projects are now urged to mobilize their resources even if they receive support from the American headquarters. The overseas projects in poor countries, even totally dependent on aid from the headquarters in the United States, are urged to tithe for fellow projects in their countries and other countries of the world. Moreover, there is now a move within Habitat for Humanity International to nationalize itself: a country where Habitat builds is expected to constitute a national board of directors which in turn is expected to take over the role of control and supervision of the activities of Habitat from the international.[29] Instead of international partners working with overseas Habitat projects, Habitat International is now trying to train people from the countries concerned who are to carry out the task previously carried out by the international partners, calling them national partners.

But what is to be noted is that this introspection points more to the structural reorganization of Habitat rather than to any rethinking on its part on the questions of interreligious dialogue, attitude to other cultures, and transnational consciousness. It is no wonder then that the formation of national organizations within

Habitat and the nominal erasure of the distinction between the affiliates and the sponsored projects have been accompanied by a shortening of the period of the IP training, for a period of six weeks compared to the previous eleven. Though the restructured IP training programme aims at putting more emphasis on "trainee's spiritual development and management exercise" (Habitat World, April 1992: 6), the agenda of what Robertson (1996: 22) calls a "moral-global education", to prepare the IPs for confronting the task of building a global covenant and living in communities of communities in the contemporary globalized world, does not figure anywhere.

RELIGION, GLOBALIZATION AND THE WORLD SYSTEM

Scholars such as Robertson (1992, 1993, 1994, 1995c; also Beyer 1994)) urge us to understand the complex link between religion and globalization. The ethnography of Habitat provides us with an appropriate case for exploring some of these issues. The first question in this regard is the issue of "global spirituality" as a defining mark of our times. E.H. Cousins, building on the seminal work of Teilhard de Chardin, tells us that "at this point of history, because of the shift from divergence to convergence, the forces of planetization are bringing about an unprecedented complexification of consciousness through the convergence of culture and religion" (Cousins 1985: 15). For Cousins, there is the rise of a global spirituality now which is characterized by two processes: a "creative encounter" and dialogue between religions and cultures, and a practical and spiritual turn in all religions in as much as they "rediscover the material dimensions of existence and their spiritual significance" (Cousins 1985: 17). Insofar as the measure of dialogue between cultures and religions is concerned, there is very little of it at work in Habitat. But insofar as the other measure of a practical and spiritual turn is concerned, Habitat's "theology of hammer" presents us a different picture. The actors of Habitat think that one cannot think of one's spiritual life if one's "physical life is roach infected." They consider building homes as indispensable for their spiritual striving. Moreover through the act of building, actors of Habitat overcome their denominational and doctrinal differences, supporting the noted theologian Johannes B. Metz's (1970, 1981) contention that the quest for unity of faith has itself to be transformed into a practical quest of ameliorating the suffering of men and women (see also, Giri 1995). Of course, their notion of spirituality, as we have seen, is more individualistic, emphasizing individual salvation and self-realization rather than an integral transformation of societies.

The second issue here is that of the relationship between religion and the world system. Scholars such as Csordas (1992) argue that there is a tenuous link between the emergent global religious movements and the logic of the world system. Csordas argues, for instance, that while Methodism corresponds to the stage of industrial capitalism, Pentecostal Catholicism corresponds to the phase of transnational capitalism. Csordas shows how it is the middle-class actors who bring the message of community as well as different services to the poor in the transnational movement of Pentecostalism. While the leaders of the movement occupy a privileged position in the contemporary global economy, the beneficiaries are mainly the migrants in the world system and the very poor in the local area.[30] For Csordas, in such an encounter while the middle-class leaders are more interested in "conversion to Christ" (in a spiritual sense?), rather than in "concern for the poor," the squatters begin to abandon "individualistic materialism" and emulate "the middle-class for an increasing communitarianism and pride of status" (Csordas 1992: 135).

The study of Habitat corroborates two important descriptive remarks of Csordas: that the leaders of transnational movements are predominantly middle-class and usually occupy a privileged position in the world economy, while the "beneficiaries" are the poor and migrants; and that the leaders are more interested in their spiritual salvation rather than service to the poor. For instance, in case of the Habitat project in Immokalee, Florida, the migrant labourers are the primary beneficiaries of Habitat (see Giri 1994a). The leaders have riches that they want to share with the poor.

Even the leaders of Habitat in the developing world are those who have contact with the global flow of information and resources and are usually agents of international aid programs or world mission activities in the local area. Here we might remember the extensive global networks of local Habitat leaders such as K. Azariah and George Thomas. The second proposition that such movements are more interested in "conversion to the Christ" rather than in "concern for the poor" needs some qualification. The study of Habitat urges us to understand the relationship between them deeply—in accordance with the frame of reference of the actors. It is undoubtedly true that the majority of leaders of Habitat look at it as primarily a spiritual quest, rather than simply as the instrumental act of helping the poor. At the same time, it has to be noted that some Habitat leaders, for instance, Millard Fuller (see, Fuller 1977, 1986), do not look at these two kinds of concerns as necessarily opposed to each other. "Conversion to Christ" and "concern for the poor" can be part of the same transformative quest at least in the vision and practice of some actors.

CONCLUSION

International organizations and transnational initiatives, originating from the affluent countries of the world, now proliferate in the global domain. These initiatives mobilize resources and goodwill from the citizens of their countries for ameliorating the condition of the disadvantaged and the needy today. The involvement of people with such transnational initiatives is looked upon as the manifestation of a "culture shift" in advanced industrial societies, characterized by a search for meaning in one's life over and above the familiar categories of money and power and an urge to share one's time and resources with the less fortunate of one's country and in the poor parts of the world (Inglehart 1990). But the work of international organizations and transnational initiatives is not innocent of the play of power and the urge for control. Thus behind the rhetoric of global partnership in a transnational organization like Habitat for Humanity we see the dynamics of control at many levels: the lack of partnership between the homeowners and the entrepreneurial leaders in sponsored projects corresponds to the lack of partnership between the sponsored projects and Habitat for Humanity International. For an international partner such as Shelly, this asymmetry finally corresponds to the unequal partnership between God and Man: God being a senior partner, and man a junior partner.

How does the ethnography of Habitat widen the universe of discourse of globalization? The differential embodiment of Habitat not only in different projects but also in different villages in the same project as in Khammam Habitat for Humanity shows that our models of globalization must be sensitive to the critical role of local structures and cultures. The present ethnography of a transnational initiative also shows that theories of globalization must be sensitive to the dialectical relationship between the local and the global. Though theorists of globalization such as Robertson, Appadurai, and Hannerz have sensitized us to the interface between the local and the global, they neither describe nor theorize how the local and the global dialectically constitute and transform each other.[31] Robertson's (1995a) concept of "globalization" points to the global constitution and production of the local but does not describe the way the local reflects, refracts, and transforms the global. While prevailing theories seem to erase the hyphen between the local and the global the present ethnography urges us towards a dialectical view of the global-human condition today.

The present ethnography also shows that what proponents of structural globalization such as Friedman call "encompassment" and cultural globalization, "relativization", are simultaneously at work in the global dynamics of a transnational initiative like Habitat. Self, societies, national system of societies—three of Robertson's four variables—are simultaneously at work in Habitat but it also works as an encompassing system and the comparative engagement with Csordas's study of Pentecostalism shows that it is also an integral part of the contemporary global political economy. But Habitat's global mobilization also brings to the fore creative roles of self, culture, and communicative action which cannot be adequately captured by the world system approaches of theorists such as Wallerstein and Friedman. One of these relates to the significance of the very spirit of covenant. Habitat seeks to build a global covenant through a covenantal approach, as opposed to a contractual approach (see Bromley and Busching 1988). Though at one level, the image of covenant has something definitely Biblical about it and to that extent people of other religious faiths do not belong to it, at another level, covenant also means relationships of trust and spiritually-based mutual commitments among actors which provide a deeper alternative to contractual relationships which predominate in the modern world (Bromley and Busching 1988). Habitat regulates the relationship between its different projects not through contracts[32] but through a spiritual covenant (even though the relationship between a specific project and its beneficiaries is governed by legal contract) and this has a wider significance today. As globalization is on its ascendancy today, we are being told about the need for a global democracy (Connolly 1991; Held 1991). But our models of global democracy are still based on models of "possessive individualism" and legal contracts between actors who are its bearers, while Habitat's covenantal approach to the global condition can help us widen and deepen these to embody covenantal relations based on mutual trust and unconditional ethical obligation of the self to the other (cf. Bauman 1993; Giri 1996).

In fact, it is the idea of a spiritual covenant which can now provide us with a transformative content to Robertsons' fourth variable, namely the notion of humankind. The ethnography of Habitat also shows that those who are to be bearers of a spiritual covenant are not only bound to their nationalism but also to their religious dogmas. The narratives of international partners of Habitat for Humanity teach us that in the international domain those who are to overcome the asymmetries of power and be sensitive to differences in religion and culture are still victims of their American ways of looking at things. In this context, Habitat's ideal of building a "Kingdom of God" and building a global covenant on earth continues remains a challenge of which there are only a very few dedicated takers. Considering their Biblical origin, perhaps there is a need to take heed of the arguments of Rienhold Neibuhr on the part of the actors of Habitat for Humanity International:

> We cannot expect even the wisest of nations to escape every peril of moral and spiritual complacency; for nations have always been constitutionally self-righteous. But it will make a difference whether the culture in which politics of nations are formed is only as deep and as high as nation's ideals; or whether there is a dimension in the culture from the standpoint of which the element of vanity in all human ambitions and achievements is discerned. But this is the height which can be grasped only by faith... The faith which appropriates the meaning in the mystery inevitably involves an experience of repentance for the false meanings which the pride of nations and cultures introduces into the pattern. Such repentance is the true source of charity; and we are more desperately in need of genuine charity than of more technocratic skills (Niebuhr 1952: 149-150).

NOTES

1. For instance, for a scholar such as Robertson, globalization involves a duality of objective and subjective processes: "Globalization refers both to the compression of the world and to the intensification of the consciousness of the world as a whole" (quoted in Friedman 1995: 70). For Robertson, through a heightening of "self-consciousness" at multiple levels, globalization simultaneously leads to "relativization of societies" and "relativization of self-identities" (Robertson 1992: 27).

2. By the "perspectival" nature of the construction of the global today, Appadurai urges us to understand how these constructs are "influenced very much by the historical, linguistic and political situatedness of different sorts of actors..." (Appadurai 1990: 296).

3. In the words of Friedman: "Globalization refers to the formation of

global institutional structures, that is, structures that organize the already existing global field, and global cultural forms, that are either produced by or transformed into globally accessible objects and representations" (Friedman 1995: 75).

4. While individual refers to the sociological identity of a person, self refers to something much more than that, captured by what Giddens (1991) calls a "reflexive self" (see, Giri 1996; Mauss 1979; Taylor 1989). But to be fair to Robertson, he demonstrates sensitivity to the significance of such reflective distinction and its potential for planetary consciousness in his recent works, for instance, in his work on global moral education (see, Robertson 1996).

5. Ingold makes this distinction in the following manner, a distinction which has enormous significance for thinking about reflective self, globalization, and "metacultural" engagement:

To regard the human being simply as an individual culture-bearer is to reduce his social life to an aggregate of overt behavioural interactions, which serve to reproduce the elements of culture just as the phenotypic behaviour of organism results in the reproduction of elements of the genotype. But if he is regarded as a person, that is as a locus of consciousness, then social life appears as the temporal unfolding of consciousness through the instrumentality of cultural forms. Whereas the individual is a vehicle for culture, his mind a container for cultural content, the conscious life of the person is a movement that adopts culture as its vehicle. Thus, culture stands, in a sense, between the person and the individual; worked by one, it works the other (Ingold 1986: 293).

6. To be fair, Robertson does talk about "metaculture" which has the potential to radicalize both culture and self. For instance, Robertson writes: "there is a need for more discussion of what I call metaculture as a way of addressing the varying links between culture and social structure and individual and collective action" (Robertson 1992: 34).

7. Robertson criticizes the tendency in some quarters to assume that globalization overrides locality and emphasizing the global constitution and production of the local through his concept of "glocalization," he urges us to study models of "practical glocalization" (Robertson 1995a: 26). Such a model erases the hyphen between the global and the local and is sensitive neither to the dialectic between the two nor to the dynamics of "local initiative and local response" in the "so-called world system" (Mintz 1977). Sidney Mintz's essay under the same title probably intended to draw our attention to this dialectical dimension of the

global human condition; but when one goes through this essay one finds very little local initiative and local response in it.

8. Take, for instance, the description of the transnational initiative of the sister-city movement offered by Wilbur Zelinsky (1991). Zelinsky writes:" Something new and remarkable, if not revolutionary, has been going on in the social geography of our late-twentieth century world: the sister-city phenomenon. Over the past fifty years, more than 1000 twinings have been formalized among a wide variety of communities in at least 150 countries — people to people relationships, one is inclined to believe, which are generally inspired by quite laudable ideals" (Zelinsky 1991: 2).

9. Following the trajectory of cultural objects in a transnational space shares the methodological insights of scholars such as Sidney Mintz (1987) who argue that a cultural object might originate in a particular area but when it diffuses to another area, it acquires a life of its own and is not simply a passive reflection of the cultural properties of the area of origin. Multi-locale ethnographies which follow and describe the trajectories of global flows, processes, and movements enable us to create "mixed-genre texts" which evoke and describe the "inner lives of the subject" and the "nature of the world political economy" (Marcus 1986: 172). The strategies of multi-locale ethnography and "mixed-genre text" help us "weave together the multiple genres of self and society in our contemporary global condition, not in any mechanical integration, nor in any contrastive presentation, but in a creative delineation of transnational discursive themes and a careful comparison of their local embodiments and manifestations" (Giri 1993b: 285).

10. In the words of Millard Fuller, "First, we're in partnership with God.. Second, we're in a partnership with each other.. With this dual partnership as our foundation we are going to arouse the consciences of individuals and organizations around the world, challenging them to join in this cause. And together, we are going to get rid of the shacks. All of them" (Fuller 1986a: 21-22)

11. It has to be noted that the United Church of Christ (UCC), the denomination in which Millard Fuller was raised has been one of the pioneers in this frontier. The same also can be spoken about MCC (Mennonite Central Committee). But none of them had taken up housing as a form of ministry. So, though the style of Habitat's need addressal has some pre-existing evangelical forms, its content and substance is a significant departure.

12. It is important to realize the significance of images in contemporary

cultural politics (see, Ewen 1989). Ginsburg's (1989) ethnography of anti-abortion activism in the contemporary United States tells us about the significance of the image of the fetus in its mobilization and it provides an interesting parallel to the image of the shack in Habitat (also, see, Giri 1989).

13. In Immokalee, Florida, most people live in dilapidated trailers. A selected homeowner is required either to burn or destroy the trailer that he/she used to live in, until moving to the newly constructed Habitat home. A homeowner indeed has no choice about this policy of the local Habitat. He or she cannot give it to relatives even though they might be paying $100 a week to rent an even more dilapidated trailer in a trailer park. Sometimes even a prospective Habitat homeowner has to spend $500 in carrying off his or her condemned and forbidden shack to be disposed of in the dumping ground. The immokalee project director explains that if the shack is not worthy of habitation on the part of one individual, then it should not exist for another, and hence must be destroyed.

14. The primary distinction between the sponsored project and the affiliated project is not that the former is overseas and the latter is domestic. The issue here is one of funding and financial autonomy. Habitat projects in Canada and Australia are called affiliates because they are self-supportive while those in India and Mexico are called sponsored projects. It must also be noted that Habitat has recently termed all its projects affiliates, an issue I discuss later in the text.

15. I had a look at the original project proposal that Azariah had submitted to the headquarters on behalf of Khammam Habitat in 1984, as well as at its proposal for expansion submitted to the headquarters on May 23, 1988. It is interesting to look at the response of the local Habitat to some of the key questions from the International and the comments of the-then Habitat area director, Keith Branson, on this proposal. On the question as to how the local committee educates the homeowners about Habitat's house-building ministry, Khammam Habitat writes: "in ground breaking and dedications and also when we have visitors from U.S.A." Branson comments: "It seems inadequate and shallow." He also wants to know why there are no community meetings. On the selection of the beneficiaries, Branson remarks: "Insufficient information, how is community survey taken? How is target location decided? How is information publicized?....We want to know how you actually do these things." On the question "What will people do or contribute to the building of their own houses?" it was written in the project proposal: "sweat

equity." Branson writes: "We know the theory of sweat equity. But how is it practiced in your project?" To the question, "What is the Christian community's commitment to the housing development?" the answer was "prayer" which made Branson comment: "If this is true, what does it say about the community backing for a project devoted to Action?" To the question, "How will you determine whether the homeowners are able to pay for the house?" Khammam Habitat replies: "Personal Knowledge." Keith Branson comments: "How does 'personal knowledge' reflect in such a case where Khammam has been in severe repayment difficulty for nearly the whole of the project life?" Khammam Habitat writes in this proposal that being a volunteer in this project means being a partner and an advisor. Branson asks: "What does your answer mean?"

16. Fuller writes: "For example, one of the basic principles of the covenant is that the local affiliate can not charge interest to the Habitat homeowners. If a local affiliate did start charging interest, we would disaffiliate them" (personal communication). Thus the relationship between covenantal and contractual dimension in the work of Habitat is complex. The relationship between the homeowner and the local Habitat project is guided by legal contract so that any breach is fraught with consequences such as eviction. But this is not so in case of the relationship between the local project and Habitat for Humanity International. For instance when a local project has serious problem, Habitat does not take recourse to the court of law. Habitat for Humanity was not satisfied with the work of its sponsored project in Hubli. It built expensive houses and allotted these to some rich people of the locality. The leaders of Habitat International as well as directors of other projects in Hubli persuaded the project director of the sponsored project in Hubli to step down. But such a transition does not happen smoothly in all cases.

17. This unique manifestation of Habitat in Palladugu strikes even the international partners. In a letter to the headquarters, an international partner writes: "I shall be investigating the why of numbers for villages. Why did Penugolanu [one of the Habitat villages] fall behind and why did Palladugu move ahead and others are really stagnant?"

18. But the process of this identity formation is complex. The identity of Habitat volunteers is crucially dependent upon the performance of the homeowners. Homeowners must repay regularly, which help Habitat volunteers to feel secure in their identity of belonging to a movement where their money and labor are not given as a dole or a charity but become a link in an ever-widening circle of "Revolving Fund for

Humanity." They feel threatened when the homeowners default. In order to secure this identity from all probable threats the actors of Habitat would not hesitate to impose their own middle class identity upon the homeowners by insisting on the destruction of the dilapidated trailer of a selected homeowner. Some of them also would not feel the prick of conscience in throwing out a defaulting homeowner to the streets of Chicago in a cold winter night (that this actually happened in the Chicago Habitat affiliate was once reported widely in the newspapers in the United States about which Habitat World had also written a commentary) or suggesting taking out the roof of a poor farmer's Habitat house, thus blurring the thin separating line between vicarious and creative identity formation.

19. Finally, after all this, the headquarters approved Khammam Habitat's proposal for the fourth phase house-building.

20. Anthropologist Constance Perin argues that in American culture, homeownership is not simply a matter of "economic externality and possession," it is a precondition of the very constitution of the American self, linked almost ritually to adulthood, independence and coming of age. In her words: "One climbs the ladder as the 'natural progression' through the stages of the life-cycle—from renting an apartment or to owning a single family detached house. In taking the ladder rung to rung, the movement is altogether upward, an evolutionary progress as well, toward salvation from 'lower forms' to a 'final, divinely ordained form' " (Perin 1977: 47).

21. Newsletters are the letters that the IPs write regularly to their supporters and friends back home. These letters are always full of the description of the natural beauty of the locality and pictures of persons, houses, and activities. Very rarely these discuss the problems that they and Habitat face in the overseas countries.

22. Martin Bavink (personal communication) also points out to me that this has to do with the attitude to physical labour: the high-caste and the rich in India think that physical labour is degrading and there is nothing worthwhile in such engagement.

23. Subsequently Dolly got married to a Hindu in Kerala with whom she fell in love and had to resign from her position as an international partner.

24. The Hubli project was temporarily put on hold, and subsequently closed because of financial mismanagement and gross violation of Habitat norms by the local leaders. Tom and James tried to develop another committee and a leadership structure that could take care of the

Habitat project in Hubli. They worked with the poor who would actually be beneficiaries of Habitat homes, but they found these local young boys lacking in proper leadership, organizational and communicative skills, thus paving the way for the final closure of the project.

25. Tom's thoughts about the practice of a more austere lifestyle is noteworthy. In fact, this is what Habitat for Humanity encourages its volunteers to emulate and practice. It is written in the manual for Habitat IPs:

   Life-style is an expression of one's faith, attitude and servanthood. International Field Personnel should develop greater sensitivity to local people through participation in the life of the local community. This enhances understanding and communication. International Field Personnel should live on a level that Habitat homeowners could reasonably aspire to. From Habitat's perspective, life-style should be one of moderation. It must be remembered that even though one intentionally seeks a moderate life-style, a Partner may receive five to ten times more income than does the "national" with whom he or she works, who may have to support an entire family on a limited salary.

   But the resistance to some of Tom's suggestions also suggests a gap between this formulation and the practice of the IPs.

26. In another context, Robert Bellah (quoted in Wuthnow 1988: 255) has argued that civil religion in America seems to function best when it apprehends "transcendent religious identity..as revealed through the experience of the American people"; yet the growing interdependence of America with the world order appears to "necessitate the incorporation of vital international symbolism into our civil religion" (ibid). This helps us understand the global orientations of Habitat.

27. This is a programme of Habitat International where those US or European volunteers interested in Habitat get a chance to spend a week or so building houses in developing countries. While many Habitat volunteers see in this an opportunity to be "citizen diplomats spreading the word of brotherhood and sisterhood through action not words," others have a more critical view. As one of the participants writes: "Half of the cost of the global village sent to a sponsored project could purchase much more labour thus ceasing the poverty / unemployment cycle" (Giri 1994a: 64).

28. To spread its message as well as mobilize resources, Habitat for Humanity periodically organizes what it calls "consciousness-raising walks". Some of these walks such as the 1988 Habitat Walk from Portland, Maine to Atlanta, Georgia are called transnational walks in which leaders of Habitat from the overseas countries also participate. These

overseas representatives speak in Habitat rallies and talk to the American audience about the work of Habitat in their communities. They also solicit contributions for their projects.

29. A recent communication from Habitat International states that the number of national organizations stands at thirty at present.

30. According to Csordas, those "who are attracted to the movement are part of the 'excess population' created by international monopoly capital" (Csordas 1992: 11). Of the Catholic Pentecostal movements in Latin American cities, Csordas also writes: "Cooperative ventures organized among Catholic Pentecostals in Mexican squatter settlements or poor neighborhoods of Santiago constitute religiously motivated innovations or organization for the provision of 'services and home-made goods' at costs below those possible by the dominant sector (Csordas 1992: 135).

31. It is perhaps for this reason that Jonathan Friedman (1995) states that he finds very little "disjunction" in Appadurai's model of globalization.

32. Again a recent communication from Habitat for International makes it clear: "The Habitat for Humanity International Covenants (National and Affiliate) are not legal instruments. The are spiritual agreements between HFHI [Habitat for Humanity International] and its national organizations and affiliates but these Covenants are not enforceable in courts of law. HFHI does, however, own the name Habitat for Humanity as a service mark."

REFERENCES

Appadurai, A., 1990, "Disjuncture and Difference in the Global Cultural Economy", in Mike Featherstone (ed.), *Global Culture: Nationalism, Globalization and Modernity,* London: Sage.

——, 1991, The Global Ethnoscape: Notes and Queries for a Transnational Anthropology", in R. G. Fox. Santa Fe (ed.), *Recapturing Anthropology: Working in the Present,* New Mexico: School of American Research.

Bauman, Z., 1993, *Postmodern Ethics*, Oxford: Basil Blackwell.

Beyer, Peter F., 1994, *Religion and Globalization*, London: Sage.

Bromley, David G. Bruce C. Busching, 1988, "Understanding the Structure of Contractual and Covenantal Social Relations: Implications for the Sociology of Religion", *Sociological Analysis* 49, S: 15-32.

Chekki, D., 1988, Transnational Networks in Global Development: Canada and the Third World, *International Social Science Journal.*

Cousins, E.H., 1985, *Global Spirituality*, Madras: University of Madras Press.

Coleman, S., 1991, "Faith which Conquers the World: Swedish Fundamentalism and the Globalization of Culture", *Ethnos* (1-2): 6-18.

Connolly, W.E., 1991, *Identity/Difference: Democratic Negotiations of Political Paradox*, Ithaca: Cornell University Press.

Cox, H., 1988, *Many Mansions: A Christian's Encounter with Other Faiths*, New York: Simon & Schuster.

Csordas, T., 1992, "Religion and the World System: The Pentecostal Ethics and the Spirit of Monopoly Capital", *Dialectical Anthropology* 17 (1): 3-24.

Ewen, Stuart, 1988, *All Consuming Images: The Politics of Style in Contemporary Culture*, New York: Basic Books.

Featherstone, M. and S. Lash, 1995, "Globalization, Modernity and the Spatialization of Social Theory: An Introduction", in M. Featherstone (ed.), *Global Modernities*, London: Sage Publications.

Foucault, M., 1972, *The Archeology of Knowledge*, New York: Pantheon.

Frieberg, M. and B. Hettne, 1984, "The Greening of the World: Towards a Non-Deterministic Model of Global Processes", in H. Addo et al., *Development as Social Transformation,* Tokyo: United Nations University Press.

——, 1988, "Local Mobilization and World System Politics", *International Social Science Journal* No. 117: 341-360.

Friedman, J., 1990, "Being in the World: Globalization and Localization", in Featherstone (ed.), *Global Culture,* London: Sage Publications.

——, 1994, *Cultural Identity and the Global Process*, London: Sage Publications.

——, 1995, "Global System, Globalization, and the Parameters of Modernity", in M. Featherstone et al. (eds.), *Global Modernities,* London: Sage Publications.

Fuller, M., 1977, *Bokotola*, Chicago: AP / Follett.

——, 1980, *Love in the Mortar Joints*, Clinton, NJ: New Wing Publishing,

Inc.

——, 1986a, *No More Shacks: The Daring Vision of Habitat for Humanity*, Waco, Texas: Word Publishing House.

——, 1986b, "Faces of Faith: Building Homes for Humanity", The Other Side, January-February: 40-43.

——, 1994, *The Theology of the Hammer*, Macon, GA: Smith & Hellwys.

Fuller, M. and L. Fuller, 1990, *The Excitement is Building, How Habitat for Humanity is Building Roofs over Head and Hopes in Hearts*, Dallas: Word Publishers.

Giri, A., 1989, "Narratives of Creative Transformation: Constituting Critical Movements in Contemporary American Culture", *Dialectical Anthropology,* 14: 331-343.

——, 1993a, "Housing Movements in Contemporary India: Some Examples from Kerala", *Social Action,* April: 193-209.

——, 1993b, "Critique of the Comparative Method and the Challenges of a Transnational World", *Contributions to Indian Sociology,* (N.S.) 27 (2): 267-289.

——, 1994a, *In the Margins of Shacks: The Vision and Practice of Habitat for Humanity*, The Johns Hopkins University, Baltimore: PhD thesis.

——, 1994b, "Some Contemporary Notes on Method", *Man and Development,* XV1 (2): 16-26.

——, 1995, *Building in the Margins of Shacks: Towards a Hermeneutics of Recovery*, Madras Institute of Development Studies: Working Paper.

——, 1996, *Self, Other, and the Challenge of Culture*, Madras Institute of Development Studies: Working Paper.

Ginsburg, Faye D., 1989, *Contested Lives: Abortion Debate in an American Community*, Berkeley: University of California Press.

Harvey, D., 1989, *The Condition of Postmodernity*, Cambridge, M.A.: Basil Blackwell.

Hannerz, U., 1990a, "Cosmopolitans and Locals in World Culture", in M. Featherstone (ed.), *Global Culture: Nationalism, Globalization and Modernity,* London: Sage Publications.

——, 1990b, "Culture Between Center and Periphery: Towards a Macroanthropology", *Ethnos,* (3-4): 200-216.

——, 1992, *Cultural Complexity*, New York: Columbia University Press.

Hegedus, Z., 1990, "Social Movements and Social Change in Self-Creative Society: New Civil Initiatives in the International Arena", in M. Albrow & E. King (eds.), *Globalization, Knowledge, and Society,* London:

Sage Publications.

Held, D., 1991, "Democracy, the Nation-State and the Global System", *Economy and Society,* 20 (2): 138-172.

Hettne, B., 1990, *Development Theory and Three Worlds*, Essex: Longman.

Inglehart, R., 1990, *The Culture Shift in Advanced Societies*, Princeton: Princeton University Press.

Ingold, T., 1986, *Evolution and Social Life*, Cambridge: University Press.

Kothari, R., 1987, "On Humane Governance", *Alternatives,* XII: 277-290.

——, 1988, *Transformation and Survival: In Search of a Humane World Order*, New Delhi: Ajanta Publishers.

Kuper, A., 1994, "Culture, Identity and the Project of a Cosmopolitan Anthropology", *Man,* (N.S.) 29: 537-554.

Marcus, G., 1986, "Ethnography in the Modern World System", in G. Marcus & J. Clifford (eds.), *Writing Culture: Politics and Poetics of Ethnography,* Berkeley & Los Angeles: University of California Press.

Martin, L.H. et. al., 1988, *Technologies of Self: Seminar with Michael Foucault*, Amherst: University of Massachusetts Press.

Mauss, M., 1979, "A Category of the Human Mind: The Notion of Person, the Notion of Self", in *Sociology and Psychology*, London: Routledge and Kegan Paul.

McAdam, D., 1988, "Social Movements", in N. J. Smelser (ed.), *Handbooks of Sociology,* Newbury Park: Sage Publications.

Mansbach, R., 1971, *The Web of World Politics: Non-state Actors in the Global Systems*, Englewood, NJ: Prentice-Hall.

Mintz, S.W., 1977, "The So-Called World System: Local Initiative and Local Response", *Dialectical Anthropology,* 2: 253-70.

——, 1987, Author's Rejoinder, Symposium Review of *Sweetness and Power, Food and Foodways,* 2: 171-97.

Metz, J.B., 1970, "Does Our Church Need a New Reformation? A Catholic Reply", *Concilium,* 4 (6): 81-91.

——, 1981, "Towards the Second Reformation: The Future of Christianity in a Post-Bourgeoisie World", *Cross Currents,* XXX1 (1).

Moore, M., 1986, "A New Look at the Nayar Taravada", *Man,* (n.s.) 20: 523-41.

——, 1989, "The Kerala House as a Hindu Cosmos", *Contributions to Indian Sociology,* (n.s.) 23 (1): 523-41.

Neibuhr, R., 1952, *The Ironies of American History.*

Neville, R. C., 1974, *The Cosmology of Freedom*, New Haven: Yale University Press.

Perin, C., 1977, *Everything in its Place: Social Order and Land Use in America*, Princeton: University Press.

Robertson, R., 1992, *Globalization: Social Theory and the Global Culture*, London: Sage.

———, 1993, "Community, Society, Globality, and the Category of Religion", in E. Barker et al. (eds.), *Secularization, Rationalism and Sectarianism: Essays in Honour of Bryan R. Wilson*, Oxford: Clarendon Press.

———, 1994, "Religion and the Global Field", *Social Compass*, 41 (1): 121-135.

———, 1995a, "Globalization: Time-Space and Homogeneity-Heterogeneity", in M. Featherstone et. al. (eds.), *Global Modernities*, London: Sage.

———, 1995b, "Globality and Transnationality", Introduction to Ananta Giri, *Global Transformations: Postmodernity and Beyond*, (forthcoming).

———, 1995c, "The Search for Fundamentals in Global Perspective", in L. van Tijssen et al. (eds.), *The Search for Fundamentals*, Kluwer Academic Publishers.

———, 1996, "Values and Globalization: Communitarianism and Globality", *International Journal of Sociology and Social Policy*.

Simons, H. and T. Media (eds.), 1989, *The Legacy of Kenneth Burke*, Madison: University of Wisconsin Press.

Stosez, E., 1993, "Stosez Sets Goals 93: An Interview with Edgar Stosez", *Habitat World*, 10 (1): 5.

Stewart, C.J. et al., 1984, *Persuasion and Social Movements*, Waveland Press.

Taylor, C., 1989, *Sources of the Self*, Cambridge, MA: Harvard University Press.

Zelinsky, W., 1991, "The Twinning of the World: Sister Cities in Geographical and Historical Perspectives", *Annals* of the Association of American Geographers (1): 103-126.

Wallerstein, I., 1991, *Geopolitics and Geoculture: Essays on the Changing World-System*, Cambridge: University Press.

Wuthnow, R., 1988, *The Restructuring of American Religion: Society and Faith Since World War II*, Princeton: Princeton University Press.

Chapter Eleven

THE QUEST FOR A UNIVERSAL MORALITY:
JURGEN HABERMAS AND SRI AUROBINDO

I think there are a few aspects of contemporary civilization where the structural non-contemporaneity (or synchronism) of different sectors of socio-cultural development is more striking than in the dimension of conventional morals, especially if it is compared or confronted with the actual requirements of a common and joint responsibility for the global consequences of human activities.....What we need today is indeed a universally valid ethics for the whole of humankind, but that does not mean that we need an ethics that would prescribe a uniform style of life for all individuals or for all different sociocultural forms of life.

—*Karl Otto-Apel* (1991: 261)

[The self is] conscious of its ideal universality that can distinguish value from appetites, pleasures and selfish interests and can become the moral subject....The order of our social world is that of value-based norms arising ultimately from the idea of the person as the supreme value. The being or reality of person is in self-consciousness which contains within itself a tension between ideality and actuality....Correspondingly the categories relevant to the comprehension of social reality can only be definitions of norms based upon value which itself is truly apprehended in terms of self-enlightenment.

—*G.C. Pande* (1982: 113-115)

Moral universalism is a historical result... . To be sure the gradual embodiment of moral principles in concrete forms of life is not something that can safely be left to Hegel's absolute spirit. Rather, it is chiefly a function of collective efforts and sacrifices made by sociopolitical movements.

—*Jurgen Habermas* (1990a: 208)

THE PROBLEM

Globalization is one of the main signs of our times. Our contemporary moment is characterized not only by a global interpenetration of cultures but also by the globalization of our everyday lives. With the help of modern science and new technologies, we are able to annihilate space and time. Social, political and economic processes in our contemporary world break down our boundaries and insularities, compelling us to participate in a global flow of culture and consciousness. In the evocative words of anthropologist Clifford Geertz, "foreignness doesn't [now] start at the water's edge but at the skin's" (Geertz 1986: 112). The globalization of our lives and the rise of a transnational world pose enormous moral questions both within a particular society and in its relationship with another. To begin with, "..moral issues stemming from cultural diversity...that used to arise mainly between societies now increasingly arise within them" (Geertz 1986: 115). As cultures and societies participate in a global flow of consciousness, their ways of worldmaking and institutional bases are increasingly subject to a moral critique, which originates from a "view from afar" of a more meaningful "good life" that has been made possible here on earth. Globalization of our condition provides us a glimpse of a more meaningful "good life" in another society, an experience and knowledge of which provides us a global vantage point both to appreciate and criticize our own taken-for-granted institutions and traditions. At the contemporary phase of globalization, it is difficult to insulate our cultural frames and institutional mores from the moralizing gaze born of this global awareness.

While the emergence of a transnational world in the domains of economics and politics is relatively more pronounced today, with the rise of transnational corporations, and movements embodying a transnational ethos, its evolution in the field of culture and consciousness leaves much to be desired. While our contemporary global existence urgently calls for "certain readjustment in both our rhetorical habits and our sense of mission" (Geertz 1986: 119), our culture and consciousness is still bound to the conventional morals of state and society. It is perhaps for this reason that political theorist William Connolly writes: "...globalization of contingency is the defining mark of late modernity, but unfortunately our reflection on issues posed by this condition is shifted to the margins of state-centered political discourse" (Connolly 1991: 25). At the same time, there is an increasing realization in many of us that "...conventional morals...can no longer cope with the new challenges of human responsibility for the distant consequences of our action" (Otto-Apel 1991: 261). Otto-Apel (1991: 264) best articulates this sensibility:

> Thus, it appears that in both dimensions of cultural evolution, namely that of technological interventions in nature and of social interaction, a global situation has been brought about in our time that calls for a new ethics of shared responsibility, in other words, for a type of ethics that, in contradistinction to traditional or conventional form of ethics, may be designated a (planetary) macroethics.

While globalization of our contemporary condition calls for a planetary macroethics and a universal morality, developments within individual social systems simply mock at them. Our contemporary phase of social evolution, name it modernization or postmodernization, is characterized, as it was bound to be by pervasive structural differentiations. In the words of Habermas, "morality gets no clear status in the construction of a structurally differentiated lifeworld" (Habermas 1987a: 92)[1]. Insightful critics of contemporary advanced societies such as sociologist Robert Bellah, have argued that our contemporary "institutional dilemmas" are primarily "moral dilemmas" (Bellah et al. 1991: 38). Bellah and his colleagues observed that Americans have to articulate a new moral language to think about their institutions as they are now ridden with "unprecedented problems" (Bellah et al. 1991: 42). In the face of the present challenges and the dislocations of the postindustrial transition Bellah et al. argue that now there is an urgency to think of "democracy as an ongoing moral quest" not simply as a political process—"as an end state" (Bellah et al. 1991: 20). They plead for a new "moral ecology" to think creatively about institutions—their predicament and possibility— since "the decisions that are made about our economy, our schools, our government, or our national position in the world cannot be separated from the way we live in practical terms, the moral life we lead as a people" (Bellah et al. 1991: 42).[2]

The imperative for a moral grounding of our institutions can be better understood by a critical reflection on two examples of persistent social conflicts that Habermas discusses in one of his recent papers (Habermas 1990b). The first is the persistent question of poverty and disadvantage in advanced industrial societies. For Habermas, while in the classical phase of capitalism capital and labour could threaten each other for pursuing their interests, today "this is no longer the case" (Habermas 1990b: 19). Now, the underprivileged can make their predicament known only through a "protest vote" but "without the electoral support of a majority of citizens...problems of this nature do not even have enough driving force to be adopted as a topic of broad and effective public debate" (ibid: 20). In this situation, a moral consciousness diffusing the entire public sphere is the only way. As Habermas argues: "A dynamic self-correction cannot be set in motion without introducing morals into the debate, without universalizing interests from a normative point of view" (ibid: 20). The same imperative also confronts us in addressing our contemporary global problems such as environmental disaster, world poverty, and the inequality between the North and the South. It is "clear that the increasing gap between the First and the Third world raises some of the most difficult moral questions of the modern world" (Hosle 1992: 229). Habermas also argues that in addressing these problems we need a moral perspective. In the words of Habermas:

> These problems can only be brought to a head by rethinking topics morally, by universalizing interests in a more or less discursive forms.... . The moral or ethical point of view makes us quicker to perceive the more far-reaching, and simultaneously less insistent and more fragile, ties that bind the fate of an individual to that of every other-making even the most alien person a member of one's community (ibid: 20).

The imperative for a moral point of view in thinking about ourselves and thinking through our problems, necessitated by the developments within our social systems and the rise of a transnational world, is paralleled by what can be called a restructuring of moral theory. Morality in the sociological and anthropological discourse has been looked upon as a construction of culture and as an appendage to social norms. In the conventional sense, moral development means learning the norms of a particular culture. But such a notion of morality and moral development ignores the question of the Being and the universal issue of justice, well-being and freedom. In this context psychologist Lawrence Kohlberg speaks of a "post-conventional" stage of moral development when the individual differentiates "his or her self from the rules and expectations of others and defines his or her values in terms of self-chosen ethical principles" (Cortese 1990: 20).

The unease with strict sociologism that the idea of a "post-conventional" morality embodies is paralleled by efforts in political discourse and moral philosophy to break away from a strictly politicized view of morality. For Edelman, western philosophical tradition from Plato to Hobbes, and even unto Rawls, is characterized by what he calls "politicization of morality"—"the attempt to derive moral principles from...political considerations" (Edelman 1990: 108). In such traditions "the raison d'être of moral practices" lies "in the limitation or adjudication of conflict among men" (ibid: 8). In such accounts of morality "the purpose of moral practices is to secure and maintain for men mutually advantageous social arrangements" and "the content of 'morality'...is a product of the requirements of the 'polis' " (ibid: 9). But Edelman argues that:

> In none of the accounts of morality belonging to this tradition are the needs, interest and desires whose satisfaction is at issue themselves characterized as specifically 'moral' needs, interests or desires. That is to say, we do not begin with any moral discrimination concerning them. The conception of morality at the root of these accounts itself rules out that possibility. Morality here is simply the means of escape from, or the means of keeping free of, that predicament characterized by conflict and the frustration of desire, a predicament that would inevitably ensue were 'morality' not allowed to do its work (ibid).

For Edelman, the politicization of morality removes the "inner life from the sphere of the moral" and "makes it impossible to articulate proper moral concepts" (ibid: 53). In this context of the pervasive discourse of the "politicization of morality" Edelman pleads for articulating an adequate language of morality where "it will no longer be conceived of as a satisfaction of individual interests" and a servant of the "polis"; instead the "polis" will be a servant of justice and morality. This requires a break from the discourse of politicized morality and to realize that the source of morality lies in morality itself. For Edelman, the idea of a common good which is not simply an aggregation of individual interests or a sum total of aggregated interests but a "metaphysical" conception is important for an adequate conceptualization of morality and the required quest for its embodiment.

The present essary looks into the issue of universal morality in the context of this structural and discursive restructuring. It critically examines the work of the German philosopher Jurgen Habermas and the Indian spiritual prophet Sri Aurobindo from the point of view of the discourse of morality and its universal import.

THE QUEST FOR A UNIVERSAL MORALITY: LINGUISTIFICATION OF THE SACRED AND THE AGENDA OF "DISCOURSE ETHICS"

Habermas has argued that at the contemporary juncture where the sacred no longer has the unquestioned authority that it once did, morality cannot be grounded in religion. Rather, it has to emerge out of and be anchored in a process of rational argumentation where the actors participate in undistorted communication as members of a community of discourse. To understand Habermas' moral theory, we have to understand his perspective on social evolution, which, following Durkheim and Parsons, is mainly characterized by structural differentiation and the "uncoupling of the system and the life world" (Habermas 1987a; also Habermas 1979). For Habermas, the rise of the public sphere of rational argumentation and rationally-motivated communicative action goes hand in hand with the relocation of the sacred from the domain of the "unspeakable" to our everyday world of language, making it both an object and medium of our ordinary conversation. Habermas's moral theory has to be understood in this evolutionary framework of the "linguistification of the sacred" (Habermas 1987) and the *Structural Transformation of the Public Sphere* (Habermas 1989). Habermas (1987a: 77) has described:

> The disenchantment and disempowering of the domain of the sacred takes place by way of a linguistification of the ritually secured, basic normative agreement; going along with this is a release of the rationality potential in communicative action. The aura of rupture and the tenor that emanates from the sacred, the spellbinding power of the holy, is sublimated into the binding/bonding force of criticizable validity claims and at the same time turned into everyday occurrence (Habermas 1987a: 77).

Habermas (1987a: 91) has explained the implications of such

an evolutionary shift:

> Norm-guided interaction changes in structure to the degree that functions of cultural reproduction, social integration, and socialization pass from the domain of the sacred over to that of everyday communicative practice. In the process, the religious community that made social cooperation possible is transformed into a communicative community striving under the pressure to cooperate (ibid: 91).

Habermas has argued that any agenda of morality in modern society inevitably faces this challenge of the decline of the sacred and the creation of the new linguistic and public spheres for the search for meaning. At the same time, he has argued that morality, anchored in and emerging out of the rational arguments of participants in discourse, can fill the void created by the demise of the sacred order. According to him (1987a: 122), "...only a morality, set communicative aflow and developed into a discourse ethics, can replace the authority of the sacred...In this morality we find dissolved the archaic core of the normative, we see developed the rational meaning of normative validity."

TOWARDS A RATIONAL SOCIETY

The idea of a rational society and an "ideal communication community" is central to Habermas's agenda of morality. For Habermas (1987a: 95), "the projection of an ideal communication community serves as a guiding thread for setting up discourses." Those who participate in this communication community have an urge to participate in not only communication but also in a discursive transformation, where "in the relationship between the Self and the Other there is a basic moment of insight" (ibid). Habermas (1987a: 15) has quoted George Herbert Mead, whose work he values a lot and whom he considers as one of the main inspirations for his theory of communicative action, programmatically: "What is essential to communication is that the symbol should arouse in oneself what it arouses in the other individual". According to Habermas (1987a: 94), "I think all of us feel that one must be ready to recognize the interests of others even when they run counter to our own, but the person who does that does not really sacrifice himself, but becomes a larger self."

But Habermas' ideal of a rational society must not be confused with a technological society where the Cartesian reason reigns supreme. Habermas's agenda is a profound critique of modern positivism, scientism and technological determinism. Expressing his nostalgia for the classical integration of theory and practice and his abhorrence towards its divorce under the regime of modern positivism he said (1973: 84):

> While in the classical Natural Law the norms of moral and just action are equally oriented in their content toward the good-and that means the virtuous life of the citizens, the formal law of the modern age is divested of the catalogues of duties in the material order of life, whether of a city or of a social class. Instead, it allows a neutral sphere of personal choice, in which every citizen, as a private person can egoistically follow goals of maximizing his own needs.

FROM CATEGORICAL IMPERATIVE TO THE DISCURSIVE FORMATION OF WILL

It is the participation in a "wider common world of rational beings" that makes morality a matter of public discourse and enables it (i.e., morality) to replace the "[Kantian] categorical imperative with a procedure of discursive will-formation" (Habermas 1987a: 94). For many commentators, such as philosopher Thomas McCarthy, "In his approach to moral theory Habermas is closest to the Kantian tradition" and "like Kant Habermas distinguishes the type of practical reasoning and corresponding types of 'ought' proper to questions about what is practically expedient, ethically prudent, and morally right" (McCarthy in Habermas 1990a: vii). Both for Kant and Habermas, "calculations of rational choice generate recommendations relevant to the pursuit of contingent purposes in the light of given preferences," and "when serious questions of value arise, deliberation on who one is, and who one wants to be, yields ethical advice concerning the good life" (ibid). Like Kant, Habermas understands "practical reason as universal in import: it is geared to what everyone could rationally will to be a norm binding on everyone else" (ibid). But there is as much discontinuity between Habermas and Kant as there is continuity. McCarthy has elaborated upon it: "His discourse ethics, however, replaces Kant's categorical imperative with a procedure of moral argumentation...This shifts the frame of reference from Kant's solitary, reflecting moral consciousness to the community of moral subjects in dialogue" (in Habermas 1990a: viii).

In order to understand Habermas's agenda of morality and the practice of "discourse ethics" that makes it possible, we have to understand Habermas's view that an urge for justification of norms that guide individual action is very much part of being human. Though Habermas is dismissive of questions of ontology he proceeds with two basic assumptions about man, namely that he/she has a need for communication and an urge for justification.[3] Habermas (1990a: 20) has argued: "from the perspective of first persons, what we consider justified is not a function of custom but a question of justification or grounding". This universal need for justification has a special manifestation in modern social systems. For Habermas all norms have now "at least in principle lost their customary validity" which makes the need for justification all the more urgent in modern societies (Habermas 1988: 227). The idea of morality has to be understood in the context of both this specific and general need for justification. The procedure of rational argumentation, which is the other name for "discourse ethics", fulfills this need of and for the "discursive redemption of normative claims to validity" (Habermas 1990a: 103).

Taking a Hypothetical Attitude to Culture

For Habermas, the procedure of rational (moral) argumentation enables the participants to take a hypothetical attitude to their own form of life, which nonetheless presents itself as the best possible form of "good life".[4] For Habermas, "practical issues" are issues of "good life," which in the form of "ethical formalism" has a "literal" incisiveness not only in the "totality of a particular form of life" but also in the "totality of an individual's life history" (1990a: 104). In this context, "Individuals who have been socialized cannot take a hypothetical attitude toward the form of life and the personal life history that have shaped their own identity" (ibid). It is here that participation in the procedure of practical discourse serves as a redeeming process. First of all, it breaks the illusion of the "good life" that has been associated with a particular form of life by the force of custom and habit. The procedure of moral argumentation subjects the self-proclaimed goodness of a particular form of life to a critique from the point of view of justice. While the formal ethics of a society binds us to its order and scheme of evaluation, discourse ethics breaks this bondage and enables us to understand our own self as well as the validity of our culture from the point of view of not only culturally prescribed norms of righteousness but also from the point of view of justice. According to Habermas, "the universalization principle [of practical discourse] acts like a knife that makes razor-sharp cuts between evaluative statements, and strictly normative ones, between the good and the just" (ibid).

Habermas makes two crucial distinctions: one, between the taken-for-granted goodness of society and the challenge of universal justice and the other between ethics and morality. While ethics and the taken-for-granted goodness of a society are natural attributes of a form of life, morality is a matter of conscious deliberation and enlightened "discursive formation of will". For Habermas, the ethical life is not usually subject to a discursive critique, and for the most part remains unproblematic. However, the development of a moral point of view, for Habermas, "goes hand in hand with a differentiation within the practical into moral questions and evaluative questions" (Habermas 1990a: 108). In this context, it is a theory of justice that is central to Habermas's idea of morality. Thomas McCarthy has added: "If taking modern pluralism seriously means giving up the idea that philosophy can single out a privileged way of life..., it does not in Habermas' view, preclude a general theory of a much narrower sort, namely a theory of justice" (cited in Habermas 1990a: viii).

A Thrust Towards Problematization

It is this concern for justice that creates an incessant thrust towards problematization, laying bare the moral problem within our taken-for-granted culture. For Habermas, a "thrust toward problematization" is essential for moral consciousness to emerge and to be at work in the context of the life world (1990a: 107). He has explained (1990a: 109) how in the normal circumstances of what he has termed "ethical formalism" this problematization is not possible:

> Within the horizon of the life world, practical judgments derive both their concreteness and their power to motivate action from their inner connection to unquestioningly accepted ideas of the good life, in short, from their connection to ethical life and its institutions. Under these conditions, problematization can never be so profound as to risk all the assets of the existing ethical life. But the abstractive achievements required by the moral point of view do precisely that (ibid: 109).

Participation in discourse ethics enables the participants to look at one's own culture critically, where criticism means discovering whether the "suggested modes of togetherness genuinely hang together" or not (see Neville 1974: 189). For Habermas, the practice of discourse ethics is an instance of both self-criticism (facilitated by and accompanying self-discovery) and cultural criticism. As a total critique, practical discourse is "linked with two other forms of argumentation: aesthetic and therapeutic criticism" (Habermas 1990a: 105). Habermas has argued that "for the hypothesis-testing participant in a discourse, the relevance of the experiential context of his lifeworld tends to pale. To him, the normativity of existing institutions seems just as open to question as the objectivity of things and events" (1990a: 107). At this stage, "moral judgment becomes dissociated from the local conventions and the historical coloration of a form of life. It can no longer appeal to the naive validity of the context of the life world" (1990a: 109).

However while describing the thrust towards problematization Habermas himself acknowledges that culture is no mere convention. In another context, Indian philosopher G.C. Pande has argued that cultural consciousness is characterized primarily by the actors' seeking for value and the quest for self-transcendence. For G.C. Pande, "the idea of culture...is the idea of an autonomous order of values, of ideal modes of self-realization. Cultural apprehension begins with the discrimination of the ideal and the actual where the ideal is necessarily presented or expressed through a symbol" (Pande 1985: 11). In this perspective, cultural items are items "in an evolving context of meaning that is to say items in the quest of self-realization" (Pande 1989: 20). Though Habermas reserves this critical attribute of self-realization and transcendence to moral consciousness, he himself realizes that "cultural values too transcend de facto behaviour...through which subjects can distinguish the good life from the reproduction of mere life" (Habermas 1990a: 208). But ordinarily it is the established convention of society which shapes "the identities of groups and individuals in such a way" that even the culturally constituted idea of a "good life" is not what moves the actors. It is in this context that "discourse ethics" performs a redemptive and transformative function. For Habermas, "under the unrelenting moralizing gaze of the participants in discourse...familiar institutions can be transformed into so many instances of problematic justice" (1990a: 108).[5]

Critical Discussion of the Idea of Discourse Ethics: Habermas's Self-Criticism

Habermas has argued that the abstractive requirements in discourse ethics provide actors a cognitive advantage—a capacity for distantiation. But this cognitive distantiation is not enough either for the practice of discourse ethics or for the quest for universal morality. It calls for parallel emotional maturity and growth. Habermas has argued that "cognition, empathy, and agape" must be integrated in our moral consciousness especially when we are engaged in the "hermeneutic activity of applying universal norms in a context-sensitive manner" (1990a: 182). Reminding us of Christian imperatives for love and care, he has said that "concern for the fate of one's neighbour is a necessary emotional prerequisite for the cognitive operations expected of participants in discourse" (ibid). This integration of cognitive distantiation and emotional care is particularly required when the initial separation between morality and ethical life is to be overcome. Habermas is aware of the difficulties that this separation poses for the practice of morality. Thus, he is not content to leave his agenda only at the "deontological level" like Kant. He is interested to bring back morality as a guide for action and reflection into practice. Habermas (1990a: 179) has written:

> Moral issues are never raised for their own sake; people raise them by seeking a guide for action. For this reason the demotivated solutions that postconventional morality finds for decontextualized issues must be reinserted into practical life. If it is to become effective in practice, morality has to make up for the loss of concrete ethical life that it incurred when it pursued a cognitive advantage.

Thus, it is "an integration of cognitive operations and emotional dispositions and attitude" that characterizes "the mature capacity for moral judgment" (1990a: 182).

Moral consciousness is characterized by an integration of the "ethics of love and ethics of justice" (ibid). What is required for moral consciousness is not only an "ability to think hypothetically about moral-practical issues" (1990a: 186) but an appropriate emotional growth. According to Habermas, "even if the passage to the postconventional level of moral judgment has been successful, an inadequate motivational anchoring can restrict one's ability to act autonomously" (1990a: 183). Though a notion of universal human justice is central to Habermas' idea of universal morality, he has taken great care to emphasize that morality must obey both the principles of justice and solidarity. While the first "postulates equal respect and equal rights for the individual," the second "postulates empathy and concern for the well-being of one's neighbor" (1990a: 200). For Habermas, these cannot be pursued in an either/or fashion in our moral engagement. He has noted (1990a: 179):

> It is an imperative to see that both principles have the same and the one root: the specific vulnerability of human species, which individuates itself through sociation. Morality thus cannot protect the one without the other. It cannot protect the rights of the individual without also protecting the well-being of the community to which he belongs.

What is important to note is that both these concerns, for Habermas, "should flow from an adequate description of the highest stage of morality itself" (1990a: 182).

Concern for Solidarity and the Work of "Connected Criticism"

In the Habermasian agenda the concern for solidarity and community has as much a transformative potential as the concern for the cognitive distantiation. It is this concern that enables the passage of "return" to society from the initial phase of "withdrawal" from the world of taken-for-granted norms and social orders, to borrow the words of Toynbee. It is this concern for community that creates an incessant urge within the seekers and practitioners of morality to engage themselves in a continuous conversation with the fellow members of their society as a "connected critic", where a critic "earns his authority or fail to do so by arguing with his fellows" (Walzer 1988: 33). Walzer (1988: 32) has described for us the practice and challenge of what he calls "connected criticism", which is not possible by a one-sided pursuit of cognitive distantiation, which at best can make us "marginal men". It is not the marginal man but a "connected critic", who practices an integration of ethics of love and ethics of justice, that can act as a regenerative seed of transformation since, as Walzer rightly noted, "marginal men and women are like Simmel's strangers in but not wholly of their society. The difficulties they experience are not difficulties of detachment but of ambiguous connection" (ibid: 32). The critical consciousness that characterizes Habermas's ideal stage of morality is one of "connected criticism".

The significance of "connected criticism" for our needed moral unity in the face of diversity of morals that characterize the human condition must be appreciated. "Connected criticism" makes possible criticism "from within a tradition" and "this possibility of transcendence from within is what holds out the prospect of moral unity" (Mohanty 1989: 148). Mohanty has explained this. What Walzer calls "connected criticism" is similar to what Mohanty calls "transcendence from within". In the words of Mohanty (1989: 146):

> The diversity of morals concerns each tradition's own Sittlichkeit [a Hegelian word, meaning ethical standards]. The unity consists in the possibility on the part of each member of that tradition to rise above an unreflexive immersion in that ethical substance, and to critically reflect on its internal coherence from an external point of view... . As a person, situated in time and history, I belong to a tradition which has already defined for me the parameters of my ethical life.... But, for that reason, to say that I can at most try to 'understand' it, but can never be a critic, goes against my moral intuitions. In order to be a critic of my tradition, I need, in some measure to transcend it-while still, as a person I belong to it. I play the dual role of a person and a transcendental ego.

Towards Hermeneutic Supplements

At the beginning of his discourse, Habermas has openly admitted that its strategy of practical discourse is only a procedure. But towards the end of his treatise, *Moral Consciousness and Communicative Action*, he has noted that "discourse ethics, though organized around a concept of procedure, can be expected to say something relevant about substance, more important perhaps about the hidden link between justice and the common good" (Habermas 1990a: 202).

Being aware of the limitations of "discourse ethics", Habermas had observed that "...the discursive justification of norms is no guarantor of moral insights" and "discourse cannot by itself insure that the conditions necessary for all concerned are met" (1990a: 209). Discourse ethics also requires an appropriate institutional climate, where institutions facilitate human creativity rather than constrain it (see Unger 1987). When material living condition is not adequate and when individuals are plagued by "poverty, abuse, and degradation" it is difficult to pursue the quest for universal morality (ibid). Habermas has clearly argued that the incidence of a universal morality is "contingent upon a complimentary form of life" (1990a: 210).

For Habermas, the quest for morality poses two crucial challenges to the actors: how to apply universal moral norms in specific situations and how to anchor moral insights in our motivational Being. For Habermas, "these two problems can be solved only when moral judgment is supplemented by something else: hermeneutic effort and internalization of authority" (1990a: 179). The authority to be internalized here is not the authority of the existing systems and naturalized conventions. Rather it is the authority of universal moral insights, born of the practice of "discourse ethics".[6] Moreover this internalization ought to be reflective, which helps the actors not only to build the creative bridge between the universal and the particular but also saves them from the danger of turning their insights into a dogma.[7] Hermeneutic effort, indeed, provides such crucial reflexivity. For Habermas, hermeneutics is a practical communicative skill as well as a "reflexive engagement" (Habermas 1987c). The hermeneutic engagement not only enables the actors to understand and "making oneself understood" in one's natural language but also to "translate from any language to any language" (Habermas 1987c: 177). For Habermas, the basis of this reflexivity and translation is the fact that "every natural language has its own meta-language" (ibid). This "reflexive structure of natural language" provides the native speaker with a "unique metacommunicative" skill which not only enables one to understand distant traditions but also at times exposes "the already understood context of one's own world" as being "incomprehensible" and "questionable" (Habermas 1990a: 176).

If such is the hermeneutic claim to universality and its redemptive role in transforming strictly conceived cognitively distantiated view of universal morality then what role does pragmatics play? For Habermas, communicative competence that is at the root of speech has "as universal core as linguistic competence" (McCarthy in Habermas 1979: xviii). The task of universal pragmatics is to make us aware of the universal import in speech as it reconstructs "the ability of adult speakers to embed situation in relation to reality" (Habermas 1979: 68). While comprehensibility is the criterion of validity of grammatical sentence, the validity of a speech depends upon

> whether it is true or untrue, justified or unjustified, truthful or untruthful, because in speech, no matter what the emphasis, grammatical sentences are embedded in relation to reality in such a way that in an acceptable speech action segments of external nature, society, and internal nature always come into appearance together.

Habermas has used both hermeneutics and pragmatics to lay the blocks of universal morality. This universal morality, though embedded in language and speech and an extension of the universal import embedded in these two communicative practices, is critical, reflexive and post-conventional. In developing his idea of universal morality Habermas has been influenced by psychologist Lawrence Kohlberg's seminal work on moral development. However, compared to Kohlberg, Habermas has laid more emphasis on stages of reflection as crucial to understanding different stages of moral development as he has noted: "the relevant distinction is concerned solely in terms of the stages of reflection" (Habermas 1990a: 172). At the highest stage of moral development, which Kohlberg calls postconventional, Habermas has argued that internal nature is thereby moved into a "utopian perspective" (Habermas 1979: 93). At this stage, internal nature is not subjected to the "demands of ego autonomy; rather through a dependent ego it obtains free access to the interpretive possibilities".

Habermasian "Discourse Ethics": Some Critical Remarks

Despite Habermas's plea for post-metaphysical orientations in our moral engagement a careful reading of Habermas would show that he is deeply aware of the limitations of his agenda. He has admitted that his agenda is anthropocentric and man-centered. According to him, "compression for tortured animals and the pain caused by the destruction of the biotopes are surely manifestations of moral intuitions that cannot be fully satisfied by the collective narcissism of what in the final analysis is an anthropocentric way of looking at things" (Habermas 1990a: 211). For Habermas, the criterion of justice is central to the idea of universal morality but according to Agnes Heller the idea of justice cannot be meaningfully pursued unless it involves a profound anthropological revolution. For Heller, without a conception of the Beyond and its transformative influence in our lives, the idea of justice, confined only to the political and the legislative domains, remains only a mirage, as we have seen in the last two centuries of modern western experience. In the words of Heller (1987: 273):

> ...a just procedure is the condition of the goodlife—of all possible good lives—but is not sufficient for the good life...The good life consists of three elements: first, righteousness; secondly, the development of endowments into talents; and, thirdly emotional depth in personal attachments. Among these three elements, righteousness is the overarching one. All three elements of the good life are beyond justice.

By "Beyond" Heller means that it must be beyond and deeper than mere socio-political legislation. Justice is embodied when "goodness becomes character" (1987: 325-326). For Heller, "...Beyond has the connotation of 'higher' and not only of being 'different'" (ibid). But it is this intimation of the "Beyond" and a transcendental height that is missing from Habermas. Habermas might not care to take note of it but he cannot justify his post-metaphysical thinking as a self-proclaimed truth and as a self-validating system. The rise of not only religious fundamentalism (not only in the so-called irrational societies but also in the "rational societies" of the West) but also what one sensitive commentator has called "global spirituality" (Cousins 1985) shows that Habermas must justify his own neglect of the critical potential that a transcendental Sacred has in rethinking existing social arrangements and transforming our conventional institutions which chain human dignity in many guises. In this context the work of political scientist Roberto M. Unger calls for our attention. Unger (1987: 576) has noted:

> Imagine two kinds of sacred reality. The first is a fundamental reality or transcendent personal being; the second, the experiences of personality and personal encounter that, multiplied many times over, make up a social world. Whereas the first of these two sacreds is illusive and disputable and requires, to be recognized, the power of vision, which is the ability to see the invisible, the second seems near and palpable. Whenever they can, men and women try to identify the first of these two sacreds with the second. They want to see the social world graced with the authority of an ultimate reality. But the progress of insight and the disclosures of conflict prevent this bestowal of authority. If there is a common theme in the history of human thought and politics, it consists precisely in failure to sustain claims of unconditional authority on behalf of particular ways of talking, thinking, living, and organizing society. As the two sacreds lose their contact with each other, the distant one fades away into an ineffable, longed- for reality without any clear message for understanding and conduct. The nearby becomes profane and arbitrary.

The above quotation shows how in the contemporary political discourse the idea of a transcendental sacred is being invoked as a frame of criticism and transformation. Habermas must take note of Unger for Unger is a political theorist and not merely a preacher or a theologian. For Unger, when people are only bound to the sacredness of the existing social contexts, "nothing is left to them but to choose one of these worlds and to play by its rules" (Unger 1987: 577). These rules, though "decisive" in their influence, are ultimately "groundless" (ibid). For Unger, the decisiveness of the present social world, presenting itself as a sacred order, "arises precisely from its lack of any place within a hierarchy of contexts" (ibid). Then, "there is no larger defining reality to which it can seem as the vehicle or from whose standpoint it can be criticized" (Unger 1987: 577).

It is perhaps for these reasons that Dallmayr does not look at Habermas' "discourse ethics" as a categorical shift from the Kantian deontological morality. "Discourse ethics," Habermas has observed, "picks up the basic intent of Hegel's thought-in order to redeem it with Kantian means" (quoted in Dallmayr 1991: 117). For Dallmayr, there is no scope for genuine redemption in the Habermasian agenda. Dallmayr has argued that the "supportive life forms" that Habermas requires for his "discourse ethics" to be embodied are those "which can be happily found in modern western societies" (Dallmayr 1991: 120). For Dallmayr, concrete life forms "persist less because, than in spite of, decontextualized universalism" since "more reason is abstracted and universalized" "enclaves of moral life have increasingly been denuded or stripped of prudential-rational resources." But in the contemporary thrust towards universalization and globalization it is important to realize that "the western way of life is not universalizable" (Hosle 1992: 247). Articulation of universal morality coming from the West, either via Kant or Habermas, must face the problem that Hosle has recently posed: "Is it really legitimate to wish for a world society built according Occidental values?....It is the Occidental culture that has brought mankind to the verge of ecological disaster; and it is our way of life which is not universalizable and therefore immoral" (Hosle 1992: 258-259). Especially in our current phase of globalization where universalization means westernization and Americanization there is the crucial urgency to explore "the possibility of penetrating other and less familiar strategies of social reproduction in their articulation with world economic and political-as well as cultural-processes" (Lash and Friedman 1992: 29). Despite his recent plea for a moral orientation on the part of the people of advanced societies towards global problems, Habermas has not faced these issues squarely. For Andre Beteille, Habermas's interest in an other society such as India is even less compared to what his hero and fellow German critic Max Weber had at the turn of the century (personal communication). Thus, Dallmayr has argued that Habermas "makes reference to the alleviation of suffering or of 'damaged life'—but only as a marginal gloss not fully integrated in his arguments" (Dallmayr 1991: 126).

The Quest for Universal Morality: The Limitations of the "Discourse Ethics" and the Promise of the "Synthesis of Yoga"

Habermas (1990a: 202) has noted: "The agreement made possible by discourse depends on two things: the individual's inalienable right to say 'yes' or 'no' and his overcoming of his egocentric viewpoint." But how can an actor genuinely overcome her / his ego and in that quest of overcoming arrive at a synthesis between the ego and the Other? Even long before his pointed articulation of discourse ethics in *Moral Consciousness and Communicative Action*, Habermas had written in *Knowledge and Human Interests*: "Hermeneutics derives its function in the process of genesis of self-consciousness. It does not suffice to talk of the translation of a text; the translation itself is reflection: 'the translation of what is unconscious to what is conscious'" (Habermas 1972: 228). But without a deeper reflection on the nature of the unconscious, what is that the Habermasian hermeneutics going to make conscious? Here Sri Aurobindo's critique of the Nietzchian idea of "superman" can be applied to Habermas' "discourse ethics" as well: "But then the question of questions is there, what is our Self, and what is our nature?" (Sri Aurobindo 1962: 219).

In his insightful paper, "Moral Development and Ego Identity", Habermas has argued that moral development is characterized by the formation of an ego identity, which replaces the role identity (Habermas 1979). But for Sri Aurobindo (1962: 606-607):

> The ego is not the true center of the Self; the law of mutuality which meets it at every turn and which it misuses, arises from the truth that there is a secret unity between our Self and the Self of others and therefore between us and the lives of others.[8]

Habermas has used rational argumentation as the key to the founding of a universal morality. Sri Aurobindo does not discount the significance of reason for the origins and growth of morals but wants us to have a proper perspective regarding "The Office and Limitations of Reason" (ibid). Like Habermas, Sri Aurobindo has argued that reason and rational development have played a key role in our being human. In his discussion of "The Curve of Rational Age" in *Human Cycles* Sri Aurobindo argues that "the present age of mankind" is characterized "from the point of view of a graded psychological evolution" by an attempt to "discover and work out the right principle and secure foundations of a rational system of society" (Sri Aurobindo 1962: 181). Reminding us of Habermas, Sri Aurobindo (1962: 179) has observed that "an attempt to universalize first of all the habit of reason and the application of intelligence and the intelligent will to life" has played a crucial role in the shift from the "infrarational" to the "rational" age. Further, he also wants us to appreciate the crucial significance of reason in understanding the validity of traditions. According to Sri Aurobindo (1962: 183):

> Reason can accept no tradition merely for the sake of its antiquity or its greatness; it has to ask, first, whether the tradition contains at all any still living truth and, secondly, whether it contains the best truth available to man for the government of his life. Reason can accept no convention merely because men are agreed upon it; it has to ask whether they are right in their agreement, whether it is an inert or false acquiescence. Reason cannot accept any institution merely because it serves some purpose of life; it has to ask whether there are not greater and better purposes which can be best served by new

institutions. There arises the necessity of a universal questioning and from that necessity arises the idea that society can only be perfected by the universal application of rational intelligence to the whole of life.

Like Habermas' plea for undistorted communication, Sri Aurobindo also sensitizes us to the distortion that power can introduce in the working of a rational discourse and the realization of even its inherent emancipatory potential. In the words of Sri Aurobindo (1962: 184):

> The reason which is to be universally applied, cannot be the reason of a ruling class; for in the present imperfection of the human race that always means the fettering and misapplication of reason degraded into servant of power to maintain the privileges of the ruling class.... It must be the reason of each and all seeking for a basis of agreement.

But even though reason is so important for moral development and evolution (both phytogenetic and ontogenetic), it cannot be a sole foundation of morality. Sri Aurobindo accords this role to spirit, not to reason. For him, both order and evolution in life involves "interlocking of an immense number of things that are in conflict with each other" and discovering "some principle of standing-ground of unity" (Sri Aurobindo 1962: 201). Reason cannot perform this function because "the business of reason is indeterminate....In order that it may do its office, it is obliged to adopt temporarily fixed viewpoints." When reason becomes the sole arbiter of life and morality, "every change becomes or at least seems a thing doubtful, difficult and perilous....while the conflict of viewpoints, principles, systems leads to strife and revolution and not to basis of harmonious development." For Sri Aurobindo, harmony can be achieved only when the "soul discovers itself in its highest and completest spiritual reality and effects a progressive upward transformation of its life values into those of the Spirit; for they will all find their spiritual truth and in that truth their standing-ground of mutual recognition and reconciliation...." (ibid).

For Sri Aurobindo, the inadequacy of reason to become the governor of life and morality lies in man's transitional nature—half-animal and half-divine. According to him, "the root powers of human life, its intimate causes are below, irrational, and they are above, suprarational." It is for this reason that "a purely rational society could not come into being and, if it could be born, either could not live or sterilize or petrify human existence" (Sri Aurobindo 1962: 114). Sri Aurobindo (1962: 206) has argued:

> If reason were the secret, highest law of the universe...it might be possible for him by the power of the reason to evolve out of the dominance of the infrarational Nature which he inherits from the animal...But his nature is rather transitional; the rational being is only a middle term of Nature's evolution. A rational satisfaction cannot give him safety from the pull from below nor deliver him from the attraction from above.

He has used reason but unlike Habermas does not think it as the end all and the be all of life. For him:

> The solution lies not in reason but in the soul of man, in its spiritual tendencies. It is a spiritual, an inner freedom that alone can create a perfect human order. It is spiritual, a greater than the rational enlightenment that can alone illumine the vital nature of man and impose harmony on its self-seekings, antagonisms and discords.

An ideal society, for Sri Aurobindo (1962: 211), is not a mere "rational society" but a "spiritual society". A society founded on spirituality is not governed by religion as a mere social organization where society uses religion "to give an august, awful and ...eternal sanction to its mass of customs and institutions." A spiritual society is not a theocratic society but a society guided by the quest of the spirit. A spiritual society regards man not only as a "mind, a life and a body, but as a soul incarnated for a divine fulfilment upon earth, not only in heavens beyond, which after all it need not have left if it had no divine business here in the world of physical, vital and mental nature" (Sri Aurobindo 1962: 213).

Sri Aurobindo's idea of the highest stage of morality is close to the Kohlberg-Habermas idea of the post-conventional stage of moral development. Like the Habermasian idea of post-conventional stage of morality, Sri Aurobindo's idea of morality is not an extension of the collective egoism of a particular society. But what distinguishes Sri Aurobindo's idea of morality is the invocation of God not only as a tertiary factor but also as a constituting factor in the dyadic relationship between the Self and the Other, as he has said, "The seeking for God is also, subjectively, the seeking for our highest, truest, fullest, largest Self" (1962: 136). For him, "ethics is not in its essence a calculation of good and evil in action of a laboured effort to be blameless according to the standards of the world, these are only crude appearances, it is an attempt to grow into divine nature" (ibid: 143). Sri Aurobindo (1962: 141) has talked about the probable more reassuring route towards a universal morality:

> ...ethics only begins by the demand upon him of something other than his personal preference, vital pleasure or material self-interest; and this demand seems at first to work on him through the necessity of his relations with others. But that this is not the core of the matter is shown by the fact that the ethical demand does not always square with the social demand, nor the ethical standard always coincide with the social standard. His relations with others and his relations with himself are both of them the occasions of his ethical growth; but that which determines his ethical being is his relations with God, the urge of the Divine whether concealed in his nature or conscious in his higher self or inner genius. He obeys an inner ideal, not to a social claim or a collective necessity. The ethical imperative comes not from around, but from within him and above him.

The Ideal of Human Unity

Sri Aurobindo (1962: 262) wrote way back in 1919: "Today the ideal of human unity is more or less vaguely making its way to the front of our consciousness." For him, "the impact of different cultures upon each other" has been accentuated by the "conditions of the modern world" (ibid: 300). This process of mutual interpenetration and interpretation of cultures is not simply a mirror reflection of the diffusion of Western modernity. He has observed: "The earth is in the travail now of one common, large and flexible civilization for the whole human race into which each modern and ancient culture shall introduce its necessary element of variation" (ibid).[9] For him, this "new turn of impact of cultures shows itself most clearly where the European and the Asiatic meet" (Sri Aurobindo 1962: 302). He is not a categorical critic of modernity as he is not a categorical defender of tradition. Sri Aurobindo appreciated the fact that the meeting between the East and the West is pregnant with creative potentials for both the sides. He has noted: "The East is on the whole ....willing...to accept really valuable parts of modern European culture, its science, its curiosity, its ideal of universal education and uplift, its abolition of privilege, its broadening, liberalizing democratic tendency, its instinct of freedom and equality" (ibid). But while accepting the West the East is also engaged in a reconsideration and reconstruction of both tradition and modernity and wants to teach the West her forgotten spiritual and human values. In the words of Sri Aurobindo (1962: 302):

> But at a certain point the East refuses to proceed farther and that is precisely in things which are deepest, most essential to the future of mankind, the things of the soul, the profound things of mind and temperament. Here again, all points not to substitution and conquest, but to mutual understanding and interchange, mutual adaptation and new formation.

An awareness of this new formation at work—what Dumont calls "the heritage of global modernity" and Appadurai, "global ethnoscope"—is essential for realizing the ideal of human unity in our continued quest for universal morality (Appadurai 1989; Dumont 1986). But this awareness is only a first step. The next important step to take note of is that while modern science and technology has facilitated this global interpenetration of cultures, our method of realizing human unity must be primarily spiritual. While "intellectual and material circumstances" have contributed towards this, Sri Aurobindo wants us to realize that the "very commodity of the material circumstances", unaccompanied by any spiritual awakening, "may bring about the failure of the ideal" (1962: 263). For Sri Aurobindo, "when material circumstances favour a great change, but the heart and mind of the race are not really ready—especially the heart—failure may be predicted unless indeed men are wise and accept the inner change along with the external readjustment" (ibid).

For Sri Aurobindo, it is only through a spiritualized religion of humanity that the ground for universal morality can be led and the realization of the ideal of human unity be possible. But this religion of humanity, unlike the 19th century positivistic approach, is not an intellectual religion but a religion of the spirit.[10] According to Sri Aurobindo (1962: 136):

> We begin to see through the principle and law of our religious being, through the principle and law of our aesthetic being, the universality of a principle and law which is that of all being and which therefore we must hold steadily in view in regard to all human activities.

The Inadequacy of the Idea of the State

It is important to note that while describing his vision of the ideal of human unity Sri Aurobindo provides us an insightful sociological analysis of the work and the evolution of social aggregates in human history. To strive for human unity does not mean to be part of a huge conglomeration and a megastructure though Sri Aurobindo does not rule out the possibility of such an imperial formation. Rather, it means to strive for both meaningful belongingness in one's culture as well as for developing one's transnational, universal and cosmic orientations. To put it in our contemporary idioms, Sri Aurobindo is sensitive to the simultaneous need for localization and globalization. Sri Aurobindo is a fervent critic of modern megastructures such as State which stifle individual and social creativity. For him, it is within a small scale that human creativity blossoms. Citing examples of the remarkable height of human creativity during the period of the Greek city states and the small kingdoms of India, Sri Aurobindo has noted: "If we consider the past humanity....we find that the interesting periods of human life....were precisely those ages and countries in which humanity was able to organize itself in little independent centres acting intimately upon each other but not fused into a single unity" (1962: 263). At the same time, Sri Aurobindo is a critic of the organized state since it is one of the greatest barriers to the ideal of human unity. Sri Aurobindo has not accorded modern state a *sui generic* reality, this he accords to nations. For Sri Aurobindo, while "the nation is a persistent psychological unit which nature has been busy developing throughout the world in the most various forms", "the organized state is neither the best mind of the nation nor is it even the sum of communal energies....It is a collective egoism much inferior to the best of which the community is capable" (1962: 291, 280).[11] Sri Aurobindo has offered a profound moral critique of modern state on grounds of collective egoism and the quality of people who man the machinery of the state. For Sri Aurobindo (1962: 279),

> ...the modern politician...does not represent the soul of people or its aspirations. What he usually represents is all the average pettiness, selfishness, egoism, self-deception in him...Yet it is by such minds that the good of all has to be decided...to such an agency calling itself the State that the individual is being more and more called upon to give up the government of his life.

According to Sri Aurobindo, "when the state attempts to take up the control of the co-operative action of the community, it condemns itself to create a monstrous machinery which will end by crushing out freedom, initiative and serious growth of the human being" (1962: 282). This is close to Habermas' description of the internal colonization of the lifeworld under the machinery of the modern state. Habermas' thesis of "internal colonization states that the subsystems of the economy and state become more and more complex as a consequence of capitalist growth, and penetrate ever deeper into the symbolic reproduction of the lifeworld" (Habermas 1987a: 367). The ascendancy of the state, its "hypertrophic growth of media-steered subsystems" (Habermas 1987a: 332) leads to "cultural impoverishment and fragmentation of everyday consciousness" (Habermas 1987a: 355). Under the conditions of cultural modernity and the modern nation-state, "everyday consciousness is robbed of its power to synthesize, it becomes fragmented" (ibid). Under these conditions "the imperatives of autonomous subsystems make their way into the lifeworld from the outside—like colonial masters coming into a tribal society—and force a process of assimilation upon it" (ibid). This makes it impossible for co-ordinating "the diffused perspectives of the local culture" to grasp "the play of the metropolis and the world market from the point of view of periphery" (ibid).

This colonization of the life world by the system world of the state leads to the "legitimation crisis" of state under advanced capitalism. As this makes the legitimacy of the state problematic in the eyes of the concerned citizens, it also gives rise to "transnational identifications" (Hettne 1990: 31). The colonization of the life world leads to the search for new meanings and new practices of "de-differentiation" on the part of the actors (Habermas 1984). This search takes place in the context of what political scientist Ronald Inglehart calls "culture shift" in advanced societies, which is characterized primarily by shift from "materialist" to "postmaterialist values" (Inglehart 1990). According to Inglehart (1990: 156),

> ...as a result of the historically unprecedented prosperity and the absence of war that has prevailed in western countries since 1945, younger birth cohorts put less emphasis on economic and physical security than do older groups...[They] tend to give a high priority to nonmaterial needs, such as a sense of community and the quality of life.

The rise of postmaterialism as a widespread social value blurs the familiar boundary between the Left and the Right and plays a crucial role in "the rise of the wave of the new social movements" such as the ecology movements, which are not solely confined within individual nation-states but also are transnational in their mobilization and cross-cultural vision. Sister City Movement, Ecology Movements and Habitat for Humanity are some of the familiar examples of transnational movements emerging from the advanced industrial societies. Hettne (1990: 31) tells us that "high level of education and welfare" in advanced societies are now "transformed into transnational identifications and concerns embraced by a reasonably large segment of the population." "The latter type of identification are expressed for instance through the new social movements which due to their global concerns also challenge the legitimacy of the state" (ibid).

The above description points to the fact that Sri Aurobindo's emphasis upon proper unit of human association is shared by Habermas and other contemporary political theorists and ethnographers. To think of the ideal of human unity is to refashion the "mediating relationships that link the individual household with the planetary ecosystem" and to be "aware of the middle range between the local and the global level" (Bellah et al. 1991: 14). This is best articulated by Hettne (1990: 34):

> Alternative solutions are generally antistatist and usually have two, but not necessarily contradictory points of reference: the local community and the earth...The relevant actor on the local level would not be the state but issue-oriented social movements whose global operations transcend the nation-state as the dominant mode of political organization.

Beyond the Technology of Power: Synthesis of Yoga and the Technology of Self

The ideal of human unity requires a new technology of self. Elsewhere Habermas has argued that modernity is solely preoccupied with technology of power and not sensitive to the challenge of developing an appropriate technology of self (Habermas 1987b).

Habermas has discussed at great length self-consciousness, but for him this is born of psychoanalytic therapy and the dialogue between the analyst and the patient. Sri Aurobindo, on the other hand, discovers this through the practice of yoga. For Sri Aurobindo (1950: 2), "yoga is a methodological effort towards self-perfection by the expression of the potentialities latent in the being and a union of the human individual with the universal and transcendent existence" (Sri Aurobindo 1950: 2). Yoga is a practical psychology of self-perfection to help God complete his unfinished task of creation. Its objective is transformation and making possible a higher stage of evolution here on earth, not individual *moksha* (salvation). Yoga helps us to overcome our "separative ignorance" (1950: 618). The practice of yoga helps us to go beyond altruism and egoism, good and evil where we are able to "take a wider psychological view of the primary forces of our nature" (ibid). Through the practice of yoga "there grows an immediate and profound sympathy and immixture of mind with mind, life with life, a lessening of the body's insistence on separateness, a power of direct mental and other intercommunication and effective mutual action which helps out now the inadequate indirect communication and action..." (1950: 615). Yoga enables individuals to have a right relation with the collectivity where the individual does not "pursue egoistically his own material or mental progress or spiritual salvation without regard to his fellows, nor does he "maim his proper development" for the sake of the community but sums up in himself "all its [community's] best and completest possibilities and pour them out by thought, action and all other means on his surroundings so that the whole race may approach nearer to the attainment of its supreme potentialities" (1950: 17).

By the Way of Conclusion: Towards a Comparison of Comparisons

The crisis of our times requires a moral perspective both locally and globally. To come to terms with the fundamental questions of our times our individual social systems as well as our international system are in need of a moral anchorage. Jurgen Habermas and Sri Aurobindo help us to think creatively about morality as a practice of transformation. Both of them sensitize us to our emergent ideal of human unity and the need for the quest for universal morality. Habermas offers "discourse ethics" as a procedure while Sri Aurobindo presents "The Synthesis of Yoga" as a practical psychology of self-realization. Though these are two different agendas of action and reflection they are not necessarily opposed to each other. Neither does Sri Aurobindo oppose spirituality to rationality nor Habermas defend functionalist reason. Both Habermas and Aurobindo are fervent critics of the idea of the state and urge for cultivating transnational, universal identifications.

Hence in our quest for universal morality there is no point in reifying the obvious that Habermas has emphasized "rational argumentation" while Sri Aurobindo has stressed spiritual realization for moral development and the planetization of our consciousness (see Chardin 1956; Giri 1992b). Taking inspiration from Sri Aurobindo our task is to discover the common ground as we strive to transcend our superficial distinctions between traditions and points of view in order to be able to contribute to social transformation and human evolution. The task for comparative engagement then is not to produce fixed wholes but to create a portrait of a "discursive formation", which ultimately enables us to transcend our taken-for-granted assumptions (see Giri 1992a). When we are confronted with the task of understanding a "discursive theme," according to Foucault, the task is to "describe system of dispersion," rather than simply "reconstitute chains of inference" and "draw up tables of differences" (Foucault 1972: 37).

Universal morality has been the discursive theme in our comparative engagement here. Describing its trajectory of dispersion in Habermas and Sri Aurobindo it has not been our objective to provide an either / or comparison between them but to explore the potential for transformation in both of them, which has a global relevance. In another context, Alasdair MacIntyre has argued that "the key to comparative studies is the comparison of comparisons" (MacIntyre 1991: 121). He has pointed out that while comparing two philosophical traditions—say Confucianism and Aristotelianism—"we cannot find any legitimate standing ground outside the context of points of view" (ibid). Drawing inspiration from Pande (1992) and Toulmin (1990), we can situate Sri Aurobindo and Habermas in both historical and perspectival contexts of Indian and European Renaissance. This comparison of comparisons can show us the global relevance of the retrieval of these two traditions of Renaissance as both India and the West are entering the third millennium.

In reflecting upon the Indian Renaissance Pande has argued that modern Indian thinkers "discounted any basic contradiction between the values of liberal modernity and those of spiritual religion" (Pande 1991: 438). This is also true of the vision and the experiment of Sri Aurobindo. For Pande, "that Sri Aurobindo has been the prophet of a new cultural hope should not make us forget that he was one of the most brilliant leaders of Indian Renaissance" (Pande 1992: 1). Sri Aurobindo felt that the Indian Renaissance if it took place fully would be "a thing of immense importance both to herself and the world" (Sri Aurobindo quoted in Pande 1992: 15). The Indian Renaissance was not simply an imitation of modern ideals but an effort to purify them by the "reaffirmation of the ancient spirit" (ibid). It was "no mere return but restatement" (ibid). For Sri Aurobindo, "probably, here lies the key of the Indian Renaissance, in a return from forms to depths of a released spirituality which will show itself again in a pervading return of spirituality upon life" (ibid). Both for Sri Aurobindo and Pande the retrieval of this Renaissance tradition of synthesis and spirituality has much relevance now not only for India but also for the whole world.

Europe is also now confronted with a parallel task of the retrieval of the tradition of her humanist Renaissance in the contemporary context of ontological doubt and social despair. Stephen Toulmin (1990) is the clearest exponent of such a point of view. For Toulmin, there is a modernity of Renaissance as there is a modernity of the Cartesian rationality. The modernity of Renaissance was an effort of creative reconciliation between late medi-evalism and the challenge of the emergent modern world. According to Toulmin (1990: 25), the writings of the Renaissance humanists such as Erasmus, Michel de Montaigne and Shakespeare revealed an

> urbane open-mindedness and skeptical tolerance...they regarded human affairs in a clear-eyed, non-judgmental light that led to honest practical doubt about the value of 'theory' for human experience-whether in theology, natural philosophy, metaphysics or ethics. In spirit, their critique was not hostile to the practice of religion [but] they discouraged intellectual dogmatism..

Montaigne has articulated this creative urge for synthesis when he writes: "Philosophy is very childish, to my mind, when she gets up on her hind legs and preaches to us that it is a barbarous alliance to marry the divine with the earthly, the reasonable with the unreasonable..." (quoted in Toumin 1990). For Toulmin, "the stage in western culture and society that we are now entering—whether we see it as the third phase in modernity, or as a new and distinctive 'postmodern' phase—obliges us to reappropriate values from Renaissance humanism that were lost in the heyday of modernity" (ibid: 201). But this retrieval and reappropriation has to take place in our contemporary context. The task is to humanize modernity rather than to condemn it. Toulmin (1990: 180) has elaborated on this agenda for humanizing modernity:

> We are indebted to Descartes and Newton for fine examples of well-formulated theory, but humanity also needs a sense of how theory touches practice at points, and in ways, that we feel on our pulses. The current task, accordingly, is to find ways of moving on from the received view of modernity—which set exact sciences and the humanities apart—to a reformed version, which redeems philosophy and science, by reconnecting them to the humanist half of modernity. In that task, the techniques of 17th-century rationalism will not be enough: from this point on, all claims of theory—like

those of nationhood—must prove their value by demonstrating their roots in human practice and experience.

Jurgen Habermas's discourse ethics is a humane integration of theory and practice and a sharp critique of their positivist divorce. Though neither Toulmin nor Habermas himself have located his work in this humanist tradition to a comparative eye this connection is clear. Habermas's stress on human practice and his nostalgia for the unity of theory and practice in the classical mode reminds us of the remarkable cultural creativity of European Renaissance and its modernity. It is the heirs of European Renaissance such as Vico, not Descartes and his positivistic children who are Habermas' heroes (see, Habermas 1973). Our quest for universal morality via a comparative meditation on Habermas and Sri Aurobindo points to the global significance of both Indian and European Renaissance. But from Sri Aurobindo we learn of the urgent need to spiritualize our humanity as we are beginning our work of humanizing our modernity.

NOTES

1. Jonathan Sacks (1991: 42) has articulated our predicament when he noted: "Something quite revolutionary has happened to our ways of thinking: what I would call the demoralization of discourse. We now no longer know what it is to identify a moral issue, as something distinct from personal preference on the one hand or technique on the other".

2. It is interesting to note that another key commentator of our times Stephen Toulmin (1990) uses the phrase "ecology of institutions" to describe an ideal society.

3. In this context we might take note of what William Baldamus (1990: 102), an insightful commentator on Habermas, writes. According to Baldamus, "...there can be no doubt that Habermas' graphical diagrams

are created intuitively. Ironically, in his own terminology this means they have no rational foundation, although in logical terms their credibility may be unquestionable".

4. On the question of taking a hypothetical attitude to one's existent social arrangement and be drawn towards an ideal, we can remember the seminal work of philosopher Vaihinger. Please see, Vaihinger, *Philosophy of As If.*

5. According to David Bidney (1967: 453), "An individual is said to be morally free insofar as he acts in conformity with the requirements of his "true good" and his "true self"...Moral freedom and cultural freedom don't coincide".

6. Habermas's emphasis that even the actors with communicative morality must internalize authority reminds us of a similar argument by Ortega Y. Gasset. Gasset has drawn a distinction between the aristocrats and the masses. Aristocrats are the ones who give much to society and are its perennial critics. But Gasset also makes clear that still the aristocrats must obey some commands. Needless to mention that this command is not of society but one's own conscience. Please see, Ortega Y. Gasset, *The Revolt of the Masses.*

7. Here we can take note of the insightful arguments of Verma who has observed: "The dialectic by itself does not explain the possibility of cultural change or critique of culture...What is important to add in this dialectic is that the internalization can be reflective or unreflective" (Verma 1991: 534).

8. Of course to be fair to Habermas the Habermasian ego is much more than the ego of the possessive individual. It is sometimes close to the Aurobindian Self. But the spiritual unity between the Self and the Other as constituted by an all-pervasive divine reality is missing from Habermas.

9. Louis Dumont's recent discussion and description of what he calls "the heritage of global modernity" deserves our attention here. He (1986: 18) has noted: "A more complex process...is found in the domains of cultures and results from their interaction. To the extent that the individualistic ideas and values of the dominant culture are spreading worldwide, they undergo modifications locally and engender new forms. Now-and this has escaped notice-the new, modified forms can pass back into the dominant culture and operate there as modern elements in their own right. In that way the acculturation of each particular culture to modernity can have a lasting precipitate in the heritage of global modernity."

10. According to Margaret Chatterjee (1991), this was also the argument of S. Radhakrishnan.

11. In this context Jonathan Sacks' (1991: 45) observation needs to be noted: "The problem of our moral ecology is that we have thought exclusively in terms of two domains: the state as an instrument of legislation and control and the individual as the bearer of otherwise unlimited choices...We have neglected the third domain: that of community."

REFERENCES

Appadurai, Arjun, 1989, "The Global Ethnoscape: Notes and Queries for a Transnational Anthropology", MS.

Baldamus, William, 1992, "Understanding Habermas's Method of Reasoning", *History of the Human Sciences,* 5 (2): 97-115.

Bellah, Robert et al., 1991, *The Good Society*, New York: Alfred A. Knopf.

Bidney, David, 1987, *Theoretical Anthropology*, New York: Shocken Books.

Chardin, Teilhard de, 1956, *Man's Place in Nature: The Human Zoological Group*, London: Collins.

Chatterjee, Margaret, 1991, "Reflections on Religious Pluralism in the Indian Context", in Eliot Deutch (ed.), *Culture and Modernity*, Honolulu: University of Hawaii Press.

Connolly, William E., 1991, *Identity / Difference: Democratic Negotiation of Political Paradox*, Cornell.

Cortese, Anthony, 1990, *Ethnic Ethics: The Restructuring of Moral Theory*, Albany: State University of New York Press.

Cousins, E.H., 1985, *Global Spirituality*, Madras: Madras University Press.

Dallmayr, Fred, 1991, *Life World, Modernity and Critique: Paths Between Heidegger and Frankfurt School*, Polity.

Dumont, Louis, 1986, *Essays on Individualism: Modern Ideology in Anthropological Perspective*, Chicago.

Edelman, John T., 1990, *An Audience for Moral Philosophy?* London: Macmillan.

Evans, J.D.G. (ed.), 1987, *Moral Philosophy and Contemporary Problems*, Cambridge.

Gasset, Ortega Y., *The Revolt of the Masses*.

Geertz, Clifford, 1986, "The Uses of Diversity", *Michigan Quarterly Review* Winter Issue: 105-23.

Giri, Ananta, 1992a, *Critique of the Comparative Method and the Challenges of a Transnational World*, G.B. Pant Social Science Institute, Allahabad: Occasional Paper.

———, 1992b, "Chetanara Uttarana: Samrpratika Biswamayita o Rastrottara Andolona" [an article in Oriya meaning, "The Transcendence of Consciousness: Contemporary Globalization and the Transnational Movements"], *Eshana,* December 1992.

Foucault, Michel, 1972, *The Archaeology of Knowledge and the Discourse on Language*, New York: Pantheon Books.

Habermas, Jurgen, 1972, *Knowledge and Human Interests*, Cambridge: Polity Press.

———, 1973, *Theory and Practice*, Cambridge: Polity Press.

———, 1979, *Communication and the Evolution of Society*, Cambridge: Polity Press.

———, 1987a, *A Theory of Communicative Action, Volume 2: Life World and System: A Critique of Functionalist Reason*, Cambridge: Polity Press.

———, 1987b, *The Philosophical Discourses of Modernity*, Polity.

———, 1987c, "The Hermeneutic Claims to Universality", in Michael T. Gibbons (ed.), *Interpreting Politics*, Basil Blackwell.

———, 1988, "Law and Morality", in S.M. McCurrin (ed.), The *Tanner Lectures on Human Values*, Volume VII, Universities of Cambridge and Utah.

———, 1989, *The Structural Transformation of the Public Sphere*, Cambridge: Polity Press.

———, 1990a, *Moral Consciousness and Communicative Action*, Cambridge: Polity Press.

———, 1990b, "What Does Socialism Mean Today? The Rectifying Revolution and the Need for New Thinking in the Left", *New Left Review* No. 183: 3-21.

Heller, Agnes, 1987, *Beyond Justice*, Basil Blackwell.

Hettne, Bjorn, 1990, *Development Theory and the Three Worlds*, Essex: Longman.

Hosle, Vittorio, 1992, "The Third World as a Philosophical Problem", *Social Research* 59 (2): 227-262.

Inglehart, Ronald, 1990, *Culture Shift in Advanced Industrial Societies*, Princeton.

Lash, Scott and Jonathan Friedman, 1991, "Introduction: Subjectivity and Modernity's Other", in Scott Lash and Jonathan Friedman (eds.), *Modernity and Identity*, Basil Blackwell.

MacIntyre, Alasdair, 1991, "Incommensurability, Truth, and the Conversation Between Confucians and Aristotelians about the Virtues", in Eliot Deutch (ed.), *Culture and Modernity*, Honolulu: University of Hawaii Press.

Mohanty, Jitendra Nath, 1989, *Transcendental Phenomenology*, Basil Blackwell.

Neville, Robert C., 1974, *The Cosmology of Freedom*, Yale.

Otto-Apel, Karl, 1991, "A Planetary Macroethics for Humankind: The Need, The Apparent Difficulties, and the Eventual Possibility", in Eliot Deutch (ed.), *Culture and Modernity*, Hawaii.

Pande, Govind Chandra, 1982, "On the Nature of Social Categories", in Ravinder Kumar (ed.), *Philosophical Categories and Social Reality*.

——, 1985, *Aspects of Indian Culture and Civilization*, Varanasi: BHU Press.

——, 1989, *The Meaning and Process of Culture as Philosophy of History*, Allahabad: Raka Prakashan.

——, 1991, "Two Dimensions of Religion: Reflections Based On Indian Spiritual Experience and Philosophical Traditions", in Eliot Deutch (ed.), *Culture and Modernity*, Honolulu: University of Hawaii Press.

——, 1992, "Sri Aurobindo: Cultural Perspectives", paper presented at the national seminar on Sri Aurobindo at Pondicherry.

Sacks, Jonathan, 1991, *The Persistence of Faith*, London: Weidenfeld and Nicholson.

Sri Aurobindo, 1950, *The Synthesis of Yoga*, Pondicherry: Sri Aurobindo Ashram.

——, 1962, *The Human Cycles, The Ideal of Human Unity, War and Self-Determination*, Pondicherry: Sri Aurobindo Ashram.

——, 1970, *The Life Divine*, Pondicherry: Sri Aurobindo Ashram.

Strong, Tracy B., 1992, "What Have We to Do With Morals? Nietzsche and Weber on History and Ethics", *History of the Human Sciences* 5 (3): 9-18.

Toulmin, Stephen, 1990, *Cosmopolis: The Hidden Agenda of Modernity*, New York: The Free Press.

Unger, Roberto M., 1987, *False Necessity: Anti-Necessitarian Social Theory in the Service of Radical Democracy*, Cambridge: University Press.

Vaihinger, *Philosophy of As If*.

Verma, Roop Rekha, 1991, "The Concept of Progress and Cultural Identity", in Eliot Deutch (ed.), *Culture and Modernity*, Honolulu: University of Hawaii Press.

Walzer, Michael, 1988, "Interpretation and Social Criticism", in S.M. McCurrin (ed.), *The Tanner Lectures on Human Values*, Universities of Cambridge and Utah Press.

Chapter Twelve

UNITS OF ANALYSIS AND THE FIELD OF STUDY: ANTHROPOLOGICAL ENCOUNTER WITH THE POST-INDUSTRIAL SOCIETIES

> If we take, for example, late capitalism as our problem and try to describe the culture of late capitalism and treat it as an aggregate of understandings (that we observers aggregate), ...then its wholeness does not consist in its being a discrete and bounded entity out there, but rather it is a discrete and bounded entity in our formulation of it and its parts, that is an abstraction which we have constructed.
>
> —David Schneider (1988: 7)

The relationship between the units of analysis and the empirical field of study is a contentious and complex one in anthropology. When anthropologists used to study only the so-called "primitive" societies, they assumed that their units of analysis (e.g., tribe, village, etc.) matched exactly their field of study and took this assumption for granted. But the assumptions of this kind are challenged when anthropology turns to western societies in general. The lack of fit between the unit of analysis and the empirical field of study and the accompanying need for a creative and thoughtful construction of unit which is not bound to a localized field is more prominent when anthropology attempts to make sense of the contemporary postindustrial societies. Constituting appropriate anthropological units for ethnography's encounter with the contemporary advanced societies requires a critical reflection on the nature of construction of units in case of primitive societies and meditation on the emergent properties of culture and social organization of the post-industrial societies.

In recasting the relationship between the unit of analysis and the empirical field of study in the anthropological encounter with the post-industrial society, we must realise that even when anthropologists studied "primitive" societies, their unit of analysis did not exactly match the empirical field of study. For Fried, "tribes seem to be secondary phenomenon, product of processes stimulated by highly organized societies..." (Fried 1968: 35). For Colson (1953), the Makah Indian tribe was created for administrative purposes. For Beteille (1986), the concept of tribe as a "self-contained unit" does not recognize its complex link with caste and "civilization". Unlike North America and Melanesia, "tribes have existed at the margin of Hindu civilization from time immemorial" (Beteille 1980: 827). But even in the case of primitive societies, anthropologists have gone beyond the bounded units of analysis: Boas focused on how cultural traits are "transmitted over large cultural areas..." (Appadurai 1988: 38), and Leach took structural types such as "Gumsa" and "Gumlao", rather than "tribe" as his unit of analysis (Pandey 1986). Dumont (see Srinivas 1975) and Hardiman (1982) have argued a similar inadequacy of village as a unit of analysis. Hence, the notion of an exact match between units of analysis and the field of study was an assumption which played its role in the "invention of primitive society" (Kuper 1988).

These assumptions are further challenged when anthropology turns to modern western societies in general. But the challenge to the anthropological "domain assumptions" (cf. Gouldner 1970) has its pedigree in the study of complex societies (Mintz 1981). One obvious reason behind this challenge lies in the nature of modern western social and cultural reality. The organizational bases of the modern western society are not kinship, tribe and caste, but the capitalist world economy, nation-state, class and industrial urban centers. In western society, small towns exist in mass society (Vidich 1957). Even as early as 1929, Lynd acknowledged the impossibility of studying Mid⁴le Town as a "self-contained community" (1929:271). Becau.se of the high mobility of individuals in modern western society and their units of sociality and community often transcending a bounded locale, the self-contained framing of social units by anthropologists freezes the study from the beginning. But the deeper reason behind this challenge to the classical anthropological assumptions is the challenge of studying one's own society: studying the "familiar and the exotic" (Martin 1987) simultaneously in a highly charged discursive context where unlike Obeyesekere's ideal situation, the participants are not only fellow, "cultural-conscious" anthropologists (Obeyesekere 1990), but also alert citizens, a watchful media and a predatory state. The nature of a constructed unit and its boundary in studying one's own society has immediate political implications for the anthropologist in both contemporary developing and developed societies. The challenge to classical anthropological assumptions and anthropology's turn to modern western society have occurred simultaneously and are part of the global process of decolonization and an ascendant "politics of awareness" (Nandy 1987). But the reason behind this challenge is also to be explored in the emerging political trends at home: the New Right's return to power in Britain and the United States, cutbacks in social science research grants, and the challenge of asking anthropological questions in a political climate where fundamentalism has largely set the terms of public discourse.

Recasting the relationship between the units of analysis and fieldwork in dealing with post-industrial societies has to start with a critical reflection on the constitution of units (objective as well as analytical) in postindustrial societies. Though units of study are properties of "analysis", (Trouillot 1986) they must correspond to the "emergent properties" of the system (Barth 1978: 259). The effort of formulating appropriate units of analysis must be linked to a discovery procedure (Barth 1978: 254). Hence, while formulating units of analysis in dealing with post-industrial societies, it is essential to discover the emergent properties of the social organization in the light of the post-industrial transformation. "Post-industrial culture is already postmodern; it is marked by boundary crossing" (Aronowitz 1989: 146). Post-industrial production is characterized by "flexible forms of work organization" (Cuomo 1988; Piore and Sabel 1984), "informal economy" and a high-tech work place where the boundary of the "internal labor market" is transcended (Noyelle 1987). The emerging post-modern culture transgresses the boundary between what is inside and what is outside of the cultural text, between reality and representation (Lash and Urry 1987). Post-industrial politics in the new social movements defy the boundaries between private and public, religion and politics (Cox 1984; Wuthnow 1988). "Postmodern self" and "post-industrial psychology" embody a "post-individualist" development and a "charismatic reaction to the contradiction between formal and substantive rationality embodied in the modern self" (Wood and Zurcher 1988:137). As a result, late capitalistic social discourse defies the bounded logic of law and is characterized by the dialogical open-endedness of "interpretation" (Bauman 1987).

Units in post-industrial reality not only defy boundaries, they are marked by their global constitution. Post-industrial societies exist in an international system of production, distribution and exchange, in which new forces such as multinational corporations and the "global assembly line" play a vital role in the issues internal to these societies. For instance, the post-industrial city is a "global city" (Sassen 1988). Post-industrial reality is characterized by "space-time compression" (Harvey 1989) where the "related reductions in time-space distanciation undermines the construction of unproblematic national subjects" (Lash and Urry 1987: 6). Here transnational socio-cultural forms challenge the conventional construction of units. Different private citizens in transnational social movements have "increasingly intruded in world politics without reference to government or interstate organizations", undermining "not only the concept of sovereignty, but also the adequacy of regarding nation-state as the sole actor in world politics" (Mansbach 1976: 22).

But global determination in the constitution of units is not all there is to the society and culture of advanced societies. "Local" also plays a significant role. Postmodernism as an all encompassing cultural movement arising out the structural context of the postindustrial societies celebrates the coming of the local as a significant category and field of thought and action in contemporary theory and praxis. Postmodernism is characterized by the collapse of the great "summarizing discourse" and the rise of local narratives (Portoghesi 1983: 28). Postmodern architecture emphasizes "vernacular traditions, local history", "with a much greater eclecticism of style" (Harvey 1987: 162). The rhetoric of the grassroots occupies a central place in the postmodern discourse of social transformation. As Harvey so aptly argues, "yet a global strategy of resistance and transformation has to begin with the realities of place and community" (ibid: 281).

Formulation of units of analysis in the ethnographies of postindustrial societies reflect some of this transformation. In Martin's (1987) study, the cells of microbiology are studied in the context of the discourse of "nation-state". In Murphy's (1987) ethnography of the disabled, the boundary between the "self" and the "other" is transcended. In Newman (1988) and Perin (1988), the informants do not come from a bounded community but from all over the USA. In Neville (1987), the unit of kinship study is an "intentional community". In Fernandez-Kelly (1988) and Lozano (1985), informal work is studied in the interstices of the boundaries of state and formal work. In Harvey (1985), urban consciousness is studied as a "particular configuration" of "different loci of consciousness formation": individual, family, community, class and state.

Recasting the relationship between units of analysis and the field of study also has implications for devising an appropriate fieldwork design which is sensitive to Geertz's challenge: "Ethnographies have now to do with realities with which neither encyclopaedism nor monographism, world surveys or tribal studies can practically cope" (Geertz 1988: 148). The way out is to break away from the notion of what Trouillot (1988) calls "the ethnographic trinity" (one observer, one time, one place) where it is necessary to do a "multi-locale" ethnography, each locale "explored ethnographically and mutually linked by the intended and unintended consequences of activities within them" (Marcus 1986: 171). Mintz's method of following the trajectory of a commodity such as sugar in a global space in the context of the Boasian historiographical tradition can sharpen this field work design (Mintz 1985, 1987). A related challenge is to make systematic use of multiple units of analysis and developing a multidimensional view of reality.

To deal with post-industrial societies, it is also essential to do strategic ethnography where "the ethnographer constructs the text around a strategically selected locale, treating the system as background" (Marcus 1986: 172). But in this move, special care has to be taken to see that the ethnography of the locale is not lost in the "ethnography of mediation", as it seems to be happening in Trouillot (1988).

But rethinking fieldwork in dealing with post-industrial societies also poses the challenge of incorporating the emerging units in ethnographic study. The emerging transnational culture is a case in point. For Marcus, conducting multi-locale ethnography requires some notion of the world system, the formulation of which cannot be left solely to the political economists. Hannerz's project on "The World System of Culture" is especially concerned with transnational culture and cultural flows in the twentieth century, as well as with local and national responses to these" (Public Culture 1988:54). Furthermore, Tyler's (1986) argument that postmodern anthropology is the study of man talking challenges us to study discourse and narratives that are central in contemporary culture (Tyler 1986). In the context of the increasing centralization in the contemporary societies, the ethnographer has also to "study up" (Nader 1969; also Marcus 1983) and do fieldwork in centers such as the Wall Street and the Smithsonian

Mall (Adams 1988). It is also crucial to study "everyday life" in the "groundfloor" (Wallerstein 1987) of late capitalism.

But this recasting of the relationship between units of analysis and fieldwork has to be part of a political struggle. Producing an ethnography of the center requires a transformed discursive climate where the representatives of the center consider anthropology as important as economics (Tambiah 1985). As Edward Said (1989: 213) argues: "To practice anthropology in the United States is.. not just to be investigating "otherness", and "difference" in a large country; it is to be discussing them in an enormously influential and powerful state whose global role is that of a superpower" (Said 1989: 213). Fieldwork has also to be conducted in the light of a post-industrial theory of society such as Giddens' (1984) "structuration theory", Touraine's (1977) theory of "self-production of society" and Michael Foucault's (1972) theory of "discursive formation", which provide us new ways of thinking about self, culture and society in tune with the structural and discursive transformation characteristic of our times.

The methodological implication of this recasting for the practice of fieldwork is to move away from the self-contained framing of cultural units to a "view of cultural situation always in flux" (Marcus and Fischer 1986: 78). The challenge for the practice of fieldwork is to "acknowledge the relevance of both history and political economy, at the very least, to delineate boundaries of our units of analysis" (Trouillot 1988: 290). The recasting also implies a critical reflection of scale: "small-scale vs. large-scale should not be confused with micro vs. macro aspects of social system: large-scale systems are also to be embedded in the events of encounters of persons" (Barth 1978: 256). Finally, following Schneider (1988), the fieldworker has to reformulate the relationship among place, society and culture with the ethnographer as both part and definer of "the field".

REFERENCES

Adams, Robert, 1988, Keynote Address to the Society for Cultural Anthropology, Washington, D.C. May 20.

Appadurai, Arjun, 1988, "Introduction : Place and Voice in Anthropological Theory", *Cultural Anthropology* 3(1):16-21.

Aronowitz, Stanley, 1989, "Working Class Culture in the Electronics Age", in I. Agnus and S. Jhally (eds.) *Cultural Politics in Contemporary America*, Routledge.

Barth, Frederik (ed.), 1978, *Scale and Social Organization*, Oslo: Universitiesforlaget.

Bauman, Zygmunt, 1987, *Legislators and Interpreters: On Modernity, Post-Modernity and Intellectuals*, Cambridge: Polity Press.

Beteille, Andre, 1980, "On the Concept of the Tribe", *International Social Science Journal* XXXII(4): 8225-828.

———, 1986, "The Concept of Tribe with Special Reference to India", *European Journal of Sociology* XXVII(2):297-19.

Colson, E., 1953, *The Makah Indians*, Manchester: University of Manchester Press.

Cox, Harvey, 1984, *Religion in the Secular City: Towards a Post-Modern Theology*, New York: Simon and Schuster.

Cuomo, Mario, 1988, *The Cuomo Commission Report: A New American Formula for a Strong Economy*, New York: Simon and Schuster.

Fernandez-Kelly, M.P. and A.M. Garcia, 1989, Informalization at the Core: Hispanic Women, Home Work and the Advanced Capitalist System", in A. Portes and M. Castells (eds.), *Informal Economy,* Baltimore & London: The Johns Hopkins University Press.

Foucault, Michel, 1972, *The Archaeology of Knowledge and the Discourse on Language*, NY: Pantheon.

Fried, Morton, 1968, "On the Concepts of Tribe and Tribal Society", in J. Helm (ed.), *Essays on the Problem of Tribe*, Washington, D.C.: American Ethnological Society.

Geertz, Clifford, 1988, *Work and Lives: Anthropologists as Authors*, Stanford University Press.

Giddens, Anthony, 1984, *The Constitution of Society*, Berkeley & Los Angels: University of California Press.

Gouldner, Alvin, 1970, *The Coming Crisis of Western Sociology*, New

York: Basic Books.

Hardiman, David, 1982, "Indian Faction: A Political Theory Examined", in R. Guha (ed.), *Subaltern Studies,* Delhi: Oxford University Press.

Harvey, David, 1986, *Consciousness and the Urban Experience*, Baltimore and London: The Johns Hopkins University Press.

——, 1987, "Flexible Accumulation Through Urbanization: Reflections on Post-Modernism in the American City", *Antipode* 19(3): 260-86.

——, 1989, Between Time and Space: Reflection on Geographical Imagination, Keynote Address: Annual Meeting of the American Geographical Association, Baltimore, March 20.

Kuper, Adam, 1988, *The Invention of Primitive Society*, New York: Routledge.

Lash, Scott and J. Urry, 1987, *The End of Organized Capitalism*, Madison: University of Wisconsin Press.

Lozano, Beverly, 1985, *High Technology, Cottage Industry: A Study of Informal Work in the San Francisco Bay Area*, Ph.D. Dissertation, U.C. Davis.

Lynd, R.S. and H. Lynd, 1929, *Middletown: A Study in Contemporary American Culture,* New York: Harcourt.

Mansbach, Richard et al., 1976, *The Web of World Politics: Nonstate Actors in the Global System*, Englewood, N.J.: Prentice-Hall.

Marcus, George, 1986, "Contemporary Problems of Ethnography in the Modern World System", in James Clifford and George Marcus (eds.), *Writing Culture*, Berkeley: University of California Press.

——, 1983, "Repatriating an Interpretive Anthropology: The American Studies / Cultural Criticism Connections", *American Anthropologist* 85 (11): 859-65.

Marcus, G. and M. Fischer, 1986, *Anthropology as Cultural Critique: An Experimental Movement in the Human Sciences*, Chicago: University of Chicago Press.

Martin, Emily, 1987, *Woman in the Body: A Cultural Analysis of Reproduction*, Boston: Beacon Press.

Mintz, Sidney, 1981, "Afterword", in Ahern, Emily and Hill Gates (eds.), *The Anthropology of Taiwanese Society.*

——, 1985, *History, Evolution and the Concept of Culture: Selected Essays of Alexander Lesser*, Cambridge: Cambridge University Press.

——, 1987, Author's Rejoinder, Symposium Review on Sweetness and Power, *Food and Foodways*, 2:171-97.

Murphy, Robert, 1987, *Body Silent*, New York: Rienhart and Court.

Nader, Laura, 1974, "Up the Anthropologist: Perspectives Gained from Studying Up", in D. Hymes (ed.), *Reinventing Anthropology*, New York: Pantheon.

Nandy, Ashis, 1987, *Tyranny, Tradition and Utopia: Essays in Politics of Awareness*, Delhi: Oxford University Press.

Neville, G.K., 1987, *Kinship and Pilgrimage: Rituals and Reunion in American Protestant Culture*, New York: Oxford.

Newman, Katherine, 1988, *Falling From Grace: The Experience of Downward Mobility in the American Middle Class*, New York: Free Press.

Noyelle, Thierry, 1987, *Beyond Industrial Dualism: Market and Job Segmentation in the New Economy*, Boulder: Westview Press.

Obeysekere, Gananath, 1990, *The Work of Culture: Symbolic Transformations in Psychoanalysis and Anthropology*, Chicago: University of Chicago Press.

Pandey, Triloki Nath, 1986, Further Notes on Indian Identity.

Perin, Constance, 1977, *Everything in its Place*, Princeton: Princeton University Press.

———, 1988, *Belonging in America*, Madison: University of Wisconsin Press.

Piore, Michael and C. Sabel, 1984, *The Second Industrial Divide: Possibilities for Prosperity*, New York: Basic Books.

Portoghesi, P., 1983, *Postmodern: The Architecture of the Post-industrial Society*, NY: Rizzoli.

Public Culture, 1983, The Bulletin of the Project for Transcultural Studies, Edited by Carol Breckenridge.

Said, Edward, 1989, Representing the Colonized: Anthropology's Interlocutors, *Critical Inquiry* 15:205-25.

Sassen, Saskia, 1988, *The Mobility of Capital and Labour*, Cambridge: Cambridge University Press.

Schneider, David, 1988, Yet Another Note on 'Culture', 'Society', and 'Place', Paper presented at the Society for Cultural Anthropology, Washington D.C., May 20.

Srinivas, M.N., 1975, "The Indian Village: Myth and Reality", in J. Beattie and R. Lienhardt (eds.), *Studies in Social Anthropology*.

Tambiah, Stanley, 1985, "An Anthropologist's Credo", in S. Tambiah, *Culture, Thought and Action: An Anthropological Perspective*, Cambridge, MA: Harvard University Press.

Touraine, Alain, 1977, *The Self-Production of Society*, Chicago: University Press.

Trouiliot, Michael-Rolph, 1988, *Peasants and Capital*, Baltimore: The Johns Hopkins University Press.

Tyler, Stephen, 1986, "Post-Modern Anthropology", in P. Chock and J. Hyman (eds.), *Discourse and the Social Life of Meaning*, Washington D.C. : Smithsonian Institution Press.

Vidich, A., 1957, *Small Town in Mass Society: Class, Power and Religion in a Small Community*, Princeton: Princeton University Press.

Wallerstein, I., 1987, "The World that Sugar Made", *Food and Foodways* (2): 109-12.

Wood, Michael and L. Zurcher, Jr., 1988, *The Development of a Postmodern Self*, New York: Greenwood Press.

Wuthnow, Robert, 1983, *The Restructuring of American Religion Since World War II*, Princeton: Princeton University Press.

Chapter Thirteen

CONNECTED CRITICISM AND THE
WOMB OF TRADITION

We are apt to be misled here by the ideological uses to which the concept of a tradition has been put by conservative political theorists. Characteristically such theorists have followed Burke in contrasting tradition with reason and the stability of tradition with conflict. Both contrasts obfuscate. For all reasoning takes place within the context of some traditional mode of thought, transcending through criticism and invention the limitations of what had hitherto been reasoned in that tradition; this is as true of modern physics as of medieval logic.

—Alasdair MacIntyre (1981:206)

..an antithesis of tradition and modernity confuses different contexts and arises out of cultural vanity, historical mis-comprehension and utopianism masquerading as social science. It needs to be replaced by a synthesis where modernity would simply be a new phase of the seeking to grapple with the problem of securing utilities for the mass of mankind. The contrast which would then remain would be a contrast between the diversely expressed age-old tradition of man's deeper awareness of eternal verities, and a newer tradition absolutizing the technology of manipulating matter for the sake of ephemeral utilities.

—G.C. Pande (1989: 105-106)

THE PROBLEM

At present many of us—concerned human beings, citizens, and scholars—are engaged in a critical evaluation of the agenda of modernity—its discourse as well as practice. This critical evaluation has been prompted by our experience of living in the modern world and both the progress and disenchantment that it has brought about. This critical appreciation of the world of modernity has manifested itself in many forms, from extremist fundamentalism of all kinds to varieties of postmodernism, including the cultural reconstructions of modernity in traditional societies. At present, the critique of modernity has expressed itself primarily in the form of a cultural critique which has involved simultaneously critiques of existing modes of social organization and codes of collective representation. In this cultural critique participants are also bringing the perspective of tradition to bear upon our contemporary reflections, since culture can not be genuinely thought of without belonging to a tradition or locating one's cultural sensibility or aspirations in a tradition. For instance, certain forms of contemporary postmodernism such as post-modern architecture or postmodern spirituality are essentially critical interpreters and practitioners of the emancipatory perspectives within the womb of tradition. While the idea of vernacular architecture is central to varieties of post-modern conceptions of space and an ideal human habitat, certain traditions of embodied religiosity are central to post modern strivings in religion and spirituality.

Though tradition has not been altogether missing from our contemporary reflections it is nonetheless not central to the practice of cultural criticism. This is partly because of the fact that the actors and schools of thought which set the terms of debate in our increasingly monological global discourse do not live out any nimating tradition. The only way they can speak of tradition is y analyzing it as a piece of object or by inventing it. Thus it is ittle wonder that the current discussion is totally exhausted by the omehow incestuous quarrel and sibling rivalry between moder- ity and postmodernity and the dynamics of tradition has been onspicuous by its absence. But it is essential to include tradition n order to participate in the contemporary trigonometry of criti- ism and creativity with tradition, modernity and postmodernity s an engaging trinity.

This paper critically examines the relevance of tradition in the ontemporary context by a critical exploration of styles of criti- ism available within the womb of tradition and the prospect for videning the universe of discourse that these styles embody. It xamines the possibility of criticism within the womb of tradition, vhich is not perceived as an externalist rejection of its frames of ulture. It focuses on a genre of criticism of tradition which is nternal to it but at the same time work towards its desired trans- ormation. This style of criticism of tradition is called "connected riticism" by Michael Walzer (1988) and "internal criticism" by Martha Nussbaum and Amartya Sen (1987). Coupled with a de- cription of connected criticism as a mode of critical engagement, s a discussion of the implication for cultural criticism when it akes tradition seriously and the relevance of tradition in the ontemporary context which is characterized by a global inter- enetration among the cultural forms of tradition, modernity and ostmodernity.

VALUATING TRADITION: FROM INTERNAL CRITICISM O CONNECTED CRITICISM

3y connected criticism Walzer refers to those styles of criticism vhere the critics criticize a prevalent way of life as meaningful iterpreters of tradition, and not simply as their outright icono- lasts. Tradition has an eternal dimension and the contingent imension. Tradition is an embodiment of the seeking for value nd good life within a particular social group but because of the vork of power the seeking for eternal values within a tradition

gets fossilized into a few customs and institutions which instea
of pointing the individuals to the Divine even chains the Divine i
the prison of the caste system. This tension between value an
power creates the perennial need for criticism of tradition even i
as a cultural form it might be a representation of perennial phi
losophy so that the distortion of power is corrected and traditio
becomes a base for the realization of an ideal society again (Gir
1993).

Criticism of tradition, however, is a difficult task, "nearl
always full of peril—especially when they involve... going agains
some group's deeply held beliefs. It is frequently felt that an
modification of tradition, especially through scientific and/or ur
ban rational criticism, must be an unacceptable external imposi
tion upon traditional culture" (Nussbaum and Sen 1987: 15). Bu
this simultaneous need for criticism on the one hand and respec
for the cultural integrity of tradition—embodied in the critic'
immersion in tradition's essential props—challenges us to prac
tise a style of criticism which is internal and immersed—interna
because it uses "resources within the culture itself in order t
criticize certain aspects of culture"; and immersed rather tha
detached because its norm of evaluation is based upon "the poin
of view of experienced immersion in the way of life of a culture'
(ibid: 15). In such a style of criticism the critic earns his authorit
to criticize a tradition and create a space for moral reflection o
taken-for-granted norms within a people "by arguing with hi
follows" (Walzer 1988: 33) in their own idioms. Practitioners o
connected criticism thus are not "marginal men and women" and
have overcome both the difficulties of detachment from and am
biguous connection with tradition through their love and action
As criticism is an inquiry into "whether the suggested mode o
togetherness genuinely hangs together" (Neville 1974: 189) in a
tradition, its criterion of judgement cannot be detachment since
"detachment, in any area, yields not objectivity but incoherence'
(Nussbaum and Sen 1987: 22).

Connected criticism as it is deeply immersed within a tradi
tion is also not bound by it either in its source or in its scope. It

immersion is accompanied not only by a "transcendence from within" (Mohanty 1989: 146) but also by exposure to views from afar. Its inspiration for criticising a tradition often occurs out of a cross-cultural encounter; yet the style of criticism is still internal because the view from afar that it brings comes not through an astronomer but through a prophet. As Nussbaum and Sen have argued: "An external critique cannot ignore internal facts, but does not preclude response to other societies and to an extended plurality of cultures" (ibid: 32). In fact, values of one part of the plurality of cultures can "enter in an integral way in an internal critique of another part..."

In its task of objective evaluation of tradition connected criticism does not stop at the taken-for-granted assumptions of a culture in the name of functionalism or structuralism or even descriptive pragmatism but proceed to "conduct a reflective dialectical examination" of people's views within a tradition (Nussbaum and Sen 1987). Thus connected criticism is also a normative criticism of tradition which performs a redemptive and transformative function and under whose moralizing gaze familiar institutions of society are perceived as "instances of problematic justice" by the actors (Habermas 1990: 108). Internal criticism has a thrust towards problematization of the "unquestioningly accepted ideas of the good life" within a tradition where the relevance of the experiential context of people tends to pale (Habermas 1990: 105). Connected criticism, as it is based upon immersion within tradition, also involves taking a hypothetical attitude to culture, where the "philosophy of as if" becomes a guide to transformative action. But because such criticism is practised by those who live the very tradition and have even rivalled the faithful in their authentic living of it, their hypothetical attitude to culture engages the mind and heart of the actors. Even if such critics are crucified on the charges of heresy and blasphemy by the powers that be they don't suffer from the problem of incomprehension and lack of communication with the actors of tradition.

INTERNAL CRITICISM AS A RATIONAL DELIBERATION

There can be two kinds of connected criticism—philosophical/ rational and prophetic. In the philosophical mode of connected criticism it is the philosopher who conducts the critical inquiry while in the latter it is the prophet who is the archetypal critic. In Nussbaum and Sen's agenda of internal criticism it is the rational philosopher—whose guide is Aristotle—is the critic while in Walzer's it is the prophet. These two agendas involves different assumptions and have different implications for the appreciation of traditional vision of good life in the contemporary world.

For Aristotle, all evaluations of tradition must be internal, proceeding with the values that people held dear. While "for Plato, the opinions of finite and imperfect people, as embodied in their traditions, are hardly a sufficient basis for an account of what is really good, even *good for those* very same people" (Nussbaum and Sen 1987: 17), Aristotle urges the critics to "seek conviction through arguments using the traditional beliefs as our witnesses and standards" (Nussbaum and Sen 1987: 23). But at the same time, evaluation of tradition in the Aristotelian agenda also involves a movement "beyond the superficial desires of participants to a deeper and more objective level" (Nussbaum and Sen 1987: 22). "Aristotle insists that these two goals—individual clarification and communal attunement—can be achieved together, by a cooperative critical discourse that insists upon the philosophical virtues of orderliness, deliberateness, and precision" (Nussbaum and Sen 1987). This is a deliberative process which "confronts the reflecting participant with all of the alternative views on a topic, leads him or her through a thorough imaginative exploration of each," leading to modification of their many "unconsidered positions" (Nussbaum and Sen 1987: 24). Yet, as Nussbaum and Sen make clear: "this modification, if it takes place, will take place not as imposition from without, but as a discovery about which, among that person's own values, are the deepest and the most central. This is self-discovery and discovery of one's own traditions" (1987: 24).

In Nussbaum and Sen's agenda of the Aristotelian criticism of tradition there is a commitment to a "tradition of rational argumentation" (1987: 29) and a "rational criticism of culture that proceeds by utilizing material internal to the culture itself" (ibid: 30). But they leave untouched the question of the cultural construction of rationality itself. In applying their scheme of criticism to evaluate Indian tradition they argue that the representation of Indian tradition as mystical has ignored the internal criticism of it in the work of rationalist critiques of it. But the opposition between the mystical and the rational that Nussbaum and Sen take for granted is itself a universalization of a particular cultural agenda, viz. the agenda of modernity. Therefore one is not clear as to why an internal criticism of a tradition has to be a rational one, when rationality means anti-mysticism. Sri Aurobindo's work suggests that there is no opposition between the spiritual and the rational though they belong to different levels in an encompassing hierarchy (Sri Aurobindo 1950). In fact looking at Indian tradition through Aristotelian gaze makes Nussbaum and Sen look for dualism where in fact exists a transcendental unity.

Nussbaum and Sen's presentation of "truth in ethics" lying in moves beyond the superficial desires of participants immediately reminds one of Habermas' critical theory and his agenda of "discourse ethics" (Habermas 1990). But Habermas himself tells us that such processes of rational argumentation are inadequate in themselves in transforming the taken-for-granted assumptions of the participants in discourse, since "the discursive justification of norms is no guarantor of moral insights" (Habermas 1990: 209). But though Habermas himself is in search of hermeneutic supplements to overcome the limits of rational deliberation the farthest he can go is towards neighborhood solidarity and "internalization of authority" (1990: 179). This supplementary hermeneutic effort is not very different from the discovery of the self as a "relational" agent in Nussbaum and Sen's agenda of internal criticism (1987: 25). They argue that the deliberative process "is viewed not in any simple way as the transcending or sacrificing of self; it is a further part of the discovery of self, since the self is understood in its very nature to be a relational entity, and its own ends are understood as shared ends" (1987: 24-25).

But are these two processes--transcending or sacrificing self and discovering self--opposed to each other as Nussbaum and Sen seem to be assuming and suggesting? Is such an assumption about the ontology of man traditional or modern? Without essentializing the traditional mode one can still argue that in all traditional orders the emphasis upon ritual sacrifice suggests that one cannot really discover oneself without sacrificing oneself and transcending oneself (Nagendra 1971). If, as G.C. Pande argues, "the whole process of self-realization is the process of realizing that the non-self is the self" (Pande 1989: 40) then self-sacrifice and self-discovery are part of the same process of interrogation of the self in search of transcendence. From a very different background Roberto Unger makes a similar argument when he writes that the citizen in empowered democracy renounces not only because of the constitutional guarantee offered to him but because of "higher spiritual significance", which consists in "the assertion of transcendence as a diurnal context smashing" (Unger 1987: 579).

In another context, Mark Warren (1992) has argued that a theory of discourse is not a theory of self-transformation, and without self-transformation how can criticism of tradition as a transformative movement be possible? The problem with Martha Nussbaum and Amartya Sen's Aristotelian internal criticism is that they fail to realize that "reflective dialectical examination" also requires "reflexive self" (Giddens 1991) and "transcendental sacred" (Unger 1987) as frames of criticism without which critical exercise is incapable of performing the task of transformation. To talk of transcendental sacred is not necessarily to evade reality by being mystical. It refers to a frame of criticism and a "dimension of ground" (Laclau 1992) from which we can judge whether

he society which we have treated as god is really fair to human
beings or not. For Unger, even though the transcendental sacred is
"elusive and disposable and requires, to be recognized, the power
of vision, which is the ability to see the invisible" without this
there is in fact no choice left to people especially as the kings and
the priests of the social worlds present them as "graced with the
authority of an ultimate reality" (Unger 1987: 576). In such a case
the decisiveness of the social world "arises precisely from its lack
of any place within a hierarchy of contexts" (ibid: 577). And it is
interesting that Unger, a political theorist—not a "mystic"—argues that when the social sacred loses its touch with the transcendent sacred "there is no larger defining reality to which it can
serve as the vehicle or from whose standpoint it can be criticized".

TOWARDS PROPHETIC CRITICISM

Thus not only the internal criticism of a tradition can be both
rational and spiritual there is a perennial need for making the
rational internal criticism a part of the encompassing engagement
of spiritual criticism. Such an agenda would carry much conviction in the traditional societies where social criticism has manifested itself in varieties of Bhakti movements. Not only in traditional societies but also in varieties of contemporary societies
criticisms of modern institutions—colonialism, slavery, etc.—
have been the work of the prophets—be it Gandhi or Martin
Luther King Jr. who, it must not be forgotten, have used the name
of God to build their movements against forces of oppression.
Even in modern critical social movements one is "back to the
beginning", to use the words of Michael Walzer, where social
critic is a prophet.

As in the case of philosophical internal criticism prophetic
criticism of tradition is not an external one, it also uses the idioms
of tradition to criticize it. As Walzer (1988: 63) argues:

Although there is conflict between the prophets and the established
priesthood, prophecy does not in any sense constitute underground

or...a sectarian movement. In the dispute between Amos and the priest Amaziah, it is the prophet who appeals to religious tradition the priest only to reason of state...Prophecy aims to arouse remembrance, recognition, indignation and repentance.

When we are confronted with the challenge of the criticism of tradition the prophetic mode of criticism is more internal compared to the philosophical mode as it uses the idiom of religion which is at the heart of the traditional order (Bellah et al. 1991 Sacks 1991). Its touch with the transcendent and its encompassment of the rational mode of argumentation as an essential evolutionary step has a special need today when existing forms of critical theory have degenerated either into narcissism or to a detached critique of the political order where one is more busy in fighting against the negativity of the Other rather than to transform oneself and thus, lay the invincible blocks for the criticism of culture (see Apter 1992; Laclau and Pantham 1989).

THE CONTEMPORARY RELEVANCE OF TRADITION

The experience of modernity in the last three centuries has taught us the virtues of "hermeneutics of suspicion" in putting all received traditions into question—examining their relevance and coherence. But modernity, even postmodernity in several guises of deconstruction, has taken the hermeneutics of suspicion to an extreme. It has to be now supplemented by a "hermeneutics of recovery", and this supplementing has to be a process of synthesis. In Sri Aurobindo's words, the challenge here now is no less than for a "synthesis of yoga". And in this yoga of synthesis tradition can provide us spiritual insights, which has a special significance in the contemporary world which is dominated by money and power as the ultimate measures of good life. It is an immersion within tradition which can teach us that "the essence of man is 'faith', not 'reason,' much less 'labour' " (Pande 1989: 54) and faith is nothing but *shradha* (Pande 1991).

REFERENCES

Apter, David E., 1992, "Democracy and Emancipatory Movements: Notes for a Theory of Inversionary Discourse", in Jan N. Pieterse (ed.), *Emancipations, Modern and Post-Modern*, London: Sage.

Bellah, Robert et al., 1991, *The Good Society*, NY: Alfred A. Knof.

Giddens, Anthony, 1991, *Modernity and Self-Identity: Self and Society in the Late Modern Age*, Cambridge: Polity Press.

Giri, Ananta, 1993, "The Quest for a Universal Morality: Jurgen Habermas and Sri Aurobindo", Indian Institute of Management, Ahmedabad: Working Paper.

Griffin, David, 1988, *Spirituality and Society: Postmodern Visions*, Albany: SUNY Press.

Habermas, Jurgen, 1990, *Moral Consciousness and Communicative Action*, Cambridge: Polity Press.

Harvey, David, 1987, "Flexible Accumulation Through Urbanization: Reflection on Postmodernism in American City", *Antipode* 19 (3).

Laclau, Ernesto, 1992, "Beyond Emancipation", in Jan N. Pieterse (ed.), *Emancipations, Modern and Postmodern*, London: Sage.

MacIntyre, Alasdair, 1981, *After Virtue*, London: Duckworth.

Mohanty, J.N., 1989, *Transcendental Phenomenology*, Cambridge, MA: Basil Blackwell.

Nagendra, S.P., 1971, *The Concept of Ritual in Modern Sociological Theory*, Delhi: Academic Journal of India.

Neville, Robert C., 1974, *The Cosmology of Freedom*, New Haven: Yale University Press.

Nussbaum, Martha and Amartya Sen, 1987, "Internal Criticism and Indian Rationalist Traditions", Helsinki: WIDER Working Paper.

Pande, G.C., 1989, *The Meaning and Process of Culture as Philosophy of History*, Allahabad: Raka Prakashan

———, 1991, "Two Dimensions of Religion: Experience based on Indian Spiritual Experience and Philosophical Traditions", in Eliot Deutch, *Culture and Modernity*, Honolulu: University of Hawaii Press.

Sacks, Jonathan, 1991, *The Persistence of Faith*, London: Weidenfeld Nicholson.

Sri Aurobindo, 1950, *The Synthesis of Yoga*, Pondicherry.

Unger, Roberto M., 1987, *False Necessity: Anti-Necessitarian Social Theory in the Service of Radical Democracy*, Cambridge.

Walzer, Michael, 1988, "Interpretation and Social Criticism", in S.M. McCurrin (ed.), *The Tanner Lectures on Human Values*, Universities of Cambridge and Utah Press.

Warren, Mark, 1992, "Democracy and Self-Transformation", *American Political Science Review* 86.

INDEX